History/Writing

History/Writing

ALBERT COOK

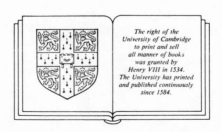

The right of the
University of Cambridge
to print and sell
all manner of books
was granted by
Henry VIII in 1534.
The University has printed
and published continuously
since 1584.

CAMBRIDGE UNIVERSITY PRESS

Cambridge
New York   New Rochelle   Melbourne   Sydney

Published by the Press Syndicate of the University of Cambridge
The Pitt Building, Trumpington Street, Cambridge CB2 1RP
32 East 57th Street, New York, NY 10022, USA
10 Stamford Road, Oakleigh, Melbourne 3166, Australia

First published 1988

Printed in the United States of America

Library of Congress Cataloging-in-Publication Data
Cook, Albert Spaulding.
History/writing / Albert Cook.
p.   cm.
Bibliography: p.
Includes index.
ISBN 0 521 36049 8
1. Historiography – History.   I. Title.
D13.C668   1988
907'.2 – dc 19   88–5005
CIP

British Library Cataloguing in Publication Data
Cook, Albert, *1925–*
History writing.
1. Historiography
I. Title
907'.2

ISBN 0 521 36049 8

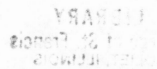

For David and Paul
and in memory of Kathleen

CONTENTS

PREFACE

IN ONE SENSE this book began at The Center for Advanced Study
in the Behavioral Sciences, where I began rethinking some of these
questions when Jack Hexter was posing them there, during 1966–67.
Yet I had already begun more than a decade before in working over "The
Merit of Spengler," written well before its publication in 1963 – the earliest
writing in this book, since I have borrowed some paragraphs from that
essay here.

All of my critical books are addressed to the underlying conditions of
the expressive use of language or other constructions of signs, and in one
sense these studies are continuous with one another. Indeed, my books of
the past few years could be grouped as studies of the referent under deep
domination by foregone matrices (*Myth and Language*); or in the "silent"
communications of art (*Changing the Signs: The Fifteenth-Century Break-
through*; *Figural Choice in Poetry and Art*; and the forthcoming *Dimensions of
the Sign in Art*); or under conditions of revelatory indeterminacy (*Thresholds*)
– or here, under conditions where the referent is both subverted and foregrounded by the very mode of expression, historiography, that the writer
has chosen.

As always, I have myself chosen a particular mix of theory and practice
that I hope will strike the reader as carrying through its attempt to explore
these questions.

ACKNOWLEDGMENTS

THANKS ARE ABUNDANTLY DUE TO: The Center for Advanced Study in the Behavioral Sciences; The Fondation Hardt; Clare Hall, Cambridge, where I did some crucial writing and planning; Brown University, where my discourse has been fostered by the general climate, and especially among my colleagues in Comparative Literature, Classics (with its many highly literate historians), and English.

Those who have read and commented on all or part of the manuscript: Edward Ahearn, Marshall Brown, Henry Kozicki, Thomas MacCary, Naomi Schor, Charles Segal, Evan Watkins, and especially Hayden White, as well as anonymous readers for this and some other publishers. My accomplished and resourceful research assistant, Dr. Blossom S. Kirschenbaum, who has handled many phases of the manuscript and the materials contributing to it with great discrimination and dispatch.

The journals are to be thanked that have published parts in earlier versions: "The Merit of Spengler," *Centennial Review* 7, no. 3 (1963); "Particular and General in Thucydides," *Illinois Classical Studies* 10, no. 1 (1985); "Reference and Rhetoric in Historiography," in Bucknell Review, *Criticism, History, and Intertextuality*, ed. R. Fleming and M. Payne (Lewisburg, Pa.: Bucknell University Press, 1988); "The Crosscurrents of Time: Burckhardt and Michelet," in *Proceedings of the 16th International Congress of the International Federation for Modern Languages and Literatures* (1984; Budapest, 1987); "The Gradual Emergence of History Writing as a Separate Genre," *Clio* 16, no. 2 (Winter, 1986); "Scale, Psychological Stereotyping, and Style in Tacitus," *Maia*, n.s., 38, no. 3 (Sept.-Dec. 1986); " 'Fiction' and History in Samuel and Kings," *Journal for the Study of the Old Testament* 36 (1986), 27–48.

As always I am grateful to my wife, Carol, for constant advice and encouragement, and for the reassuring fundament of a loving life together.

I

INTRODUCTION

DISCOURSE ABOUT DISCOURSE engages the attention of writers in many of what have been taken to be separate disciplines, and discourse about the writing of history has drawn the converging attention not only of historians, philosophers, and social theorists, but also of those who are identified as literary critics. History writing is a form of literature; it could be said that it began as such. But it carries, in its very conception, an especially sharp angle on what it designates. It lays claim, both rhetorically and actually, to a validity of correspondence to the public processes of the real world. What the commanding historians of the past, remote and recent, have written constitutes a set of texts, of multiply coded verbal constructs that seem in certain ways to exceed the just demands of the claim to validity by means initially of veracity to evidence and then to a sense behind all the evidence so concatenated. But the concatenation, if successful, turns these writings into "works"; it is their achieved discourse that manages to answer the claims of validity and veracity by concatenating them. How they manage to do so turns out to be puzzling, whether looked at from the point of view of the single detail or from that of the overall bearing of an entire work. Each point of view multiplies questions as it is examined. As with many deep issues, the questions resist being settled; they provide other questions.

My initial aim is to keep in view the two seemingly contradictory constraints on historiography, the validity that in one form or another the theorists of historical explanation single out for discussion, and the "rhetoric" analyzed by recent writers who stress the literary structure of historiography. I want to show how these two constraints combine to enable, rather than to inhibit, the presentation of meanings in temporal sequences of events.

For R. G. Collingwood the sense inhering in a historiographic work amounts to understanding the thinking of an agent. As he says, following Hegel, "All history is the history of thought."' Having found and approved this notion in Hegel, he goes on to specify the historiographic task as that of intuiting the thought behind a "specific" event. In "penetrating to the inside of events" (214), the historian will "re-enact" them in his mind – but as "individuals" (passim), in such a way that he is seen effectually to be taking them up singly, one by one. Collingwood's notions are frequently apposite, and they are based on a complex definition of thought in relation to emotion.[2] Finally he confines what is an understanding of social processes to important agents in the social process. As with many theoreticians, his attempt to account for causes tends to focus preponderantly on the individual event, and it is just here that his conclusions are problematic – which is to say at the very center of his question.

There is, along these lines, not just from Collingwood but generally, a tendency to raise questions about causality by inspecting very simple, sentence-long propositions. This is the approach of Morton White, for example, as he runs through regularities, explanations, and other technical questions in philosophy. White's discussions typically confine themselves in such a way that they do not effectually address the enchainment of events in actual works of history, though they do apply forcefully to summaries and small, sentence-length propositions.[3] The ground for the relations among sentences, and through a whole discourse, must be addressed in accounting for how a causality has been presented by a work of history. The elusiveness of causality in a work of history limits the critiques that are brought to bear from a causal point of view on specific historiographic discussions, as in W. H. Dray's critique of Lawrence Stone's "three causes" for the English Civil War:[4] "The nearest thing to system in his account is an attempt to classify his causal factors into long-term *preconditions* which made the outcome no more than possible, shorter-term *precipitants* (up to a dozen years in length) which began to make it probable, and, finally, *triggers* in the form of particular events or human decisions which were decisive in the end." But Stone need not have been systematic in his as-signment of cause to be valid, nor, indeed, would he need even to have been frequently explicit in the assignment of cause, as in their intrications the best historians often, and characteristically, are not. Nor are overlaps in time and other partial inconsistencies sufficient evidence for invalidity even with respect to this particular trio of causes – again because of the perpetual hermeneutic supplementation that the historian has to engage in. He never works in a closed field. This condition holds true for the related question of necessity, brought to bear by Rex Martin on this essay of Dray's.[5] Necessity can be hinted at or even propounded but never estab-lished in history, except perhaps, in some views, for the kind of "isolated" event that is itself subhistoric.

At the other end of the spectrum, the sort of general accounts of regularity in human nature, Hume's "uniformity" as the ground for understanding and explanation in history, while perhaps philosophically consistent, cannot be brought to bear without tautology on the "evidence" within a work of historiography, if that evidence is taken in the essential matrix of interconnections it would have to have been the business of the writer to establish. It is not these "laws" themselves and whether they hold or do not hold that should concern us. Rather we must finally assess the applicability of their connection to the acts of written understanding before us.[6] Even if one is rigorous, in short, one can be too particular or too general in seeking causal explanations in history, because historiography proliferates in concatenations of events. It produces thereby the intrications of a human conception of time; in the terms of Paul Ricoeur, the historian avoids a simple mimesis of static correspondence (his "Mimesis I") for an intrication of events in time (his "Mimesis II"), which leads to the reader's perception of the text in a "Mimesis III." As Ricoeur points out (he is adapting from Plato's *Sophist* the notions of same, other, and analogy and applying them to history), to stay exclusively public in historiography and to offer no future is a sort of double temptation.[7] Yet even Ricoeur would too quickly equate the "intrication" of the "intrigue" in historiography to the patterns offered by Aristotle for Greek tragedy.[8]

Although an extreme skepticism would want to reject summarily any causal ascriptions, most historians would not do so, nor need one do so in order to see that the validation of single causal connections will not serve to explain, one way or the other, what is happening in the overall sense conveyed by the historian. In the case of Gibbon, for example, as Lionel Gossman has shown, a number of interlocking notions are propounded in the *Decline and Fall*, along with, and contributory to, the thesis that Christianity chiefly brought about the long decline of the Roman Empire.[9] As Gossman says, "What is given as the 'design' of Chapter XVI, on the attitude of the Roman government to the Christians – 'to separate, (if it be possible) a few authentic as well as interesting facts from an undigested mass of fiction and error, and to relate in a clear and rational manner the causes, the extent, the duration, and the most important circumstances of the persecutions to which the first Christians were exposed' – can be taken *mutatis mutandis* as the design of the entire History. It is for the sake of the 'order and perspicuity' of the narrative . . . that the historian carries out a rigorous selection among the chaotic and obscure materials that press upon him" (95). Further, it may be said, the historian preserves in his style, and also in the "excessive" proliferation of detail, at once a sense of that pressure, and of the chaos against which his order will stand – an order neither subsumable to a logically formulable causal argument on the one hand nor independent of causal implications on the other. Or as Gossman well says, " 'Order and perspicuity' are not, in short, immediately perceived; they are not given in the material, but proposed by the reason that contemplates and evaluates the material" (97). And, as Gossman further points out, Gibbon's personal attitudes toward authority were doubly transmuted into the text. "One of the central problems in the *Decline and Fall* – the problem of the foundation of truth and authority – thus reappears in relation to the rhetoric and epistemology of history, as a central problem of the work, the problem of the truth and authority of the text" (111). So Gossman can consistently find in Gibbon's *Decline and Fall* conclusions that parallel the views of Locke on the one hand and Rousseau on the other, as well as the views of other eighteenth-century thinkers often compared to his.

Since the time of Plato – and indeed, since Heraclitus – the relationship between the individual and society has been considered crucial for understanding social processes in time. These questions have been referred for clarification to the understanding of the psychological processes that enter into the determination of events. History includes both. Just as the writing of history may draw on ideas but not exemplify ideas in ways that are fully extrapolable – without turning into a historical tract buttressed by examples – so the subject it must address inescapably mediates between the individual and the social. Paul Ricoeur emphasizes this intermediate status, deriving his notion from Schulz, Husserl, and Weber.[10]

All these, and many other theoretical notions, go beyond the nearly tautological injunctions of Ranke to tell events "as they were," *wie es eigentlich gewesen.*" On the side of verification, historiography inescapably emphasizes the referent, which then leaves open the question of validating one fact or event with reference to another. The theoretician, to address historiography in an adequate, and even in an apposite, way, is obliged to depart somewhat from recent critical notions about endless regress toward the referent – even though such notions, with all their limitations, have proved fruitful in the past two decades. With respect to the veracity of the individual datum, and the enchainment of data, the "misplaced concreteness" of a work of history is of the same ontological order, in its preassumed conditions, as that which has not been misplaced: that is, events left out of the work have the same status in being possible referents as do the events left in it, because they "were" (and so remain). Therefore the same assertion may be made of the large referent, the single large event comprising many smaller events, themselves comprising details that could be accorded the status of an event.

What counts as an event is in itself initially unstable and cannot be fully stabilized. The development of Turkish economic policy in Braudel's *La Méditerranée* is at once an event, a complex of events, a contributory demographic tally, and a part of a historiographic work that is not simply an accretion, and not a work whose sense is simply solved by attributing it to "*la longue durée.*" The originality of Braudel's principle of selection for his enormous array of detail is apparent from the fact that there is no prior work framed on such a principle, and no succeeding one either, except his own. And if there were really an Annales method that produced kinds of histories, then there would be a whole array of such works. Of course, there is such a "school," and they share some common principles; but the principles do not provide conditions sufficient (or, for that matter, necessary) for predicting the sense or the character of such works.[11]

Looking at a single instance, we may take what could be considered an arbitrary detail in Gibbon (and many details in most historians are arbitrary), his account of the deification of his wife by the emperor Marcus Aurelius:

> In his Meditations, he thanks the gods, who had bestowed on him a wife, so faithful, so gentle, and of such a wonderful simplicity of manners. The obsequious senate, at his earnest request, declared her a goddess. She was represented in her temples with the attributes of Juno, Venus, and Ceres; and it was decreed, that on the day of their nuptials, the youth of either sex should pay their vows before the altar of their chaste patroness.

According the name "Ceres" would be an event, as distinct from the more general term "goddess," in the public ascription of official names, by perlocutionary force, as it were, to the wife of Marcus Aurelius; this would become explicitly clear, for example, in a study of Demeter-Ceres from Archaic Greece through the Middle Ages. In such a study we could measure exactly the illustrative force of this detail. The study would be monographic rather than historiographic, and in that presentation we could judge its relevance and even its necessity in the work, which we cannot do when we ask either why this detail is included in the *Decline and Fall* or what its status is as an event. Gibbon effectually interprets the "fact" as an event, and like any historian he cannot escape doing so. We cannot tell whether it is an event or a detail contributory to an event; and we cannot judge the necessity of its presence in his presentation. But we should have to be able to do both before we could approach historiography directly as an enchainment of causes, as Jack Hexter has vigorously pointed out.[12]

In a work of fiction, on the other hand, the fictional precondition would give a different status to events inside and outside the work. If a Braudel-inspired historian of the nineteenth century were to omit the Napoleonic Wars – as Braudel himself gives them slight attention in his history of technology – they would still be "there," having the same status as (in this case only potential) referents and events, to be adduced by some other historian, who might then assimilate the Braudel-like data for enchainment with his own contributory events and also his Big Event. But in a famous instance, Jane Austen's novels never mention these wars, which were going on at the time of the action she delineates in her novels. And the precondition of fiction precludes our bringing the Napoleonic Wars to bear upon the views she presents as she presents them. (A historian, however, might write a large work in which both her novels and the Napoleonic Wars would figure.) Of course, these events of the war can be taken globally, like any other data connected with human beings from crop records to lists of court honors, and put into various kinds of enchainment in a historiographic work.

Causal connections come into play the moment the writer, a historian or a theoretician of history, would want to assert a necessary connection between one fact or event and another. But the facts that the historian draws on seem from one point of view potentially gratuitous when he adduces them; does it really add to the *Decline and Fall* that Marcus Aurelius deified his wife? That he called her Ceres? And from another point of view the facts are never "complete"; and the "misplaced concreteness" of those that he does not adduce are "present" (as having happened in the past) for possible supplementation of, or modification of, any written interpretation of the past. This circumstance importantly qualifies any attempt to close the link of cause – or to prove that it cannot be closed. The possibility of hermeneutic supplementation subverts any attempt to close the logic of the causal pattern. Narrative overcompensates, indirectly, for the radical deficiency of full proof by offering "more" data, and by rhetorical shapings, which keep the inescapable linearity of a discussion or a narrative from proceeding unqualified by implications. From the systematic point of view adopted by Hempel, an "explanation sketch" becomes more "probabilistic" as it brings more data to bear on some supposed isolated question. "What the explanatory analyses of historical events offer is, then, in most cases, not an explanation in one of the meanings developed above, but something that might be called an *explanation sketch*. Such a sketch consists of a more or less vague indication of the laws and initial conditions considered as relevant, and it needs 'filling out' in order to turn into a full-fledged explanation. This filling-out requires further empirical research."[13] Hempel's discussion gives an admirable account of how to handle hypotheses in science. But in acts of historiographic understanding, new data, in fact, will not necessarily clarify understanding or increase probability. They may blur the historiographic perception in one direction, and they may also slant the account toward simplification in another. Again, the special function of the possibility of hermeneutic supplementation in the task that faces the historian places special conditions on that task, and on the results. These conditions will not yield to the usual laws of causal analysis, for the reasons given; nor can they in turn be handled so as by themselves to produce general laws.

The discussions about cause in history are carried on with great rigor, whether they issue in a general law, a covering law, or merely an "explanation sketch." But all of them, proceeding on the assumption that a logically formulable justification for causal connection can be deduced from historiography, center on the pattern of predication, either for a single event, "Caesar crossing the Rubicon," or for the movement from a state of affairs to a situation, "the causes of the rise of the gentry . . . of the English Civil War . . . of World War 1." Or even "the decline and fall of the Roman Empire." The patterns of causation, since they are never total, will not effectually work when applied to the plethora of happenings in the human past. It is effectually to get around this situation that historiography was evolved, in Greece somewhat *after* the earliest evolutions of philosophy, to account for social developments under the constraint of this impossibility. We can attribute the impossibility even to Herodotus, who begins with a "cause" (*aitia*) and singles out one man as a cause ("I shall proceed by signaling this one man," "*touton séménas probésomai*" [1.5.3]). This one man, Croesus, will very soon get buried in the complexities of a narrative to which his own career is necessarily contributory but also necessarily not fully commensurate.

Verbal structures in the historian's writing compensate for, and partially overcome, this situation. These verbal structures can be seen as "tropes" involving kinds of "emplotment." Speaking generally, metaphor, metonymy, irony, and synecdoche can be attributed as emphases, one by one, to the work of individual historians.[14] Or all four of these tropes can be found on principle to be present in the writing of any historian. Or, more neutrally, all of these tropes, and others, too, can be classified as kinds of synecdoche. Self-consciousness in the style and organization of the historian must mime the open-endedness of the process it would understand. Hayden White's notion of emplotment, indeed, has the clarifying effect of throwing the emphasis on the wholesale intrication carried through by a work of historiography, above and beyond the causal nexuses it might employ.

Indeed, in the relation between causal connections and verbal structures lies the sense that the historian tries to convey in his writing. It provides its own implicit justification and critique of emplotments and of events.

The algorithm of the slash in my title, *History/Writing*, is open to several interpretations, but the activity upon which it is meant to converge is not, or not finally, to be replotted. The term "event" has been based on an assumption that this is the case, in old-fashioned relativism on the "history" side, and in new-style semi-structuralism on the side of "writing." Mediately it would be so, and the *Dinge an sich* of "events" cannot be separated from the act of writing, or fused with it either. "Events" and "writing" would both, and paradoxically, have to engage the attention before the two could be provisionally rejoined.

If looked at in its strategy of expression, a work of history can be found to present puzzles about language. If looked at for its sequences, it presents puzzles about time. And if looked at for the connections among its events, it presents puzzles about causality. These three puzzles are as extensible as any philosophical discourse may be, and their interconnections are also infinitely extensible, especially the interconnection between language and causality. Most who discuss such questions therefore quite arbitrarily limit the discussion to the logician's domain of the individual sentence, which effectually removes the interconnections among events, and thereby removes the large and crucial reference of the individual sentence. So, even if time is adduced as a marker for the sentence, its complex presence in sequences cannot function as one or more of a series of points in the past as related to present and future, as Ricoeur's expansive demonstration about time in historiography has demonstrated.

If E. P. Thompson's *Making of the English Working Class* can be described as running serially through the series of metaphor, metonymy, synecdoche, and irony,[15] then it would differ from White's ascription to a usual emplotment under the "master trope" of one of them, and would thus escape a dominant mode; seriality would itself be a metamode, or metatrope – leaving aside the possibility that the unity of tone in Thompson would argue for the simultaneous intrication of these (or other) tropes into it – as well as the thrust of other suppositions.

The presence of emplotment, in fact, is so deeply integrated into the historical work that it at once lends itself to characterization by such models and deeply resists them, to the point where the co-presence of all four in any work would argue for just one model, with the possibility of emphases within a work, serially or globally. Or, to put it differently, the model-making itself would be subject to hermeneutic aspectualization – for not one but any number of "metahistories." The flexibility of this particular quartet of models would argue for the possibility of other models and other typologies – perhaps as many as there are "authentic" works of history writing.

If White's four tropes may be matched, as he impressively matches them, diachronically with the governing principles of Piaget's stages of childhood development (8–14), with Vico's stages of cultural epochs (94–95; 145–146), and with the sequences of Foucault's "*epistemes*" from the Middle Ages to the present (250–255); and if these tropes may be matched synchronically with the mechanisms of the Freudian dreamwork[16] (13–14), then they have a function too general to characterize the sense of a particular historiographic act, even if we do take the tropes in some sense as "syntactic" constituents, and even as partial determinants, of the work.

It remains to ask what the emplotment of the *Decline and Fall* might be that it would, unconsciously, as it were, enlist a type (or a reverse type) of the very text that stands at the center of those factors to which it is at great length ascribing the "Decline and Fall." The paradox of emplotment is engaged, ipso facto, when the paradox between verification and rhetoric, or single (ever aspectualized) event and multiple enchainments, has been effectually joined into words. In fact the emplotment can itself be taken as an overall illustration and also as an implicitly dialectical sublation, of a large event, multiply aspectualized so that it may appear plausibly as a single large event with all its contributory enchainments. What is then given will result finally in no pattern of causations, though mediately it may enlist causations of various sorts.

A historical narrative thus both illustrates and supersedes the tropes under which one could classify it. And historiography remains both an intellectual procedure and a "genre" of writing. The procedure may be present when the genre is not clearly demarcated, both before the genre came into existence and much later. In any case, all the paradoxes enlisted in a successful act of history writing complicate it in such a way that the various rhetorical presences in it cannot be abrogated: "the imagination" is present, but not in ways that confine it to "the imaginary" (in a Lacanian or other sense) – because its large referent in reality is present, as are the real details it intricates. Indeed, the reality is saliently present, even if not "proved," in and through the very act, where the last paradox, that between imagination and reality, is unresolvable other than by some such circular ascription as "authenticity." The narrative or quasi narrative offers a pattern both that it imposes (it has manifestly selected and organized the data) and that is really there (the pattern has been discovered in the events themselves, as could have happened no other way but in the narrative). The communicative act of the intentionally grounded historical writing brackets, as well as comprises, this paradox. Something like this also happens in fictions, the fictions of prose and of drama – except that the initial conception of them as fictions frees them from having to use actual events. That freedom gives them a different communicative set; but ultimately they, too, refer to the real world, for all the imposed patterns of their arbitrary structures. If they did not, they would not be intelligible. In all cases the reference of the writing, historical or other, is to the real world. How adequately the real world has been interpreted is another, very large question, on which all the issues of hermeneutics and of literary criticism must continue to be brought to bear.

The ten following chapters of this book, focusing for the most part on individual historiographers, explore the implications of these interrelated questions as they are involved in our apprehension and interpretation of what is communicated by historians. Although my main concerns are systematic, what I have to say does bear on developmental questions in the practice of historiography over the past twenty-five hundred years or so. That is, this book implies not exactly a history of historiography but rather a historicized perspective of its manifestations in some cultures.

The book is divided into two parts. The first part, "Encompassing Instances," brings the practice of individual historians to bear on these general questions. The second, "Strategies of Inclusion," deals with the attempt to universalize, or to refuse to universalize, historical sequences by particular philosophical or organizational techniques, in scriptural historians, philosophical historians, and the typically self-critical historians of our own time. For a conspectus of what I am about here, I should like to indicate briefly what each chapter addresses.

PART I. ENCOMPASSING INSTANCES

2. "The Problematic Emergence of History Writing as a Separate Genre": In the introductory chapter I examine the presence of an impulse to understand the past in works where the historiographic purpose has not yet been fully disengaged from myth and legend.

3. "Particular and General in Thucydides": There is a paradox implicit in historical knowledge. This knowledge always purports to be *causal*, both for some set of cases in point and with respect to a conception of general historical laws. Thucydides works his way steadily and alertly through this paradox. The speeches in his work offer him an indirect, "double" mode of introducing interpretation while maintaining neutrality.

4. "Reference and Rhetoric in Historiography (Gibbon)": Verification and narrative, or verification and rhetoric, run inescapably together in the true historiographer's work. On the surface this union appears in the tendency for every single sentence to carry an interpretive as well as a documentary force, though of course in a string of narrated details the interpretation is just implied.

5. "Scale, Psychological Stereotyping, and Style in Tacitus": Psychology is at once nearly impossible to justify in historiography and indispensable in all such enterprises but those on the largest scale. It shares this character with narrative, of which it is often a strong constituent. Psychology throws into relief the historiographic dilemma between individual and society, and also between random event and cause. Psychology in a work of history, indeed, since it purports to build a bridge between the individual and society, and also between random event and cause, cannot escape these dilemmas any more than historiography can, which must proceed as though they had been resolved, or as though a properly sequenced presentation could resolve them.

6. "Temporalizing the Abstraction of Indeterminacy: Machiavelli and Guicciardini": In this chapter I discuss the likenesses and differences between the approaches of these two historians, as they introduced questions of temporal scope, and of multiple factors, in ways that were furthered by modern historians.

7. "The Crosscurrents of Time: Burckhardt and Michelet": It is synchronic

presentation that constitutes the particular force of Burckhardt's historiographic method, a synchronic presentation that pulls against, aspectualizes, and throws into relief the diachronic material he is manipulating. Burckhardt transforms synchronicity, a standard Enlightenment approach to argument by the characterization of society, an approach shared by Montesquieu and Rousseau. But Burckhardt intends no program for the future to lie behind his work. Consequently, he has powerfully reversed a sequential presentation so as to bring temporal sequence into a sharper focus, rather than to abrogate it.

"*L'histoire,*" said Michelet, "*c'est le temps,*" history is time. The "romance" of the French people's struggle against tyranny and division and their attainment of a perfect unity during the first year of the Revolution is progressively distanced by the growing awareness in Michelet of the resurgence and (at least temporary) victory of the blocking forces. Michelet's temporality shows its hand, and evidences the power to which it is subject, in the fits and starts of his discourse.

PART II. STRATEGIES OF INCLUSION

8. "The Contractions and Expansions of Biblical History": As Auerbach trenchantly demonstrates, the narratives in the Torah are contracted, or "in the background." Yet the progression of time in these narratives is not evenly uniform, and there is a marked unevenness to their acts of foregrounding, which follow no simply formulable principle but are too assured to be random, as well as too referential and too public to be seen primarily as "fictional."

9. "The New Testament in Its Historiographic Dimension": The New Testament increases the "totalizing" focus of the Old by splitting up its historiographic approaches; by centering on a single figure who combines priest, king, prophet; and by making his life and doctrines the pivot of the crucial turn in the historical process.

10. "The Implications of Scope: Totalizing Explanations in History": Those philosophically oriented historians who are also philosophers of history, tend to foreground in their work the assumptions and governing notions that appear in any historiography whatever, because the relation they establish between general and particular for facts or events, and between individual and society for actional complexes, tends toward a totalizing one.

11. "Kinds of Synecdoche in Modern History Writing": A historical work is and must be synecdochic for having chosen and connected its details from a number of others that have been omitted.

In this way historiography must therefore necessarily lack, to some extent, one characteristic of scientific hypothesis or explanation. It cannot be "disverified," because one can only either check it against itself or contrast it to other data. Nor is it an "explanation sketch," but complete in itself, for all its omissions and discontinuities. The sense of an explanation only hovers over the work as the historian plays structure against event to contrast moment with moment in his narrative "ironically." Various modern historians have written in implicit awareness of these conditions, and I close my discussion by examining a variety of their practices.

PART I

ENCOMPASSING INSTANCES

2

THE PROBLEMATIC EMERGENCE
OF HISTORY WRITING
AS A SEPARATE GENRE

I F W E A S K exactly what it is that the historian is writing about, then
modern historiographic practice is fairly easily described, if not justified.
Addressing a question about the human past that has some connection
to public life, or to public events, the historian consults the documents and
other evidence he judges to be relevant, and then he writes an account of
some sort that he believes to be accurate and illuminating, an account that
may involve a main thesis. This formulation of historical practice, however,
will not fully describe the enterprise of earlier writers who may have mixed
"fiction," "legend," or myth into their inquiries. Such an admixture, if the
writer sifts facts for accuracy and interprets public events, does not disqualify
the writing from being characterized as "history." Thucydides, to be sure,
would have disqualified unnamed predecessors for being "mythy," and he
is usually thought to be indicating Herodotus. But the prevailing judgment
of subsequent times has regarded Herodotus the way he regarded himself,
as a historian.

Herodotus aims to be much more systematic and documentary than Homer, but Thucydides is still willing to cite Homer as an authority on historical facts, even though Homer's admixture of fiction and legend is much
stronger than that of Herodotus. Indeed, one finds in the range of Western
practice many admixtures, some of them more marked or more puzzling
than the traces of myth and legend in Herodotus that led Thucydides to
call him "mythy." Usually the modern concern for a purified professional
historiography will overlook the historiographic element in such admixtures, classifying them oversimply as fiction, when actually they may be
performing the historiographic task of organizing data around a central
question about the past much more probingly than many an additive chronicler will have done.[1]

Historiography is a genre of writing, like the novel or poem. But, like
philosophical discourse, historical investigation is also an intellectual enterprise that transcends such generic classification. A poem may use philosophy
in certain ways and still be recognizably a poem. Philosophical discourse
may quote a poem, but it does not thereby get assimilated to poetry, nor

does it resemble poetry in other than an access to metaphorical language. And metaphorical language cannot be taken as essential to philosophy without denying the intentional thrust of the discourse. Because that thrust aims first at explanation, philosophy is not fiction, however many attributes it may share with fiction, whereas poems, plays, novels, and the like, can initially be called fiction, since their intentional thrust starts as a make-believe, even though it must entail some reference to some sort of experience or it would lack communicative possibility. History writing, like philosophy, is not a discourse that conforms just to the canons of a literary genre, "historiography." Beyond its literary canons, and in a sense logically prior to them, history writing conforms to its conditions of inquiry: It must attempt to explain the actions of the past in some domain more than private. Suetonius and Plutarch are thus historians, not just biographers, because their *Lives* envisage comparisons and sequence in the arena of public action.

Of all modes of discourse, historiography is most firmly connected to the beginning of writing, and it may be said to call for writing insofar as it stands at a fixed remove from the past for the shaping and heightening of its patterns. To write history also implies an attitude to the past. "Oral history" usually refers simply to transmitted genealogical lists in primitive societies, or to taped accounts by elderly survivors of data they remember from their youth. Such oral history may occasionally shape and heighten a true tale, and thus qualify minimally as historiography. Yet such marginal possibilities in oral expression are not so broad or so central for historical discourse as is for philosophy the presumably abundant and unrecorded oral argument among the pre-Socratics – or in a modern department of philosophy. Plato, as in so many other ways, stays at the quick of his discursive mode in the oral formulation of his dialogue form, as in the discussion of the *Phaedrus* about the relative merits of oral and written presentation. For poetry, too, because of the initial conception of the discourse, the vast amount of verse composed and transmitted for oral delivery holds a more important place than prewritten materials can for history.

To write history is to engage in what Herodotus called *historiē*, an inquiry.[2] Yet an impulse to understand the past finds discursive expression in works where the historiographic purpose has not yet been disengaged from legendary and poetic, even from fictional, material. Homer shows such an impulse, becoming most explicitly historiographic in "The Catalogue of Ships." In that segment of the *Iliad*, a detailed account of the marshaled forces is given with an approach to completeness comparable to such accounts in Thucydides and Gibbon, or even to accounts of political forces in the work of historians still alive today. Yet "The Catalogue of Ships" finds so little of a coherent place in the cyclic scheme of the *Iliad* that it has often been adjudged the addition of another hand. Homer in that poem provides an understanding, and not just a chronicled account, of the forces of the Trojan War. Indeed, the *Iliad*, taken as a whole, can be called historiographic in that it refers its understanding to a systematically balanced structure of interaction that keeps the Wrath of Achilles in a foreground, allowing for a social picture while still not broaching a view of historical development.

In the Catalogue of Ships, Homer's focus sharpens; he is suddenly conscious, as the historian would be, of the detail pressing in upon him, and of the necessity to select from it. At the very moment when he begins the Catalogue of Ships, he reinvokes the Muses (plural here, though singular in the first line of the poem). As he says just before embarking on his list of the various local fighting contingents, "I could not tell of their throng nor could I name them / Not if there were mine ten tongues and ten mouths too, / And an unbreakable voice, and a bronze heart were within me" (2.488–490). As Herodotus was later to do expansively, Homer adds formulaic but incidental bits of geographical detail in this account: "rocky Pytho" (2.519); the "well-established citadel" of Athens (2.546); the "fragrant vale" of Lacedemon (2.581); and the like. The framework of the poem is large enough to permit of such shifts, and its conception, for all the tightness of the action, is loose enough to prevent our characterizing such details as the supernumerary ones of Roland Barthes, given to create an "effect of the real."[3]

Indeed, Homer is already beyond the Flaubert with whom Barthes begins his discussion of historical discourse. By attenuating, and even at points denying, the actuality of reference to the real in historiography, Barthes also oversimplifies the very "effect of the real" it has been his insight to point out. The effect of the real in Flaubert differs crucially from such an effect in history because it is governed by no prior validating process. Though Homer works from memory, presumably, and not from documents, his lists have been subjected to such prior validation. In historiography as it later comes into definition, it is clear that the presence of such validation, and the disconnection of the seemingly superfluous detail, has also the effect of making that particular detail float away from the more ordered ones. The superfluous detail's relative lack of coding, even if it turns out to have some faint traces of coding, must do more than create a momentary effect of the real to be effective. Heaping up such details would quickly dissipate the effect of the real, and Homer's early use is too bristling to carry such an impression. Normally, indeed, to heap up such uncoded details would quickly dissipate the "effect of the real"; to be salient, the uncoded details must not saturate the coded ones. Especially as historiography comes into sharp definition as an approach to the past, the uncoded details in historical discourse do not only create a momentary or local effect of the real. They also implicitly endorse the validity of the historian's entire presentation, as an implied a fortiori: "If this detail rings true and is uncoded, then the entire narrative may carry conviction as well as a sense of meaning underlying the story." Further, as a corollary, the uncoded detail furnishes an implied pointer to that underlying sense: "If both coded and uncoded details flow together in this narrative, then there is a sense they are evolving which has to lie beyond the distinction between structured codes and the absence of such codes; the coherence will be found elsewhere than in a structure of argument."

In fiction such details must be governed by some extension of a principle of verisimilitude. In history they must only be preverified to carry such functions as Barthes has prevented himself from seeing by somewhat precluding an attention to verification.

All the details of the Catalogue, in their formulaic character, have an ethnic as well as a geographic dimension. In this, too, they resemble the separate accounts that Herodotus gives of the Egyptians, the Scythians, and others. But these details are not pulled into relation with the rest of the scheme of the *Iliad*, whereas in Herodotus a coordinating scheme reminiscent of and perhaps developed from Homer's takes the *"Egyptioi logoi"* and the *"Skythioi logoi"* up into a double historical analogy. Athens in Homer, for example, plays no special role between the bronze-greaved Achaeans and the long-gowned Trojans, except to be classified under the former; and it is obvious in the massing of troops that the Trojan side is numerically inferior as well as less warlike (that term itself characterizing the Achaeans). In Herodotus, however, the Lydians and the Persians, and then the Greeks, are implicitly compared to the Egyptians and the Scythians, in a first analogy. This comparison should be assumed because the accounts of these groups are introduced into the narrative after Herodotus has explicitly declared his subject to be the cause of the war between Greeks and Persians. Before that war gets under way, the Persians attack these other groups (so that there is the further implied comparison between military operations against Egyptians, Scythians, or Babylonians on the one hand and against the Greeks on the other). Then these analogies converge, to the second degree, as it were, for both sides of the climactic battles, to measure the Greeks and the Persians, who are now compared fully and directly but implicitly with each other in the unfolding of the ultimate conflict. There is a separate account of Persian history, but not of Persian customs. Thus are the various peoples intricated, and they are placed in a temporal relation that the doubled logical analogies subserve, whereas in the *Iliad*, the peoples are more or less randomized, except for their affiliation to Greek or Trojan. So, too, the story has a plot from the beginning in the *Iliad*; the emplotment is schematic. In Herodotus the complications are at once cumulative and proto-dialectical. Having been presented on the linear time line, the complications press upon the combatants of his three final books as the Greeks move silently toward the life of victory that has been the horizon of the writer's own present time, while defeat seems to make the Persians act more rigidly and perversely, a behavior they retained, again, into the present time of Herodotus.

In a different pattern, the sequence of ages in Hesiod's *Works and Days* complexly aligns its stages of human development, through the traits that characterize the ages of gold, silver, bronze, heroes, and iron respectively.[4] There are thematic overlaps – analogies of one age to another. But there are no actual societal overlaps from age to age, since Hesiod declares that each age comes to a definite close, except the last. The thematic overlaps are not reasoned about; they are simply nested into the vocabulary. As Hesiod starts this part of his poem, he makes it a departure; he says he will "give the high points of another account."[5] The present age is the iron one, and it is unclear whether any cyclic possibilities reside in the pattern. And the causality for the massive transition from one phase to another is assigned not to human action but to the gods. The ages of Vico, by contrast, are cyclic; and they are also historical in that they derive from the declared actions and thoughts of men; they are "poetic" or imaginatively man-made in Vico's special sense of the term. Hesiod's ages of man offer a macro-historical series, as well as an anthropology, though in a context dominated by ethical and poetic concerns. The same is true for Plato, with allowance made for differences.

When Hesiod speaks of touching the high spots (*ekkoruphôsô*), he implies that he has chosen to omit detail, just as Homer claims to have been obliged to omit detail.[6] Yet after his summary of the ages of man, Hesiod once again shifts his conception, going on to tell the "fable for kings" of the hawk and the nightingale. The historiographic set has been engaged, but it has not yet been disengaged from myth, from the "lies like truth" (*Theogony* 26–34), or from modes of fiction – or for that matter, in this prephilosophic age, from what amounts to an equivalent for philosophy.

In historiography proper, the writer asserts as well as states the validity of his referent, and that makes his statements point initially and finally outward. Consequently the detail in a historiographic work cannot strictly speaking be assigned to the "effect of the real," because its asserted verifiability makes it more than a mere effect. To use another of Barthes's terms, the detail in history cannot be designated a "punctum," a uniquely focusing detail, as in a photograph.[7] In a sense the linearity of a historical work puts everything on a par, from the accident that happens to bring about one ruler's premature death (Herodotus' Cambyses) to the complex of strategic purposes that leads another to pull out an entire vast army and leave a second army behind to continue the fighting (Herodotus' Xerxes). A fictional work gives a sense of an ending, and an ending as well; nothing happens after it that the writer does not tell. But history is open-ended in more than a formal sense. Even for Hesiod there will be a future to the iron age, which may mean its continuation or may mean other ages, like or unlike the past ones. The patterns of similarity and dissimilarity that Hesiod has mounted imply as much.[8] He initially matches the five ages of man to the story of Prometheus and Pandora, another account of effects on origins. And as Nestor's accounts in the *Iliad* remind us, there is a dim past to the Trojan War, just as the poem keeps reminding of a threatening future – one that, in its historiographic dimension, is the real future of a real Greece.

Both because of its assertive and "flat" relation to its referents, and because of its necessary openness to real past and real future, a historical work cannot subsume its details under the categories of the "ornamental" or the "diegetical" – if this last fashionable term, a rough equivalent of "narrative," can be made to carry more theoretical weight (as it can for fiction and film) than "narrative" would for the discussion of sequences in historiography. The very notion of an "effect of the real" implies such a distinction, and implies a coherence into an essentially fictional conception for the details that are not supernumerary. In a fiction the coherence of the details allows other details to be "left over" for the effect of the real. In earlier terms, the distinction made by Percy Lubbock (though of scenes rather than details) between the "pictorial" and the "dramatic" has been abrogated by the initial referential and linear conception of a historical work.[9] And the "psychoanalytic" dimension of the detail, which would refer it to defensive and repressive structures in the private life, while not meaningless, would itself be another detail to the second degree in a historical work; it will not go far toward interpreting Herodotus to psychoanalyze the depression of Cambyses.[10]

History permutes the general and the particular along a time line while addressing the real. There is no other logic than the historical work itself that can make past and present permute with general and particular so as to give a sense of events that does not immediately and simply subsume the general under the particular. Of the many paradoxes of which historiography cannot be divested, the relation between the general and the particular is the initial one. The particular in a work of history must be subsumed or it would not be illustrative, and yet it cannot be wholly subsumed or it would lose its raw distinctiveness. This paradox, then, must apply to the historiographic work as a whole, by a sort of inversion, and not just to a puzzling detail. Put differently, the distinction between individual and particular becomes obscured, since any particular detail is a sort of permanent candidate for characterization as the individual of a class that the historian is in the process of defining. This happens by a perpetual implied application, so to speak, of what Charles Sanders Peirce calls "abduction," the entertaining of a hypothesis that remains interrogative – to the degree in the case of history that it is unformulable.

And, of course, in historical discourse the typical is not ruled out either. That is a special category that corresponds to the general by characterizing it as a law – and Hegel, along with Derrida, White, and Foucault after him, has signaled the tendency of historiography both to follow Law and to enunciate law. The special (Hegel's *Besonderheit*) is a category of the particular that highlights its incipiently contrastive nature to other particulars. As Max Weber so elaborately explained in discussing "ideal-types," the typical may be held in thought while there are subsumed under it particular cases no one of which perfectly embodies the type.[11] The typical, and even the general, in the frame of an actual past brought present by an act of writing, can then shadow the particular, and be felt to interact with it. Aristotle, as often (or, indeed, one may say, typically), isolated most of the factors but combined them in ways that do not really help definition:

> The difference between the historian and the poet . . . is this: the one tells what has happened, the other the kind of things that can happen. And in fact that is why the writing of poetry is a more philosophical activity, and one to be taken more seriously, than the writing of history; for poetry tells us rather the universals (*to katholou*), history the particulars (*kath'ekaston*).[12]

Critics from Sir Philip Sidney on have been seduced by this oversimplification, in which one obvious fact, that poetic fictions are invented and histories cannot be, is brought to bear arbitrarily on a different question, the relation between general, or type, and particular in the writings of poets and historians. As it happens, though, the poet (in ways Aristotle helps us to see) melds the general and the particular, just as the historian does. The deep difference of the historian's manner has here deflected Aristotle into an indefensible exclusion – though in making it he has isolated what remains a final, and perhaps unsolvable, puzzle in the historian's work, his radical enlistment of detail.

Annals and chronicles, king lists and the like, cover a past that necessarily involves a time sequence, but they preserve that sequence rather than interpret it, even if their formulation, like any human utterance whatever, rests on the substratum of an implied phenomenology. Such writings contain, in the timeworn phrase, the materials of history rather than history itself. Even the Gilgamesh epic, insofar as it characterizes the hero as both a benefactor to the society for which he builds cities and a problem because of his rampages, begins to do some of the discursive work that may properly be called historical. E. A. Speiser makes a good case for a sense of the past among the Sumerians and the Akkadians, and even for the materials in their literature from which may be reconstructed a series of phases in history.[13]

In the Bible historiography begins by the concatenation of previous records. Such, even more saliently, is the practice in China, where chronicles give way to the *Spring and Autumn Annals*, which are included in the canonical list of classics and form the basis for the beginning and continuation of actual historiography in the work of Ssu-ma Ch'ien. His enterprise and principles served as the basis for further such writing, and for amplified commentary upon commentary, throughout two millennia.[14] In the work of Ibn Khaldun, on the other hand, an independence from the particular phrasing and data-selection of prior records manifests itself in a range that carries a full historiographic force, with an attention to the long view that is reminiscent of Herodotus, Vico, and even Braudel.

Medieval Latin historians were rarely so free in organization or so clear in discursive purpose as the great Arabic historian. Gregory of Tours abounds in details and in random stories, and a careful study of his work would find an interpretive historiographic residue in it as well as the materials of use to later historians. However, the pattern of the actions he narrates, in the parts I have looked at, conforms simply to the patterns of saints' lives or the opposite. And his moral purpose remains statically Christian, as his statements in the preface to his first book clearly show. In the preface to his fifth book he begins to weary – as he well might, finding no other pattern in them – of the details (*diversitates*) of the Franks' civil wars, referring them to a predictive citation in Matthew.[15] The passage from Matthew can interpret the actions of the Franks religiously but not historically, being remote from the historical context and so lacking even the particular historical force of Jeremiah and 2 Isaiah, who write from and toward the same context as the actions they assess. Unlike Matthew, Gregory has drawn no historical inferences; he has simply noticed a plethora of troubles. Growing tired of them, he has drawn on this scriptural passage to give them a moral dimension. Indeed, in its own historical context, the New Testament passage, as Christ gathers the twelve to send them out into the world, warns them of severities that are on the horizon because something like an apocalypse is at hand. Gregory's use of the passage is moralistic and somewhat static; he wearies while writing about what seems a very long progression of horrors. Christ says in the next verse, "he that endureth to the end shall be saved," in a historical orientation absent from Gregory's citation (though not wholly from his actual historical accounts).

The Carolingian historian Einhard is more Plutarchian in approach as he shapes his portrait of Charlemagne, but the encomiastic-religious purpose dilutes the historiographic one.[16]

Quo tempore imperatoris et augusti nomen accepit. Quod primo in tantum aversatus est, ut adfirmaret se eo die, quamvis praecipua festivitas esset, ecclesiam non intraturum si pontificis consilium praescire potuisset. Invidiam tamen suscepti nominis, Romanis imperatoribus super hoc indignantibus, magna tulit patientia.

It was on this occasion that he accepted the titles of Emperor and Augustus, which at first he disliked so much that he said he would never have entered the church even on this highest of holy days if he had beforehand realized the intentions of the Pope. Still, he bore with astonishing patience the envy his imperial title aroused in the indignant Eastern Roman emperors.

(Chap. 28)

The crowning as Holy Roman Emperor is here placed in a context where Charlemagne exhibits the magnanimity of modesty, which has a political force, while he exercises de facto a power that has thrown a protective mantle over this particular beseiged pope. Later historians might question the extent of the envy actually felt by the Eastern potentates, wrapped up as they were in their own power, but at the same time Einhard's sense of Charlemagne's achievement holds. Aside from some incidental personal details of the sort that his model Suetonius provides for his Caesars, Einhard presents mainly an uncluttered, succinct account of the gradual, and highly impressive, spread of Charlemagne's empire, and then of the preparations for preserving it through orderly succession. In that way he has given more than a monographic cast to his biography, while at the same time not wholly escaping the encomiastic mode, and also not attaining to the sort of comparative sense of changes in historical time that Suetonius does manage by presenting a sequence of rulers. Here Einhard's selection of material and his organization of it is historiographic, as is his preponderant confinement of Charlemagne's life to its public and imperial activities. At the same time, the encomiastic purpose holds him slightly and firmly short of the scrutiny of events, the interpretive focus, that we expect from the out-and-out historian.

An interpretive focus is what we do get in the constantly bewildering mix of history and fiction of the Old Norse narrative "Njalsaga," which presents an intricate, coordinated series of collective actions and judgments by small groups and individuals over a period of nearly a hundred years. It stays close to what it considers the facts, and it is more historiographic than the work of Gregory or Einhard – even though the constant effect of actions by individuals makes it read for us like "fiction." And for Arthurian material, the early medieval poet Wace may be said to be more historiographic than his source, the medieval Welsh historian Geoffrey of Monmouth, to the degree that he (1) cuts Geoffrey's "Prophecies of Merlin," (2) seems to have applied the criterion of historical validity in using his sources, (3) made a Herodotus-like research trip to southern Britain to check out some legends, and (4) invokes eye witnesses or oral traditions.[17] Even Wace's statement that what he tells is part truth and part lie sets a dividing line between historiography and fiction inside the work itself.[18] We are not much further ahead today for criteria about Arthur, whose existence and particular identity remains an open question for which fresh evidence keeps being discussed.[19] The equivocation is imbedded in the very term "hystorye," as this term is used in the preface to Malory's works by Caxton, his editor and publisher. In one sense "hystorye" means "story" and allows a slant toward fiction; but in another sense – aligned in the phrase "hystoryes and actes" about events told in the historical portions of the Bible – it designates an interpretative, sequenced account of actual past events, a sense emphasized in what Caxton says of "Arthur, whos noble actes I purpose to wryte in thys present book here folowyng."[20] Malory, indeed, is much more encyclopedic in approach than the earlier Arthurian writers, as though he is gathering all the evidence he can. But, of course, the element of fiction remains in him as well, to be distinguished but not disentangled from the historiographic element that is often ignored.

There is a historiographic element in drama, indeed, from the *Persians* of Aeschylus to the very recent *Civil WarS* of Robert Wilson.[21] This last is a nearly wordless attempt to establish congruences between public and private in social action, and in modern time between Frederick the Great, the American Civil War, and future wars. Shakespeare's history plays constitute an interpretation of British history more attentive to collective action, as well as, of course, more composed, than their source in the chronicles of Holinshed.

Ezra Pound said early that an epic poem is a poem that includes history. Pound has produced in the *Cantos* a work that interprets congruences between principles of governance and the long span of Chinese history – represented by sharply selected details. The principle changes from section to section. In "Rock Drill" he makes a point of isolating the details for their singularity as "core samples," to carry out the "rock drill" metaphor, revelatory early statements, often single words or ideograms, about the forces and conditions of the transition from the Shang to the Chou dynasties in the China of the second millenium B.C. and analogues to them across history.[22] In a poetic perspective these details are emblematic and ideographic. But they are verified details; Pound has gone to documents for them, and often quite out-of-the-way documents like legal records (for England, the sources of Coke) or the letters of political figures (those of John Quincy Adams and Jefferson for America), as well as, in his later handlings of China, to the same early historians that Chinese compilers themselves use. The details, moreover, are set in a pattern of temporal sequence that gives some of them the discursive character of historiography. In this they also function like the details of such totalizing historians as Spencer and Toynbee.

Pound's all-embracing theory does not simply pretend to document its principles about usury, governance, and spiritual coherence at one moment of time. It also takes them across time, from the eighteenth century to the present, especially in America, and analogously in China for three millennia, and in Italy for a fifty-year period of troubles centering around Malatesta, as well as in the rule of the Lombards, and at other points, too, always sharply focused, in Western history. Pound's abrupt changes of perspective, both from small segment to segment and from large section to section, have the effect of heightening the relation between general and particular, of clarifying the analogies, and of suggesting their expansibility.[23] Yet, of course, in this nearly contemporary work the mix of "history" and "fiction" remains, and the discursive intention is not just to understand sequences in the public past. The poetic image-cluster and the historiographic event-cluster are fused.

Fused with intense, subtle, and increasingly condensed poetic procedures are these sharp acts of collocated historical interpretation, which it is hard for us to see initially as such because of the modern division of labor that assigns history to professional historians, and also because Pound verges on a one-thesis, obsessive, and sinister explanation of some events. Still, his notions of "sensibility" and "points of rest" are not so different in their organizing force from the *virtù* of Machiavelli or the various prudential principles that historians tend to adduce.

In the opening of the "Rock Drill" section, for example, Pound takes the points of Chinese history synchronically, when in his earliest mentions of China he had merely praised Confucius, and in the "Chinese" cantos he had given a lengthy and detailed, if severely selected, account of two millennia of Chinese history, beginning before the Shang, to whose demise he here returns:

LXXXV

Our dynasty came in because of a great sensibility.
All there by the time of I Yin.
All roots by the time of I Yin.
Galileo index'd 1616,
Wellington's peace after Vaterloo.

chih

a gnomon,
Our science is from the watching of shadows;
That Queen Bess translated Ovid,
Cleopatra wrote of the currency,
Versus who scatter old records
ignoring the hsien form

25

The ideogram Pound prints (and which I have not reproduced) means "sensibility," and it is quoted from the Chou King, a Chinese classic of history.[24] The ideogram comprises signs for "heaven" over "cloud" over "raindrops" over "ritual," and in Pound's handling is itself a complex artifact, almost like an archeological object, handled for its historiographic (as well as for its poetic) resonance. He will recur to it several times as he concludes the *Cantos*, but in this first, late appearance he lodges it firmly both in a document and a historical context. It is what the Duke of Chou said in 1753 B.C. to the just-conquered remaining officers of the Shang Dynasty: "Our dynasty came in because of a great sensibility." This, presumably, denies that the military power, by which the Shang was conquered, can be assigned causal primacy. Such sophistication, such Periclean self-possession in an early conqueror, already constitutes for Pound an instance of the sort of governmental management that I Yin, named in the next ideogram ("that one/ruler"), would have had to face as the last chief minister of the Shang Dynasty (1766–1753 B.C.). So that it is "All there by the time of I Yin," and this governmental sensibility, in Pound's agrarian-derived populism (and Fascism) connects to natural processes, to the growth of trees. "All roots" are there too.

For mutual historical illumination this situation is succinctly and compactly juxtaposed (in what Pound's literary critics call a "thought rhyme") to some Western ones, first the late but deplorable indexing of Galileo, which compares poorly with what Pound sees as Chinese moderation. Next it is matched to the skillful diplomatic close of the Napoleonic Wars, which is a worthy analogue to the Chinese because Wellington managed to stave off territorial disasters by his "sensibility." The German pronunciation of "Vaterloo," taken with other items in these cantos, delicately but definitely brings into the comparison what Pound sees as the bungled resolutions after World War I and World War II. All of this, taken together, can be seen as the next ideogram, *chih*, a place of rest or pivotal point from which a constant Confucian judgment can be brought on these epochal historical developments. *Chih*, the "ground whence virtuous action springs" (as it may also be rendered), has itself served as a sort of "gnomon" or measure of shadows throughout the *Cantos*. Pound uses the *chih* ideogram to conclude Canto 52, in which at the beginning of his run through two thousand years of Chinese history, he matches it against England, Spain, and Italy. He quotes it again in Canto 79, in a context where he himself is offered as a sort of salient example, the Pisan cantos. Again, its other occurrences are in these still later cantos. "Our science" could be the editorial "we"; these events all cast shadows. And it could also be "the West," since the West as well as the East used the gnomon in both senses as sundial and as columnar shaft. Elizabeth I, an encourager of a simple science that had not yet broken, as Chinese science had not, from its astrological connections, is here addressed by her nickname, whereas in Canto 66 she is seen in the aspect of one who uses rituals for an instrument of terror; in Canto 108, as concerned with taxes on grain; and in Canto 109, as the sponsor of Coke, the great jurisprudent who for Pound carries the weight of something like Chinese sensibility in government.

To translate Ovid, as "Queen Bess" did, does not just evidence culture; it, too, is a compacted historical evidence, a rock-drilled core sample of what that culture and its leaders were like. Ovid resembles Pound in a skillful long-range view of metamorphoses, and of the proper civic uses of religion, as well as in managed notions about Eros. Ovid, like Pound, has also been condemned by the authorities; and so he is both an analogue and a source for the *Cantos*, as well as a litmus test as to the extent of culture in the governed (a test Malatesta passes in Canto 76 by having seen to a fine edition of Ovid). What connects to culture in Pound – it is his one-thesis obsession – is the currency, and that queen in the Roman Empire whom we know for her military connections, her beauty, and her position in the Ptolemaic dynasty, is here singled out by Pound for having given attention to what Pound sees as crucial matters, just as the Chou put sensibility ahead of military force. "Cleopatra wrote of the currency," an act which for Pound makes her at once aware of where the true forces lie, decisive enough to turn her attention to them, and cultured enough to write about them – as distinct from the nameless others with whom these two model rulers are contrasted. The last quotation, too, is from the Chou king, encapsuling Elizabeth and Cleopatra further in Chinese discriminations based on *hsien*, "virtue" or "the good."

So the *Cantos* proceed, increasingly preoccupied with history as they progress, in a condensed presentation that is not just poetic but also interpretative in the manner of Hegel or any other philosophical historian.

To define the discursive domain of historiography as it attains the self-realization of a relatively unmixed utterance, it is not sufficient, as Dominick La Capra has remarked, to have recourse to the conventional criteria of unity, continuity, and mastery of a documentary repertoire.[25] Nor will just a rhetorical analysis do, even one that has been updated to include modern reshaping of ancient categories and modulated through philosophical manipulation. The aim or intent of the writer goes deeper than merely a desire to adhere to, or even to remold, accepted canons of persuasion in an "interpretive community," to use a current critical locution. The historian's aim defines an area that has a logical validity; an inquiry is conducted under conditions where detail is necessary but not explicitly full in its coherence, where data is tested for factuality but only at the outset, and where causality is envisaged but cannot, for the nature of the inquiry, be rigorously enchained.

Herodotus begins talking about the assignment of "cause," and he says he will "proceed by singling out one man," Croesus (1.5). However, the Croesus he fingers at the beginning has wholly disappeared, except by implication, once Herodotus engages the major presentation in his last three books of the final confrontations of Greeks and Persians. The causal pattern has not been abandoned, but its implication is so deep that the links in the chain cannot irrefutably be enumerated.[26] In what is now a receding past, the Lydian king Croesus has been conquered (1.76–84), and has been an adviser at the Persian court (1.155–156; 3.14), serving as a wise man the way Solon served him (1.28–33). His kingdom is so fully absorbed into the Persian Empire that Sardis, the former Lydian capital, has become the traditional western limit of Persia, "from Sardis to Susa."

As though in a shadowy reference to that expanding span, a message is sent from the still more distant Athens all the way to Susa after Xerxes has conquered that city (8.54). And it is at this point, where it is functional in the time sequence, rather than earlier, that Herodotus gives his famous summary of how reliable these Persian messengers are, "not stayed by snow, rain, heat or night" (8.98). Lydia in Asia Minor lies in territory that already borders on the Ionian Greeks; geographically as well as psychologically, Croesus' vanished kingdom is intermediary between mainland Greece and Persia. The Ionian Greeks are an easier problem, for bordering upon the Persians, but still a difficult one because they are Greeks, rather than Lydians or Scythians or Egyptians. Negotiations with and hostilities against Ionian Greeks occupy much of the middle ground of Books 4 through 6. In Book 7, finally, Darius slowly undertakes the vast, final expedition, which has been in the historian's view from the beginning, the attack on mainland Greece that culminates in the defeat of Marathon. This is picked up and played out a decade later by his son Xerxes, whose expedition culminates in the defeats of Thermopylae, Salamis, and Plataea.

While Herodotus follows the military detail in a geography that has ominously gone into more microscopic focus and lost all its demographic dimension, the strategy constantly interacts with the buildup of temporal factors to the point of combat, and also with the psychology of the participants. In this regard Herodotus demonstrates, finally, an accord with Collingwood's too summary prescription (it would exclude Braudel among others), "All history is the history of thought."[27] It is finally, the psychology that is crucial, and the psychology reflects the ethnic style. King Xerxes takes advice; the democratic Greeks hold councils. This difference determines the outcome of the war, as the royal leader makes mistake after mistake, assuming that the enemy is cowardly rather than strategic; or that the potential division among the several Greek states is something his side alone can see (8.68) when Themistocles has registered identical advice from Mnesiphilus (8.57); or that he can override his officers' recalcitrance before listening to the advice of his skillful female admiral Artemisia (8.69; 8.101–103).

As references to wide space shrink in these last books, so do references to distant time; but they will crop up now and then as they irrepressibly bear on the factors at hand; so the foundation of Athens by Ion bears upon the difference between Ionians and Peloponnesians (8.45). It is told in a context of exact temporal and strategic bearing, when the Greeks are marshaling at Salamis. Here Herodotus' "Catalogue of Ships" has multiple and specific causal and temporal links that Homer's lacks. And the pattern of the future after the war, the time from the last battles of 479 to Herodotus' first writing around 430, gets touched in through a number of details that become sequent conditions more than just random episodes. There are twenty of these "future" details, enough to suggest the complexities of continuity but not so many as to overshadow the strong linear progression of the central actions in time.[28] In addition to these, a sense of later developments is worked into the history, for Pericles and his clan, for Themistocles, and in other respects, as Charles Fornara points out.[29]

In its overall presentation, however, the strong linear progression pulls together, and flattens, the historical account that has thus realized itself. Gibbon, indeed, shows a marked difference in style between his history on the one hand and his memoirs and critical writings on the other. To take a different kind of discourse oriented toward the depth explanation of factual events in time, the case histories of Freud exhibit among them different sequences of general discourse, analysis, temporal sequence, and fullness of key event.[30] They are freer in this regard than the historical discourse can be, which departs only marginally from its time sequences. By the time such a vast buildup has been carried off as Herodotus manages, the thematic echoes can carry fairly far, and without displacing the fundamental temporal order. The last large series of events in the *Histories* is an adulterous intrigue managed by Xerxes, a sort of epiphanic psychograph of his frustration, distraction, and persisting pride (9.108–113). The narrative of the intrigue registers and exemplifies the state of affairs the Persians have come to with respect to the Greeks. It has, indeed, all the air of a conclusion, not a beginning. This is the crucial, temporal difference between this final episode and the one it echoes thematically, the intrigue between Candaules' stealthy exhibition of his naked queen and her ultimatum that Gyges either assassinate her husband or die, an intrigue that put Gyges on the Lydian throne and began the whole sequence of Herodotus' history (1.11–14). These real intrigues, at the beginning and at the end, stand in a sort of thematic contrast to the less proximate, and less accurately adduced, causes of the hostility between Greeks and Asians, the famous erotic episodes that Herodotus takes upon himself to dismiss rather elaborately before getting to Croesus, the abductions of Io and Helen of Troy (1.1–5). The linearity, again, flattens out these various intrigues into long-range juxtaposition; they characterize the beginning and end, not the middle.

At the very end Herodotus appends an anecdote about the crucifixion of a Persian by Greeks on the Chersonese (9.120). This victim happens to be the grandson of a man who long before gave Cyrus a fairly detailed plan so that he might undertake the very same vast attempt at imperial expansion that Cyrus' descendants did carry out, and largely with the successes Herodotus has recounted. They carried it out everywhere except among the mainland Greeks and the more remote of the Scythians. Cyrus, ironically we may say, refuses this plan, saying that to broaden conquest would *soften* (not harden!) the Persians (9.122). In its temporal scope this recollected statement recapitulates to before the beginning of Herodotus' history. In its systematic measure it eases out of its merely anecdotal frame to cut several ways.[31] The Persians listened to Cyrus and held off; then they forgot. They did in fact fulfill his prophecy by softening, by becoming proverbial for their luxurious softness in the time of Herodotus. Yet during the Persian Wars they are hard, perhaps weak for being too hard. Indeed, at the time of Herodotus' writing the Athenians themselves, who were expanding their empire, were also becoming more and more known for a possibly unreliable softness; and they were also hardening toward their allies.

The possibilities of applying connections here are multiple. In having intently followed through his "inquiry" so that it suggests constant causal connections in its large but limited sequences, Herodotus brought to expression, and to interconnection, such possibilities of multiple application as both close and project a truly self-realized history. Herodotus has not just lined up his details in temporal sequence, like a chronicler, nor has he made them either supernumerary or expansive, a literary view of personal relations, like Homer in his "fictional" aspect. The public bearing, and the causal nexus, appear at every point, but at every point they are subjected to the temporal sequence. The final intrigue of Xerxes is both appended and illustrative, as though its disconnection from the factors of the war – rather than its causal connection to the war – can help it serve as a capping illustration of the war's effects. Such a presentation would not have been possible without what we have come to realize as a historical sense, one that sets into interdefinition the large interactions of two opposing peoples and the developing fates of the leaders involved.

3

PARTICULAR AND GENERAL IN THUCYDIDES

I

ERODOTUS DISENTANGLED PROSE sufficiently from myth, setting Thucydides a standard of comprehensiveness and purity that he could better only by a more rigorous purity. If, indeed, Herodotus is included in the nameless writers whose principles he abjures (1.20–22), he abjures not all of Herodotus but rather, among other things, Herodotus' penchant for the exotic and *fait divers*. Thucydides' pejorative for him, *muthōdes*, "story-like" or "mythy," can certainly be stretched to cover Herodotus' sense. It is because Herodotus exercises a somewhat loose control on particulars that with him, or those like him, the details "prevail into the mythy."

Thucydides states, as he inserts his statement of principles between the "Archeology" and the account of the war, that he rests upon inference (*tekmērion*),[1] and also on inference with a rigorous linear connection to his subject, "all inferential data in order" (*panti hexēs tekmēriō*; literally, "every datum"). "All" points out explicitly that every particular detail is sifted, taken with "inferential data." Taken with "in order" it starts to remind us that Thucydides' focus will shortly change and that everything he says will bear still more directly on the war.

Writers who do not follow this recommended process may be poets (*poiētai*), an activity that engages them in setting up another kind of order: they write not *hexēs* but *kosmountes*, an "ordering" that is at the same time an adorning, in a dead spatial metaphor that implies a comprehensive *kosmos* and not a linear sequence. Poets are here coupled with those whom the reader, after Herodotus had written, and in the climate Havelock describes in *Preface to Plato*,[2] might be tempted to distinguish from poets. These are the *logographoi*, or "prose writers," who also put their material into order. Their procedure of doing so is designated by yet a different locution, *xunethesan*, "put together." The three terms of ordering (*hexēs, kosmountes, xunethesan*) align the three types of writers according to the principle on which they organize their material. Thucydides is a fourth kind, and it may be

31

said that he here emphasizes testing his data rather than ordering it himself because his ordering must evolve in the long presentation he is beginning.

The *logographoi* "put together" their material, Thucydides says, so as to be more attractive to the *hearer* – and the term "hearer" assimilates them back to the more automatic persuasiveness of oral reception. The term *prosagōgoteron*, "more attractive of access," also comes close to a notion of *fait divers*. They are "more attractive than true," and Thucydides then returns in this passage to his single explicit positive criterion, the checking of evidence datum by datum.

It is, to be sure, a distance in time, and not in space or in logical ordering, that by his account will make presented data "prevail with incredibility into the mythy," "*apistōs epi to muthōdes ekneninēkota.*" The compound verb *ekneninēkota*, which might also be rendered "win over," indicates a dynamic process. It suggests struggle to control detail that the writer loses because he does not understand how deep for the historiographer this question goes. The writer whom Thucydides rejects gradually succumbs to a "mythy" element in his data by failing to scrutinize it. As if in still fuller deference to what he has articulated here, he couples his declaration in the next chapter, that he has constructed or reconstructed the speeches on reliable evidence, with the assertion that in any case they bear directly on the war. Both of these statements may be taken as an implied rejection of Herodotus' scope. Thucydides' term *zētēsis*, "inquiry by scrutiny," steps up the rigor of Herodotus' *historiē*, "investigation," a term Thucydides wholly avoids using. As for his initial look at events remote in time, Thucydides has already shown them to bear directly on the factors of the war. His opening is similar to Herodotus', except that Herodotus begins almost at once with a narrative as a causal explanation. Herodotus, after setting his theoretical premises briefly, immediately starts sifting stories in the search of a single cause for the enmity between Europe and Asia so as to account for the beginning of the Persian War. He settles on a single particular, Croesus, "pointing out this one man" (*touton sēmēnas*). It is from that vantage that he gets into his narrative; "pointing out this one man I shall proceed into the further presentation of my account" (*es to prosō tou logou*) (1.5).

Thucydides, by contrast, makes no attempt, as he sets up his background, to make a particular datum carry the burden of his general account. He stays on the plane of factorial semi-abstraction until he reaches the point in time and space that immediately involves his particular war, deferring even the fifty years preceding it, the "Pentēkontaetia," till somewhat later. In the still longer range of the history from Homer to the Persian Wars, the "Archaeology," though he sees the particular details as subject to the dimming and mythologizing falsification of extended time, Thucydides has proceeded by what he calls "most explicit signs" (*epiphanestatōn semeiōn*), "sufficiently" (*apochrōntōs*). This final adverb suggests that in this instance he has contented himself with something like a minimum of data, but after having tested evidence that did prove testable. A sufficient condition has been met for moving from particular to general. The signs were "explicit" – for those who could test them. Again, if this is a revision of Herodotus, it is still very much along Herodotus' lines, except for the adjustment of particular to general, though it could be asserted that Herodotus, even when he doubts, does not usually hint that his evidence is at a low state of verifiability. And the possibility here implied by Thucydides, that evidence might somehow be at once scanty and adequate for explicit reading, puts him in a different realm from Herodotus by raising the criterion not just of verifiability but of sufficiency (*apochrōntōs*).

None of this is directly countermythological, though it works even harder than Herodotus does the countermythological substructure of its organizational principle. This principle tests for validation a relation between particular and general, whereas the myth is always easily both particular (Oedipus or Apollo) and general (man or god). Applying the myth, as the poet does, requires intelligence but not testing. On the contrary, the poet is free to invent within the outline of his story, as well as to emphasize some aspect of a known story. The historian must establish the aspects of a story that has happened but that he must coordinate from scratch. Plato strains his dialectic, as it were, to restore myth's easy congruence between particular and general without recourse to story, except as a supplement or as a movement onto another plane. For Plato connections between the planes, between dialectic and myth, are left mysterious, and the philosopher's enterprise is neither confined nor fully defined by story-bound pattern types. The ideas are in heaven, but they are history-less, unlike either men or gods.

None of this is exactly countermythological either. Thucydides is of course still more negative than Plato on the uses of myth as a factor in the progress of his main narrative. "Having prevailed into the mythy," the abjured practice of others, suggests also for them an intellectual process – one that logically could include Plato's – to mediate that which has been allowed to become "mythy." Such a softening of rigor would work against Thucydides's task in hand.[3]

Thucydides leaves Herodotus' ethnographic inquiries almost wholly behind. He does not need those particulars. He differs from Herodotus more notably in that restriction than he does in his attitude toward the gods.[4] Thucydides does differ from Herodotus in addressing a collective action that was going to be a failure rather than a success. It was also going to transform the Greek world, for the time being, much more radically that the larger-scale Persian conflicts did. Since he could not have known these two large results when he set himself the task of writing his history, his initial vantage could not have been conditioned by Cornford's sense of a tragic sense in him. Still, it is well to keep Cornford in mind, though at a distance, if we wish to understand how Thucydides, like his younger contemporary, Plato, took the tack of rejecting much previous discourse and much of the previous conditions thereof, as an impetus for his own.

In the complicated dispute that he reports over the Athenians' drawing water in sacred temple precincts when the Boeotians themselves abstained (4.97–98), Thucydides intrudes no doubt about the many factors implicit and explicit.[5] One factor stated, indeed, is that the Athenians and the Boeotians share the same gods (4.97.4). Nor does Thucydides question the myth of Tereus (2.29) when he distinguishes a different Tereus in the background of Sitalkes. He actually provides the detail that poets have memorialized the nightingale incident, asserting in the same sentence that the distance between the countries would make a closer origin plausible (*eikos*) for the better-known Tereus. As the scholiast says, "It is significant that here alone he introduces a myth in his book, and then in the process of adjudication" (*distazōn*, literally "doubting").[6] The significance would lie not in confirming his rejection of myth,[7] and still less in his subordination to it, but rather in the austerity of a focus that rarely allows a myth to obtrude. Still, in this instance, even the veracity of a mythical past may be brought in as a tool to sift facts. And when he later brings in the myth of Alcmaeon (2.102), it serves to define a region. Even a myth will do as a focusing particular.

2

In the reckoning of time and the marking of stages for his *History*, Thucydides abstracts his work at the outset, demarcating time as related just to his event-series; he numbers the years according to the war, usually by summers and winters. "And the eleventh year ended for the war," he says (5.39). This particular time there is a tinge of ironic emphasis in the statement, since it marks events after the "Peace of Nicias" in 421. The flat statement works to keep his progression relentlessly even. His movement forward implies a prior reasoning: "If anyone were to doubt that the war continued just because a much-broken treaty of truce was in force, I will use the word 'war,' as I did before, to characterize this particular year too." Such sentences as "And the eleventh year ended for the war" place a purely temporal mark on the event-series, coming as they do regularly but unpredictably in the work, and sometimes with his own name attached to them. Their neutrality reinforces their inexorability.

This writer of prose has left behind him the ambition of Herodotus or of Ion of Chios. He can rest with his method, and with his verbal means. The relation between oral and written is not a problem for him, as it is posed in the *Phaedrus* of Plato and felt all through Plato's work. Nor is Thucydides' prose simply a convenient instrument, as it is for Lysias, Anaxagoras, and the medical writers. Thoroughly grounded in his principle of testing, Thucydides' written account can then re-include the oral, and spectacularly, in the form of the complexly structured speeches of the work. His principle of testing reassures him to the point where he asserts he can reconstruct these speeches, if necessary, on the basis of reports of what the main arguments would have been ("the way each of them seemed to me to have spoken most likely what was needed [*ta deonta malista eipein*] about what the present situation each time was," 1.22). Such a confidence implies that the oral, to be congruent with the written and narrated, need not be poetic. The memorable need not be poetic.

Plato's speeches, of course, are not remembered speeches. They are mostly fictive reports of conversations imagined to have taken place. Plato's initial fiction corresponds to Thucydides' reality. Thucydides asserts that in their essentials these speeches really did take place. The essentials are points in an argument, which thereby and therewith are put on a par with other historical happenings, the *logoi* with the *erga* – and in this passage he contrasts the two terms, words and deeds. This pair remains a key duet of terms throughout his work. The speeches show that a sequence of points in an argument is a sequence of constated particulars. The enchained generalities and abstractions for which the speeches are notable actually attest to their verifiability. The generalities guarantee that the particulars have been tested by sifting.

What was spoken in the past, then, assimilates to, as well as assesses, what was done in the past – so long as it is within the living attention-span of the writing historian.

This vision of the public experience arises from a new privacy of the literary act. The philosopher, the poet, the tragedian, and even the medical writer, had an audience defined somewhat by social subgrouping and personal contact, or else by a ritualized occasion. If Heraclitus was a private writer, he would seem to have taught, and he is said to have laid his book, in the temple of Artemis. In carrying out lessons before a band of faithful auditors, Socrates, and Plato himself, conform to the pre-Socratic prototype for the thinker's posture to an audience. The historian, however, from Hecataeus on, is committed not only to prose but to the written book freed of such social constraints. The exile of Thucydides here offers a literary dimension as well as a vantage for research. He intensifies these conditions. He has no immediate audience for his book, but a long wait. And a certain randomness defines his potential readership; he has no theater or academy or group of poetry enthusiasts or ritual throng or law court in which it will be taken up.

It is in the act of writing history that the comparatively free audience-expectation of the modern book suddenly comes into existence.

Moreover, while Herodotus undergoes a comparable wait, and compasses a long work in comparable privacy, he can expect some national accolade from the very success of the Panhellenic effort he so fully accounts for. There is a tradition that he read his work aloud to general acclaim. As with Livy, there is an element of patriotism in his history. Thucydides, however, resembles the gloomy Tacitus. Even before the failure of the war, since, as he in effect tells us, he set himself the task before knowing its outcome, his testing of factors implies a neutrality toward the parties that has a sharper cutting edge that Herodotus'. Thucydides' vision of public events, while highly generalizable, is intensely private and personal, the more so that its generalities are based not on a prior social code, and not even on Herodotus' neutral ethnographic stance, but on the writer's principle of inference as it governs the enunciation of factors. Thucydides proposes no community, as Plato does, and in a sense he does not himself describe a community, though he lets other do so. Brasidas is as noble as Pericles, and there is more in his actions than the specifically Spartan. Instead, Thucydides provides a basis in action for the principles on which community rests, though unlike Machiavelli he does not turn explicitly to such questions. The high degree of communal energy that characterizes Athens in Pericles' Funeral Oration, on the evidence, is a momentary increment from the prosperity whose evolution is described in the Archaeology and the Pentēkontaetia. As Schadewalt says, Thucydides "indicates general horizons for events (*das Geschehen*) and carries within himself a mode of the theory of categories. Both aspects determine the picture Thucydides offers us . . . in tension with each other."[8]

The social implications of the "achievement laid up forever," the *ktēma eis aei*, lodge Thucydides in a lonely universality, even though *ktēma* in its regular Homeric and post-Homeric sense suggests personal use in a social context. Looking personally backward, his events have to have been lived through in order to have validity, and they must be tested in order to have general relevance. Looking ahead, their effectiveness is indifferent with respect to the group that might be imagined as consulting the *History*.

Yet in one sense Thucydides is conservative and by implication community-minded. His narrative concentrates on military history, to as great a degree as the *Iliad* does. Thucydides is a military historian to the point that the coherence of so striking a cultural tribute as the Funeral Oration becomes a problem for the interpreter. In this Thucydides is closer to Homer than Herodotus was. For the military hero that a poet celebrates, too, the poem is a perpetuation of his fame to generations that might otherwise forget, as Pindar reminds us. The poem, too, is a *ktēma eis aei*. What Thucydides memorializes, however, are events not only unique but also explicitly patterned and exemplary. So are Homer's events, to be sure, but the poet, in his social role at least, seems to be organizing the pattern to enhance the uniqueness, whereas for Thucydides it is the other way around.

So forceful is this difference of priorities between the patterned and the unique, the general and the particular, that almost alone it sets the conditions for the kind of unity, for the historiographer. Homer had already taken the giant step of transforming the sort of battle frieze to be seen on Mycenean reliefs, late geometric vases, and later on classical pediments. He transformed this persistent Near Eastern celebratory focus on awesome clashes by setting organizational principles over the clash. Thucydides goes Homer one better by reversing the order of priorities, and also by abstracting the principles, but clashes are still far more particularized in his history than the clashes of Herodotus.

Thucydides' concentration on military operations also throws them into perspective through the touching in of power motives, the more strikingly that the military is so preponderant.

In depicting military events, Thucydides is linear, but also expansive. The same thorny problem-states – Thebes, Corinth, Corcyra, Potidaea, Platea, Mytilene, Amphipolis, Syracuse – keep turning their thorns to the event. A complex particular moves in time toward generality. Yet in the imposition of power considerations, Thucydides' view seems to be at once cyclical and general. The same factors keep applying; the course from inception of campaign or attack to resolution keeps taking place. He demonstrates the fact that failure or success may not be clear, and he is consequently careful to point out those occasions when both sides claim victory. In Thucydides the word *kuklos*, "circle," is always just spatial, though he uses the verb *kuklousthai*, "circumvent," in a way that combines the linear and the cyclical. The verb implies making linear progress in getting past something by using a circular movement.

If we cannot press the buried metaphors in Thucydides so far, the sense he creates of constant ratiocination invites us to look for it in his very diction.

3

The war is involved uninterruptedly, though with unpredictable particular variations, in a forward linear flow. Thucydides shows it at every point gathering up, and pulling against, assumptions and causes – to such a degree that defining his uses of terms like *aitia*, "cause," and *prophasis*, "pretext," entails intricate comparisons and discriminations.[9] In Herodotus the large, understood forces pause, as it were, for stocktaking. In Thucydides they never rest from their dynamic interaction. The spreading pool of ignorance about the past that Thucydides stresses can be taken to imply some ignorance about the present. And ignorance, signally the Athenian ignorance about the complexity of politics in Sicily, operates itself as a factor, dynamically. The speeches exhibit the tension, and the syntactic intricacy, of trying to construct present-oriented rationales for specific behaviors. This is true even of Pericles' Funeral Oration. Its high abstractions and graceful definitions are aimed toward the propaganda purpose of boosting morale. Pericles takes an opening backward look at the past superiority of Athens, and this is adduced as a factor in giving the Athenians an extra edge in the coming conflicts. He ends the speech in a well nigh Hitlerian injunction to replace the dead soldiers with living children who may grow up to fight for Athens (2.35–46).

Still, there remains always such a surplus of factors and emphases that they get out of hand – not counting such natural disasters as the plague, which follows very soon after this oration. The plague brings still more deaths, deaths that only most tangentially can be connected to the war. The multiplicity of factors jerks the linear flow ahead, as is shown in pairs or larger groups of speeches – the normal case. A second speaker will exhibit a generalizing intensity of recombining particulars as against a first speaker, by his reliance on inevitably different emphases and possibly different factors, even when the geopolitical assumptions are the same. The speeches show general and particular in the process of refocusing their relations, at a level above the level of the narrative that includes the speaker. The contrast between these two levels creates a third one, that of the historian himself, whose discourse resembles the speeches in abstract texture while it subsumes them into and against the grainier texture of narrative.

Such is the pressure from many quarters that events tend to outrun Thucydides' translinear account of them. Often something has happened that his unavoidable focus at one point has kept out of his narrative in its proper sequence. Occasionally, and revealingly, he violates strict chronological order.[10] So, in a specific instance, the very relaxedness that a new peace implies, and the necessity to realign forces once they are not firmly marshaled against one another, leaves participants in a position of overreaching themselves through an inevitable incapacity to cover all the factors. This is the case at the beginning, when Athens incurs the wrath of Sparta by trying to manage forces at the perimeter of her league. It is the case after the peace of Nicias once again, when in 420 many states – Argos and its confederacy, the Athenians and Alcibiades personally, the Boeotians, the Corinthians, the Megarians, and the Spartans – all re-expose themselves by negotiations in more than one contradictory direction.

Those Spartans "who most wanted to dissolve the treaty" (5.36) secretly urge the Boeotians and the Corinthians to ally themselves first with Argos (and its allies), and then subsequently with Sparta. They thus call into play the factor of internal factionalism, as Alcibiades will soon effectually do. This project, if it were to be actualized by these hostile Spartans, would, as often in Thucydides, kill two birds with one stone. It would offend the Athenians by violating the condition of the truce that no new alliances be formed, and by forming them it would strengthen Sparta. However, on their way home from Sparta the Boeotians (5.37) encounter, again privately, some Argives who are waiting there for the purpose of urging the very same alliance; persuasion turns out not have been necessary. Back home the rulers of Boeotia endorse this policy, but the four councils that constitute the decision-making group in Boeotia see it differently:

> Before these oaths could be carried out with Corinthian, Megarian, and Thracian envoys, the Boeotian rulers publicized these events to the four councils of the Boeotians, who carry the whole authority, and advised them to carry out oaths with those cities who would wish to swear a common oath for defense (*ophelia*). But those who were in the Boeotian councils did not accept this rationale (*logon*; also "speech"). They feared to act in opposition to the Spartans by swearing a common oath with the Corinthians, who had defected from them. For the Boeotian rulers did not tell the councils the events in Sparta, that among the Ephors Kleoboulos, Xenarches, and their friends had advised allegiances with the Argives and Corinthians to be carried out first and then allegiances with the Spartans. They thought that the councils in deliberation (literally, singular, *boulē*), even if they did not tell them this, would not vote otherwise than they themselves had determined beforehand and advised. The affair thus took a contrary position, the ambassadors from Corinth and Thebes went off, and the Boeotian rulers, who had previously intended, if they had persuaded them of this, to try to make an alliance with the Argives as well, no longer brought anything about the Argives before the councils, nor did they send to Argos the ambassadors they had promised, but there was a certain lack of care (*ameleia*) and delay in all these matters.
>
> (5.38)

"Lack of care" and "delay" are constant threats in the tension between the forward progress of events and the instability of factors pressing upon them. Shortly, in fact, Alcibiades plays a double game by courting both Sparta and Argos, which is itself playing the double game of courting both Athens and Sparta. Alcibiades is actually playing a triple game because, by lying himself, he tricks the truthful Spartan envoys into looking like liars before the Athenian Assembly (5.44–45). But then another factor, one from the different realm of natural catastrophes, supervenes over this already complicated situation: "But an earthquake occurring before anything had been confirmed, this assembly was adjourned."

In the war a state is itself a complex factorial entity, and mounting the factors as action progresses keeps setting general and particular into tension. The weight or permanence of one such factorial entity – say Corcyra or

Sicily – cannot be assessed in its magnitude of importance with relation to that of another entity, until "after the fact." The "fact" itself is a state of affairs that would neither be summarized by the particulars that constitute it nor accounted for by the generality of a covering abstraction. So the "state of affairs" stands, and constantly evolves, as a tension between these two. Corcyra in this initial state of affairs could not have been assessed beforehand as incurring the set of events that would place it at the center of the conflict between Athens and Sparta over her handling of Epidamnus (1.25–56), which drew the Spartans' protesting attention and helped precipitate the huge war. Four years and a vast complex of events later, this trouble spot, as it turns out, re-erupts, and the same dominoes tumble against one another in a different order – Epidamnus–Corcyra–Corinth–Athens. This time the crisis centers on the sort of internal struggle between oligarchy and democracy that later develops as a parallel threat to Athens itself (3.69–85). Corcyra is caught as an entity in a linear sequence of power-events, whose unstable timing of recursion in a stable repertoire of factors is guaranteed by the steadiness, and the dynamism, among those factors. A census of the relevant factors would include Corcyra's (or any other entity's) geographical distance from a friendly or a hostile power, its relation to colonial ties, both originally (Corcyra is a colony of Corinth) and as it develops (Epidamnus is a colony of Corcyra). Financial status, too, is an important factor, stressed by Thucydides in the Archaeology: the ability of a state to translate its resources into an army, a navy, and defensive installations. There are, further, the local political factions, and also a state's prior relations to such more powerful entities as Athens or Sparta, as well as the history of the state's prior role in the common effort of the Persian War. A state's geography comes into play somewhat differently, too, through its relation to war operations in close or distant theaters, and even to holding operations on or near its own terrain.

By adducing all these factors and at the same time often keeping them implicit, Thucydides allows for their permutation, for the subjection of their particular manifestation to the linear progression, and also for their coordination into usually unstated generality. The factors are never quiescent and never isolated, he implies – even though his conception obliges him to be silent about them when, as inevitably on these very grounds, his attention is drawn elsewhere. The naiveté of the Athenians in not seeing, and in not listening to Nicias about, the inevitable interplay of such factors on the large Sicilian terrain, is implied by what has already been shown to bear on the picture. If this is so with little Corcyra, all the more so with huge Sicily. The roll call of the Sicilian allegiances as they have shaped up (7.57–58) carries with it an implied demonstration of how force, racial ties, prior allegiances, prior colonial ties, and geographical proximity all permute beyond the power of Athens to control them, or even to influence them very much.

As against the interrelations of the political entities in Herodotus, which happen pretty much on a binary or a ternary basis, those in Thucydides permute in the face of a common but relentlessly evolving situation that presses on each state differently, but on all alike. The forces are, as it were, centripetal, in spite of the geographically centrifugal relations – often across much water or over rugged mountains – of the Greek states. The relations in Herodotus may be themselves called centrifugal: a state, once it has resolved a stress point, is left to itself for a while in a stable condition. There is no general center of common interest or high permutation of factors between Persia and Ionia, or between Persia and Lydia. And for the big conflict mainland Greece has pretty much been left out, except for occasional consultations, until Persia turns by elimination in her direction. State marriage in Herodotus (never except remotely in space or time for Thucydides) may involve a number of state groups, as that of Astyages involves the Medes, the Persians, the Lydians, the Scythians, the Cilicians, and the Babylonians (Herodotus 1.73–77).[11] But the factors are static, and separable. As these peoples go their separate ways, or take up their places within the Persian Empire, they tend to stay in place.

The speeches, either antithetical or propagandistic in character, serve to externalize the counterpoise of forces in Thucydides' *History*. Just so the forces drawn up for conquest will meet either prevailing or succumbing counterforces. But then, whichever the case may be, still other forces will be operating against them. And the speeches are oriented to the military action that their own situation orientation and usually their antagonistic stance serve to mirror. The speeches address the war; they are the speeches of those "either about to make war or already in it" (1.22).

This practical relation of the speeches to force, and their subjection to force as in some ways just another manifestation of it, differentiates Thucydides from debaters in the law courts, from philosophers like Protagoras and tragedians like Euripides, to whom he has been compared.[12] Any lawyer is less involved, any philosopher more theoretical, any speaker in a tragedy more oriented to his own subjective needs, than the speakers in the *History*. Even Alcibiades, the most self-centered of his actors, must try to force a yield of personal gain out of collocating unremittingly public factors. Those are, therefore, the forces to which he addresses himself, like everybody else in Thucydides. In this sense we can almost see the leaders in the *History* bringing to bear upon events the critical view of the historian himself. And, though he may not offer the abstract political science of Machiavelli, he does, indeed, show a "latent systematization of power."[13] The generalities are always being tested, from the very first sentence of the

History, by the particulars held in a tension that reveals the force organizing them.

In the *History* a speaker may be said to aim at an equilibrium, a stability among factors. "Stable," *bebaios*, is a favorite term of Thucydides. He has Pericles say that the Spartans, as farmers, will offer their bodies rather than their material resources (*chrēmata*), because the latter "would not be stable against the possibility of being exhausted" (1.141). The envoys of threatened Mytilene, speaking at the Olympic banquet upon Sparta's urgency, speak of a "stable friendship," while twice invoking *aretē* in international relations. They go on to say that if all states were independent, they themselves would have been "more stable against innovating" (3.10). In urging death for the men of the rebel city, Cleon declares "the worst thing of all is when nothing remains stable in what we are concerned about" (3.37). Brasidas' excellence creates a "stable expectation" that other will be like him (4.81). Under the upheavals and proscriptions caused in 412 by the Four Hundred, a 'stable mistrust" is created (8.66).

Moreover, as these quotations illustrate, the term "stable" is applied under the most diverse circumstances. There is no set of general principles that would allow Thycydides to enunciate laws governing stability. In military operations – and they are his subject – he may give specific tactical rationales, but he is not only silent, as Gomme points out, about the relation of tactics to strategy.[14] He must be silent, except about specific factors at a given place and time, on the principles we may deduce from the *History*. Especially is this the case in a Panhellenic conflict taking place in what might be called a weak macrosystem: Corcyra, Corinth, Potidea, Naupactus, Thebes, Samos, Lesbos, Melos – to say nothing of the various Sicilian states. All are subject, taken together, to an idiosyncratic congeries of factors, even if the factors taken singly are the same. It is a stable fact that they will be unstable, and variously unstable. The tension between general and particular operates unpredictably in accordance with predictable laws. The weak macrosystem is balanced, by contrast, against what might be called a microsystem, one that is stable or at least potentially stable, based on the internal organization of a given state by itself, whether small like Melos or large like Athens and Sparta. And the event-moment in space and time – say the siege of Mytilene – is itself a stable microsystem, rendered in turn unstable by the incursion of other systems. This is borne out vividly by what Dover calls "the complexity of classification" in the lineup of combatants before the Sicilian conflict.[15]

Buildups have a tendency, as in this impressive one, to work up to a grand slam of alliances. Since the kind of equilibrium that will obtain at a given moment is unpredictable, in the linear progression of the *History* the length and complexity of a buildup may be cut short at any time. So in one among other earlier intrusions of Athens into Sicilian affairs, twenty ships are sent in the summer of 427 to aid Leontini against Syracuse; and then the Athenians establish themselves at Rhegium. Thucydides reports this buildup right after, and implicitly as a consequence of, the petering out of the Corcyrean rebellion. He makes his transition by the lightest of contrasting particles, a *de*. Such a *de* introduces the next transition, qualifying and curtailing this buildup; the second plague in Athens; and then earthquakes. Consequently it might be said – this time a *men* marks the transition – that the Athenians turn away from their original purpose when they attack the islands of Sicily (3.88), and unsuccessfully. Then the following summer they do prevail at Mylae and win Messina, other events intervening to give the buildup and deployment a still further twist. Finally for this campaign, they sail from Sicily to Locris, an action they perform in implied concert with a prior Athenian force there (3.96–98), and become masters (*ekratēsan*) of Locris. The whole final development is swift enough to be recounted, as though by interrupted aftermath, in a single not lengthy sentence (3.99).

The balance between predictable factors and their unpredictable development correlates with the principle governing the speeches, which take up a fourth of Thucydides' text. Cornford makes the distinction in the speeches between "infiguration," or fitting in what is already known, and "invention," or adding new matter.[16] As the Corinthians say while pressing their case for war at the beginning, "war least of all proceeds on specified conditions (*epi rhētois*), but manages the many factors (*ta polla*) of itself according to contingency (*paratunchanon*)" (1.122).

This stated rule succeeds in a simultaneous declaration and ironic qualification, a contradiction of effects it can imbed because the "contingency" can be either predictable, if seen for its factors, or unpredictable, if seen for the impossibility of knowing what direction the particular combination of their multiplicity (*ta polla*) may take. The Corinthians are, in fact, here revealing their ignorance and overconfidence – traits that elsewhere in Thucydides, as here, accompany bloodthirstiness. We have the curious mechanism of whistling in the dark by calling the dark dark. The speeches are, in Schwarz's words, "willed showpieces (*Glanzleistungen*) of his political-rhetorical thinking."[17] In them the intelligence of the historian converges with the intelligence of the participants. He attains his pitch by assuming they can rise to his intelligence on occasion. He envisages an intricacy in their thought comparable to his own by putting it on the same plane as his own. "Intelligence," *xunesis*, is a special word for Thucydides, and as he uses it the prefix, *xun*, "together," is active.[18] It is an active intelligence, brought to bear on keeping particular events open to the possibility of the sort of general subsumption that the historian brings to bear on his narrative. Twice Thucydides pairs the term with *aretē* (4.81; 6.54). Intelligence here allows for the "reckoning by probability" (*eikazein, eikos*), and for an attempt to avoid that "irrationality" (*paralogon*) that characterizes human life generally (8.24) and especially wars (3.16; 8.28; 8.61). Intelligence is the chief safeguard against that which it cannot reach to, the "unapparent" (*to aphanes*).

The long range is distinguished from the short. It is only after his death, on a long range, that the long range of Pericles'"foresight" (*pronoia*) becomes apparent. The Spartans expect it to be the short war they have no firm grounds for conjecturing; thus expectation works against "good sense" or "the best opinion," *para gnomēn* (5.14). *Gnomē* is a term Thucydides uses well over a hundred times, more than twice as many times as Herodotus. In this term intelligence is conceived as an activated natural faculty, often spoken of as "applied" (*prosechein*) to the particulars of a situation.

Nicias, in the debate before the Sicilian expedition, declares that his reasoned speech would be weak (*asthenēs ho logos*) if he did not try to avoid speaking against his best opinion (6.9). Pericles links the possibility of stability to the active use of intelligence: "Overconfidence (*auchēma*) can come about through lucky ignorance even for a coward, but disdain is our resource who can rely on good sense (*gnomē*) to prevail over our enemies. And under equal fortune an intelligence (*xunesis*) on which his superiority of feeling depends will provide a more tenacious daring; and it relies less on hope, which is the strength of someone without resources, than it does on good sense from the resources it had, a good sense of whose foresight is more stable" (2.62). This complicated sentence at its conclusion comes down hard on three key words: "good sense's stabler foresight," "*hēs (= gnomēs) bebaiotera pronoia*". Mere hope, *elpis*, is often given a pejorative cast in Thucydides.

In the stylistic flow of Thucydides' own presentation, these definitions of the mind at work on events crop up with special saliency in the speeches. They evidence a high self-consciousness in the speakers. In the narrative they tend to cap a presentation, as Regenbogen[19] points out of the moment when the Athenian ships are setting sail and "the foreigners and the rest of the crowd came for the spectacle as to a conception (*dianoia*) that was sufficient [to draw so large a crowd] and incredible" (6.30). The term I have rendered "conception," *dianoia*, is hard to translate here. Presumably the unprecedentedly large fleet is visible evidence of a thought process in the leaders of Athens. It is the result of thought, not thought itself, the usual sense of *dianoia*. Thucydides has been consistently proceeding at a level of factor-collocation that would justify the odd transfer here from thought to what it produces. As for the crowd, the sight is "sufficient" to draw them (*axiochrēon*), but at the same time "incredible." The crowd has a somewhat easier thought process than the leaders, that of wonder, and their reaction may be taken as part of a cautionary series with the earlier dissuasions of Nicias and the much earlier warnings of Pericles against such expeditions.

In his repeated corrections about the overthrow of the Pisistradae (1.20;

44

6.54–59), Thucydides uses a particular fact, the distinction between Hippias and Hipparchus, as the thread that will provide the proper sequence for an interactive situation. "Factual accuracy," Edmunds emphasizes, "is not the sufficient condition for history in the Thucydidean sense, but only the necessary condition for *to saphes*" ("that which is clear").[20] The rebels from Mytilene use the same term during a summary moment of their defense at Olympia, "Possessing such demonstrable grounds (*prophaseis*) and motives (*aitias*), O Spartans and allies, we revolted; they are clear enough to make our hearers know (*gnōnai*) that we have acted in accordance with sound inference (*eikotōs*)" (3.13). Here, actually, the term "clear" is an adjective, *sapheis*, applied to two terms that are themselves intricate, separately and in relation to each other, *prophaseis* and *aitias*. Further, *sapheis* here gathers up and organizes a whole interlocking set of intellections: the lengthy ones of the Mytileneans, the inference of the Spartans and their allies, and the Mytileneans' thought that what they have thought will make the Spartans and their allies think (*gnōnai*) they have carried out their thought on sound inferential grounds (*eikotōs*).

Nathan Rotenstreich speaks of a "paradox implicit in historical knowledge. This knowledge is always *causal*, yet it is not based on material *laws*."[21] Thucydides works his way steadily and alertly through this paradox. "Pretext" is a more ordinary sense of *prophasis* in Greek[22] and "cause" of *aitia*. Taking the terms that way, they would provide a ladder of certainty for the principals in the *History*. But they cannot be taken just that way. They are ridden with the complexities of connection and the doubts about cause, implied in questions that get examined soon in the philosophers of the following century. The ladder of certainty is always collapsing because the situation changes so radically and frequently as to suggest at once the inadequacy of these intellections and the presence of some force of the same type beyond the reach of summary, though comprising the same factors. For all their alertness, the Mytileneans do not extricate themselves. Nor in the whole *History* do the Athenians either. Later, replying to the Athenian claim that the weak go to the wall (5.89), the Melians enunciate Thucydidean principles, "It is useful not to dissolve the common good, but for what is sound (*ta eikota*) and just to prevail in the danger as it is perpetually coming about; and for who is persuasive, even when what he says is somewhat short of accuracy (*akribeia*), to be able to have the advantage of them." Still the Melians are massacred.

"Everything that has to do with war is difficult," Hermocrates tells the Sicilians (4.59). Archidamus says much the same thing to the Spartans, "Things having to do with war are unclear" (*adēla*, 2.11). Gomme observes that the reflection is a recurrent one in the *History*,[23] and Thucydides, from the beginning, adduces the terms "clear" and "unclear" as alternate characterizations for the dispositions of particular events.

4

The elusive factors bear impersonally on states, but it is men who personally make the decisions that activate them. The contrast between factors and persons, brought to a head in Thucydides' method, carries within it at once a permanent disparity and a perilous resolution. Such a contrast is another aspect of the oscillation between clarity and its opposite, an oscillation that operates in any successful historiography between explanatory subsumptions and selected ongoing events. Men are generalizing particulars in a particular situation that is governed by general factors reshuffled through time. Thus is a comparable interaction in Herodotus made dynamic. Resolution into clarity, in a sense, always bears on any specific situation Thucydides depicts, since the factors can only be activated, and thereby raised, as it were, to the second degree, by being taken up in the calculations of participants. After the peace of Nicias, and on the heels of a calculated rapprochement with Argos, the Spartan ambassadors who go to Boeotia decide to return the Athenian prisoners they have been given and to announce the razing of Panactum to the Athenians, who had been promised it back (5.43). The different interpretations put by the Athenians and by the Spartan envoys upon this double announcement, and the different weight given to each event, precipitate a hostility that immediately opens a path for Alicibiades and his rivalry with Nicias (5.44).

Events, by their very nature as crystallizations of decisions, lead to persons, and to particular kinds of persons. The Spartans may be slow and the Athenians swift, as the Corinthians tell the Spartans (1.70). However, the clarity, the resignation, and even the particular brand of selfishness in Nicias, transcend national boundaries and heavily qualify the notion that he is weak. Thucydides rarely expresses estimates of his persons directly[24] and when he does so, he is, as it were, assessing the man as by himself an extraordinary factor, as in the praises of Themistocles (1.138) or the cautionary words about Alcibiades (6.15).

Leaders, in fact, under whatever form of government, are clearly shown in Thucydides to determine initiatives. They manage the forces to which, in turn, they cannot help being subject. These forces include other leaders; Nicias loses to Alcibiades the debate over the Sicilian expedition, and he reconciles himself to it, leading the expedition. But then he is subject to another constraint on the lives of statesmen. Unless they have the precocious gifts of an Alcibiades, they will be along in years when at the helm. And war itself increases the risks of mortality. Nicias suffers through the Sicilian expedition and dies there, as Pericles had died and Archidamus, Demosthenes, and Brasidas, Phormio and Kleon.

Precocity brings with it another risk, which Alcibiades has come to stand for more than anyone else, the risk of brilliant narcissism. He might trick the Spartan envoys, but over the long run a man's character shows. It was inevitable, whatever his guilt, that he would be accused of the sacrilege against the herms and the Mysteries. Thucydides underscores this inevitability by giving us insufficient evidence to decide his guilt either way, where usually it is accuracy in just this sort of affair that he seeks. The fact that Alcibiades is accused, as he inevitably would have been, impels this rapid and adaptive politician to avoid probable death by fleeing when the Athenians send to have him returned for trial. Other Athenians had fled to avoid prosecution, not always so successfully. Later, Alcibiades repeats this success, slipping away from a Spartan death sentence to the entourage of Tissaphernes. He would inevitably be using his talents to intrigue with the Persians and with the Spartans. Through the irony of developments, he escapes the disastrous Sicilian campaign he had urged, contriving his way back finally into the good graces of the Athenians.

The forces, at every point, are there to be managed, and the very change of their configuration from present moment to present moment provides a clever man with the opportunity to take them up without necessarily being impaired by the way he had done so before. Finally Alcibiades' selfishness and skill at diplomacy come into their own under the conditions that prevail after the Sicilian disaster, in the eighth book. This, as Westlake reminds us, is "packed with reports of secret negotiations and intrigues."[25]

The disintegration of the Athenian empire entails a decentralization of forces that permits playing one force against another without effective checks. In this way the person of Alcibiades, at this moment in the war, functions doubly as an agent upon the factors and as a mirror of where they stand. Indeed, the very mode by which agency combines with mirroring will differ. Pericles' particular bearing on the general situation is resumed into the speeches that exhibit him. These speeches exemplify a particular phase of the war and serve as agencies to influence a particular kind of policy – or not to influence it, since they are partially unheeded.[26] "When he died his foresight about the war was still further unrecognized" (2.65). For Nicias, and for the dark events around Syracuse, the man and the time are characterized first by a reasoned speech not forceful enough to prevail, and finally by the relative silence of desperate defensive maneuvers. The individual in this instance would seem to have developed under the pressure of circumstances, since at an earlier moment Thucydides has asserted that Nicias urged the peace "to leave a name to later time" (5.16).

Thucydides' managed silences, too, as Reinhardt and Schadewalt have emphasized,[27] preserve a neutrality. "What [your] nature always willed has been tested to the point of truth" (3.64). Literally "the things (*ta*) which your nature always wished" are plural and particular. The wish is general, and the truth is singular, a generalizing abstraction (*to alēthes*). So the Boeotians say to the Plataeans, but the notion will apply to the whole *History*.

Most of Thucydides' uses of "nature" (*physis*) mean "human nature." Of the twenty times he uses *physis*, "human," or its equivalent is attached in nine. This quality, however, is not taken for granted, nor does it operate on the surface. It must be "tested to the truth" by the participants, and overridingly by Thucydides himself, whose *History* constitutes such a testing.

Nor is war a special case. "Many difficulties (*polla kai khalepa*) fell upon the cities in the uprising," he says of the Corcyrean revolution, "Occurring and always bound to occur so long as the nature of man is the same, though more peaceful and changing in their forms according to how the particular transformations of events (*xuntuchiōn*) may impinge (*ephistōntai*)" (3.82). "For all things by their nature (*pephuke*) do indeed diminish" (2.64), Pericles reminds the Athenians at the moment when he is assuring them that the glory of their empire will survive in memory. Nature, necessity (*anankē*), and customary behavior (*to eiōthos*) are linked in his presentation.[28]

Thucydides' neutrality extends even to the presentation of himself in the third person both as a writer and as a participant (4.104). And it is significant that in his "second preface" Thucydides adopts for a few sentences the grammatical sleight of an imagined, neutral observer. "If someone should not consider the intervening truce to be accounted war, he would not judge rightly. Let him look to the events as to how they are discriminated, and he will find it not a likely thing (*ouk eikos ion*) to assess it peace" (5.26). The elaborate negatives here, and the six different verbs for mental sifting, establish, as though through syntactic struggle, the neutrality of viewpoint that Thucydides everywhere aims at. A sense of the severity with which he maintains this steadiness of view impends upon this neutrality, and a sparkling clarity of presentation holds his details in unwavering coordination. The neutrality heightens the relational interaction between general and particular.

Many constraints bear on the historian's task generally, and some obligation to preserve neutrality is one of them. Neutrality is the attitudinal aspect of the obligation to narrate events "*wie es eigentlich gewesen.*" Another constraint obliges him to report only facts he can be reasonably sure were the case, Thucydides' "accuracy" (*akribeia*). Still another constraint obliges him to select them for some kind of congruence to his purpose, as Thucydides is a military historian. Another constraint inhibits the historian from avoiding a mediation of his events, inducing him to adjudicate between general and particular in any case. He is obliged to steer somewhat clear of what could be taken for bare reportage. On the one hand he must suspend judgment while suspending his long-range connections. On the other hand mediation requires that he not give just a flat summary of events; he must not simply offer a chronicle. The balance of mediation obliges the historian to steer a constant middle course between tract and chronicle. Thucydides not only understood this requirement, as Herodotus had. The speeches offer him an indirect, "doubled" mode of introducing interpretation while maintaining neutrality.

In this sense he must hold to the narrative, and his skillful management of all these constraints strengthens his narrative, allowing it to take on details for which the necessity cannot be argued on any logical framework. In the case of Thucydides, these details sometimes stun through similarity; particulars worked on by a coordinating intellection evolve into generality. The narrative of the Sicilian campaign would presumably carry a comparable sense of the action if it were divested of half its details, and yet the extra details do not diffuse the narrative, but rather sharpen it; the particulars function as cumulative demonstration, and in the narrative mode a sense of their necessity does not vanish once a general view is sensed.

Any historian is thus pulled in two directions by the particular and by the general. The mystery of his task resides in striking a balance between them that will operate along a narrative line. To quote Paul Ricoeur again, "it is the place of universals in a science of the singular that is at issue,"[29] though even the word "science" is misleading here, since in the historical narrative hypothesis and conclusion are fused together. There is a mix of the two in the ongoing narrative that the historian mediates, and may mediate differently within a given work. Particular and general have different relationships in the speeches of Thucydides[30] and in the more directly narrative portions. The speeches have a double role as explanatory pauses establishing a general case, and as subsumed particulars globally aligned with details of action, along the lines of Thucydides' constant distinction between *logoi* and *erga*, words and deeds. A whole speech, composed of words, is itself a sort of deed.

Thucydides' statements about persons or events are briefer than his narrative presentation of them. This seeming disproportion or spareness of interpretation actually creates, together with the management of other constraints, a sense that a general view is being gradually furthered. It permits Thucydides sharply to enunciate what all successful historians must, the partial synecdoche that constitutes his *ktēma eis aei*. Particular events have to have been selected for some general aim for them not to be a chaotic mass. The selection is partial even of those the historian can know; for Thucydides these are only the events that have not been inescapably lost in the dimness of time. As particulars they suggest a generality to which they relate; they are inescapably synecdochic. But the synecdoche does not operate the way it does in poetry; there is no whole for which the parts can stand. The whole is only adumbrated, and the synecdoche remains only partial, mediating perpetually between general and particular.

This mediation entails a sense of irony, and for Thucydides, as for all or nearly all successful historians, one event is bound to throw another into an ironic light. The overlooking of Pericles' advice, the escape of Alcibiades from the war he had urged, the fruitlessness of the articulations of the Melians to save their lives, the failure of the overweening Athenians in Sicily – the ironies of event multiply in Thucydides, who rarely makes an out-and-out ironic remark. Some irony in the historical narrative is unavoidable through the initial chaos of the referent, and yet an overall irony is impossible if the historian retains the order of the referent as a goal. The ironies play over the work as a sort of multiple running check against sliding back to mere particulars or against wholly backing some oversimplifying generality that would undo the tension of the narrative. The interpretative touch of ironic statement in later historians like Tacitus or Gibbon or Burckhardt will jog the narrative along. Thucydides, we may say, shows his earliness in the intensity by which he stiffly refrains, by and large, from such touches.

The speeches, again, serve to double the ironic possibilities, not only between event and event, but between what is said and what happens, between *logos* and *ergon*. Any speech, as a complex of ratiocinative recommendations aimed at the immediate future, is bound to be tested by that future, and bound to miss its mark somewhat, generating the implied irony of contrast. And even if the speech hits its mark, there is the irony that still the speech may not be heeded, as Nicias' apt speech is not. There is generally an impelling onward movement toward conquest through the whole *History*, against which any speech, or any sequence of speeches, protests in vain. So there may be said to obtain a further, deeper irony between momentary if tensely reasoned arguments and silent, overriding motives. The Athenians do not listen to Pericles when he recommends restraint about campaigns, at his point of maximum prestige and maximum social authority. "Our knowledge (*epistēmē*) is better than any other force that has good fortune (*eutuchosēs*)" (7.63). So Nicias says to troops whose morale is low as the Sicilians are pressing them hard. Not only does the disastrous outcome render these words ironic. Thucydides' own principles do, since "knowledge," here meaning military skill, ought to be sufficient to know that it will be a decisive factor only if other factors are equal. This is what Pericles had insisted long before, weighing up the whole balance of factors. There is also the irony that Nicias, who seems to be imitating Pericles, is inadequate to his model. Of the factors that count, it is precisely strength or force (*rhōmē*) and happenstance (*tuchē*) that figure large.

So particular is the narrative of Thucydides that it often stays close to the maximum point of particularity. In its onward flow, however, it pauses most notably for the speeches, which do not halt the action but poise on the brink of futurity and decision. They themselves, seen not as ruminations over the events but as themselves an event, particularize still further. They are given not word by word as uttered, but word by word to delineate the arguments presented. This summarizing function makes each clause, and sometimes each word, a microscopic encapsulation of dialectical relations between particular and general. Their reference is to a moment in an idea, and as such the terms in the speeches present a double face. With respect to their referents they are reconstructively concrete, and their character as signs must work more actively just because the individual words are constructive rather than reported. But the actual words tend to be abstract with respect to their lexical origin, and also with respect to their syntactic function.

Because of his onward flow, and his intermittent nervous adduction of qualifying abstraction, Thucydides is not felt to be slipping from particular to general, or from concrete to abstract. He can get back again very fast. For this reason, as well as for those Finley gives,[31] he operates, in a sense, midway between the paratactic (*lexis eiromenē*) and the hypotactic or subordinate (*lexis katestrammenē*). Actually, even to describe him so may obscure the fact that the coordinates on which he operates permit of the occasional combination of these two styles, but not for their discrimination. His partial synecdoche makes him always potentially a subordinator, but the stringing of one event onto another in the narrative line pulls against this tendency.

To use G. E. L. Lloyd's terms for persistent tendencies in Greek thought,[32] Thucydides implicitly subsumes both the polarity that would make him subordinate his particulars under a general heading and the analogy that would make him coordinate them. Polarity and analogy are readapted to the constantly testing linearity of his presentation. In the sentences, frequent in his work, which seem to derive from, and distort, the *isocola* formalized as stylistic desiderata by Gorgias, the balances between clauses are almost always subverted. The feeling given by Thucydides' wrenching style is of too much pressing upon the sentence to be distributed out in even clauses. Only in the tendentious argumentation of an advocate uttering a speech will they be pressed into balance, or in the high piety and enthusiasm of Pericles' Funeral Oration. And even in such instances the abstractions brought into balance are themselves terms not usually polarized.

The compression of thinking into these terms individually shows in their somewhat unusual contrast collectively. Dionysius of Halicarnassus takes Thucydides to task for a number of stylistic sleights. All of these could be redescribed as distortions of language into imbalance under pressure: the substitution of noun for verb and of verb for noun; of active for passive and of passive for active; the change of tenses; the frequent use of parentheses and involution; the substitution of person for thing and thing for person. Dionysius speaks, too, of Thucydides' enthymemes. These logical proofs with one term left out will serve well to indicate the onward "slippage" of Thucydides' demonstration.

As Wille says of Thucydides, "Formal analogies can cover actual differences, while actual analogies are concealed in formal variations."[33] This happens especially when he is moving from more particular to somewhat less, and from concrete description to abstract reflection, as spectacularly in his transition to general observations after the Corcyrean rebellion:

> Every form of death occurred, and as is wont to happen in such cases, there was nothing that did not transpire and yet more extremely. Yes, and father slew child, and people were dragged from the altars and killed upon them, and some were walled up and died in the temple of Dionysus.
>
> So the raw strife proceeded, and, because this was the first example of it, it seemed even worse than it was; later, practically the whole of the Greek world was stirred up, because in every state quarrels gave occasion to the democratic leaders to ask for aid from Athens, to the oligarchs to ask Sparta. In peace, without the excuse and indeed without the readiness to summon them; but in war and with an alliance at hand for either side, to injury for their enemies and to advantage for themselves, inducements were easily furnished by those wishing to innovate. Many were the calamities that befell the Greek states through this civil strife.
>
> (3.82; Gomme, revised)

Intermediate abstraction has already begun in the sentence about the father killing the son. This is not one instance but a type case of which there could have been more than one instance, though one single salient instance of horror, the walling up of supplicants in the temple of Dionysus, brings the sentence to its climax. The typification of the first instance modifies the horror of the last, while the actuality of the last instance concretizes the whole passage even further. There is also a shift between singular and plural for the verbs here, and for "temple" (*hieron*), though the cases are suspended differently between particular and general.

The jump to much higher generalization in "raw strife" (*ōmē stasis*) reveals, and incorporates, the horror. Thucydides controls and compresses his diction while his syntax forces itself into extreme torsions here. He goes on to describe another kind of slippage than the one his mastery is enlisting, a slippage of diction:

> So as the affairs of the cities kept going into revolt, the later outbreaks, by knowledge of what had gone before, were marked by ever-increasing novelty of rationales, shown both in the ingenuity of attack and the enormity of revenge. They changed the customary validation of terms as men claimed the right to use them to suit the deeds: unreasoning daring was termed loyal courage; prudent delay specious

cowardice; moderation the cloak of timidity; an understanding of the whole to be in everything inactive.

(Gomme, revised)

"As men claimed the right to use them," translates the single term *dikaiōsis*, "adjudication," a term usually applied to court actions, and sometimes to the punishment assigned after judgment. All these senses tinge Thucydides' use without modifying it. *This* word refuses to refer to that which it describes and unwittingly exemplifies – the "judgers" are "judged" by Thucydides; indeed, they are even effectually self-punished by destroying the use of the language to get them out of such later enterprises as the Sicilian expedition or the rule of the Four Hundred. Under such stress, however, the language must respond by a corresponding compactness and agility, as in this extraordinary case Thucydides is exemplifying when he takes the fairly unimportant Corcyrean rebellion as a typifying instance. When he gets to still bigger and more crucial events, he cannot digress for so long.

The increasing pressure not to digress confines Thucydides' presentational variation simply to relativizing his linear detail. Sometimes he offers a great deal of detail, in campaigns important for the war or for their emblematic force. Less often he scales down the amount of detail he gives. We cannot be sure that his omission of speeches in Book 8 indicates incompleteness and not the writer's decision to foreshorten from this point on. It could be said that, having been initiated to the argumentative processes of speeches, the informed reader is in a position to make do with summaries so as to move forward more cogently.

The principle of relevance in the *History* operates simply at first; every detail must relate to the one all-embracing war. But the *History* starts out at a higher level of complexity and generality than the one it maintains, since Thucydides delays his prefatory theoretical remarks till after the Archaeology and delays the Pentēkontaetia ("Fifty Years History") till after the beginnings of conflict. The shifts from one to another of these four initial units might tempt a critic to provide schematizations,[34] but the onward pressure of events will undo such large-scale structural deductions. Thucydides cannot be found to have invented a structure more complex than his implied rule of explaining only what time has brought new to the condition of the war. He could have built the *History*, after all, on a version of Herodotus' more complex pattern, the intertwining of distant with close time-frames, and of ethnographic monographs with narratives. As it is, his narrative almost mimetically changes course as the war changes course. The Olympian viewpoint of the Archaeology and the Pentēkontaetia cannot be brought in to provide a Herodotus-like expansive disquisition about Persian politics in Book 8.

By that point Thucydides has established his theoretical control over the factors governing the narrative. Those come as a gradual revelation, and their increasing explicitness reinforces the simple but elusive near-pattern he is single-mindedly elaborating. The synecdoche can only be partial, but its theoretical force holds.

Plato, and later Aristotle, devised categories that would solve problems about the relation of general and particular. In the *History*, Thucydides offers an ongoing instantiation of how one kind of relation evolves between general and particular through a complex temporal sequence.

4

REFERENCE AND RHETORIC IN
HISTORIOGRAPHY (GIBBON)

I

IN A WORK OF HISTORIOGRAPHY, attention to time tends to double against, and to reinforce, the necessarily temporal progression of sentences. Taken together, the time of the referent and the time of the rhetoric both converge and interact so as to produce a sense that there is something lurking under the story being told.[1]

At no point can we attend just to the rhetoric of a historiographic presentation, because historiography has meaning only by its relation to a series of referents taken singly and together. Its intentional purpose is undercut if that crucial relation is slighted in favor of rhetorical constructs. So much must be preserved of the injunction of Ranke, ambiguous and at the same time simplistic as it is, that history must tell the event or events "as it actually was," "*wie es eigentlich gewesen.*" But rhetoric cannot be dismissed either, since it enters the best historiography as a repertoire of modes for delineating whatever lurks under the story or must be left implicit in it. All human utterances imply conditions for themselves and so are metalinguistic. But the high performances of Herodotus, Thucydides, and Gibbon enlist and energize their presuppositions much more complexly.

Verification and narrative, then, or verification and rhetoric, run inescapably together in the true historiographer's work. On the surface this union appears in the tendency for every single sentence to carry an interpretive as well as a documentary force, though of course in a string of narrated details the interpretation is just implied. But if the writer verges too close to the limit of interpretation – if he is just making a case – he tends to lose his diachronic doubling; the work is synchronized, and he is merely arguing for a particular interpretation of the institution of slavery in the American South or the debilitating effect of religion in the Roman Empire. But the fact that someone who does not accept Gibbon's thesis can still assent to the historiographic validity of his narrative, partial as it must be, means that Gibbon has escaped a full analogy to the legal brief.

Length does not bear on this question, because some legal briefs are as long as Gibbon; nor does detail, because they can be very detailed.

At the opposite pole, if the historian approaches the limit of mere verification – of just listing cattle in the Anglo-Saxon Chronicle or of just describing the administrative structure of the Roman provinces in some more descriptive substitute for Gibbon – then he is approaching the limit of bare description, even if his work is widely compendious and scrupulously sifted, like Roland de Vaux's *Ancient Israel*. Gibbon only inserts his survey of the provinces in an ongoing narrative the way historians since Herodotus (with the *"Egyptioi logoi"*) have tended to do. So he always stays inside the historian's implied limits, even though he concludes his history, arrestingly and puzzlingly, with some deductions about the actual physical Rome and its buildings in space. He retains, in the diachronic doubling of his sentences, some correspondence to the diachronic progression of his events. And thus, in ways we may continue to discuss, he remains ironic, or tends toward an implied irony even though he has recourse only intermittently to the explicit ironic sentences that tend to be a constant feature of narratives written by historians of any persuasion.

Irony, indeed, inheres in the very conception of historiographic presentation as a sort of guarantee that the work in hand provides a sense of overall coherence not wholly subsumable under a flat thesis. Further, some factors in the presentation will be more prominent than others, as for Gibbon personal probity involving a tolerant attitude toward various religious practices is more important than geography and for Braudel the other way around. Since this is so, the pre-selection of factors will induce the partfor-whole air of synecdoche. The very relation between moment and overall sense makes a historiographic work tend toward a part-and-whole presentation: toward synecdoche. An overall conception, as a factor becomes of leading importance, will embody itself in some datum that attaches slanted characterizing terms, and the presentation will verge on metaphor. When a given factor moves toward capital importance for the historian, he will tend to embody that factor in given expressions or even in given figures, and in this sense he may be said to employ metaphor.

Moreover, both the ongoing progress of his words in time and the fact that time itself is the medium and the condition of a diachronic narrative means that one sentence will follow another and one event will either follow another as presented – the regular mode – or be perceived as actually following in time, when the historian takes the liberty of looking back or ahead. In all this he may be said to be metonymic.

The terms "irony," "synecdoche," "metaphor," and "metonymy," then, are applicable to the writing of any valid historian at all. Hayden White shows considerable ingenuity in having selected these four terms to characterize the rhetoric of history, even if there are problems with the lack of coordination among them.[2] And though he wishes somewhat exaggeratedly to characterize particular historians of the nineteenth century by forcing them predominantly under one of the four headings, he is in turn forced to combine these terms – often with great appositeness – really to account for what they are doing. He does so actually at the cost of seeming to assimilate them fully to the "trope" in question, and thus by overdefinition to an oversimplification.

Moreover, in any historiography at its outset, an implicit tension develops between the synchronic view of the moment and the diachronic presentation of whatever series may be induced to explain it. This tension enters the narrative itself as a pull away from balance in the sentences and also as a tendency for less than full congruence to appear between one fact or set of facts and another. The moment full congruence is lacking, the state of affairs enters into an ironic contrast as presented, and the historian himself may be tempted to superadd ironic comment or language to this contrast. However, if he shows full congruence, there may be an air that he has nothing left to explain. He verges up to his synchronic limit of the explanatory brief as he moves away from the diachronic limit of mere chronicle.

Irony, then, inheres implicitly in a historian's work when he emphasizes one datum or group of data over another, something he is bound to do the minute he makes the kinds of discriminations that differentiate his writing from flat chronicle. The time contour he produces, regardless of his personal attitude toward the beginning and the end of the series he is presenting, will also contain within itself contrasts, when a datum or group of data either fulfills or resists the ongoing development he is delineating. If the data do nothing but fulfill an ongoing development, all the data will present such salient similarity that once again we will be in the domain of chronicle.

The divergence of historiography from flat chronicle implies that some moments in the narrative presentation will be more prominent than others, and also that one moment will contrast with another in a way that will already come to seem somewhat ironic, even without the comment of the historian. The structuring of the work toward some kind of closure, also implied in any narrative that is more than a chronicle, will induce further contrasts through the work. Put differently, some of the events the historian presents will be resistant to the tendencies he is disengaging from them. If not, his act of intellectual disengagement will not appear, and once again chronicle will be the result. These contrasts, again, cannot but have an ironic cast to some degree. What we have, in other words, almost unavoidably in historiography, is some version of what I have discussed in an earlier work as irony of event.[3]

Irony enters historiography almost at the outset, in Herodotus. While the books of Samuel and Kings in the Bible are constrained away from irony by the unfolding of the sacred nation and by the solemnity of the inspired writer, an irony of event still obtains between Saul's initial attitude to David and his final submission, between Saul's daughter Michal's rejection of David's dancing and her father's absorption in his music, and between the selfishness and erotic self-expression (also implied in the dancing) that leads David to set Uriah at risk of death and the flexible governance that this king puts at the service of his nation. In all this, ironies of event obtain that link this narrator into the mode of Thucydides and Gibbon, Michelet and A. J. P. Taylor. While the *Iliad* provides a vast network of contrasts and even paradoxes,[4] it is proto-historic; and so it can remain shy of irony in its very conception, as much so in the music of its verse as music itself must.[5]

The elaborate modern attempt to discriminate and assess the principles of verification in history, and to equate this necessary condition with the sufficient condition of a reasonably coherent view, has tended to obscure the fact that all such questions are preliminary.[6] As Louis O. Mink maintains in stressing the paradoxes between what we may call verification and rhetoric, "the narrative combination of relations is not subject to confirmation or disconfirmation, as any one of them taken separately might be [in questions] about historical narrative: as historical it claims to represent, through its form, part of the real complexity of the past, but as narrative it is a product of imaginative construction, which cannot defend its claim to truth by any accepted procedure of argument or authentication."[7] Form is here an unfortunate term to have to use, since in historiography as in literature generally, and as White has abundantly argued if not always shown, form is inseparable from content, and content seems to be composed of the discrete particulars of the historian's presentation, though this is the sort of paradox Mink focuses on, since the "facts" must somehow undergo "interpretation" – and, indeed, perhaps multiple interpretation – through the "form."

2

For verification taken by itself, there is no case of a great historian who makes anything like the percentage of errors that would lead us to disqualify the view his work presents. So the question of how many times a historian can be factually in error need not really be settled, even if we had firmly defined the criteria to set such percentages. And to go through the levels of verification will point up the way they tend to shade into the historian's interpretation.[8] Gibbon mistakenly defined *capitatio* in describing the land taxes set by Constantine (chap. 17, 1:554; references here and throughout are to the two-volume Modern Library edition). The assessment of Constantine's managerial style, as the error about his defeat at the hands of the Goths (chap. 17, 1:574) feeds into the assessment of his military prowess.

Gibbon in his assessment is not just providing the eulogy for which he criticizes Eusebius (chap. 16, 1:501), and so these errors do not much impair his assessment. At a more general level of verification, he is alleged to have misjudged the amount and frequency of Constantine's distribution of food to the people (chap. 17, 1:518), but in order to assess the role played by this particular directive in the generosity of Constantine, or even the Christianity of Constantine, it would have to be matched by comparisons to the exact kind, and the specific continuity, of other such distributions. The level of factuality involved in defining Constantine's Christianity is so complex that a number of views thereof will always be possible for the historian – many "right" and some "wrong." (There is perhaps an infinite number of wrong views, but we would not in practice get many instances of these from people who had taken the time to go over the evidence and prepare a view.) Here the specific question moves under the aegis of the general constraints on any hermeneutic practice whatever, questions that are in turn subsidiary to the ongoing progress of a narrative in which Constantine is only one among many other figures.[9]

As against such constraints, we can in fact dispose rather quickly of the narrower set of hermeneutic constraints involved in interpreting a document with a prevailingly factual content or even a definable context. To locate such a document in a series that the historian himself chooses is already to move onto the terrain of his full-scale interpretation by the selection and sequencing of events. And in doing so we will have left the terrain of how accurately he read a given document (in general we may assume a moderately adequate reading) for the terrain of how he fits it into his narrative. He must start with the sort of neutrality that Eusebius may be said to have abandoned, but his own prior neutrality gets absorbed into the ongoing act of composing his work and according it into the developing coherence of his narrative view. As Nancy S. Struever says, "The tangential nature of rhetoric can provide a model for the simultaneous detachment and commitment of the historian."[10]

And in the prior selection of documents, too, the historian should be judged positively by how his presentation makes them hang together, rather than negatively on what he has left out. Gibbon, for example, had to leave out many inscriptions that were not available to him. And he had to slight the explanatory dimensions in a vast number of Christian apologists during the times he writes about. At the same time, relative attention to documents is a question of degree, and there is a point at which passing over relevant documents will discredit a work, as would often be the case with early Christian apologists or contemporary Soviet historians.

The pull between diachronic and synchronic is matched in the historian's work by the pull between general and particular. The two pulls are related but not to be fully identified with each other. We cannot discriminate neatly in the text what Roland Barthes discriminates for the photograph, the "*stu-dium*" of the social environment and the "*punctum*" of the particularly fo-cused detail. All details in a history are part of the focus, furthering a general point while escaping a complete subsumption under the case or thesis prof-fered.[11] The pull on the detail in a fictional narrative is manifold. It will resonate with an overlay of echoes within various mythic systems, as again Barthes, according to one scheme, has laid it out.[12] In history it is not so much, pace Barthes, that a given detail is uncoded, but rather that there is a slippage among the possibilities of coding it. In a historical narrative, by contrast with fiction, a mythic plot is present only in the loosest sense and a mythic echo is at best weak and episodic. For reasons I have discussed elsewhere, historiography becomes possible when myth is effectually aban-doned even when it is not severely criticized.[13] To call Thucydides tragic, and in that sense a myth-historian, tells us no more than to call Gibbon or Burckhardt so – or Tocqueville, whom White wishes to call tragic because of his conservative cast and because he envisions a certain decline from the *ancien régime* to the revolution or from Europe to America. Such sense as the narratives or quasi narratives of all these historians enunciate lies else-where than in such prior fictional templates.

Consequently, the detail in a work of history often, and even character-istically, does not have a manifold symbolic character pulling it into con-gruence. And the detail in a history does not pull back or refer proleptically ahead the way it would in a fiction. The detail is entered in an ongoing aim that carries the temporary character of further documentation for a case being built. And at the same time it escapes that character. That character is only temporary or virtual, however, and can only be so if the work is to escape the limit of just making a case. Then it dwindles toward syn-chronicity. The narrative in history builds from a possible explanation (rather than a mere sketch of an explanation) to the effect of an actual one. It is only an effect, however, and the vast cumulation of Gibbon is not summarizable into his thesis that Rome declined because of the Church, nor is it qualified by his afterthought that he should have begun in the first century A.D. rather than with the Antonines.[14] Possibility and actuality converge in the detail:[15]

> In his Meditations, he thanks the gods, who had bestowed on him a wife, so faithful, so gentle, and of such a wonderful simplicity of manners. The obsequious senate, at his earnest request, declared her a goddess. She was represented in her temples with the attributes of Juno, Venus, and Ceres; and it was decreed, that on the day of their nuptials, the youth of either sex should pay their vows before the altar of their chaste patroness.

The monstrous vices of the son have cast a shade on the purity of
the father's virtues.

The father here is Marcus Aurelius Antoninus, and the son is Commodus.
We are here (chap. 4, 1:74) at the first and arguably the most momentous
large turn toward decline in the Roman Empire, when, as Gibbon has said
a page earlier at the beginning of this chapter, "The mildness of Marcus,
which the rigid discipline of the Stoics was unable to eradicate, formed, at
the same time, the most amiable, and the only defective, part of his character." Here Marcus is shown as the unwitting prisoner of both his own
personal power and the machinations of a servile senate, well-meaning and
ineffectual at the same time. The automatic deification of his wife at the
hands of the senate, the detail here given, illustrates both his well-meaning
posture and his ineffectuality, since what the youths of either sex do at their
nuptials will in no way mitigate the cruelty and depravity of his successor
Commodus. That ruler is given a free field because of the very servility of
the senate, and because his indulgent father seems not to think of mounting
any constraints upon his choice of successor. The detail of deification that
Gibbon has here chosen to give us – out of many he will have omitted from
the principate of Marcus Aurelius – is pregnant with ironies from the now
distant Republic, and also toward the gradually worsening Empire. It can
be said to point ahead – this complex of family, religion, state, and succession – to the various models and mixes found in the rules of Constantine
and Alaric, Justinian and even Rienzi.

Given the constant additions of such pregnant detail, the process of verification is not only covered by the writer but manipulated by his rhetoric.
The first sentence in the series of these three declarative sentences puts
Marcus Aurelius in the third person, thereby overlaying the datum, which
could have been conveyed more directly by a quotation from the *Meditations*,
with the attitudes of Gibbon. These attitudes are complex: They include a
nostalgia toward the golden age of the Antonines that could produce such
an emperor; an admiration for his gratitude about his wife, which comes
to a head for Gibbon in the rhythmic emphasis he has placed on "wonderful"; a monitory regret that this will soon pass; a gentle irony about the
emperor's blindness; perhaps even some relief that he would be spared the
knowledge; and an enjoyment of the superabundant domestic bliss that is
named in the bursting cornucopia of the last in the series of three attributes,
"so faithful, so gentle, and of such a wonderful simplicity of manners."
The next sentence, a slightly shorter one, puts the senate on a par grammatically with the emperor: both are in the third person, and the decree of
the senate matches the effusion of the emperor: "he thanks the gods"; they
"declared her a goddess."

There is something wrong here, and it is built into the first adjective:

"obsequious." In that light, the disproportion gets reflected in the shift of tenses from present "he thanks" to past "they declared." The senate is not on a par with the emperor, and the mere personal virtue of the author of the *Meditations* has not risen to work on that situation. So "wonderful" takes on a tinge of ominousness that makes the last, long sentence more so, since it will be abruptly cut off by the first sentence of the next paragraph, "The monstrous vices of the son have cast a shade on the purity of the father's virtues." Gibbon's rhetoric has already been creating that shade. And the extravagance of the organized detail in the third sentence makes it in context something more sinister than a cornucopia. Given such content, a heavy relentlessness comes through the resting balances, in which the short, short, long of the first sentence's concluding phrases matches the short, short, long of the three sentences making up this paragraph. Summary inheres in the further shift of tenses, into the perfect "have cast a shade." And that sentence further offers an equilibrium of balanced phrases, with the expanded verb phrase of the fulcrum, "The monstrous vices of the son / have cast a shade / on the purity of the father's virtues." As against this, the first and third of the sentences preceding it have a cumulative rotundity. But the middle sentence is also balanced, and also in three different members, "The obsequious senate / at his earnest request / declared her a goddess." The shade is already being cast here, on earnestness, and the pushing of the rhythmic balance between these two sentences reminds us of the (inter-preted) fact.

The detail is interpretative detail in itself, then; it sets a value on the point of its inclusion after verification, and the rhetoric interprets it further. Yet the detail cannot be said to be required for any of the interpretations it serves, including the arguably limited characterological ones, the uxorious-ness, piety, and mild temper of Marcus Aurelius, which are seen at once as a logical development, both positive and negative, from the good gov-ernment of the Antonines and as an accidental tonality introduced at what happens to be the last moment when their good government prevails. To put it differently, Commodus could have had a different character and it would only have postponed the decline, or Marcus Aurelius could have been less pious – or even less oblivious of needs for succession – and a military despotism of a sort already known in the Julian dynasty would have taken over anyway.

Again, as Paul Ricoeur says, "it is the place of universals in a science of the singular that is at issue."[16] The narrative as it goes along at its most effective will manage the universal and the singular without subsuming the singular under the universal, and thus is qualified Paul Veyne's assertion that in historiography the facts are considered either as separate individu-alities or as phenomena behind which an invariant hides. Actually, I have been arguing, the facts work both ways, as in Ricoeur's reinterpretation of Saint Augustine's notion of time.[17]

These various suspensions also have the effect, finally, of loosening a tight causality. A historiographic narrative is offered in place of – but again not as a sketch of – the full causal explanation that is in principle impossible. Thucydides' pattern is repeatable in its factors but unique in the mix it presents of power and character. Gibbon's modern age presents survivals from Rome as well as the decline he gradually delineates. And at any point in his narrative it is theoretically possible, though in actuality less often the case, that some great man will once again demonstrate the virtues of the Antonines. Tocqueville's trenchancy of analysis cuts through any filiation to the politics of his context and gives an air of seamless absoluteness to the *ancien régime* or to America indifferently, for all the differences of his attitude to both. Put in the falsely alternative position of choosing between causality and chance, Veyne must consistently assert that historiography is fatally a tychography.[18]

Tacitus well embodies the paradoxical stance of the historian who must have some impetus to have chosen his particular material and yet must treat it with something that looks like impartiality. He must work between the prior partiality of Eusebius and the impassivity of Mommsen (which itself, of course, has chosen attitudes built into a specific discourse, as well as "superadded" attitudes like pro-Caesarism). Yet the *nil admirari* that approaches Stoicism has no place in historiography. *Nil admirari* will ultimately lead to *nil scribere*. Or else to mere documentation, to some still more austere Mommsen.

Assuming that the necessary condition of checked data has been met, the paradox obtains in historiography that the rightness of an explanation must both precede and follow the act of writing. This means that historiography taken globally (once the condition of some accuracy has been met) can be experienced and judged but not disconfirmed. And at the same time we cannot escape the paradox between verification and rhetoric to opt just for the latter. It cannot be disconfirmed because it can only be checked against itself, vetted for occasional inaccuracies, or compared with other, comprehensive narrative accounts. Even then we may disavow its central thesis and still find its narrative convincing. The devout Christian need not reject Gibbon, nor need the modern historian replace him wholly by Mommsen, Rostovtseff, Runciman, Syme, or others.

In this state of affairs one would be tempted to ascribe Gibbon's method to some combination of idea-currents in his time; Gibbon would then be a product of Robertson plus Hume plus Montesquieu plus, perhaps, Voltaire. But the invention of a millenial comprehensive history cannot really be derived from an Enlightenment catena, and still less can it be wholly in-

terpreted as some form of irony. The search for deep structures in historiography, specifically with White or generally with Reinhart Koselleck,
leads ultimately to still another paradox, that the historian can only write
with an implicit theory but that this implicit theory cannot be derived and
redeployed in analytic form.[19]

The ongoing presentation of the historian admits of, and actually benefits
from, divergences among opinions that he will have received prior to the
work. So Gibbon will now adopt the skepticism of Hume or the relativism
of Montesquieu and again will seemingly contradict these views by the
posture of the moralist and patriot. It will explain nothing for us to derive
his blame of militarism from the first or his praise of militarism from the
second. Such derivations will neither resolve the implied contradiction nor
mount the implied contradiction in place as a lever to deconstruct his work.
And the contradictions, or at least the changes of focus, inhere in his focused
subject matter as well as in what might be called his asides. The asides
themselves have a functional effect, not just a rhetorical one in the pejorative
sense. This effect remains itself a mystery to be resolved, if we take seriously
the principle of coherence that must be attributed to so unified a work. In
the area of causality, an overriding cause obtains, Christianity, as producing
the decline of Rome. At no point, really, does the residual moralism of
Gibbon enter to qualify this assessment. But other causes intermittently
supervene, prominently at the end, when in a massive coda before he summarizes the overall temporal progression of the work in his last paragraph,
he deals not with time but with space, the visible space of the city of Rome,
with the sight of which he tells us he began. He quotes at length not a
contemporary description, but one from Poggio in the fifteenth century.
This sets up two converging time frames for the spatial picture, that of
Poggio and, in the last sentence of the work, Gibbon's own contemporary
prospect of the physical city that led him back at the beginning to begin
the *Decline and Fall*. These two time frames, in turn, nest another two times,
that of an anonymous thirteenth-century writer who has testified pretty
much to what Poggio has said, but at a considerably less advanced stage of
decay, since "the principles of destruction acted with vigorous and increasing energy in the thirteenth and fourteenth centuries" (chap 71, 2:1040).
The fourth time is that of the pristine Rome, with all its imperial additions,
the ideal time of the Antonines conceived as also an ideal space.

Gibbon, however, here shifts to four causes, rather than one, and four
causes that are not commensurate with each other: "I. The injuries of time
and nature. II. The hostile attacks of the barbarians and the Christians. III.
The use and abuse of the materials. And IV. The domestic quarrels of the
Romans." And in addition to this surprising miscellany of his conclusion,
he adduces throughout his long work local causes distinct either from his
large overriding one or from some such sets as these four. He often delineates

particular characterological mixes in individuals, the mode of Tacitus; he even adds touches of geographical determinism for the Germans or the Egyptians, the mode of Montesquieu or, for that matter, Herodotus. In all this, space and time have been brought into a partial polyphony, a polyphony well served by the orotundity of Gibbon, large-lunged enough to accommodate a summary of the more than a millennium that he has covered in a single sentence of his final paragraph, and at the same time fine-tuned enough to pick up one or more of the many telling details in the progress of the narrative.[20]

In that final paragraph he returns the space of the city once more to the time of his overall presentation via the "pilgrims" who have a touristic and not a religious purpose in visiting the Rome of his own present time. Since Gibbon admires the pre-Christian period of the Roman Empire and believes in its administrative capacity and moral fiber, the word "pilgrim" is at the same time not wholly ironic:

> The map, the description, the monuments of ancient Rome, have been elucidated by the diligence of the antiquarian and the student; and the footsteps of heroes, the relics not of superstition, but of empire, are devoutly visited by a new race of pilgrims from the remote and once savage countries to the North.

> Of these pilgrims, and of every reader, the attention will be excited by a history of the Decline and Fall of the Roman Empire; the greatest, perhaps, and most awful scene in the history of mankind. The various causes and progressive effects are connected with many of the events most interesting in human annals: the artful policy of the Caesars, who long maintained the name and image of a free republic; the disorders of military despotism; the rise, establishment, and sects of Christianity; the foundation of Constantinople; the division of the monarchy; the invasion and settlements of the barbarians in Germany and Scythia; the institutions of the civil law; the character and religion of Mohammed; the temporal sovereignty of the popes; the restoration and decay of the Western empire of Charlemagne; the crusades of the Latins in the East; the conquests of the Saracens and Turks; the ruin of the Greek empire; the state and revolutions of Rome in the middle age. The historian may applaud the importance and variety of his subject; but, while he is conscious of his own imperfections, he must often accuse the deficiency of his materials. It was among the ruins of the Capitol that I first conceived the idea of a work which has amused and exercised near twenty years of my life, and which, however inadequate to my own wishes, I finally deliver to the curiosity and candor of the public.

Gibbon's somewhat contradictory mix of purposes for his historiographic enterprise – the antiquarian-scholarly, the Enlightenment-serving, and the moralistic – appears, without detriment to his overall purpose, in the fore-shortened attributions of his last two nouns, where "curiosity" can be subsumed under the antiquarian purpose and "candor" under the Enlightenment one, with no word at all reaching very far into the moralizing fundament for these. The mix also appears in the shift of senses within given words like "amuse," in which the older Oxford Dictionary meanings, "2, to occupy the attention of," which is still alive in the eighteenth century, and even the still older "1, to cause to muse or stare, to puzzle," also still alive in the eighteenth century, cannot be excluded from Gibbon's reference to his preoccupied attention. But the normal modern sense – first coming into prominence in the eighteenth century – "3, to divert the attention of," must still be allowed to operate, especially in conjunction with the putative reader's matching curiosity.[21] The causal mix, along with the verbal shifts, can be observed throughout Gibbon's work, as for example at the point where he moves into his last two quarto volumes and offers still another summary of the events he has told:

> The Monophysite churches resounded with a song of triumph, "that the sheep of Aethiopia were now delivered from the hyaenas of the West"; and the gates of that solitary realm were for ever shut against the arts, the science, and the fanaticism of Europe.

This sentence has a marked position as the end of chapter 47, and also as the end of the first two-thirds of the entire work. It, too, carries a spatial as well as a temporal function. Ethiopia is at an actual spatial limit of the domain he writes about. The Ethiopians themselves have made their marginal but relevant military and dynastic struggles a psychological as well as a spatial limit by shutting their door on the West and allowing Gibbon the occasion and justification for henceforth excluding them from his history. The Roman dimension of the word "triumph" may ironically measure how far the Empire has come for these Christians deep at its borders to be able to use a Roman mode in rejecting what has become of Rome. There is a further, related irony that churches should not be resounding with songs of military triumph. They call themselves sheep in the Christian sense, but Gibbon by quoting this line of their song is calling them sheep in still another sense. "Hyaenas of the West" contains both straight and ironic designations, since the slur shows the Ethiopians to ignore the complexity of Western life to which the various fusions of barbarian, Roman, and Christian in Gibbon's preceding narrative offer elaborate testimony. In resisting those they are too willing to call simply barbarians, they are rejecting civilization, as his last sentence declares. Yet Europe has not only "the arts, the science," but also "the fanaticism," and the Ethiopians are right after all to call them "hyaenas," except that they themselves are fanatics by Gibbon's testimony, just as Gibbon might well lump the European "hyaenas" together under "sheep" too.

In the ensuing transition to his last two volumes, Gibbon changes some of his presentation with a change of scale, and he proceeds simply in chapter 48 to a somewhat briefer account of the later Byzantine emperors than he had given of the first:

> I have now deduced from Trajan to Constantine, from Constantine to Heraclius, the regular series of the Roman emperors; and faithfully exposed the prosperous and adverse fortunes of their reigns. Five centuries of the decline and fall of the empire have already elapsed; but a period of more than eight hundred years still separates me from the term of my labours, the taking of Constantinople by the Turks. Should I persevere in the same course, should I observe the same measure, a prolix and slender thread would be spun through many a volume, nor would the patient reader find an adequate reward of instruction or amusement. At every step, as we sink deeper in the decline and fall of the Eastern empire, the annals of each succeeding reign would impose a more ungrateful and melancholy task.

Here, so far as cause is concerned, he foreshortens casually and even more abruptly than he did at the end. We are given not one cause, not four, and not a miscellany of local characterological matrices, but rather a pure randomness, "the prosperous and adverse fortunes of their reigns." The simple up and down of the designation links Gibbon's "fortunes" not just superficially to the ongoing events but also to some faint echo of the medieval Wheel of Fortune, and through that, perhaps less faintly, to the Roman Fortuna. This seems to be just casual eighteenth-century usage. But certainly it is not ironic. It must, though, contradict all his prior causal buildups, and his successive ones too. How can we justify its presence in the work? Only, I would urge, as a kind of place marker, and only as the sort of backhand attribution that throws into relief what precedes. It is as though he said "one would be forced to call this 'random fortune,' had I not done the labor of bringing causes, and one Big Cause, to bear on what precedes." It also, quite differently and contrastingly, throws light on what follows, "these Byzantine reigns are so deep in decline that they offer really only annals, and a sequence of random causality becomes so prominent in their work that it would be unprofitable to examine it for deeper ones." The "fortunes," in this sense, as they somewhat falsify Rome but somewhat appositely characterize Byzantium, themselves mirror, as the word itself consequently does, the progress of the decline.

"The patient reader," that new eighteenth-century figure, becomes something like the tourist-pilgrim of the last chapter, and in this passage the word "amusement" highlights a main sense of "diversion" by contrast with "instruction," but it also allows construal in the subsidiary sense of "preoccupied attention": by amplification of "instruction."

As with Gibbon's, or any historian's, use of detail, however, we may explain such shifts and condensations while still not offering a justification for their presence in the work, which would amount to a demonstration of how omitting them would impoverish it.

The "pilgrim" side of Gibbon's reader, and correspondingly of the writer himself, appears always implicitly in Gibbon's moral judgments, and explicitly in the last paragraph of the long chapter 48 on the later Byzantine emperors (2:576–577):

> Many were the paths that led to the summit of royalty: the fabric of rebellion was overthrown by the stroke of conspiracy, or undermined by the silent arts of intrigue: the favourites of the soldiers or people, of the senate or clergy, of the women and eunuchs, were alternately clothed with the purple: the means of their elevation were base and their end was often contemptible or tragic. A being of the nature of man, endowed with the same faculties, but with a longer measure of existence, would cast down a smile of pity and contempt on the crimes and follies of human ambition, so eager, in a narrow span, to grasp at a precarious and short-lived enjoyment. It is thus that the experience of history exalts and enlarges the horizon of our intellectual view. In a composition of some days, in a perusal of some hours, six hundred years have rolled away, and the duration of a life or reign is contracted to a fleeting moment: the grave is ever beside the throne; the success of a criminal is almost instantly followed by the loss of his prize; and our immortal reason survives and disdains the sixty phantoms of kings who have passed before our eyes and faintly dwell on our remembrance. . . . The virtue alone of John Comnenus was beneficent and pure: the most illustrious of the princes who precede or follow that respectable name have trod with some dexterity and vigour the crooked and bloody paths of a selfish policy.

Some of the phrasing here could easily be paralleled in the Prophets and Wisdom literature of the Bible, and in context "immortal reason" is a curious compound not far removed from 'immortal soul" in an age of Deism. The "being . . . with a longer measure of existence" whom Gibbon here imagines and invokes can actually be found closest to hand in the dual-natured Christ of Christian theology, and to carry this being through congruently to the "immortal reason" verges on implicitly recommending an *imitatio Christi*. Certainly in this context the "virtue" of John Comnenus cannot wholly be contained, or even mainly characterized, by the *virtus* of the Romans. Indeed, to call it "beneficent and pure" continues the Christian coloring and measurers the whole long sequence of emperors by a modified Christian perspective rather than by an extrapolated Roman one, and still less by Enlightenment criteria, even though the key word "reason" stands at the center of this passage.

It would be idle to try to reconcile this quasi-religious moralism with Gibbon's other, contradictory views of the historian's work and effect. The contrary views coexist. They are reconciled not by logic or by any deep structure but by the broadness and coherence of his diachronic presentation, which admits them and assimilates them. Here Gibbon in fact curiously resembles Eusebius more than he does Tacitus, Machiavelli, or even Thucydides, who would never assimilate their historiographic purpose to a quasi-Christian *memento mori*. The effect, though, is not one of naiveté or incoherence, but rather of a demonstration of the broadness and intricacy of his events in time, which such reflections cast light on as permissible. He is, in fact, reminding us of his work's long time span, as he periodically does in his presentation.

One could point out comparable shifts and mixes in Gibbon's use of the term "barbarian," which at one moment will be an absolute pejorative and another moment will offer a sort of foil for the growth of surprising virtues. Indeed, when these virtues are military, "barbarian" is not even a foil but rather a characteristic of the rude conditions under which military virtues may flourish. But all kinds of qualifications attend the word, sometimes with irony and sometimes without. And even for the monasticism which is a main object of his scorn, there are often unironic modifications as well as the downright assimilation I have just shown to surround 'immortal reason." In chapter 37 he condemns the monks outright: "The aspect of a genuine anachoret was horrid and disgusting: every sensation that is offensive to man was thought acceptable to God; and the angelic rule of Tabenne condemned the salutary custom of bathing the limbs in water and of anointing them with oil" (2:10). Very soon, however, he is qualifying these pejoratives:

> But the more humble industry of the monks, especially in Egypt, was contented with the silent, sedentary occupation of making wooden sandals, or of twisting the leaves of the palm tree into mats and baskets. The superfluous stock, which was not consumed in domestic use, supplied by trade the wants of the community: the boats of Tabenne, and the other monasteries of Thebais, descended the Nile as far as Alexandria; and, in a Christian market, the sanctity of the workmen might enhance the intrinsic value of the work.

Here the attention to the ethnographic detail has been made to seem to force Gibbon's hand into a modified and almost benign view of the monk's economic enterprises, but he shifts his tone into an outright verbal irony in the last sentence, recovering his tonic note with what is an almost Marxist analysis of the factors; he implies something like the Marxist use-value and exchange value, in an analysis perhaps owing something to his contemporary Adam Smith.

In the middle sentence of his concluding paragraph to the whole work, which I have quoted above, Gibbon holds the attention of his "pilgrim" and runs through a paratactic summary, connected by semicolons, of thirteen moderately successive but sometimes overlapping designations for his entire sequence. These numerous large clauses, which designate time- periods, are held in suspension for the tonic note of a last periodic sentence. Their assertion remains. So does the polyphony of their rhythm as it is scored within itself, and by contrast to the following, much simpler sentence, and by the ampler but still shorter one with which he concludes the entire work. He recapitulates backward for a series of verificative summaries while attending to the coda of his rhetoric. Thus he keeps verification and rhetoric in coordination, as any historian must do in his narrative, holding together what cannot be separated in either direction without semantic loss.

3

It is not only that the developed opinions governing the *Decline and Fall* or expressed in it will escape the critic's controlling summary. This is true, too, for the millennial conception of the work itself. Machiavelli and Guicciardini, like the ecclesiastical historians who precede them, take the long view of their histories, in the fashion of Livy's "From the Founding of the City." But such Livian works do not carry Gibbon's kind of deep sense of developing social forms in time, which is already on the threshold of Meinecke's "historicity." They go from the remote past to the near present, the present offering a self-sufficient and self-explanatory terminus. Gibbon, to be sure, brings the reader to the terminus of the present in his last chapter, but complexly, and in ways that cause the cross-currents of past factors to be shown at work while buried. Unlike any of his predecessors he takes a huge segment of the past, brings it up to within nearly two hundred years of his present, and then lets the past reveal, match, and contrast with the present, as he had allowed it to do in asides throughout his work. The ancient historians took segments, but nearly all of them had a compass not much longer than a man's lifetime. And these segments were brought to bear on a near present. Saint Augustine in the *City of God* only varies this procedure by measuring a disastrous present against the vision of an ideal state. Vico is millennial but cyclical.

In fact the closest analogue to Gibbon's conception is nothing other or less than the Old Testament from Genesis through 2 Kings. In both works there is a millennial scale plotted on a time line at a past remote but still active for the presumptive compilers. Both are conflations of large documents. Both show forces operating on a charged center across a large, various, and changing geographical extent. And both see the present as dominated by beneficial, and also harmful, forces in the delineated past. While the differences are obvious, the point is worth making if we seriously ask what sorts of verbal deep structures Gibbon may have had in mind. Here the Bible fits the bill, and corresponds in a number of ways that none of the ecclesiastical historians can match, or the secular ones either.

For his own unique sense of time, then, Gibbon has no marked predecessors, but if we try to derive what his sense of time is from the *Decline and Fall* itself, we will be left with such attributions as Heidegger's "authentic" for genuine history as opposed to one which merely recounts a superficial past.[22] As Harold L. Bond well says, "Rather than moving from one assertion to another, Gibbon's prose expresses a series of relationships. He will play the general against the specific, the illusion against the reality, effect will grow out of cause, reaction out of action."[23] In this light, for Gibbon or any other great historian, it is hard to isolate an event, let alone define one. Is it Marcus Aurelius' decision to deify his wife that is the event, or the senate's ratification, or the proliferation of goddesses, Juno, Venus, and Ceres? Or is it the attenuation of old Roman virtue in the proliferation? Or the excessive family devotion? Here, as so often, event leads to cause, which leads in turn to detail, which leads in turn back to time. The question remains that Hexter rightly insists on, namely the ungroundability outside the given narrative to defend Gibbon's choice of specificity at this point by naming the three goddesses instead of just saying "deified" or "three goddesses." This question, as I have argued in my introduction, sends the critic back to notions like event, cause, and time, which in turn send him back to the necessarily sequenced detail.

As Ricoeur says, "Time becomes human time in the measure that it is articulated according to a narrative mode . . . and the telling attains its full signification when it becomes a condition of temporal existence."[24] What then? It is no accident, either logically or in the history of recent thought, that this sounds very much like Heidegger. We are forced to sound like Heidegger if we would deal with the force of the narrative element in historiography because we are forced to connect time and humanity in a circular fashion. Only a story or some account that retains narrative features – not even philosophical terminology – can compass this circle. And to break it is to break out of history altogether.

So the search for the parameters of the event will continue, without focusing fully on the point – the many-dimensional *punctum* – in a narrative,

71

as Marcus Aurelius' act of deifying his wife. Can Braudel's *"longue durée"* be an event? This question is circular in a different sense. "Action is inherently historical," says John William Miller.[25] Miller has indeed already interestingly specified how this might come through an actual historiographic work, "history is the story not of appearances, but of the differences by which appearances have been set off from reality." One could translate these terms into the "irony" of my discussion above, and the necessity of molding some differentiation among the items sequenced in narrative so that chronicle may be avoided. But the mysterious event continues to escape into the nets of the narrative work designed to capture it.[26] We are returned, inescapably, to the particular view, even to the vision, that the particular narrative affords us as the essence of its strategic manipulations of time and event through the intricate interactions of verification and rhetoric.

SCALE, PSYCHOLOGICAL STEREOTYPING, AND STYLE IN TACITUS' *ANNALS*

I

TACITUS AT HIS PEAK, in the *Annals*, reaps the advantages of suspending his actual demonstrations between the causal exposition of a gradual decline away from a Republican ideal and the delineation of a sort of inevitable and recurrent Thucydidean process. He is at once cyclic and linear, a sort of logical contradiction that prevents us from ever settling on some demonstrated case as the thesis of the *Annals* – from opting for either the psychology of the individual or the structure of society as a leading cause. His suspension returns us to the tensions and complexities of his narrative, as it enmeshes the individuals who are caught in processes of debilitation. This presentation works by silence, by aspectual change for given cases, by quasi-enthymematic breaks between one kind of event and another, and by unannounced changes of topic and scale, for space and time alike, within the annually divided segments.

In the *Annals*, Tacitus somewhat enlarges the scale of time and space he had adopted in the *Histories* and increases the variety of his topics. The *Histories*, in turn, enlarge the space under consideration and vary the topics, by comparison with the fairly original topical coherence of the two monographs preceding them, the encomiastic biography *Agricola* and the ethnographic survey *Germania*. The scale of the *Histories*, then, is large; that of the *Germania* differently so; while the *Agricola* sees its central figure too close at hand for significant patterns of public events to get under way.

At the beginning of *Histories*, Tacitus refers generally to a decline and places himself in a position vis-à-vis earlier historians that turns the disadvantage of remoteness into the advantage of the neutrality he will also stress in the *Annals*:

> I begin my work with the time when Servius Galba was consul for the second time with Titus Vinius for his colleague. Of the former period, the eight hundred twenty years dating from the founding of the city, many authors have treated; and while they had to record the

transactions of the Roman people, they wrote with equal eloquence and freedom. After the conflict at Actium, and when it bore on peace that all power should be centered in one man, these great intellects passed away. At the same time the truth of history was impaired in many ways; at first, through ignorance of public affairs as strange to them, then, through flattering agreement or, on the other hand, hatred of the master. And so between the enmity of the one and the servility of the other, there was no regard for posterity. But while we instinctively shrink from a writer's adulation, we lend a ready ear to detraction and spite, because flattery involves the shameful imputation of servility, whereas malignity wears the false appearance of honesty. I myself knew nothing of Galba, of Otho, or of Vitellius, either from benefits or from injuries. I would not deny that my elevation was begun by Vespasian, augmented by Titus, and still further advanced by Domitian; but those who profess inviolable truthfulness must speak of all without partiality and without hatred. I have reserved as an employment for my old age, should my life be long enough, a subject at once more fruitful and less anxious in the reign of the Divine Nerva and the empire of Trajan, enjoying the rare happiness of times, when we may think what we please, and express what we think.'

> (*Histories* 1.1; quotations from Tacitus are as translated by Alfred John Church and William Jackson Brodribb, slightly revised)

At the beginning of the *Annals*, however, as though the structure of society and its large scale were his paramount concern, Tacitus widens his scale to pass over specific shifts in the more than seven hundred years before Augustus:

> Rome at the beginning was ruled by kings. Freedom and the consulship were established by Lucius Brutus. Dictatorships were held for a temporary crisis. The power of the decemvirs did not last beyond two years, nor was the consular jurisdiction of the military tribunes of long duration. The despotisms of Cinna and Sulla were brief; the rule of Pompeius and of Crassus soon yielded before Caesar; the arms of Lepidus and Antonius before Augustus; who, when the world was wearied by civil strife, took over empire under the name of "Prince." But the successes and reverses of the old Roman people have been recorded by famous historians; and fine intellects were not wanting to describe the times of Augustus, till growing sycophancy scared them away. The histories of Tiberius, Caius, Claudius, and Nero, while they were in power, were falsified through terror, and after their death were written under a fresh hatred. Hence my purpose is

to relate a few facts about Augustus – his last acts, then the reign of Tiberius, and all which follows, without either ire or partiality, from any motives to which I am far removed.[2]

(*Annals* 1.1)

Here, as an introduction to his celebrated and much contested declaration of impartiality, four forms of government are announced in fewer than that many sentences. This suggests instability as well as the sort of logical series among governmental forms that Plato offers (*Republic* 544c–548d). Kings are, in this sentence, neutral and natural at an originating stage, *in principio*. The coupling of the complexly unmatched pair *"libertas"*[3] and *"consulatus"* certainly implies the embodiment of a republican ideal. But this ideal is triply subverted, first by a power-grab (*sumebantur*) on the part of dictators, and then by an unstable set of oligarchic decemvirs, and then by a short-lived extension of tribunician military power. Roman history can be taken to illustrate the difficulty of settling on the right mix among the three possible abstract types of government:

All nations and cities are ruled by the people, the nobility, or by one man. A constitution, formed by selection out of these elements, it is easy to commend but not to produce; or, if it is produced, it cannot be lasting. Formerly, when the people had power or when the patricians were in the ascendant, the popular temper and the methods of controlling it, had to be studied, and those who knew most accurately the spirit of the Senate and aristocracy, had the credit of understanding the age and of being wise men. So now, after a revolution, when Rome is nothing but the realm of a single despot, there must be good in carefully noting and recording this period, for it is but few who have the foresight to distinguish right from wrong or what is sound from what is hurtful, while most men learn wisdom from the fortunes of others.[4]

(4.33)

In the light of all this, the rule of Augustus exhibits some positive features of a model against which the later Claudian emperors are measured. The *Annals* would seem to invest a force in their point of departure "*Ab Excessu Divi Augusti*," "From the End of Divine Augustus' Reign." On the other hand, the presentation of Augustus himself at the outset shows him quietly consolidating power, outmaneuvering the triumvirs, and outdoing the short hegemony of Cinna and Sulla by possessing the Empire in a way that would cyclically recur to the possession (*reges habuere*) of the initial kings – except that they would not have been sophisticated enough to carry off the smooth duplicity that Augustus manages.

But the Principate in any case provided a mix, and not one that had been of prior deduction, nor one passively subject to the machinations of a static, duplicitous personality. Large human societies never so structure themselves. Rather, even in Augustus' supremely skillful hands, the state underwent the distortions which Tacitus implies are likely to be produced by power manipulations. Or in Syme's summary, "As a form of government the Principate was essentially equivocal, and the *nobilitas* was called to play a false role therein, forfeiting power but ostensibly retaining honor and prestige."[5]

The irony that often mobilizes the onward progress of a historian's narrative derives one impetus from a contrast between actual events and an ideal. For Thucydides this contrast would seem to lie between a perfect application of a Thucydidean Realpolitik and the various approximations of that Realpolitik, near and far, by the principals of his narrative. For Tacitus the ideal was the embodiment of Republican probity or *libertas* in a past close to Tiberius and almost to be discerned in Augustus. He offers the further twist that seeds of real corruption work the more effectively for Augustus' own supreme effectiveness. So, we may deduce, the ideal is measured against the actual not as one absolute good against an absolute bad but by the proportions and also by the ironies of a mix. These proportions appear most vividly in the complex acts of power-endowed persons, and in a consequent psychology that we must necessarily allow a complexity sufficient to carry out such far-ranging and many-factored maneuvers.

The pressure that events bring to bear on the discrepancy between ideal control and an increasing real chaos emerges in Tacitus' intense psychological summaries, but also in his near silences, what Inez Scott Ryberg calls his "art of innuendo."[6] The discrepancy she notes between Tacitus' "willingness to ascribe motive" and his "avoidance of the direct accusation of crime" (84–85) does not result in a sort of perspectivism, and still less in showing people as just "good" or "bad", even though they are always making moral choices. Rather he shows a result as so complex that the intensity of challenge produced by the ongoing events thus brought into focus will variously escape formulation. In this light the phrase "*sine ira et studio*" will not apply to specific statements or events so much as to a prior, general impartiality. This reserve may also apply to the suggested condition of the period (or history generally) as it squares the historian's adequacy beyond his expression of particular indignation (as against Livia, who was a "*gravis noverca*," [*Annals* 1.10]) or admiration (as repeatedly and indirectly for Seneca).[7] An overriding implication, as it were, corrects back into neutrality the positive or negative reactions confined to a particular statement or passage. The innuendo of comprehensiveness controls, and amounts to, a superior impartiality.

The shift of scale aids this silence, too, and Tacitus' final summary of Germanicus (*Annals* 3.16–3.19) would be unbalanced if it paused to comment on discrepancies that the more closely focused prior accounts include. All the while the constant innuendo about Tiberius' hatred implicitly portrays that hatred as appearing through the hypocritical silence that Tacitus shows to be a leading, and treacherous, characteristic of that emperor. The sentences are abrupt and contorted at times, but the passage of the narrative runs smoothly. The comments that arrest it often state psychological laws, subsuming rather than simply describing or labeling the action at hand.

So, too, in the presentation of the large and loosely coherent space of the Empire, attention to the constantly pressing periphery of the provinces carries the silent corollary of its effect on the center. And the interconnection between center and periphery bears always on the presentation of such individuals as Germanicus. The impositions of Nero's rule on Rome are silently displaced by Tacitus' repeated, prolonged attention to incipient rebellions in Germany, Parthia, and Armenia – and this amounts to a comment on the distractable psychology of that emperor.

Such manipulations and adjustments dynamize and mobilize the always disjunct factors of event presented in the *Annals*, as against the simpler list of provinces at the beginning of the *Histories* (1.2). The earlier work focuses more exclusively on the preponderance of differently located military campaigns as these bear on who will become emperor – at least in the segment of the *Histories* that remains.

2

Thucydides shows and quietly dramatizes the constraints of policy in the case of Nicias. Seeing clearly the folly of the Sicilian expedition and expounding it before the assembly, Nicias is overruled. He then accepts a command that will lead to his death, strenuously trying to counter the effects he had foretold. In Tacitus such constraints do not appear in public policy, which goes about its way. Rome is so powerful that she overbalances all her neighbors, and the encroaching difficulties in North Africa or Germany or the Near East serve mainly to test and reveal those who, if they survive, are to be participants at Rome. They lack Nicias' freedom, but not his psychological complexity.

The perversion of bureaucratic policy at Rome derives not from a faulty assessment of foreign forces, but from a willful mismanagement of forces within the Senate and the Roman leadership itself. The arena, consequentially, is not a military one, and the role of all the military action in the *Annals* is subsidiary. Tacitus' "psychology" is thus entirely appropriate to this focus, and he makes it the most promising theme of his history, a focus that distinguishes him from Livy and Sallust alike. Even in the military arena, indeed, the psychology of Tacfarinas or Vologeses, rather than their strategic capacity, governs the twists and turns of their enterprises. And that psychology is neither simple nor schematically moral. It is Germanicus' public flair, not mainly his generalship – or his virtue or vice – that leads to his downfall. The factor of psychological currents, dominant in the Senate, is shown to be traceable in less sophisticated spheres as well, and to govern the behavior of crowds.

Collingwood's indefensible assertion that historiography cannot draw on psychological inference (though inescapably "based on thought")[8] has the positive corollary of sharpening questions about the role of psychological inference in historiography. Thucydides for the most part maintains silence about the psychological factors in the tension between personality and strategy, and the reader must infer the psychology of Nicias and Alcibiades from a pattern of events. Tacitus, too, maintains a general silence about Tiberius, but his shifts of scale, and the unmanageable variability of his factors, permits him to introduce a psychological inference, often abruptly after the fact, and often with an air of the capping demonstration.

Tacitus' summary statement about Tiberius runs through his many psychological phases, preceded by the perils of psychic interaction; Tiberius had finally corrupted himself into blatant simplicity:

And so died Tiberius, in the seventy-eighth year of his age.

Nero was his father, and he was on both sides descended from the Claudian house, though his mother passed by adoption, first into the Livian, then into the Julian family. From earliest infancy, perilous vicissitudes were his lot. Himself an exile, he was the companion of a proscribed father, and on being admitted as a stepson into the house of Augustus, he had to struggle with many rivals, so long as Marcellus and Agrippa and, subsequently, Caius and Lucius Caesar were in their glory. Again his brother Drusus enjoyed in a greater degree the affection of the citizens. But he was more than ever on dangerous ground after his marriage with Julia, whether he tolerated or escaped from his wife's profligacy. On his return from Rhodes he ruled the emperor's now heirless house for twelve years, and the Roman world, with absolute sway, for about twenty-three. His character too had its distinct periods. It was a bright time in his life and reputation, while under Augustus he was a private citizen or held high offices; a time of reserve and crafty assumption of virtue, as long as Germanicus and Drusus were alive. Again, while his mother lived, he was a compound of good and evil; he was infamous for his cruelty, though he veiled his debaucheries, while he loved or feared Sejanus. Finally, he plunged into every wickedness and disgrace, when fear and shame being cast off, he simply indulged his own inclinations.[9]

(*Annals* 6.51)

But Claudius, who occasions some psychological observation, is shown as offering less mutation and less complexity. Consequently he gets no such summary from Tacitus.

It is as though Tacitus were saying, "And given this psychological law, how could this event have proceeded otherwise?" His tension obtains not between Realpolitik and the partial variable incapacities toward supreme management of it, as with Thucydides. Rather, it is the presence of tension among factors that forces the invariant psychological law forward. The very variability of the events Tacitus recounts would obviate any possible set of Machiavellian principles. Failing a *libertas* conjoined with *potestas*, the individual is powerless. He can only operate assuredly in the sort of Republican state that Tacitus implies is also susceptible to erosion from variabilities of personal temper and purpose.

The ever-increasing flattery, *adulatio*, is a shortsighted solution, even if it were not a cowardly offense against *virtus*. Flattery permits too easy an evasion on the part of the powerful. Under increasing *adulatio* Tiberius can go on enchaining silence into complex forces. Consequently those obliged to function under such circumstances are too afflicted by a sort of stupidity, a *socordia*. (This is a frequent word in Tacitus.)

Though Tacitus' psychological inferences are intermittent, the presence of psychological forces is felt over the long haul, as in Thucydides, and at the rare moment of the speeches. Where Thucydides sets one speech against another, they are nearly always single in Tacitus; and they expose the angle of the individual more fully, making him predominant over the policy countertensions that govern Thucydides' matched speeches. The contrast between the balanced rhetoric of these speeches and Tacitus' twisted style carries its own omen of doom. Even the seemingly disjunct and protractedly strategic military accounts carry psychological implications both for the man conducting the campaign, say Germanicus, and the emperor in Rome who holds the strings of power. The pressure on Claudius to admit provincials to the Senate, indeed, is episodic by comparison (11.23–25), and its episodic character testifies to the weakness of his control. Thucydides' military campaigns carry a state behind them; those in the *Histories* of Tacitus decide who will hold sway over the state. The campaigns in the *Annals* merely reveal what a given individual can muster in the contest of always supervening forces. Everyone, as it were, whether generalship is in question or a sweeping diplomacy, is measured against the salient case of the Augustus whose comparable acts are summarized at the beginning.

The abruptness of the psychological summaries in Tacitus calls the reader up short before this sudden articulation of laws that are, so to speak, held in reserve by the historian rather than simply demonstrated. Their connection may go further than the case to which they are applied; indeed, they would tend to go further than the case at hand, as a general law defining a specific situation. Where no connection obtains, Tacitus is silent; he does not mention the alcoholism of Tiberius, as Syme remarks.[10] Tacitus aims not exactly to indict Tiberius, but rather to delineate his effect on the body politic, and the drunkenness would operate too remotely for that purpose.

At every point the crucial connection shows, to a situation of power that itself will not respond certainly to the manipulations of Realpolitik because the interactions of the powerful are too rooted in individual psychology. Given this dominant uncertainty, it is no wonder that astrologers, mathematicians, and necromancers of various kinds were both consulted and proscribed (*Annals* 12.22, 12.52, 12.68, etc.). Agrippina, audacious and scheming though she is, prudently balances her domination over Claudius against a presumptive opposition – based on the psychology of their previous affiliations – in the praetorian cohorts. This prudence limits the machinations Tacitus recounts (12.41) of jockeying the emperor's stepson Nero ahead of his natural son Britannicus. "Agrippina, however, did not yet dare to set her highest purpose in motion," "Nondum tamen summa moliri Agrippina audebat."

Every emperor in the *Annals'* series of four is a psychological puzzle, but no one is like another, on the presumption that Caligula would appear distinctive in the missing books about him. And this distinctness of each in itself amounts to a principle for overall psychological portrayal.

Claudius' very easiness of temper makes him, through his power, an instrument of cruelty under the manipulations of Agrippina, "In his wonted easiness he did not veil under any external considerations what he had conceded to a single suppliant," "set Claudius facilitate solita quod uni concesserat nullis extrinsecus adiumentis velavit" (12.61). Here the suppliants are cities, or areas, Cos in this instance, and a certain randomness of policy makes the empire seethe into various unsolved problems. This happens in Judaea, Cilicia, and Byzantium, to take only the instances surrounding this statement (12.58–63). About the same time the emperor has calmly and somewhat distractedly staged two different mock naval battles, with criminals acting the parts of the real combatants (12.56–57). There is a linkage running along through these gladiatorial entertainments, the pride of Agrippina, her cruelty, her ambition, the relative ineffectuality of this emperor in managing the provinces, and his generosity. This link is to be found in the psychological temper summarized by the aphorism just quoted. Claudius' ineffectuality has its effects just because he possesses the power that links the random instances into a connection of sameness underlying the differences among them, a "facility" that makes him as pliable to the power-hungry Agrippina as he had been to the lascivious Messalina.

And the power, through another law of mass psychology, must be real and present to be effective. When Agrippina is distanced by the son whom she made emperor, her power slips fast, and Tacitus introduces his account with the psychological reason "Nothing in mortal affairs is so unstable and fluid as a reputation for power not sustained by its own force," "Nihil rerum mortalium tam instabile ac fluxum est quam fama potentiae non sua vi nixae" (13.19). And "*mortalium*" hints that when the power is at once absolute and capricious, the instability implies a danger of death; before long Nero will have killed his mother.

The psychology of a more duplicitous emperor, Tiberius, will be correspondingly more complex, and sometimes doubtful. So he raises "with a proud inscription" (*superbo cum titulo*) a monument claiming as his what has been intrinsically a victory of Germanicus', "He added nothing about himself, fearing jealousy or thinking that consciousness of the achievement was enough," "De se nihil addidit, metu invidiae an ratus conscientiam facti satis esse" (2.22).

It is a subjection to psychological effects of power, and not just intellectual position, that governs the sort of point of view other historians adopt:

> The affairs of Tiberius and Gaius, of Claudius and also of Nero while they were in power were falsified through fear; and after they had died those affairs were composed out of fresh hatred. Hence it is my purpose to transmit a few facts about Augustus – the final ones – ; then the principate of Tiberius and the others, without anger or partiality, the motives for which I hold at a remove."
>
> (*Annals* 1.1)

Thus Tacitus' understanding of psychological laws, as well as his distance in time, removes him from the subjection to them: His impartiality is reactive and dynamic, rather than just an intellectual neutrality. And it has been achieved through "deliberation" and "judgment," other senses of the word "*consilium*" that are operative upon his "purpose" here. Tacitus refers frequently to "*motus animorum*" – "arousals" and "motions," but also "causes" – in the spirit, a dominance of psychology.

There is in the *Annals* an overall psychological law, an unexpressed one, that men in supreme power will crave a trusted confidant who in turn will have fomented that confidence to his own ends and finally to their downfall. Sejanus matches Narcissus, who matches Tigellinus, and a silently presented psychological plot-pattern provides a larger patterning for the events of the four reigns under consideration.

3

Too great a concentration on structure by the historian, or on merely abstract disquisition, results in the presentation of an argued case. Too great a concentration on event, on the flow of particulars, results in a chronicle. Ethnography, which is set up to draw conclusions, may distinguish between structure and that definition of type-events which goes under the name of "function." An ethnographer may choose his emphasis on structure or function, even though structure and function, or structure and event, stand in an implicit contradiction to each other, as Jacques Derrida, among others, has argued.[12] Historiography, however, mediates between structure and event by allowing the tension between the two an ongoing, and flexible, role in the narrative. Tacitus' abrupt shifts of scale, as well as his eruption from silence into psychologizing articulation, serve the end of such a flexibility. The abruptness keeps the tension taut.

Tacitus's reaction to Nero's poetizing or Tiberius' delays or Claudius' evasions, and, of course, to the many atrocities recounted in his narrative, may be said not only to follow the individual event but to precede it by setting up the measure of a Republican ideal. Tacitus highlights the contrastive force of his discontinuities by setting his material in the annual framework that Thucydides invented, and also by organizing it into eighteen books that themselves are susceptible of a larger, tripartite division.[13]

Where Thucydides presents an intricate sameness of political factors in a state of perpetually fresh recombination, Tacitus further dynamizes his account by subjecting his ongoing narrative to inner purposes. These purposes deal always with the same large question from year to year and principate to principate – management of the bureaucratic structure from the Senate on down, careful provision for succession, military and political control of the provinces and outlying foreign territories. But the political factors do not only recombine; they twist in long-range and short-range response to the special style of the *princeps* in question. Event subverts structure, which appears only after the fact, tangentially and silently, and by a kind of buildup of analogies: The adoption of Tiberius by Augustus is matched to that of Nero by Claudius, the aspirations of Germanicus to those of Sejanus, the manipulations of Livia to those of Agrippina the younger, the trial of Piso to that of Seneca. And each *princeps* is compared to the others, while all are compared, often implicitly but in this case sometimes explicitly, with Augustus – who himself is matched against the Republican ideal.

The differences among events outweigh the sameness of the social structures into which they are molded. Idiosyncratic as are Tiberius, Caligula, Claudius, and Nero, each of the four differs markedly, for incapacity and corruption, from Augustus – who at the same time resembles all of them in an authoritarianism that is causing the decline of Rome from a Republican ideal.

Augustus is actually three-sided: First, by comparison with his successors he stands closer to the Republican ideal. Second, he has introduced the new social mechanisms, or else silently and lethally changed the old ones, keeping "the same terms for offices" (*eadem magistratuum vocabula*). Thus it is chiefly he who bears the guilt for undoing the Republic. But third, he possesses a keen, farsighted, and balanced talent for political manipulation that serves the state and not just himself, since something in him retains the vestiges of Republican altruism.

All three of Augustus' sides bear on most of what he does at the end of his life:

> Augustus meanwhile, as supports to his despotism, raised to the pontificate and curule aedileship Claudius Marcellus, his sister's son, while a mere stripling, and Marcus Agrippa, of humble birth, a good soldier, and one who had shared his victory, to two consecutive consulships; as Marcellus soon afterwards died, he also accepted the former as his son-in-law. Tiberius Nero and Claudius Drusus, his stepsons, he honoured with imperial titles, although his own family was as yet undiminished . . .

> And lo! Augustus had appointed Germanicus, Drusus's offspring, to the command of eight legions on the Rhine, and required Tiberius to adopt him, although Tiberius had a son, now a young man, in his house; but he did it that he might have several safeguards to rest on. He had no war on his hands at the time except against the Germans, which was rather to wipe out the disgrace of the loss of Quintilius Varus and his army than out of an ambition to extend the empire, or for any adequate recompense. At home all was tranquil, and there were the same titles for the magistrates; there was a younger generation, sprung up since the victory of Actium, and even many of the older men had been born during the civil wars. How few were left who had seen the republic!

> Thus the State had been revolutionised, and there was not a vestige left of the old sound morality. Stript of equality, all looked up to the commands of a sovereign without the least apprehension for the present, while Augustus, in the vigour of life, could maintain his own position, that of his house, and the general tranquility. When in advanced old age, he was worn out by a sickly frame, and the end was near and new prospects opened, a few spoke in vain of the blessings of freedom, but most people dreaded and some longed for war.[14]

(*Annals* 1.3–1.4)

An adoption that immediately taps a successor is an institution of greater force in the Empire than in the Republic. Augustus' naming of Tiberius, however, is not just a selfish act; Augustus, it may be presumed, sees in Tiberius the bureaucratic talent. Yet he could not see that when Tiberius takes over, the same talent will turn government into an instrument of his psychology and will aid him to tease and agonize the Roman state. Here the farsighted Augustus is seen as making even further provision when he forces Tiberius to adopt Germanicus, thus giving a military backup to Tiberius' managerial capacities, and also providing into the future for a putatively seasoned successor to Tiberius. But here in his arrogance *Divus Augustus* plays God. For all his *pluribus munimentis*, he cannot make provision for everything. His presumed contempt for Tiberius fails to perceive that when anyone becomes emperor he will then call his own tunes. This presentation is the first in the series that will lead to the mysterious death of Germanicus under the successfully concealed agency of Tiberius. So much for bureaucratic talent further released from the network of Republican obligations! It may be, though, that Augustus' far sight was not wholly wrong here. Of Tacitus' four emperors, one was the son (Caligula), another the brother (Claudius), and a third the grandson (Nero) of Germanicus. Tiberius alone stood at a more collateral remove to that family. So the family did prevail, as Augustus may be presumed to have planned. And in any case, none of the four emperors chose his successor with anything like Augustus' wisdom, or even his effectiveness.

So, too, in military affairs. The *Annals* are not preponderantly a military history, as are what we have of the *Histories*. Campaigns stand in dynamic relation to imperial management or aspiration. The military actions flare up constantly, and presumably because the emperor in question cannot prevent them from doing so, lacking the skill Augustus is here declared to manage. In his principate only one trouble spot appears in the whole empire, so by implied analogy Augustus outdoes the others as a farsighted peacekeeper. That was the boast; the gates of Janus were closed during the Pax Augusti. Moreover, when he sustains a campaign, he does so in this case not for equivalent gain (*dignum praemium*) or in response to attack, but rather to redress the Romans' disastrous defeat in the battle of the Teutoburger Wald. He also aims to assert the ultimate invincibility of Republican glory. Furthermore, unlike his four successors, Augustus holds too firm a rein on government to let some aspiring general accumulate a dangerous following among the troops. He has maneuvered completely free of the shadows from which he emerged, like Caesar before him – shadows that gather almost at once when Tiberius assumes the reins of government. Augustus' restraint on ambition also betrays a certain indolence (4.30) if measured against Tacitus' later praise for those who extended the empire. Still, at no point in the *Annals* does the Empire reach the point of subjection to almost purely military action, where the imperial succession is decided just by battle, as later on in Rome, beginning with the Galba, Otho, Vitellius, and Vespasian of the *Histories*. Augustus' perspicacity, then, may be said to have staved off that end, while the various blindnesses of his four successors may be said to have brought it on.

In any case, the topics of the short summary above – succession, bureaucratic manipulation, military campaigns – remain the predominating topics of the *Annals*. A series for each of these spheres, and an interaction among them in the psychology of Augustus, has been begun here. Nor does any of these submit to the sort of focus emphasized by the *Res Gestae Divi Augusti*.[15] Tacitus, as Syme says, handles his sources with powerful freedom.[16] He continues his emphasis as he varies his scale, and the revealingly incomplete matches of analogical events build relentlessly onward into the terrifyingly simpler reign of Tiberius, where many duplicities operate, but no longer with Augustus' range and mastery. The introduction to Tiberius' reign tells us as much in its blunt one-dimensionality, "The first crime of the new principate was the slaughter of Postumus Agrippa," "primum facinus novi principatus fuit Postumi Agrippae caedes" (1.6). Here Tacitus engages a rare simplicity, a rare explicitness, a rare absence of some ironic shadow, and even a rare freedom from analogy, since nothing Augustus did could quite so baldly be called a crime.

Tacitus' problem differs from Thucydides'. How does one historicize a universal bureaucracy? In the Peloponnesian War the nearness of one city-state to another results in a strategic network, as well as an ever disjunct chain of events. In one sense the Roman Empire is continuous: It spreads in all directions to its boundaries. But this simple continuity creates a discontinuity: Events in Africa do not affect those in Germany, and even those in Egypt do not affect those in outlying Armenia – except indirectly through their response to the central authority of the emperor.

Tacitus handles this strange, englobing space by making it subservient to time: Germany or Armenia, or central Rome, comes up in the annalistic sequence, which he does allow himself to break so he may carry a sequence to term, so long as he does not throw off proportion.[17] In the *Germania* he had gone Herodotus one better by inventing the separate ethnographic monograph. He distributes his discussion of this territory's space by treating first of the whole, then of the separate parts; the general is implicitly brought to bear on the specific. In the *Agricola*, Britain is simply a field for the operations that may then be eulogized. Everything in the *Histories* converges upon Rome, and even more does the *Annals* take the empire as a background field of force that admits of both converging and diverging movements. That Germanicus is shipped from Germany to the Near East, and meantime is conceded the office of consul at Rome, tells us not that he is needed everywhere in the Empire but that he remains while alive an insoluble problem for the emperor.

At a further level of spatial pressure, dignitaries from some of the provinces may aspire to be assimilated to citizenship and candidacy for offices, including the Senate. Claudius shows himself to be both mild and weak when he supports the application of Gallia Comata for this centripetal privilege. "Everything, Senators, which we now hold to be of the highest antiquity, was once new . . . This practice will establish itself, and what we are this day justifying by precedents, will itself be a precedent," "omnia . . . quae nunc vetustissima creduntur, nova fuere . . . quid hodie exemplis tuemur, inter exempla erit" (11.24). Tacitus governs his ongoing narrative by no other rule than this one he notices Claudius enunciating, though in political context the rule cuts both ways, since bad actions can serve for precedent as well as good.[18] In this instance Claudius's vacillation appears under his resourcefulness at formulation. Moreover, a correct rule can be imprudently applied. All three of these misfires are the case at this particular moment, in a sort of triple irony that coruscates through the impacted structure of the narrative. In addition to the ironies that contrast the bad side of Claudius' rule with the good, and its correctness with its misapplication, there is another irony that the whole action characterizes the incompetent Claudius at the very moment when he is adducing competence. This stands as an analogue and variant of Tiberius' incompetence when he exhibits cruelty in the very moment of pleading clemency.

Such adaptive complications in the narrative provide a principle whereby abrupt shifts of subject are brought into a coherence that is not exactly structural but rather a sort of processive equivalent for structure.

As a consequence of the very fact that all the variables bearing on an event cannot be introduced, there is no way to decide whether a given shift of subject results from randomness or from order. Claudius, since he was emperor, did carry the day: "The emperor's speech was followed by a decree of the Senate," "Orationem principis secuto patrum consulto" (11.25), a remark that carries a certain irony, in the light of Tacitus' view of the ever-increasing subservience of the Senate. The Aedui, who earlier had been at the center of a massive revolt (3.40–47), are admitted to the Senate; and then Claudius goes about shoring up the old families by enrolling senators among the patricians. And then he asks certain infamous senators to resign voluntarily, while he expels others. And then he refuses a flattering title. Then he closes the lustrum-census. "Then too" – finally – there "ended his blindness as to his domestic affairs," "isque illi finis inscitiae erga domum suam fuit" (11.25). Is his new awareness a cumulative result of all these statesmanlike actions? Or does Messalina's downfall just happen because she has finally become too flagrant even for the oblivious Claudius? Has he earned the *finis inscitiae*, the end of obliviousness, or is it just handed to him? Tacitus' ongoing suspension between structure and event will not permit a judgment either way, though the very next sentence piles ironies of contrast upon the awareness, "not long afterwards he was driven to notice and punish his wife's flagrancies, so that thereupon he would burn for an incestuous marriage," "haud multo post flagitia uxoris noscere ac punire adactus est ut deinde ardesceret in nuptias incestas." Do the *flagitia* of Messalina help legitimate the *nuptias incestas* of Claudius, himself lustful as well as now just? The force of that *ut* above is suspended over all these questions. Claudius effectuates as well as "burns for" a marriage with his niece Agrippina – a marriage that will ultimately lead to the disinheritance of his legitimate son Britannicus, and the murder of the younger man, at the hands of her son Nero, who will then kill her. For the conservative Tacitus perhaps all this sequence of horror resides embryonically in the *nuptias incestas*. The very phrase implies a sort of oxymoron in the code of the Republican family, where the *matrona* who has been the only viable candidate for *nuptias* must be *casta*, and not its opposite. Again, there is an analogue to Tiberius among his Spintrians on Capri, and to the various orgies of Caligula and Nero. Augustus, by contrast, promulgated laws intended to uphold the family and restore it to its prior sanctity, laws only mentioned in passing. And his personal life always ran on a plane that kept him from the more extreme kinds of distractions that variously preoccupied his four successors.

Further on, in fact, Agrippina first follows in the footsteps of Messalina by taking as an adulterous lover the very man who had advised her marriage and was "bound to her," "Pallas, qui obstrictus Agrippinae ut conciliator nuptiarum et mox stupro eius inligatus":

> . . . he still urged Claudius to think of the interests of the State, and to provide some support for the tender years of Britannicus. "So," he said, "it had been with the Divine Augustus, whose stepsons, though he had grandsons to support him, had flourished; Tiberius too, though he had offspring of his own, had adopted Germanicus. Claudius also would do well to strengthen himself with a young prince who could share his cares.[19]

> (12.25)

Thus, with irony playing over this little speech, Claudius is once again the duped husband. He is led to overlook the crucial difference that Augustus had no eligible son. Precedent is brought in to serve ends very different from those that the adoptions of Augustus had aimed for. All these contrasts of implied comparison are mounting further contrasts as the narrative relentlessly both builds its networks of signification and carefully refrains from endowing them with an extrapolable structure. And the effect is to highlight the psychological factor.

On another occasion Tacitus gives an account of new sumptuary laws immediately after presenting a savage execution (2.33). Each comments on the other more complexly for not being connected by ratiocinative utterance. The bareness of the narrative sequence makes the juxtaposition a forceful one because Tacitus has already manifested a controlling intelligence behind the data. He can come out and indicate his reason for bringing some affair up, as in the case of Libo's trial, the innovation of a disastrous precedent: "I shall expound with greater care the beginning, sequence, and end of his case since then first were found those practices which ate into the state for so many years," "Eius negotii initium ordinem finem curatius disseram, quia tum primum reperta sunt quae per tot annos rem publicam exedere" (2.27).

The process is a gradual one, and the pitch increases, along with the frequency, of such trials. By the latter end of Tiberius' reign Tacitus can use the word *acervatim*, "in a heap," to indicate their rapid succession (6.9). In one sense causes are delineated; all actions ultimately result from the emperor; they arise from the particular psychological style governing his capacities and limitations. In another sense, however, the very variety of events an emperor is called on to manage, and the complexity of the human personality, prevents the historian's ascription of causes to a single trait, even though a predominant one will come out over a long haul, gradually. As Syme says, "The *Agricola* expounds the moral and political ideals of the new aristocracy; not systematically formulated but emerging gradually in the portrayal of an individual and in the stages of a senator's career."[20]

This principle is endowed with many dimensions in the *Annals*, where each terrible ruler, while simpler in his vices than Agricola was to be in his virtues, is faced at the same time with more complex, more various, and far more insoluble problems. So that the strain is constantly brought to bear on the action between the system of a single structural explanation (Tiberius is a hypocritical sadist) and the range of the sequenced events (he must deal with the armies throughout the Mediterranean, with the Senate, with a changing repertoire of actual and would-be successors to power).

Consequently the analogized exempla recur through the stream of events in a sort of causal limbo.[21] Tiberius resembles Claudius and Nero in a cruel ineffectuality manifested under the semblance of rule, but there is a discontinuity among their particular personal styles. The style becomes gradually unmistakeable as each puts his stamp on the events. There is a further discontinuity between the temper of their actions and the process by which each was brought to power. No one of them was so immediately responsible for his succession that the qualities which brought them to the fore are then incorporated in their administrations. In this discontinuity, again, they differ radically from Augustus, as well as from the Flavians portrayed in the *Histories*. But, again, because Augustus' successors consequently cannot impose their wills quite the way he was able to do, the causal reins somewhat escape them, and there is a sense in which all that happens under the decline of these four principates is the result of relative impotence. From this angle the emperor is not so much a cause as an impediment on the one hand, and on the other hand someone whose psychological limitations allow other causes, particularly in the Empire at large, to come to the fore.

4

The detail itself in a historical work pulls against, as well as substantiating, the sense of process that the writer creates. The law of balancing relevance against mere listing tells with particular salience upon the detail – so much so that justifying a particular detail in a work of historiography will incur an endless regress of argument between relevance and superfluity – unless narrative is accorded its own special thrust of radically necessary communication.[22] The *fait* that is *divers* from one angle may not be from another, and the historian is well advised to use both angles.

No principle will fully substantiate – or fully ensure – Tacitus' providing more details for the suicide of Libo at the hands of his slaves than for other executions; they knocked over a lamp on the table at his side and in darkness he "aimed two blows (*duos ictus*) at a vital part" (2.31). Tacitus could simply have mentioned confusion and haste. It is possible, but not necessary, to code these details.

A seeming distraction – Tacitus' mention of his own priesthood and praetorship in Domitian's secular games (11.11) – can be justified by its extension of comparison up to his own time, Nero to Domitian, and the great age (*antiquitus*) of the institution. This, and not boasting (*non iactantia referet*), he declares to be his purpose. He mentions without summarizing them the reasons of Augustus and Nero (*utriusque principis rationes praetermitto*) without offering any details at all. Instead he refers us – by footnote, as it were – to his prior writings, in which these were "sufficiently related" (*satis narratas*). Thus he limits the *Annals*, by the detail of adducing himself, to the whole process depicted in the *Histories*.

The detail in the *Annals* provides a linchpin for the working analogy, but it also holds profoundly to the concretization of its own moment, resisting as well as furthering explanation. Indeed, the proliferation of detail here itself reveals the process of decline, since most of it might – but only might (*forsitan*) – seem small and light in the telling:

> Most of what I have related and shall have to relate, may perhaps,
> I am aware, seem petty and light to record. But no one must compare

my annals with the writings of those who have described Rome in old days. They told of great wars, of the storming of cities, of the defeat and capture of kings, or whenever they turned by preference to home affairs, they related, with a free scope for digression, the strifes of consuls with tribunes, land and corn-laws, and the struggles between the commons and the aristocracy. My labours are circumscribed and inglorious; peace wholly unbroken or but slightly disturbed, dismal misery in the capital, an emperor careless about the enlargement of the empire, such is my theme. Still it will not be useless to study those at first sight trifling events out of which the movements of vast changes often take their rise.[23]

(4.32)

In this last sentence Tacitus propounds the necessity of a deep probe (*introspicere*) of what is light at first look, and the possibility (*saepe*) that seemingly light detail will be found at the origination of great events.

It was to Tacitus that Pliny addressed his epistolary essay against brevity, as Syme points out.[24] The condensation of Tacitus' style thrusts such details as he does enlist into particular salience. Tacitus often, indeed, uses the word *causas* in the plural and links it to words like *motus* (as above), *initium*, and *origo*, in the plural, as though the events offered a complex that could only be partially disengaged by the indicative force of detail. And the use of *motus* above is unusual in its application to large and multiple events, when more regularly Tacitus applies such words to a single delimited event, often a similar one, a death or an animosity.[25]

Tacitus engages, though intermittently, in proliferation of detail, a proliferation that gradually increases through the *Annals*. It increases especially in the last Hexad, as though fleshing out the corruption of Rome with the visible trappings of its decadence. Nothing in the account of Tiberius' activities possesses the concreteness of Claudius' mock naval battle and its catastrophe of flooding (12.56–57). The narrative of Tiberius' lasciviousness on Capri (6.1), though placed for rhetorical prominence at the beginning of a book, offers next to none of the detail that fills out the debauched spectacles of Nero (15.36) – which Tacitus says he "will recount as an example so that he need not often narrate such extravagances," "ut exemplum referam, ne saepius eadem prodigentia narranda sit" (15.37). But he is not obliged for this reason to tell us that the boats were "ornate with gold and ivory and the oarsmen ordered by age and experience in lusts," "naves auro et ebore distinctae remigesque exoletae per aetates et scientiam libidinium componebantur." Upon this account follows the great fire of Rome (15.38–41), occasioning for Tacitus a descriptive panorama of the city that is logically unnecessary for his presentation of events, as though he were slowing down to register the physical completeness of this disgraced Rome. It is rendered in far greater detail than the earlier fire (6.45).

Still later over that city, with a capping intensity of detail that exceeds in both cruelty and visual extent the prior atrocities, there burn living torches, the Christians whom Nero has accused of the arson so as to throw suspicion off himself:

> an immense multitude was convicted, not so much of the crime of firing the city, as of hatred against mankind. Mockeries of them were added to their deaths. Covered with the skins of beasts, they were torn by dogs and perished, or were nailed to crosses, or were doomed to the flames and burnt, to serve as a nightly illumination, when daylight had expired.[26]
>
> (15.44)

This intensity transfigures the partiality of Tacitus. An unnatural light, the raised bodies of so many victims, shines out when daylight has failed over the ruined city. This detail, which easily lends itself to metaphorical extension, etches its concreteness on the text. It comprises an implied contradiction: Nero sets a fire to a throng of the accused to demonstrate that he has not set the earlier fire. And it carries its own intensification: not buildings, but now bodies, are burning. The executions take place not secretly, as in Nero's two attempts on his mother, or rapidly, as after some corrupt judicial conviction, but with horribly protracted slowness, on high, in the open air.

Here, too, analogy serves to intensify the detail. Nero accuses the Christians of outrageous and obscene acts (*atrocia ac pudenda*), projecting upon them the moral characterization Tacitus implies of the emperor's own orgies. Those orgies were torchlit, and here orgy and torches form a new, horrible connection not so much of cause as of the link between rumor-mongering accusation (*atrocia ac pudenda*) and cruelty. He here torches "orgiastic" figures. This is not the first imaginative recasting of the fire of Rome that Nero has undertaken, since he pretends, in his insane sensitivity, that the fire furnishes a kind of literary spectacle by imitating the Fire of Troy, inciting him to play his lyre before it in another detail that has captured the imagination of the ages ("Nero fiddled while Rome burned"). He has made the catastrophe into a display, and the burning of the Christians is a further display. The visible and the psychological, imperial power and what for Tacitus is an exotic and suspicious religion, are set to run riot in this passage.

5

Tacitus the student of rhetoric[27] must have planned the effects he in any case achieved. The annalistic method permits a seeming randomness of ill-matched topics, a procedure that throws an analogical match into even greater relief when such a match is brought forward. His method also emphasizes the power of a preoccupation when the same topic keeps coming back. The end of *Annals*, Book 1, for example, moves from the everlasting treason trials (74) to Tiberius' excessive pettiness in attending the praetor's court and his arbitrariness in granting subsidies to individuals; and then on to the flood of the Tiber. The flood serves as the occasion for another confusingly ambitious act on Tiberius' part – an analogy in a different domain – his refusal to consult the Sibylline books. The flood itself, rhetorically, is an early entry in a series of natural disasters that throw a further wild card into the already unplayable deck of public problems. At a much later point the incapacities of a further emperor will converge upon a most devastating and central natural disaster at which the emperor himself had very likely set his hand, the fire of Rome.

Here the flood of the Tiber is followed immediately not by a natural disaster but by a request from Achaia and Macedonia for tax relief (1.16). These states are given to Poppaeus Sabinius somewhat arbitrarily in 1.80. (Achaia and Macedonia recur ten more times or so in the narrative, and they are not always linked.) Then comes the social disaster of a theater riot and enough measures to handle it (77), followed by the request from the Spaniards of Torraco for a temple of Augustus and from the citizens of Rome for a reduction of sales tax, for a resultant cancellation of concessions to military mutineers (78). Finally here, Tacitus moves to the proposed measures for controlling the Tiber once again, to divert the tributary rivers and lakes. This proposal incurs protest from the settlements that would be affected either economically or in their access to religious sites and buildings.

Into the series of this frequently refocusing narrative, as characteristically, Tacitus inserts what is itself a series, his succinct summaries of interwoven and confusing causes. The discrepancy of rank that imposes when an emperor sits among the praetors amounts to a liberty-sapping hypocrisy: "While a consultation is being held with respect to truth, liberty was being corrupted," "dum veritati consulit, libertas corrumpebatur."[28] The discrepancy is strong enough to occasion a shift of tenses. The narrative of Tiberius' refusal to consult the Sybilline books when it is proper to do so illustrates the same law, though it is described in terms not of its characters but of its effects. "Tiberius refused, and so he obscured the divine and the human," "Renuit Tiberius perinde divina humanaque obtegens" (1.76). This blockage between men and gods very soon results in the aphorism that summarizes the suspended decision about why the works to divert the water from the Tiber were abandoned, "Whether the pleas of the settlers, the difficulty of the works, or superstition prevailed," "Seu preces coloniarum seu difficultas operum sive superstitio valuit" (1.79). A partial match for these factors comes up almost at once, then in the more complex inextricability of cause over Tiberius' leaving his deputies permanently in office:

> Various motives have been assigned for this. Some say that, out of aversion to any fresh anxiety, he retained what he had once approved as a permanent arrangement; others, that he grudged to see many enjoying promotion. Some, again, think that though he had an acute intellect, his judgment was irresolute, for he did not seek out eminent merit, and yet he detested vice. From the best men he apprehended danger to himself, from the worst, disgrace to the State. He went so far at last in this irresolution, that he appointed to provinces men whom he did not mean to allow to leave Rome.[29]

This practice would seem to confuse the emperor himself, who did not act when he should have. Then, though – through an extreme effect of the same *haesitatio* – he acted against his own wishes by despatching to the provinces those whom he wished to retain in Rome. The summary has been driven to a contrary-to-fact in the pluperfect future (*erat passurus*). Such confusion leads to the fundamental confusion in terminology between the words (*verba*) and a fact (*res*) (begun by Augustus when he weakened the function of a named office). The process is effectually summarized in the climactic final sentence of the book: "Things with a good face[30] in words; in the fact, empty or deceitful; and the more fully they were covered with the image of freedom, the more they erupted into hostile servitude," "speciosa verbis, re inania aut subdola, quantoque maiore libertatis imagine tegebantur, tanto eruptura ad infensius servitium" (1.81).

Tacitus introduces his speeches as moments of pause in the special emphasis of isolated pleading, to be swallowed up in the ongoing narrative. These, Syme says, he composes on the model of Sallust. "Sallust demonstrated once and for all, that the periodic sentence will not do either for narration or for picture. It has balance, subordination, amplitude, and a conclusion all too often inevitable. History stabs 'facts' one by one."[31] Tacitus, however, in the torsions of his style, strains those facts, and the result is a variation, gradual or abrupt, of his pace, among fulsome speech, curt note, and the sweeping summary. So the statement quoted above introduces Tiberius as emperor, "The first crime of the new reign was the murder of Posthumus Agrippa," "primum facinus novi principatus fuit Postumi Agrippa caedes" (1.6). This statement interrupts and changes rhythm; these stylistic features themselves encapsulate comments on the new style of rule. The isolated speech of the dying Germanicus – Augustus-like in its fusion of magnanimity and deathbed political manipulation – is followed not only by ironic contrast in the remote event: five of the six children mentioned in the speech will die, yet the sixth will be an emperor, and all three succeeding emperors will be his close relatives in the office from which he has here been finally deflected.

This speech (2.71) is followed in the immediate narrative first by succinct, narrative clauses, rounding out in a final clause of arrestingly paired abstractions:

> indoluere exterae nationes regesque: tanta illi comitas in socios, mansuetudo in hostis; visuque et auditu iuxta venerabilis, cum magnitudinem et gravitatem summae fortunae retineret, invidiam et adrogantiam effugerat.

> Foreign nations and kings grieved over him, so great was his courtesy to allies, his humanity to enemies. He inspired reverence alike by look and voice, and while he maintained the greatness and dignity of the highest rank, he had escaped the hatred that waits on arrogance.

The last statement connects Germanicus' potential constituency (he did not arouse *invidia*) with his personal self-presentation (he lacked *adrogantia*). We must *think*, to make the logical connection between (the absences of) hatred and arrogance. The style arrests and imposes as it twists. In its continuation it provokes the still further examples from the text of widespread *invidia* and *adrogantia*.[32]

This clause is balanced syntactically, as many of those in Tacitus are not. It strains its balance logically, however, by requiring a logical step to connect the two abstractions, and another to register their absence of the traits in the lauded subject. Rhetorically it functions as a litotes, without recourse to that syntactic structure. It is also doubly anticlimactic since the prior terms paired – *visu et auditus . . . venerabilis; magnitudinem et gravitatem* – were laudatory, and so contradictory to this *invidia* and *adrogantia*; and since we only learn him to be free of those vices as we get the final verb, *effugerat*.

Comparably, what is perhaps his most famous clause, "where they make a desert, they call it peace," "ubi solitudinem faciunt pacem appellant" (*Agricola*, 30), while balanced, has also a double or even a triple force, in addition to its function as the climax of a series of indictments against Rome. There is a contrast not only between "pacification" in the propagandistic sense and the real devastation an invader creates, but also between what a real peace would be and the silent chaos here called a peace. There is also the general contrast between the real state of affairs and that hypocrisy of silence, imposed on talking about it in the person of a brave Briton – a silence that the historian here is ipso facto breaking.

Silence, more variously in the *Annals*, serves as a tool for the tyrant. Tacitus describes it as a chief mechanism for Tiberius in the climactic conclusion of his first book:

> I can hardly venture on any positive statement about the consular elections, now held for the first time under this emperor, or indeed, subsequently, so conflicting are the accounts we find not only in historians but in Tiberius' own speeches. Sometimes he kept back the names of the candidates, describing their origin, their life and military career, so that it might be understood who they were. Occasionally even these hints were withheld, and, after urging them not to disturb the elections by canvassing, he would promise his own help towards the result. Generally he declared that only those had offered themselves to him as candidates whose names he had given to the consuls, and that others might offer themselves if they had confidence in their influence or merit. A plausible profession this in words, but really unmeaning and delusive, and the greater the disguise of freedom which marked it, the more cruel the enslavement into which it was soon to plunge.[33]
>
> (1.81)

Silence works also for the revelatory omission, as when Tacitus mentions that the fact was not mentioned about Blaesus that he was the uncle of Sejanus (3.35). The very silence here is a dynamic, corrupting, force upon the state. It creates and activates an *imago*, "simulacrum of freedom," "*quanto que maiore libertatis imagine.*"

In such turns, and in the changes of emphasis and scale within his narrative segments, Tacitus invigorates and complicates his account by leaving traces in his language and structure of the historian's necessary pull of the moment against the whole. In historiography the narrated moment seems simultaneously to exemplify and to transcend its potential analytic-relational context.

"Every event is a species unto itself," Paul Veyne asserts, offering one side of the tension between the moment and the whole. "History is also a shorthand," he says.[34] Tacitus' language, his control of sequence, and his attention to event-intricating psychological effects, bring him to a vision that exhibits the same sort of tension in its overall extent. On the one hand, he can be found to adhere simply to the view that power is best vested in a single person and the Republican parliamentary practices best preserve virtue (these sentiments themselves nest a contradiction, of course). On the other hand, he does achieve a version of the neutrality *sine ira et studio* declared at the outset, a neutrality that has a Stoic cast, without adherence to that world view which he seems to criticize somewhat in Seneca. The plausibility that Stoicism would become particularly attractive under the conditions that Tacitus depicts, derives from the awareness he has brought us to realize.

6

TEMPORALIZING THE ABSTRACTION
OF INDETERMINACY:
MACHIAVELLI AND GUICCIARDINI

ACTORING, AND THE BALANCING OF FACTORS, are introduced more or less suddenly into the writing of history of Machiavelli and Guicciardini.[1] This new dialectics at once forces the temporal sequences that it puts into consideration under the constantly tested principles of synchronic management, which at the same time can be regarded as derived from them. The reciprocity between event and principle dynamizes the presentation and enters the narrative chain as more than just a set of rhetorical modifiers.[2]

Machiavelli inspects the temporal dimension in given cases that he measures against a principle; his synchronic approach is subjected to a powerful diachronic dimension, a successful application of what Paul Ricoeur finds in Augustine's solution of puzzles about time, a "*distensio animi,*" or "stretching of the mind," for a "dialectic between narrativity and temporality" in which the present is modified by measures of the past and even of the future.[3]

Guicciardini, breaking free, as Pocock reads him, from the static presentation of separate events in medieval historians, aims his close-woven diachronic presentation at a coherent view.[4] This comes about through what Ricoeur calls an "intrication," a "*mise en intrigue*" in an achieved "dialectic between narrative and temporality," in which "it is the capacity of history (historiography) to be logically consecutive that constitutes the poetic solution of the paradox between distension and intention (*intentio*). . . . That history allows itself to be put into sequence converts the paradox into living dialectic."[5]

Indeed, the surface differences in style between the two historians, as well as the different "positions" that can be ascribed to them, are arguably less essential to their presentations than this defining posture toward time. They present what Pocock has called "the beginnings of a dialectical perception of history in Europe."[6]

This new dialectics did not come easily to either writer, and it was applied variously and intermittently through the career of each. Machiavelli's *Discorsi* on Livy governs itself into seriality and obliquity by casting itself in the form of a commentary. Indeed, he is deep into the commentary before he turns it to his own theoretical ends, and yet the name Livy is not mentioned very often, and not a second time till he gets some way into his discussion.[7]

If for Machiavelli, in De Sanctis's characterization, "the facts are the fixed point around which he turns,"[8] still Machiavelli offers no covering law that will compass all the facts he gives. The cases strain ahead of him, especially in the *Istorie fiorentine*. In the *Discorsi* he proceeds by putting a general law at the head of each of his trenchant, short chapters and then both amplifies it or illustrates it by cases that come from Roman, or Italian, or sometimes even Turkish, history. In the conventional modesty of his dedicatory proem, he still speaks of himself as "discoursing in many areas," "*in molte parti discorrendo.*" And he is fairly far into the work when he uses as a chapter heading the second-order generalization that underlies the rest, "Among diverse peoples the very same accidents are frequently to be seen," "In diversi popoli si veggono spesso i medesimi accidenti" (I, 31).

The fact that he is constantly, and with great originality, providing explanatory laws has led commentators to resolve his indeterminacy – which can be done so long as the historical factor, which became progressively more pronounced in his work, is curtailed from its full temporal force. Machiavelli, indeed, gives evidence that he himself wishes to curtail the historical factor; he seems convinced that the set of laws he adduces in a given instance, because they are bold and comprehensive, will serve or could serve to remove men from being "*sull' ambiguo.*" But the very nature of his intention to subject himself to the temporal conditions of the historiographer, and his declared focus on particular places and times, keeps the discrepancy between explanation and fact in a dynamic interaction that provides, as resolution would not, the impetus not to abandon particular temporal sequences.[9]

In the *Discorsi* there is a built-in double (or triple) indeterminacy, first between the incorporated ideal of Livy's Rome and the relative primitivism of its political gestures; second, between either of these and the conditions of the Italian city-states contemporary with Machiavelli; and third, between the randomness of the historical events at either time and the order that might be imposed upon them, both separately and together. The effect of all this indeterminacy is to confine Machiavelli into the disjunctions of commentary, from which he is always breaking out. The liberation of his thought takes the form of the enunciation of laws about a particular instance. There obtains, taken with his announced principles elsewhere, a further indeterminacy about how far the express law may be taken to carry. It is not always but "frequently" that "among diverse peoples the very same accidents are to be seen." On the one hand the law heading a given chapter offers a full explanation just of the given instance from Livy. But on the other hand it is usually meant to have a general force. Yet even if the law enunciated by Machiavelli be true beyond the given instance, it would not necessarily be apposite or applicable in some other instance; or he would not have enunciated some other law to cover that. Though the congruence between diachronic particular instance and synchronic general law tautens in *Il Principe*, still, there too the congruence between instance and law is reined in, so that it can be felt as the base upon which the enunciation of laws is energized. Far from being stalled by this indeterminacy, like a deconstructionist *avant la lettre*, Machiavelli is inspired by it to bring as much synchronic generality to bear as he can. The effect is a histrionic one: to master, and to project, what would otherwise be a diachronic chaos.

In the *Discorsi*, while a full narrative historical sequence lies firmly in the background (the sequency of Livy), Machiavelli himself intrudes sequences only intermittently and sparsely. At the same time the principle of diachronic sequence, as governed by the cross-hatching of political laws, is often present. Indeed, it can be built into the very maxim itself, as "A headless multitude is useless; and it should not threaten first and then invoke authority," "Una moltitudine senza capo è inutile; e non si deve minacciare prima, e poi chiedere l'autorità" (1:36). Sequence holds, as well as contingency, even when the famous factors of fraud and force are in question, "That one gets from low to great fortune more with fraud than with force," "Che si viene da bassa a gran fortuna più con la frode che con la forza" (2:10). The case of Coriolanus (1:6) engenders a whole chain of maxims laid down as abstract templates upon the moments of that sequence, "because out of it is born an offense from private persons to private persons, which offense generates fear; fear seeks defense, through defense the partisans are introduced, from the partisans are born factions in the cities, and from the factions the ruin of those cities," "perchè ne nasceva offesa da privati a privati, la quale offesa genera paura, la paura, cerca difesa, per la difesa si procacciano i partigiani, dai partigiani nascono le parti nelle cittadi, et dalle parti la rovina di quelle."

Through an inevitably more even sequence, such powerful foreshortening still keeps the temporal progression of the *Istorie Fiorentine* dynamically tautened. The detail becomes more pronounced toward the end (the death of Lorenzo di Medici) than at the beginning (the barbarian invasions). Right at the beginning the kinds of laws that served as chapter headings in the *Discorsi* are brought to bear: "These migrating masses . . . fixed their residence at Constantinople . . . by this step they exposed the western empire to the rapine of both their ministers and their enemies, the remoteness of their position preventing them either from seeing or providing for its necessities."[10] Here, as generally, the maxims are both applied to temporal sequence and put through dialectical manipulation. The geopolitical factors here permute groups and their spatial location, doubling in both cases: "both ministers and their enemies" and "seeing or providing for." In a way much more integrated into narrative sequence even than Thucydides managed, the abstractions energize the narrative:

> This government, from its establishment in 1381, till the alterations now made, had continued six years; and the internal peace of the city remained undisturbed until 1393. During this time, Giovanni Galeazzo Visconti, usually called the Count of Virtù, imprisoned his uncle Bernabo and thus became sovereign of the whole of Lombardy. As he had become duke of Milan by fraud, he designed to make himself king of Italy by force. In 1390 he commenced a large-scale attack upon the Florentines; but such various changes occurred in the course of the war, that he was frequently in greater danger than the Florentines themselves, who, though they made a brave and admirable defense, for a republic, must have been ruined, if he had not died. As it was, the result was attended with infinitely less evil than their fears of so powerful an enemy had led them to apprehend; for the duke . . . died before he had tasted the fruit of his victories, or the Florentines began to feel the effect of their disasters.[11]
>
> (3:6)

Historiographic definitions permeate and orient *Il Principe*. To begin with, the classification of the whole work is historically determined; Machiavelli declares at the outset that he will deal with just one kind of the two kinds of government that exist; he will neglect republics. This alone keeps *Il Principe* from being simply a treatise on government in general. And he tends toward a discussion of just the "mixed" principates that predominated in the time immediately before his writing. He draws, indeed, most fully on the events just after the conclusion of what would become his *Istorie Fiorentine*; he draws, in fact, on the nearly contemporary time covered by Guicciardini in the *Storia d'Italia*. Sometimes, notably in the discussion of Cesare Borgia, Machiavelli gives far fuller an account than the principle under discussion would call for. And the principle itself tends to be historicized as well. A sequence is implied in what he says of Cesare: "Whoever does not first lay his foundations could – with great *virtù* – do so later, although causing trouble for the architect and danger to the building."[12] His amplifications about Cesare constitute a foreshortened historical narrative, drawn into synchronicity by the forceful intellection of the principles that are brought to bear upon it.

While Machiavelli's illustration ranges broadly enough to include Greece and Rome, Moses, and the Turks, it focuses prevailingly on the Italy of just before his own time. And it is, in turn, usually when his own time comes into question that he is most historiographic. "Thus for the French king to lose Milan the first time, a Duke Ludovico had only to create a disturbance on his frontiers; for the king to lose it a second time, he had to have the whole world against him and his armies had to be destroyed or driven out of Italy – results of the causes mentioned above. Nevertheless, the city was taken away from the king both times."[13] This passage has reached a rhetorical fusion where it functions fully both as a synchronized historical capsule and as the illustration of a general principle, though, of course, it is rhetorically framed as the latter – just as the *Discorsi* are framed rhetorically as a version of the former, and the *Istorie Fiorentine* may be said to digest both foreshortened history and ingrained principle. Or again, the conclusion, still historicized, may be appended at the end of the encapsulated narrative: "The Venetians were then able to contemplate the recklessness of their decision; to acquire two towns in Lombardy, they made the king ruler over one-third of Italy," "E allora posserno considerare e' Viniziani la temerità del partito preso da loro; i quali, per acquistare due terre in Lombardia, feciono signore, el re, del terzo di Italia."

Even in a principate there is a constant interaction between leader and people; to this interaction the prince's very necessity to manage the people eloquently testifies. Such interactions intensify the *Istorie Fiorentine*, whereas in the *Storia d'Italia*, Guicciardini organizes his whole presentation around the actions of princes who are managing their domains through the stresses and counterstresses not so much of their own people as of other principalities large and small. This proto-diplomatic history puts a more individual stamp for the speaker on the many speeches he quotes, and it displaces from too detailed a presentation the many battles he does recount.[14] So intent is Guicciardini's focus on rulers, and so abundant and intricate the presentation, that the annual method he adopts, marking the year much as Thucydides had, does not really serve as an organizing principle. His consequent gain in the air of objectivity receives backhand testimony in the strictures against him of Montaigne, who, though he praises Guicciardini, finds that he "left nothing to say" ("*rien laisser à dire*") and fails to bring questions of religion, virtue, and conscience to bear on his narrative.[15]

Guicciardini, centering his geopolitical presentations on the statesmen who managed them, begins his history with the new imbalance brought about by the death of Lorenzo di Medici in 1492. He ends it, after decades of intricate activity, with what amounts to a persisting indeterminacy at the death of Clement VII in 1534. Much of the earlier part of the *Storia d'Italia* is taken up with delineating how one man, Ludovico Sforza, had tried to manage the imbalance to his own advantage by subtlety upon subtlety of counteraction, beginning with what can only be called the suborning of Charles VIII of France to enter Italy and tilt the balance in Ludovico's favor. But after a lifetime of such activity, and hundreds of pages of dense readjustments toward the many other states, Ludovico himself ends by dying in prison (2:14).

Even such an astute leader is subject to unpredictable factors, among which the risk of being totally checked by imprisonment figures importantly, to say nothing of mortality. Yet on the other hand, in the last sentence of the *Storia d'Italia*, "That proverb is most true and worthy of highest praise which says that the magistracy makes manifest the value of him who exercises it," "Perchè è verissimo e degno di somma laude quel proverbio, che il magistrato fa manifesto il valore di chi lo esercita." The term *valore* may be taken as an even more neutral version of its political cousin, the *virtù* of Machiavelli.

The fact that Guicciardini begins and ends with personal deaths of leaders when all men are mortal renders the coherence of his history different from that of Thucydides – even though his was perhaps not fully finished – or from that of Gibbon. The deaths have a randomness – an indeterminate relation to the other factors – in the *Storia d'Italia*, and so do the events. A related sequence serves as just a segment in time, and the sequence in its resultant indeterminacy exhibits a certain indifference, rather than a natural beginning and ending. The sequence could have begun anywhere, which is not usually the case with narrative history; and it could have ended anywhere, in spite of Guicciardini's obvious personal involvement with the events. He avoids the wide temporal focus of Machiavelli's *Istorie Fiorentine*, and yet Guicciardini's focus is spatially wide, and it seems thematically wide because the situation to be accounted for is always so intricate and so variously changeable. He declares his intention at the outset to write about what had happened within living memory after the invasion of the French; and he then goes on almost immediately to characterize events as a tossing sea – a metaphor which implies that one could enter the sequence at any point and still find the endless play of similar counterforces: "From numerous examples it will appear evident into what instability, not otherwise than a sea excited by winds, human affairs are subjected," "per innumerabili esempli evidentemente apparirà a quanta instabilità, né altrimenti che uno mare concitato da' venti, siano sottoposte le cose umane" (2:1).

The swell of events may rise higher when a powerful distant player, the Turk or the Holy Roman Emperor, enters the game. At their best the rulers will exercise the prudence much praised by Guicciardini, and his greatest exemplar would seem to be Lorenzo de Medici, who here does not come under intense scrutiny because he is a predecessor, one who "brought it about by every labor that Italian affairs kept themselves moderately balanced," "procurava con ogni studio che le cose d'Italia in modo bilanciate si mantenessino" (1:1). The events, once out of balance, slip beyond the most determined efforts of prudence, as the case of Ludovico il Moro demonstrates at length. He, of course, let himself be thrown out of balance not only by events that were too intricate and unstable even for his keen political sense, but because he was subject to the ambition that Guicciardini castigates in passing while observing it as a constant factor in the rulers who are his main players, "the pestiferous thirst for rule," "*la sete pestifera del dominare*" (1:3). Indeed, in one place he introduces a medical analogy when summing up the results of ambition, saying that things had got too far for even a truce to be a strong enough medicine, bringing "innumerable calamities and bloodier war" rather than peace (8:1).

So alone are these rulers that even asking advice is seen as an imprudent step, if an indispensable one: "Nothing is more necessary in arduous deliberations, and nothing on the other hand more dangerous, than asking advice," "Niuna cosa è certamente più necessaria nelle deliberazioni ardue, niuna da altra parte più pericolosa, che 'l domandare consiglio" (1:16).

These patterns of event go back in time to Charlemagne (1:6) or even to Hannibal (1:9). The possible perfection of balanced forces, in Guicciardini's presentation, can easily be broken not only by excessive ambition, by lack of capacity, or by too difficult a situation for the participants, but by what he, like Machiavelli, calls "accidents," *accidenti*, a term that still has a scholastic flavor, and which in a work of history may be rendered as an event that has an effect but to which no causes may be assigned of the sort that the historian has been discussing. Death is a chief such *accidente*, and a notable *nuovo accidente* is the sudden death from apoplexy in April, 1498 of Charles VIII, whose incursion into Italy had had such far-reaching effects in the first place (3:15). But Charles will be replaced by Louis XII, and the old forces will realign, always with variation, just as the disappearance of one Holy Roman Emperor, the German Maximilian, will be followed by the powerful presence of another, the Burgundian-Spanish Charles V.

Whatever their differences in principle, Machiavelli and Guicciardini always effectually subordinate principle to historical sequence. This in itself, for both writers, makes a higher principle of the enchainment of principles, though in Machiavelli the abstract discussion may obscure such enchainments, and in Guicciardini the slow buildup of intricate actions may throw the principles into the background. As Machiavelli says at one point of the *Istorie Fiorentine*:

> ... from good they [mundane affairs] gradually decline to evil, and from evil again return to good. The reason is, that valor produces peace; peace, repose; repose, disorder; disorder, ruin; so from disorder order springs; from order virtue, and from this, glory and good fortune.[16]

(5:1)

Such sequential thinking is so endemic to Machiavelli that it may crop up at any time, as at the point in the *Discorsi* where he is discussing one among many surprising conclusions, that the *disunion* between populace and senate made the Roman Republic free and powerful (1:15), "A republic may in no way be called disorganized where there are so many examples of *virtù*, because good examples spring from good education, good education from good laws, and good laws from those upheavals that many damn without thinking."[17] Indeed, "many" here would include nearly everybody, and the principle Machiavelli here adduces is only possible after the careful consideration of the dynamics that may be causally attributed to a historical sequence. In this instance, as typically, Machiavelli's theoretical power derives from and is based on his insight into a specific historical situation. As he says, in a maxim more general than anything in Thucydides, "It is very true that most men are better adapted to preserve a good course than to be able to find one for their own circumstances." "Egli è verissimo che gli assai uomini sono più atti a conservare uno ordine buono che a saperlo per loro medesimi trovare" (*Istorie Fiorentine*, 3:6).

But the causal pattern, in turn, implicitly requires the constant application of the historian's discrimination to be adjudged. As he says in the same chapter, "So many good effects were not produced by causes that were not of the best," "tanti buoni effetti... non erano causati se non da ottime cagioni." And he goes on in the next chapter to consider still other aspects of these particular upheavals. Guicciardini, whose commentary on Machiavelli's *Discorsi* criticizes them for not judging particular cases carefully enough – that is, for not being sufficiently historical – echoes Machiavelli's scrupulous determination not to accept what seem to be causes at their face value. As Guicciardini says when he is leading to the climax of Charles VIII's decision to attack Naples (1:3), "Removing causes does not always remove the effects that have had their first origin in them," "Ma non sempre per il rimuovere delle cagioni si rimuovono gli effetti i quali da quelle hanno avuto la prima origine." And he applies this rule to Ludovico Sforza's application, out of fear, of "a medicine stronger than the disease calls for" ("*medicina più potente che non comporti la natural della infermità*") when he has summoned this foreign power as a factor in his negotiations with the pope and the Venetian Senate.

Here, as nearly everywhere, Guicciardini brings everything back to the complex dealings of the princes who are the main movers of the large interactions he sequentially traces. Machiavelli, on the other hand, may be said to throw a theoretical emphasis on the prince just because other groups within a state may be effective – heads of religion and learned men (*Discorsi*, 1:9), as well as the populace (*plebe*) itself. Roman history serves him, then, not only as a traditional Renaissance exemplum, but also as one that is notable for containing and exhibiting such interactions among groups within a society.[18]

As he says in the heading of a chapter toward the end of this work (3:15), "One must pay attention to the actions of citizens, because often a principle of tyranny hides beneath a pious act," "Che si deve por mente alle opere de' cittadini, perchè molte volte sotto un opera pia si nasconde un principio di tirannide." And in a following chapter he adduces what could be called a psychological *longue durée*, a substratum of attitude in a citizenry persisting through all the twists and turns of policy: "The men born in a province observe practically the same nature through all times," "Che gli uomini che nascono in una provincia osservano per tutti i tempi quasi quella medesima natura" (3:22).

Principles must be based on historical events that have a somewhat random cast at first glance, according to Machiavelli. Like Guicciardini, he often uses the term *accidente*, "occurrence" or "happening." "Signs" or "signals" give clues to the *grandi accidenti*, but they must be interpreted.[19]

Machiavelli jumps back and forth nervously from particular illustration to general maxim, whether in the commentary of the *Discorsi*, the theory of *Il Principe*, or the history of the *Istorie Fiorentini*. A historical substratum of causes sought and then found brings into near coherence the indeterminacy which is a future for events as demonstrated by the past that has been brought forward for inspection. There is a sense of mediation constantly produced, even if the writing may be characterized as operating between extremes.[20] In Guicciardini's tendency toward amplification, a maxim is often balanced by its contrary; and yet at points of condensation, the style comes to a head in a momentary terseness.[21] Beyond these local phenomena of style Guicciardini generally floats atop a sea of humanist rhetoric, which he manages to channel toward a presentation of long, detailed sequences, much like Gibbon, and more so than like any classical historian. In both these cases we should remember that jaggedness and abruptness are the norm for the stylistic flow of the great historian, from Thucydides and Tacitus through Machiavelli to A. J. P. Taylor and Namier. So that the massive rhythmic leveling of Guicciardini and Gibbon should be taken not just as the application of the normal rhetoric of their respective times to the historian's task, but rather as the powerful departure away from the historian's norm to that of the orator in order to impose upon the flow of a discourse a sense of overriding coherence and congruent clarity. It is as though they were impelled to ingrain into the very texture of their discourse a pervasive sense of the time flow that freshly governs, and also submits to, their emplotments.

Indeed, it is just here, in the rhythmic patterning, that the difference between the time-gapping pessimism of Tacitus and the panoptic pessimism of Gibbon – for all that there is a (transmuted) Tacitean strain in Gibbon – becomes perceptible, and, one may say, even audible. Yet especially for Guicciardini this rhetoric is caught up in what its orders cannot quite manage. He deploys not only forces but the tendency toward oversuspiciousness about forces that his principles cannot escape and so cannot intricate into an order that matches the order of the discourse of the historian who co-ordinates the forces. The rhetoric is a sign of the historian's coordination, which is lacking in the time-bound referents of his discourse; and in this the rhetoric of Guicciardini differs radically from that of the humanists, who point toward some version of hoped-for order. Machiavelli, however, outplays Sallust and Tacitus in a terseness and a staccato avoidance of amplification that even more boldly masters the indeterminacies he is also presenting. The lessons to be learned from him lie in the gaps of his rhetoric of anti-rhetoric – which means that, as with Guicciardini, the style manages to suggest that the action it recommends controlling faces a silent force that resists such control.

7

THE CROSSCURRENTS OF TIME:
BURCKHARDT AND MICHELET

I

THE PROCESS OF PRODUCING a view of events in time
that allows at once for coherent dynamic development charges the
very vocabulary of Machiavelli and Guicciardini, as Pocock has
shown. Such a process continues through the achievement of Gibbon; and
after him, in the wake of the late-eighteenth- and early-nineteenth-century
philosophers of history, a repeated reprobing of the organizing principles
behind a presentation of long-term historical developments, a varied realization of Meinecke's "historicity." Michelet, who notably enlisted Vico
(as could not be guessed from the surface of his presentation) can be said
to give his own version of *la longue durée*; to be a predecessor of Braudel.
Michelet is multiply diachronic, whereas Burckhardt, whose method is so
different from his as to constitute a nearly systematic alternate possibility
of synchronic presentation, still interprets and collocates events on a foregoing assumption of his own *longue durée*. Contrasting him in turn with de
Tocqueville makes Burckhardt's time orientation abundantly clear. Contrasting him with Michelet throws into relief the fundamental and primary
character of time management in the work of this historian, whatever other
features may be found in it, and whatever other features of deep structure
he may be said to approximate.

One cannot go to Burckhardt's separately expressed political views for
a reliable index of his manipulation of themes in historical works.[1] Burckhardt, in the persisting confidence of his own intellectual projects, asserts
toward the end of his career the specially developed power of the historiographic enterprise of his time. He attributes this power not to scholarly
scrupulosity as it had become refined among such fellow professionals as
Ranke, but rather to philosophy – to Hegel, we may say:

> through the cosmopolitan traffic of the nineteenth century in general
> the viewpoints have become endlessly manifold . . . Finally there are
> added to this the strong movements in modern philosophy, significant

in themselves and steadfastly connected with general world-historical perspectives.

So have historical studies in the nineteenth century been able to win a universality that earlier ones never could.

And again:

Indeed we are dealing, as I said, not so much with the study of history as with the study of the *historical*.[2]

In Burckhardt's work it is synchronic presentation that constitutes the particular force of his historiographic method, a synchronic presentation that pulls against, aspectualizes, and throws into relief, the diachronic material he is manipulating. As though to insist on this, Burckhardt deliberately sought for a simple style, in contradistinction to the style of his contemporaries.[3] Now synchronicity is a standard Enlightenment approach to argument by the characterization of society, an approach shared by Montesquieu and Rousseau. The synchronicity of Tocqueville, whose similarities to Burckhardt are well delineated by Hayden White, carries still some of this Enlightenment tract-like force: Tocqueville means, like Montesquieu, to show that the deep traits of American democracy bode ill for its future, and for the future of any country that would follow its practices. He means to show that France could well assimilate itself with some measure of assurance to practices in prerevolutionary France. In the course of this demonstration he is arguing that these should be understood to have worked better than the proponents of the Revolution like Michelet have argued. Burckhardt, however, is not synchronic in this way. He intends no special present force, and no program for the future, to lie behind his *Age of Constantine the Great* or *Civilization of the Renaissance in Italy*. Consequently, he has powerfully reversed the sequential presentation in those works so as to bring temporal sequence into a focus heightened through the constant pressure of the synchronic, rather than to abrogate it. In this he is highly original, whereas the synchronic method of the *Cicerone* or of the *Recollections of Rubens* is just the standard method most writers would use in writing cultural guides or art-critical monographs.[4] Burckhardt specifically abjures an explicit programmatic purpose for his history.

Spirit is the power that grasps each temporal ideal . . . What was once jubilation and lamentation must now become knowledge, as really, also, in the life of the individual.

Consequently the proposition *Historia vitae magistra* holds a sense that is higher and at the same time more informed. We become through experience not so much crafty (for another time) as wise (for all time).[5]

Burckhardt goes on here to stress not only "spirit" but "the true, the good, the beautiful," and he asserts, almost as his friend Nietzsche would have done, that the true and the good take a manifold coloring and conditioning from their temporal position, "Das Wahre und Gute ist zeitlich gefärbt und bedingt" (7).

In the spirit of Hegel, Burckhardt puts *Geist* at the base of everything. Then he proceeds, as Hegel would not have done, to delineate the resultant temporal complexities, instead of assigning all traits at one temporal moment to a particular spiritual emphasis, a *Zeitgeist*. More comprehensively, in discussing Constantine or the Italian Renaissance, Burckhardt does both at the same time and thereby defines the spiritual unity in the synchronic presentation as a derivative of the complexities resulting from the diachronic development:

Since the spiritual like the material is variable and the change of times incessantly snatches up the forms which show the limit of the external life as of the spiritual, it is the theme of history generally – so that it may show and proceed from these two fundamental directions that are identical in themselves – how first of all everything spiritual, on which domain it also is perceived, has a historical side.

And he goes on:

The operation of the key phenomenon is the historical life, as it heaves forward free and unfree, thousandfold, complex, in all possible disguises, speaking sometimes through masses, sometimes through individuals, determined sometimes optimistically, sometimes pessimistically, founding and destroying states, religions, and cultures, sometimes a simple riddle to itself, led more by dark feelings that are mediated by fantasy than by reflection, sometimes accompanied by mere reflection.[6]

While Burckhardt explicitly disavows a philosophy of history – a posture of denial that he repeatedly strikes in his correspondence with Nietzsche – he is highly aware of the contradictions inherent in the original method he has chosen, and he gives it a quasi-philosophical characterization: "[Philosophy of history] is a centaur, an adjectival contradiction; for history, an act of coordinating, is non-philosophy, and philosophy, an act of subordinating, is non-history," "Diese ist ein Kentaur, eine *contradictio in adjecto*;

denn Geschichte, d.h. das Koordinieren ist Nichtphilosophie und Philosophie, d.h. das Subordinieren ist Nichtgeschichte" (2.)

Burckhardt's summary definition here is too simple to account for the
complexities of his own actual practice. But we may begin to characterize
the force of his shift into the synchronic for his own historiography by
noting that he throws a strong emphasis precisely on history as coordination.
Normal narrative through time also coordinates, but it does so on a time
line that throws a mystery over subordination; we ask, as we proceed
through events or episodes, how these details as they move strongly and
coordinately along a time line, relate, or are subordinated, to the sense the
historian is trying to evolve. It may be said that for Burckhardt it works
the other way around. Synchronicity throws subordination into the constant
foreground: Every detail is at once subordinated under a synchronic heading. And mystery lies in the coordination – how the statecraft of the Renaissance really can be described as a product of the same "spiritual"
development as its art or its religion.

In *The Age of Constantine* the synchronic presentation has an announced
diachronic purpose, to explain what it means to make the important transition from Diocletian to Constantine, Burckhardt intends to derive this
meaning from the particular qualities of interrelation among religion, family, culture, and power politics. Of separable questions such as ascertaining
"the religious consciousness of Constantine," Burckhardt departs from Gibbon by declaring that "such efforts are futile."[7] At the same time the "religious" in the bureaucratic and other actions of Diocletian and of
Constantine tends both to fill out into an almost Weberian complex of
interdefinitions, and to become obscured through its mixture with other
purposes. Religion in this work attains already the dialectical hovering for
which Lucien Febvre's impressive study of Rabelais is taken as so note-
worthy. Using Gibbon as a respected predecessor and Eusebius as both a
necessary source and a rhetorical stalking horse, Burckhardt subordinates
a narration of political and military history to a synchronic overall organization, and he narrows his time frame to focus on the shift he has in mind:

> And now there were again two Western and two Eastern rulers
> (*Regenten*), Constantine and Maxentius, Licinius and Maximinus Daia.
> But their relationship was far different from that of the harmonious
> "tetrachord" which had once bound Diocletian to his colleagues. No
> subordination and no mutual obligation was recognized; each was
> Augustus on his own account, and measured the others with distrustful
> glance. Their dominions were sharply delimited; none would venture
> to share the rule in the realm of another, but neither would any come
> to the assistance of another before he had exacted selfish terms in
> separate treaties. The Empire lay divided in four portions, and Con-

stantine, who had first broken the peace, now had the task of instituting some new bond to replace the earlier (*an die Stelle des frühen Zusammenhanges einen neuen treten zu lassen* – "*Zusammenhang*" suggesting more intricacy than "bond" and "*treten zu lassen*" a dynamic realignment of causal forces).

Yet an implied general style of rulership encompasses these reigns, and a kind of synchronicity reestablishes itself in spite of the changes Constantine's power and craft had brought about: "[Constantius'] marriage with Eusebia was barren, and so in the end the son of Constantine the Great, in consequence of the unbounded sultanism of two generations, had arrived[8] at the point from which Diocletian had departed – he was forced to resort to adoption" (279). Character does produce an effect, and this work broadly discriminates between the character of Diocletian, prudent and harmonious, and the more complex character of Constantine. In this light Burckhardt emphasizes that complexity but makes no ironic comment on it, when he describes Constantine by an anticlimactic triad of nouns, "Constantine's good fortune, talent, and cruelty succeeded in preventing this eventuality" (63). He constantly has in mind a purpose that will develop into the conspectuses of his *Renaissance*, the later purposes of Huizinga: "We must learn to understand the singular mixture of nobleness and flattery which that period produced" (62). Synchrony and diachrony bear on each other constantly, of course, and Burckhardt's strategy is to center his historiographic presentation on their interaction:

> From the midst of conditions whose history is clearly and precisely known there sometimes emerges a fact of the first importance whose deeper causes stubbornly elude the eye of the student. Such an event is the great persecution of the Christians under Diocletian, the last war of annihilation waged by paganism against Christianity. At first glance there is nothing strange in these persecutions; Diocletian had all too many predecessors upon the throne of the world who similarly wished to extirpate the Christians, and scarcely any other course was to be expected of so zealous and confirmed a pagan as he was. But the question takes on a quite different aspect when we consider the circumstances in detail.

Here something like the purpose of Gibbon has been detached from Gibbon's fixed, or mixed, viewpoint, and given a dimension that looks neutral but really has behind it the kind of instinctively ethnological and implicitly philosophical judgment that stands midway between the out-and-out synchronic categorization of Hegel and the somewhat myopic diachrony of Ranke. Still, we cannot ourselves detach and summarize these views, any

more than we can do so for the narrative burden of Gibbon, because Burckhardt has succeeded in finding a way to embody it in his presentation. In
this work Burckhardt does not just carefully select his focal points in a
restricted period of time. Further, instead of sharply focusing on one moment, he constantly tests one moment against another to ascertain how the
two may throw each other into relief, a relief that in turn will produce the
Gestalt of a synchronic picture.

In *The Civilization of the Renaissance in Italy*, he performs such operations
with much greater latitude, allowing his synchronicity a free rein through
a longer time. His second chapter organizes itself around the individual,
and his first chapter, "The State as a Work of Art," implies operations by
an individual; indeed, the second chapter can be taken as an amplification
of the first, extending his method in *Constantine* of asking just what it is
that lies behind a phenomenon. In a world where the individual is emphasized, a given person will be more important because the individual is
highlighted; but his salience will be less easily discernible than that of Constantine or Diocletian because he will be set against many other individuals.
Synchrony emphasizes the coordination of them all at a moment of time,
and the synchronic presentation, by relaxing the diachronic sequence of
events, renders that sequence as a set of instantiations rather than as an
evolution. Consequently and coherently Burckhardt in this work has become still more synchronic: He does not give us a narrative about Leo the
Tenth, as he does about Constantine and Diocletian. What lies behind Constantine is Diocletian; what lies behind Leo the Tenth is the *Kultur* (the
word translated as "civilization"). Leo the Tenth must be understood
through a variety of the cultural contexts in which he was active. The
Civilization presents as complex a portrait of Leo the Tenth as the earlier
work had of Constantine, but that portrait is fragmented and aspectualized
in a still more fully synchronic presentation that makes Leo everywhere,
however variously, contributory to the *Kultur*, which becomes the gradual
sum of his, and others', contributions.

In a way that is reminiscent of Tacitus' gradual buildup (though Tacitus
in this is simpler for following a time line), Burckhardt shows Leo the
Tenth at many moments as wholly or partially defined by, while illustrative
of, the particular chapter heading under which he happens now to be subsumed. Thus in Part Three, "The Revival of Antiquity," under chapter 2,
"Rome the City of Ruins," we are asked to contemplate the city under Leo
the Tenth in a way that will illustrate the intersection of political power,
religious power and intellectual patronage, by showing this particular pope's
mix of these activities. "Raphael undertook for Leo X that ideal restoration
of the whole ancient city which his celebrated letter (1518 or 1519) speaks
of (191)."[9] He goes on to touch in Leo as a person, continuing again with
the city:

The Vatican resounded with song and music, and their echoes were heard through the city as a call to joy and gladness, though Leo did not succeed thereby in banishing care and pain from his own life, and his deliberate calculation to prolong his days by cheerfulness was frustrated by an early death. The Rome of Leo, as described by Paolo Giovio, forms a picture too splendid to turn away from, unmistakable as are also its shadow sides (*Schattenseiten*) – the slavery of those who were struggling to rise; the secret misery of the prelates, who, notwithstanding heavy debts, were forced to live in a style befitting their rank; the lottery-like and accidental character of Leo's artistic patronage; and, lastly, his entirely ruinous maladministration of finances.

(193–194)

Here the "shadow sides" in all their manifestations are brought back to Leo's door, along with the glory, and his personal obliviousness to a whole social and spiritual chiaroscuro is juxtaposed to the "cheerfulness" (*Heiterkeit*) of his attempt to stave off death. Styles of papacy, and an emerging general view of the papacy in its relation to the functions of *Kultur*, are here percolated through the individual. The relation between psychology and event, or between large social causes and deep individual ones, here is solved by dividing the individual synchronically into various social aspects. The shadows are not just of those of Leo the Tenth; they obtain generally of the papacy, as Burckhardt says in the chapter on its dangers: "The greatest dangers appeared within the Papacy itself. Living, as it now did, and acting in the spirit of the secular (*weltlich*) Italian principalities, it was compelled to go through the same dark (*düstern*) moments as they; but its own particular nature brought into it shadows that were entirely special."

In the last chapter of "The State as a Work of Art," "The Papacy and Its Dangers," we had learned of the context in which this Medici pope arose:

Lorenzo the Magnificent, on his part, was anxious that the house of the Medici should not be sent away with empty hands. He married his daughter Maddalena to the son of the new Pope – the first who publicly acknowledged his children – Franceschetto Cybò, and expected not only favours of all kinds for his own son, Cardinal Giovanni, afterward Leo X, but also the rapid promotion of his son-in-law.

(126)

Leo's election, described in the same chapter, shows an interplay of forces comparably corrupt – though since Burckhardt deeply admires the Renaissance, we cannot take the irony here for a simple condemnatory pessimism:

In a constitution of his Lateran Council Julius had solemnly de-
nounced the simony of the Papal elections. After his death in 1513,
the money-loving cardinals tried to evade the prohibition by proposing
that the endowments and offices hitherto held by the chosen candidate
should be equally divided among themselves, in which case they
would have elected the best-endowed cardinal, the incompetent Rafael
Riario. But a reaction, chiefly arising from the younger members of
the Sacred College, who, above all things, desired a liberal Pope,
rendered the miserable combination futile; Giovanni de' Medici was
elected – the famous Leo X.

We shall often meet with him in treating of the noonday of the
Renaissance; here we wish only to point out that under him the Papacy
was again exposed to great inward and outward dangers.

(136)

And Burckhardt then lists these dangers, though the election itself is shown
as a product of a simony first banned, then revived, then deeply compro-
mised in a liberal direction by reformist forces. Those forces still cannot
keep this Medici from becoming the pope that Ficino predicted he would
become when that signal beneficiary of Medici patronage drew a horoscope
for the children of Lorenzo's house (491–492). Nor do Leo's defects prevent
Machiavelli from orienting toward this pope, in his "memorial" to him,
what Burckhardt calls Machiavelli's "most complete programme for the
construction of a new political system at Florence (104)." All these forces
have entered the psyche of Leo the Tenth, whose Rome Burckhardt characterizes as "gay" and "basically corrupt" ("*heitere*," "*grundverdorbene*")
(104).

Being a prince like any pope of the time, Leo commanded troops (65).
In the chapter on foreign policy, Romagna is described as "feeling itself
very repressed under Leo X (112)." His love of jests is cited in the chapter
on satire (165), and much later, in a nearly final chapter on the "Mixture
of Ancient and Modern Superstition," where the astrological prediction
about the future pope has been given, he turns a jest of his own at a time
when he has been discouraging alchemists, "Aurelio Augurelli, who ded-
icated to Leo X, the great despiser of gold, his didactic poem on the making
of the metal, is said to have received in return a beautiful but empty purse
(509)."

He is shown making an orator a cardinal (169), consecrating a press for
Arabic publications (210), and variously supporting humanistic and scientific enterprises (230–231, 246, 270, and passim). These include zoology
(290). He gloried in his Latin (257). As a patron of art and music he endowed
his court with great elegance (386); "Rome possessed in the unique Court
of Leo X a society (*eine Gesellschaft von so besonderer Art*) to which the history

of the world offers no parallel (381)." At the same time this pope "despised the mendicant orders" (448). Yet he "set forth a Constitution at the Lateran Council in 1513 of the immortality and individuality of the soul" (512).

As well as measuring Leo the Tenth with and against the categories of Burckhardt's chapter headings, the effect of this synchronic presentation is to align him with hosts of others who are more or less directly classified under the chapter categories – with other popes, other members of forceful ruling or mercantile families, other humanists, other clerics, other intellectuals and artists and scientists, other participants in the high life of the Renaissance. In one of his late remarks, which does strike a pessimistic note, Burckhardt limits the effectiveness a state can have if it tries to channel the activities of individuals: "The 'realization of the moral upon the earth' must founder a thousand times because of the inadaptability of man's nature generally, and that of the best in particular. The moral has essentially a forum other than the state; it is already enormously much that the latter can uphold conventional justice. The state will remain most readily healthy when it recognizes its nature (and perhaps even its essential origin) as an institution of need."[10] This statement as a late, abstract definition has vague affinities with a number of other thinkers. One can trace similarities in it to notions of Rousseau, Marx, Nietzsche, and even Heidegger. Taken with relation to the enterprise of the *Civilization* it marks a difference between individual and state that is at once illustrated in the fallible Leo the Tenth and bridged by his embodiment of the Renaissance splendors that the pervasive type of state "as a work of art" enabled both individual and state to attain.

There is, in short, a case being made for the Renaissance here by partial subversion of this principle of the state as a healthy, conscious institution of need. Burckhardt's case is made nowhere in the *Civilization* but is implied by the myriad special matches of individual and category that he synchronically provides. The nature of this case is not to provide the brief's separable thesis about the Renaissance, but rather to offer a specific mix of the particular and the general that itself will have both particular bearing to this time and place, and a general force in the understanding of the human past. Indeed, that is the goal of all historians, and that Burckhardt is able to single out a particularly optimistic high point – for all its "shadow sides" – in human history distinguishes him from many of the great historians. By contrast, Thucydides and Machiavelli, Tacitus and Namier and even Herodotus, show human events in whatever complex combination as always subject to implied general forces that are in many ways too powerful for those who would manipulate them. In this light a historiographic purpose governs Burckhardt's early emphasis on and separate treatment of individualism in the Renaissance; it ties in with a view of social process that, however cautionary, remains more optimistic than that of the other historians named, although the optimism remains too nuanced and complex to be described as a "comic" (or a "satiric") emplotment. Indeed, our access to the artistic heritage of the Renaissance functions not just as an aesthetic advantage for the connoisseur, Burckhardt and others. It also validates the permanence of their achievement, and the human incorporability of their presence. The surviving art works effectually refute both Gibbon, since the objects are not in ruins, and Hegel, since they are not sealed off in an earlier spiritual totality. Taken with the *Renaissance*, the *Cicerone* is one long testimony to this survival. This constative force in artworks, is a corollary to the large, and special, interplay between individual and society that such presentations as the "fragmented" Leo the Tenth throw into relief. Coming to an end with some remarks about Renaissance Platonism, Burckhardt need only touch in a hint of this point his very organization has been making, "One of the most precious fruits of the knowledge of the world and of man here comes to maturity, on whose account alone the Italian Renaissance must be called the leader of our age" ("*unseres Weltalters*").

As with individuals, so with states. Because the states are the framework and product of the individuals – their creation as a work of art and their milieu as active presences – Burckhardt's first section is about the state. He begins with a loose diachronic series, the "tyrants" (*Herrscher*, a plural that is somewhat more neutral than "tyrants") of the fourteenth century, followed by the ones of the fifteenth century. He then works his way from the small ones (*klein*; "petty" is too prejudicial, though now he does speak of *Tyrannien*) up to the great ones. And then, after a brief look at the "opponents of tyranny," he reaches his climax in a description of Venice and Florence, continuing on with a chapter each about foreign policy, war, and the papacy. He ends the whole with a "conclusion" on patriotism (not separately demarcated in the English translation).

The effect of this ascending series is both to provide a substitute for diachronic development and to produce as well as to reveal a feeling of élan about the chief city-states. He creates an impression of the Renaissance as he engages this recourse to the rhetorical device of climax. Further, the chapter on the papacy, the last of its section, sets an international perspective on the city-states; serves as an implied introduction to the next section, about the individual; and gives a particular temper to the morality and religion that are to be the main topic of the sixth and last section.

The individual city-states, once they have been delineated, will, of course, reappear throughout the work, as Leo the Tenth does. Their particular force and character will also be indicated by the prismatic, aspectual series of references to them. And each of the six large sections of the work itself unfolds an aspect of what has gone before. The second section, on the individual, is already implied in the impulse to willfulness shown by the rulers of the city-states, and in the "dangers" of the papacy. The transition occasions an excursus on the particularly Italian quality of subjectivity, as Burckhardt sees it. Only by the third section does a diachronic aspect, though not a sequence, become paramount, in the revival of antiquity that is again presented as lying behind what he had asserted:

> ...allein wie das Bisherige, so ist auch das Folgende doch von der Einwirkung der antiken Welt mannigfach gefärbt, und wo das Wesen der Dinge ohne dieselbe verständlich und vorhanden sein würde, da ist es doch die Aeusserungsweise im Leben nur mit ihr und durch sie.

> But both what has gone before and what we have still to discuss receives a manifold coloring from the influence of the ancient world; and though the essence of the facts might still have been understandable without it, it is only with and through this influence that it gets an external manifestation in life.

> (175)

Einwirkung is a stronger term than *Einfluss* for the influence of antiquity in the Renaissance. It is a live, operative, internal presence, an *Einwirkung*, that goes far to express in a single word the intrications of temporality that a historical work, and even such a synchronic one, can make manifest.

Just as a look at the state is balanced by a look at the individual, a look backward in time is balanced by a look forward in space and time, for the fourth section, which deals with discovery and introduces the second half of the work:

> Freed from the countless bonds which elsewhere in Europe checked progress, having reached a high degree of individual development and been schooled by the teachings of antiquity, the Italian mind (*Geist*) now turned to the discovery of the outward universe, and ventured upon the representation of it in speech and in form.

The fifth section turns, as it were, to the celebration of all this development, in "Fellowship (*Geselligkeit*) and Festivals," while the sixth carries out the principle of counterbalance by turning from merry to stern; its subject is morality (*Sitte*) and religion. In doing so Burckhardt draws a veil of impenetrability over the subject he is about to discuss, "The final assessment (*die grosse Verrechnung*) of national character, guilt, and conscience, remains a secret, if only because its defects have another side, where they then appear as national characteristics (*Eigenschaften*) – indeed, even as virtues (427)." Thus is the circle closed in the declaration of a mystery – a mystery that keeps the severity of this focus from throwing implications backward over the state of social existence Burckhardt is celebrating, and disentangling from its subjection to time. The Renaissance Italians will have the qualities of their defects as well as the defects of their qualities, and at the fullest a person or a city will roundedly exhibit all, in one synchronic result of diachronic operations. Florence, he says, "is the most complete mirror of the relations of classes of men and individual men to a variable whole" (101).

The point at which the mystery of the spirit of a nation eludes the historian lies just at that point where he would assess their morality. Since, as quoted above, Burckhardt makes a great deal of the true, the beautiful, and the good, the position he takes here cannot be characterized as a relativism, and still less as some sort of ironic cynicism. Indeed, he saved the explicit condemnation of the dark side of individualism till this section, through all the horrors of power and the contradictions in the papacy: "The fundamental vice of this character [of the upper classes] was at the same time a condition of its greatness – namely, excessive individualism" (442). He had much earlier said of Ludovico il Moro, "The Moor is the most perfect type of the despot of that age, and, as a kind of natural product, almost disarms our moral judgment," *"dem man nicht ganz böse sein kann"* (58). Burckhardt, as it were, implies and subsumes Guicciardini's sequential presentation of Ludovico's career. Yet within the limits of mystery about a deep moral bearing at a moment of time, Burckhardt will still have recourse to reconstructive inference: "Do we do him an injustice if we attribute all these measures to the strongest political calculation? To the conception of government (*Herrscheridee*) of the house of Este, as indicated above, does such a correlative use and subjugation of the religious element belong, almost according to the laws of logic." Here Burckhardt is speaking of the action taken by Ercole I of Ferrara at the fall of Lodovico il Moro, marshaling nine religious processions and summoning a live saint to deflect unrest. Indeed, such inference is constantly called for by the constant mix of the political, the aristocratic-courtly, the religious, and what may be called the artistic.

As against the elegiac note of Gibbon, Burckhardt's prose carries with it the rhythms of eulogy, a eulogy that tonally buoys up the onward progress of the critical intellect as it constantly defines, assesses, and illustrates, providing a parallel in the work of the historian for the inquiring buoyancy of the Renaissance figures whom he is discussing. The normative paragraph of Burckhardt consists of a general, measured characterization followed by an illustrative anecdote of more or less expansive length, followed in turn by another such paragraph. The change of section announces, of course, not progress in time, but a shift in the point of view, where the same procedure continues with unflagging abundance, and with the sense suggested that much more illustration could be adduced. The subsumption of small illustrations gives the chapters the double character of larger illustration and of summary by displacement to another topic. Indeed, Burckhardt's footnotes often illustrate further rather than documenting more precisely the notion under consideration. There is a curious falling off of detail in the chapter about the decline of the humanists, as though the subject itself were such a detraction to his general enthusiasm that he is unwilling to allow the documentation of it to strike too deeply into his presentation. An occasional fullness of description assists the air of constant affirmation supported by constant inference.[11] Detail rises easily to the surface to illustrate the points, and the surface takes over so powerfully that it would be hard for an ironic remark to obtrude for long. Another historian would have let irony of event draw the contrast between Cesare Borgia and Julius Caesar. In the long passage on triumphs and festivities, Burckhardt simply says, "At the carnival of 1500, Cesare Borgia, with a bold allusion to himself, celebrated the triumph of Julius Caesar in a procession that was eleven magnificent chariots strong, doubtless to the vexation of the pilgrims who had come for the Jubilee." Burckhardt's judgment easily surfaces in a single adjective, "bold" (*keck*). A prevailing synchrony has done the job of at once bringing the splendidly ostentatious Renaissance into the light and suggesting the darknesses, the contradictions, and the insoluble mysteries inherent therein.

2

"*L'histoire*," said Michelet, "*c'est le temps*," "history is time."[12] In devoting himself to the millennial history of a single nation, Michelet himself here suggests his own kind of *longue durée*; it will take centuries for France to realize itself in the Revolution. And over this long period his presentation will meld the linear approach of Machiavelli with the millennial approach of Gibbon. In fact, because Michelet continually watches his moments for signs of development, he is also analytic like Tocqueville – rather than like Montesquieu, because time always hovers over the enterprise, letting it swell, propelling it ahead beyond any Thucydidean power-plays, Tacitean degradations, or Gibbonesque decays of institution.

Two forces are at work in the *Histoire de la révolution française*, which are contradictory but not paradoxical: the deep impulse toward the people's realization of its true nature, and an ignorance of how to preserve that realization because of the very depth out of which it arises. The failure of the Revolution derives not from bad institutions, and not from missed calculations or overfacile hopes. Still less does it derive from the defects of the qualities that over a long haul created it. It derives rather from the impossibility in the mix of social action to master and control what is deeply felt enough to bring a whole society into being. For this reason Michelet, as he himself protests, is not a romantic, or not in the messianic sense of Blake or even Rousseau. He can consistently both celebrate the Revolution as a final fulfillment and deplore the brevity of its transience through the temporality of the events he recounts. The temporality resolves the very contradictions it creates, both contradictions and paradoxes cropping up in the onward movement of his presentation. Michelet stays in the conventional mode of subjection to diachronic presentation, and he is always adducing proleptic suggestions across the wide sweep of time – for example, when he compares Etienne Marcel in the fourteenth century to a revolutionary figure. He qualifies the latter procedure while insisting on the former, "History is time. This constant thought has prevented us from introducing questions before their hour, as is too often done. It is a common tendency to want to read all of today's thoughts in the past that often did not dream of them." ("Cette pensée constante nous a empêché d'amener les questions avant l'heure, comme on le fait trop souvent. C'est une tendance commune de vouloir lire toutes les pensées d'aujourd'hui dans le passé, qui souvent n'y songeait pas.")

The temporality shows its hand, and evidences the power to which it is subject, in the fits and starts of this writer's discourse, as though proleptic force and strict temporal succession were involved in an obscure but constant dialectical struggle. Michelet is not aphoristic like Tacitus or periodic like Gibbon; instead he manages his style so that the aphorisms subvert the periods, while the periods gather the aphorisms into their sweep. Nervous interruptions constantly disappear and reappear, governed by the confidence of a voice that flags and immediately recuperates itself, over and over again. Here he is in the ninth chapter of Book Three, June 1790, under the headings of "religious struggle" and "counterrevolution crushed":

> Que faisait pendant ce temps à Paris l'Assemblée nationale? Elle suivait le Clergé à la procession de la Fête-Dieu.

> What did the National Assembly do at Paris during this time? It followed the clergy in the Fête-Dieu procession.

This paragraph of question and answer begins a chapter. It is preceded by one that had ended on an exclamation point. Michelet's verbal energy picks up the exclamation point and transposes it into a question and answer that themselves, in their abruptness, are a sort of equivalent for an exclamation point. The two sentences constitute, disproportionately, an implied dialectic of three propositions: (1) The National Assembly is going about the business of disenfranchising religion, and here they are mildly devotional in their public acts; (2) this contradiction itself contradicts the bloody conflict between Catholics and nationals at Nîmes in the preceding chapter but "during this time"; (3) though the union of assembly and clergy is an allusion, that illusion will take many forms, as when Talleyrand, bishop of Autun, proposes the confiscation of clerical property, pledging it as security for the assignats, or as when Robespierre a little later defends pensions for retired priests. (A double contradiction here: The Jacobins defend the clergy; the severe Robespierre appears in a guise milder than his co-members and more conciliatory.)[13] Still, deep down, since Michelet shows the Revolution to be propelled by a profound religious spirit, there is a union between nation and devotion that will take other than illusory form. And it will undergo a number of mutations as the religious character of the Revolution comes forward, shortly to produce the national-religious composite of the pyramid-shaped *autel de la Patrie* on the Champ de Mars (704). Some thousand pages ahead (but only a couple of years) Robespierre will put "l'Etre suprême" at the head of the constitution. Priests then still see him as their friend (2:426, 430). Still later, in the midst of the Terror, the Festival of the Supreme Being will be celebrated (2:868).

The last point is taken up as Michelet changes his rhetorical key signature in the next paragraph for an evener narrative voice:

> Sa douceur plus que chrétienne, en tout cela, est un spectacle surprenant. Elle se contenta d'une démarche que les ministres exigèrent du Roi. Il défendit la cocarde blanche, et condamna les signataires de la déclaration de Nîmes. Ceux-ci en furent quittes pour substituer à leur cocarde la houppe rouge des anciens ligueurs. Ils protestèrent hardiment qu'ils persistaient pour le Roi contre les ordres du Roi.
>
> Ceci était net, simple, vigoureux; le parti du Clergé savait très bien ce qu'il voulait. L'Assemblée ne le savait pas. Elle accomplissait alors une oeuvre faible et fausse, ce qu'on appela la Constitution civile du Clergé.
>
> Rien ne fut plus funeste à la Révolution que de s'ignorer elle-même au point de vue religieux, de ne pas savoir qu'en elle elle portait une religion.

Its softness was more than Christian in all this, a surprising spectacle. It contented itself with a manoeuver that the ministers exacted from the king. He forbade the white cocarde and condemned the signers of the Declaration of Nîmes. The latter got off by substituting for their cocarde the red houppe of the old Leaguers. They protested vigorously that they persisted for the king against the orders of the King.

This was neat, simple, and vigorous; the party of the Clergy knew very well what it wanted. The Assembly did not. It accomplished then a work that was feeble and false, the civil Constitution of the Clergy.

Nothing was more damaging to the Revolution than to be unaware

of itself from a religious point of view, than not to know that it carried
a religion within itself.

(1:381–382)

These paragraphs spell out, in acts recounted and inferences drawn, the
implications of Michelet's initial question and answer. The acts recounted
function in context as both illustrations and proofs, but they are proofs that
the Revolution has not yet realized itself. Michelet's rises and falls – so
different from the swell of Gibbon or the even progressions of Burckhardt
– constantly vary their tempo, as here, indicating both the eagerness of the
writer's deep enthusiasm for the Revolution and the sense that its events
have not yet broken through for triumphant self-realization. And indeed,
they will never do so, with the result that the retrospective hope is to become
a prospective nostalgia. Both moods, contradictory as they are, score the
registers for the ongoing voice that recounts them. They encapsulate, and
vary, the *distensio animi* of Augustine that Ricoeur applies to historiography.

Each paragraph constitutes such an adjustment of voice, and the sentences
also vary, sometimes sharply and sometimes mildly, so that the intrusion
of an example, long or short, will nearly always wear the double face of a
capping proof and a suddenly appearing, imperiously assertive surfacing of
detail. After more inferences and examples about the stress between epis-
copate and clergy, enough pressure has built up for a longish example to
surface:

quitter le monde connu, et pour passer dans quel monde? dans quel
system nouveau? . . . il faut une idée, une foi dans cette idée, pour
laisser ainsi le rivage, s'embarquer dans l'avenir.

Un curé vraiment patriote, celui de Saint-Etienne-du-Mont, qui, le
14 juillet, marchait sous le drapeau du peuple à la tête de son district,
fut accablé, effrayé, de la cruelle alternative où le plaçaient les évêques.
Il resta quarante jours, avec un cilice, à genoux devant l'autel.

Il eût pu y rester toujours, qu'il n'eût pas trouvé réponse à l'insoluble
question qui s'était posée.

Ce que la Revolution avait d'idées, elle le tenait du XVIIIe siècle,
de Voltaire, de Rousseau. Personne, dans les vingt années qui s'écou-
lent entre la grande époque des deux maîtres et la Révolution, entre
la pensée et l'action, personne, dis-je, n'a sérieusement continué leur
oeuvre.

Donc la Révolution trouve la pensée humaine où ils l'ont laissée:
l'ardente humanité dans Voltaire, la fraternité dans Rousseau, deux
bases, certes, religieuses, mais posées seulement, très peu formulées.

To leave the known world and pass into what world? Into what new system? . . . An idea was needed, a faith in that idea, to leave the shore behind in this way, to embark into the future.

A truly patriotic curate, one from Saint-Etienne-du-Mont, who on the fourteenth of July marched under the flag of the people at the head of his district, was overcome and frightened by the cruel alternative in which the bishops had placed him. He remained forty days, in a hair shirt, on his knees before the altar.

He could have stayed there forever and he would not have found an answer to the insoluble question that had been set.

What the Revolution had of ideas it got from the eighteenth century, from Voltaire, from Rousseau. Nobody, in the twenty years which elapsed between the great time of the two masters and the Revolution, between thought and action, nobody I say, seriously continued their work.

Hence the Revolution left human thought where it found it; ardent humanity in Voltaire, fraternity in Rousseau, two bases which were certainly religious, but only set, too little formulated.

From one point of view too little happens in the twenty-year interval of time; from another point of view too much. In one sense there is a stasis; no new ideas have been produced since Voltaire and Rousseau, and this is a specific failing of the time, attributable to a general human tendency to fail. But on the other hand, like an electric spark leaping a gap, there has been a transition from thought to action, and the Revolution has been realizing itself after all,[14] while always carrying the double sign of glorious fruition and sad imperfection. The even progression of time – neither the stasis nor the quantum leap – most reliably allows the Revolution to follow its inevitable course; and in this, too, Michelet is proto-Marxian. Except that as he here declares and often implies, the contradictions are too much for human capacity; so they cannot be counted on to mutate into satisfactory realizations. The curate could stay on his knees in a hair shirt forever and not resolve them. This act, itself, though, as interpreted by the sequence of statements Michelet offers, may be taken as a deeply religious, honest commentary on unresolvability.

Or it may be taken as an evasion, a failure to produce the ideas that could resolve the contradiction, following in the path of Voltaire and Rousseau with what could not be deduced simply by consulting their inspiring and suggestive but finally inadequate writings. Both the "ardent humanity" of the one and the "fraternity" of the other are figured, and translated from thought into a kind of action, by the kneeling curate. In this epiphanic detail the curate's immediate prior history stands for an ironic hope that comments on the arrested hope of his forty-day silent, suffering prayer. Michelet often has recourse to what someone was doing or saying on Bastille Day. A curate marching behind the people's flag at the head of his district constitutes in his person the order of the clergy, thereby that order in the Assembly. He also expresses the deepest embodiment of national feeling in the people, and exemplifies a solid location on the map of France for representing his district. That composite icon is swallowed up in the icon of the kneeling figure, and the two responses stand also as hope to despair, and as true integration to pardonably sidetracked isolation.

The nervous lapses of time appear here not only in the considerable variety of length for the various paragraphs, but in Michelet's recourse, frequently in these passages but often elsewhere, to the rhetorical device of asyndeton, the suppression of either conjunctions or commas. The asyndeton becomes a rhythmical and rhetorical mark of the nervous syncopations of development under the pressure of superhuman conflicts among human beings. Yet these conflicts, too, have a heroic cast, and Michelet all the while creates an air of asserting not that a Thucydidean lesson could be drawn from these events, but rather that they have an arresting uniqueness. They are an inspiration rather than a model in their very failures.

Such a sense allows the intermittent intrusion of the historian himself, sometimes with a bit of biographical detail, sometimes with a touch of first-person assertion, as here, *"personne, dis-je."* He even refers to his own tears (2:399). And he has said in the larger *Histoire de France*, "Vertigo overtakes me, watching the prodigious scene of so many beings, yesterday dead, today so alive, creative."[15] This sort of intrusion, of course, violates the convention of the historian's impersonality, an impersonality derivable not just from the young university tradition in which Michelet was active but in fact at least as far back as Thucydides. Michelet uses the personal intrusion for further assertion, and as something of an indication of how serious a sequence he is recounting. "These matters are of such capital urgency," he seems to be saying, "and of such prima facie importance, that of course I am involved, of course I write from a partiality I will let out the stops to reveal."

"Chose étrange," *"chose bizarre,"* and similar expressions flow frequently from Michelet's pen, as though the Revolution were such a burning terrain of *faits divers* that he will not attempt to restrain remarking on their arresting interest of encapsulated contradiction. At one point, indeed, he claims that he is forced to rivet himself to the details, "Que le lecteur nous excuse d'avoir raconté dans un si grand détail ces tristes événements. Nous le devions," "May the reader excuse us for having told these sad events in such great detail. We had to" (2:398). In another couple of pages he will resort to italics, six in two paragraphs, beginning "L'Assemblé veut que désormais le Clergé soit l'élu du peuple, *affranchi* du Concordat, du pacte honteux où deux larrons, le Roi, le Pape, s'étaient partagé l'Eglise, avait

tiré sa robe au sort," "The Assembly wishes that henceforth the Clergy be the elected of the people, *liberated* from the Concordat, from the shameful pact in which two thieves, the King and the Pope, had parcelled up the Church, had cast lots for its garment" (1:386). This presents a contrast between the unity of religious feeling that permits a religious typology, casting lots for Christ's garment, to define an anticlerical act and the contradictory forces that come to a head in this political decision. And the contrast also gets swamped in Michelet's enthusiastic onward progress. But it also gets delineated thereby, and characterized by the buoyancy that for him is the fundamental historical fact of the Revolution.

Irony never disappears from the events, and yet it never takes over wholly to govern them. Soon through the agency of two bishops in the king's confidence (bringing into the picture a Louis XVI whom Michelet portrays as constantly timid) the assembly is given an ultimatum:

"Que nul changement ne pouvait se faire sans la convocation d'un concile." – Dans *les premiers jours de juin* le sang coule à Nîmes.

"That no change could be made without the convocation of a council." – In *the first days of June* blood runs at Nîmes."

This standoff is important enough to trigger another narrative sequence, one not so diverse or illustrative as that of the kneeling curate; a small military band is marshaled. In fact the contradictions can even be felt momentarily to disappear, "La Révolution, de plus en plus harmonique et concordante, apparaît chaque jour davantage ce qu'elle est, une religion," "The Revolution, more and more harmonious in agreement, appears more and more what it is every day, a religion." On the other hand, by the end of the chapter (395), a contradiction between king, people, and church is once more resolved. And a contradiction is once more embodied as the king's agent swears fidelity to the Revolution on his royalist sword, with an expression that must proleptically refer to the fact that before very long the king will be executed. "L'inflexible va fléchir, le Roi ordonne, il obéit; il s'avance entre eux, triste et sombre, et sur son épée royaliste, jure fidélité à la Révolution." This execution will at once put a permanent end to a very large contradiction and fulfill the Revolution by giving it a public face. But the execution will also condemn it in the eyes of the world outside France, preparing the way for a super-king and pseudo-king, the Emperor Napoleon.[16] These sentences are much more measured in rhythm, as though drawing breath for a pause in time, and as though at the same time holding back from the effusions that will accompany the most glorious or the most terrible events. The next chapter, though, keeps moving irresistibly to glory, to "the new principle" that Michelet characterizes as *"l'organization*

spontanée de la France," an expression for which he once more has recourse
to italics.

In the mightiness of the forces that are constantly at work, unity can
come about or else diversity can continue to manifest itself. The forces are
too strong to let unity either be submerged or realize itself in any persisting
equilibrium. The "people," Michelet's most dominant unifying force, is
the vehicle for carrying along the mighty stream of national realization
toward convergent goals, because its instinct is always sound. And it is also
the ground on which diversity manifests itself, since the people cannot by
definition know where it is going. The people may speak through the clergy,
"Non, *le peuple* de France n'est pas imposable à volonté," "*The people* of
France cannot be taxed at will" (51). "Man is the unity of the world, and
he appears in three figures, Montesquieu, Voltaire, and Rousseau, interpreters of the Just" (56), and "Right is sovereign of the world," "Le Droit
est le souverain du monde" (58). Even when ignorant the people will be
right; "L'Evénement trompa tout calcul. Ce peuple, si peu préparé, montra
un instinct très sûr" (80). "The event foiled all reckoning; this people showed
an instinct that was very sure." And the people always stands by, heaving
like a sea, "Tout ce monde était ému, attendri, plein de trouble et d'espér-
ance," "This whole world was moved, softened, full of upheaval and hope"
(88). A moment later Michelet feels justified in attributing to the people an
emotion corresponding to the mood proper for the procession of the Estates
General, "tous heureux de ce grand jour qu'ils avaient fait et qui était leur
victoire," "all happy for the great day they had made and which was their
victory" (89). Brilliant speakers express the thought of the masses (1847
preface; 1:7).

Between the movements of the people and the actions of individuals there
is a constantly changing counterpoint that sometimes emerges into harmony. The middle ground of this interaction between the individual and
the society in terms of organization is the club. Michelet makes much of
the ins and outs of affiliation among the revolutionary clubs, the Feuillants,
the Cordeliers, the Girondins, the Jacobins. A middle ground, too, is found
in the official assemblies. They often carry the same aspect as the clubs,
"sociétés et comités, au fond, c'était la même chose," "societies and com-
mittees were basically the same thing" (2:835).

Another major preoccupation in *L'Histoire de la révolution française* is parliamentary history, the ins and outs of speeches in the Assembly or of
machinations in the Commune. In his unremitting attention to temporal
mutations, Michelet depicts these interactions as far more dependent on the
complex dispositions of individual participants than they are shown to be
in the usual diplomatic or parliamentary histories, where the forces can be
said to follow quasi-Thucydidean laws. In the France that Michelet shows
us, the will of the people is too all-embracing and subterranean, the dis-

positions and talents of the individuals too intricate, and even too private, for the interplay of forces to be analyzed according to a version of Realpolitik. The effect, as it goes along, can be comic or tragic as the observer wishes:

> Ces subalternes dont parle Sieyès, qui succédèrent à leurs chefs (et qui leur sont bien supérieurs), furent surtout deux hommes, deux forces révolutionaires, Camille Desmoulins et Danton. Ces deux hommes, le roi du pamphlet, le foudroyant orateur du Palais-Royal, avant d'être celui de la Convention, nous n'en pouvons parler ici. Ils vont nous suivre, au rest, ils ne nous lâcheront pas. La comédie, la tragédie de la Révolution sont en eux, ou dans personne.

> These subalterns Sieyès speaks of, who succeeded their chiefs (and who are quite superior to them) were first of all two men, two revolutionary forces, Camille Desmoulins and Danton. These two men, the king of the pamphlet, the thundering orator of the Palais-Royal, before he was that of the Convention – we cannot speak of them here. They will follow us anyway, they will not let us go. The comedy and tragedy of the Revolution are in them, or in nobody.

> (1:179)

As for "comedy and tragedy," Michelet makes an easy attribution of the emotional complexes that derive from these large literary forms. Indeed, his usage is, of course, casual here, but the inferences we may draw from it, both negative and positive, are far from casual. Centrally there is the course of the revolution through time as it embodies itself in these two men. In three years' time they will find themselves imprisoned together and awaiting execution. At that point (2:801–810) the situation will not be "tragic" in the literary sense, and naturally the comic will have diminished. By that time the Revolution will have been betrayed by the Terror, of which these executions are a notable instance. Camille who is not ready to die will form a contrast to Danton who is, though they will have stuck to their guns through it all, Camille endangering himself by too direct hits against Robespierre, Danton by becoming a sadly ineffectual orator. And the Gironde, their rallying point, will long since have been superseded. The passage just quoted is introduced to qualify remarks of a negative cast uttered by a Sieyès who will himself have been superseded, along with those he has been addressing, Mirabeau, Duport, Barnave, and Lameth.

The intrication in time of these events is such that it will not respond to such characterizations, nor can its overall movement be spoken of, loosely and globally, as other than both comedy and tragedy. These terms as used here are only slightly heavier and more defining than terms like *piquant* and *amusant* (both to be found at 1:241), or the frequent *étrange* and *bizarre*. All indicate a submission to a presentation in time that sharks up *faits divers* without allowing them to be defined as either random or coherent in the large forward movement of the events. By a kind of paradox, their suspension between randomness and coherence allows them more fully to contribute to the large sense of progression that the temporal narrative brings about. The popular élan in which effective men participate will channel their efforts toward the common stream. It, in turn, will meander forcefully because of the particular traits and situations of these participants. They are composites, these men, and Barthes (80) emphasizes Michelet's penchant for describing them in terms of *"substances élémentaires"* like the grasses at the base of their diet or the flint of their environment. Michelet himself has recourse to a still more startling metaphor that almost phantomizes man: "Qu'est-ce que l'homme physique et la vie? Un gaz solidifié," "What is the physical man and his life? A solidified gas" (2:844). Still, he says this in a context where he is praising Lavoisier as a kind of positive product of the revolutionary spirit, and the effect here is to humanize chemistry rather than to dehumanize man. Man builds up pressure like a gas and has the onward movement of a solid object, so that his psyche corresponds to what Lavoisier had discovered of the transmutability of the elements. And again, these human elements are not perfectly transmutable because they are so complex, so varied in their temporal progressions.

Along with all the other complications involved in his existence, man is mortal, and the Revolution tends to shorten lives. Camille was executed at thirty-three, Danton at thirty-five, Madame Roland at thirty-eight, Saint-Just finally even younger. All had moved away from events through the intricacies of an imbalance in each person among dispositions, activities, and principles. At an earlier stage even a natural death, notably that of Mirabeau, carries omen as well as fulfillment, and also, this early, the suspicion that perhaps he was poisoned:

> La douleur fut immense, universelle. Son secrétaire, qui l'adorait, et qui plusieurs fois avait tiré l'épée pour lui, voulut se couper la gorge. Pendant la maladie un jeune homme s'était présenté, demandant si l'on voulait essayer la transfusion du sang, offrant le sien pour rajeunir, raviver celui de Mirabeau. Le peuple fit fermer les spectacles, dispersa même par ses huées un bal qui semblait insulter à la douleur générale.

(There follows a paragraph about the autopsy, of which the son of Mirabeau reports that most doctors found poison.)

Le 3 avril, le département de Paris se présenta à l'Assemblée nationale, demanda, obtint que l'église de Sainte Geneviève fût consacrée
à la sépulture des grands hommes, et que Mirabeau y fût placé le
premier. Sur le fronton devaient être inscrit ces mots: "Aux grands
hommes la patrie reconnaisante." Descartes y était. Voltaire et Rousseau devaient y venir. "Beau décret! dit Camille Desmoulins. Il y a
mille sectes et mille églises entre les nations, et dans une même nation,
le Saint des saints pour l'un est l'abomination pour l'autre. Mais pour
ce temple et ses reliques, il n'y aura pas de disputes. Cette basilique
réunira tous les hommes à sa religion."

Le 4 avril eut lieu la pompe funèbre la plus vaste, la plus populaire
qu'il y ait eu au monde, avant celle de Napoléon, au 15 décembre
1840. Le peuple seul fit la police et la fit admirablement. Nul accident
dans cette foule de trois ou quatre cent mille hommes. Les rues, les
boulevards, les fenêtres, les toits, les arbres, était chargés de
spectateurs.

En tête de cortège marchait Lafayette, puis, entouré royalement des
douze huissiers à la chaîne, Tronchet, le président de l'Assemblée
nationale, puis l'Assemblée tout entière sans distinction de partis. L'in-
time ami de Mirabeau, Sieyès, qui détestait les Lameth et ne leur parlait
jamais, eut pourtant l'idée noble et délicate de prendre le bras de
Charles de Lameth, les couvrant ainsi de l'injuste soupçon qu'on faisait
peser sur eux.

The sorrow was immense, universal. His secretary, who adored
him and who had several times drawn his sword for him, wanted to
cut his own throat. During the illness a young man presented himself
to inquire if they wished to try a blood transfusion, offering his own
to rejuvenate and revive that of Mirabeau. The people closed all spectacles and even dispersed by shouts a ball that seemed to insult the
general sorrow.

The third of April the Department of Paris presented itself at the
national Assembly, and demanded and obtained that the church of
Sainte-Geneviève be consecrated for the burial of great men and that
Mirabeau be placed there first. On the cornice these words were to
be inscribed: "To great men from a grateful fatherland." Descartes
was there, Voltaire and Rousseau were to come. "A beautiful decree,"
said Camille Desmoulins. "There are a thousand sects and a thousand
churches in various countries, and in a single nation the Holy of Holies
for one is an abomination for another. But there will be no disputes
about this temple and its relics. This basilica will bring all men together
to its religion."

On the fourth of April took place the largest and most popular funeral ever held in the world, until that of Napoleon on the fifteenth of December, 1840. The people itself served as police and did so admirably. No accident in that crowd of three or four hundred thousand men. The streets, the boulevards, the windows, the roofs, the trees, were loaded with spectators.

At the head of the procession marched Lafayette, and then, surrounded royally by twelve huissiers with the chain, Tronchet the president of the National Assembly; then the entire Assembly, without distinction of party. Mirabeau's intimate friend, Sieyès, who detested the Lameths and never spoke to them, had the noble and delicate idea of taking Charles Lameth's arm, thus covering them with the unjust suspicion that weighed on them.

(1:558–559)

There follows an account of the Jacobin club's size – itself an omen! – of the mourning period, the tardy arrival at the church, the eulogy, the crashing of all the glass in the church under the simultaneous volley of the national guard, the subsequent torchlit procession, and a wrap-up of the effect of this mass of action, sequenced into a mass of detail. "He carried with him something no one yet well knew, but only too much later: the spirit of peace in the war itself, goodness under violence, sweetness, humanity," "Il emportait avec lui quelque chose, qu'on ne savait pas bien encore, on ne le sut que trop plus tard: l'esprit de paix dans la guerre même, la bonté sous la violence, la douceur, l'humanité."

Having proleptically brought in for comparison the funeral of Napoleon, which he characterizes only by its size, Michelet continues in the next paragraph to assert that the soul and memory of Mirabeau persist, the standard pious reflection thus given an overarching place in an account of how a moment may be taken to endure. We cannot ask whether this is a valid interpretation, either in Michelet's time or in our own. This substitution of piety for historical analysis is moot, and sends us in this context back to the text of Michelet, where we may note, close to the end of this work, that the death of Robespierre following the events of Thermidor (2:990) is much more sinister, accompanied by far less detail, amplified by none of the characterological inferences or interplay of charities and enthusiasms that are exhibited in this account. The careful weaving in and out of detail, as Michelet progresses temporally through this day, here comes still more sharply clear if we compare his historiographic account of Mirabeau's death with the quasi-historiographic, but more autobiographical and judgmental, account in Chateaubriand's *Mémoires d'Outre-Tombe* (5:12), or with the account in Victor Hugo's "Sur Mirabeau."[7] Chateaubriand devotes a whole chapter to Mirabeau at the point of his death but offers little detail and almost no narrative, devoting himself instead to an elaborate contrastive balance sheet of analyses on Mirabeau's political effect. Hugo's effusive romanticism helps show up by contrast the sinewy complexity of Michelet's. As one might expect, Hugo immediately lets out the metaphoric stops over the death of Mirabeau. There is a disproportion between his effusions, and his abrupt transition to detail that is weak because of its indiscriminatory abundance. He gives most space to a summary nearly two pages long of various speeches in the Assembly on the occasion, and he goes on to present, like Chateaubriand, a synchronic assessment of Mirabeau.

In Michelet's own handling of this death, as just quoted, the details are woven together, rising easily up and down in sharpness. At any point the situation can be given broader implications: It can be taken, in various ways, as metaphoric. The young man offering the blood transfusion, the nationalist sentiment engraved on the cornice of the church, the mingling of the illustrious great with the figures in the live funeral procession of the early revolutionaries and the thronging anonymous masses – all this can be read as a metaphoric expression of where the Revolution has come. But it is also an actualization, and the mysterious fusion of the metaphoric and the actual here is largely subjected to time. Only in the passage that follows will Michelet draw the explicit conclusion of symbolizing what is taking place in the late-night torchlit streets, "Mais à mesure que le jour disparut, et que le convoi s'enfonça dans l'ombre doublement obscure de la nuit et des rues profondes, qu'éclairaient les lueurs des torches tremblantes, les imaginations aussi entrèrent malgré elles dans le ténébreux avenir, dans les pressentiments sinistres." "But accordingly as the day disappeared and the procession buried itself in the shadow doubly obscure of the night and the deep streets lit by the light of trembling torches, imaginations entered in spite of themselves into the tenebrous future, into sinister presentiments." This final asyndeton is only the last one in a variable riot of asyndetons that Michelet here allows himself. He plays back and forth across the personalities and the groups, delaying for later mention a notice that there was one man who refused to join the funeral procession because he credulously believed that Mirabeau had entered a conspiracy (1:560). That man was Pétion, whom we shall come to know as a hanger-on of Robespierre, and so too credulous in another direction. Much later he drifts away from Robespierre. He will be arrested, and finally he will commit suicide.

Time will be needed to produce these complications, and Mirabeau himself, like Napoleon much later, will be subject to the hazards of time beyond any possibility of calculation or inspiration. He has been fulfilled, but also blocked, and the roles of Richelieu, Washington, and Cromwell, were all impossible for him, Michelet declares (1:555), though to mention these three is to assert that aspects of their activity did combine in Mirabeau. He is defined a little earlier as "*l'organe même du peuple, la voix de la Révolution*"

(1:545). Mirabeau is shown as implicitly a federalist on the pattern of Brissot and Lafayette, as having had Milton's antiroyalist tract printed and then having it suppressed by its friends, as "destined to exhaust the contradictions," "*épuiser les contradictions*" (2:238). He is called a spokesman for Rousseau (1:58), a constant presence (as at the opening of the Estates General, when Sieyès is absent) (1:90). He early combats "indignities" sponsored by Robespierre (1:481). After his death he is called "the master of variations," "*maître en variations*" (1:643) by Michelet. He had begun a decline into ineffectuality before his death, which his funeral caps as the surge of positive enthusiasm necessarily ignores it.

Character interests Michelet at all turns, and he diverts a chapter of the *Histoire de France*, purportedly about "France and England," to discuss the mix of Saxon and French in the person of Becket, in a long, digressive account of his struggles with Henry II and his ensuing martyrdom. He says of Charles V, in terms almost like those he occasionally used of Mirabeau, "Ce chaos d'éléments divers s'incarne en Charles-Quint" (*Histoire de France*, 7:13). But always the complex participants are caught up in a time that moves forward evenly while impelled by deeply upwelling currents, much as the symbolizing, and then the piety, surface at the end of the detail-etched account of Mirabeau's funeral just quoted. The Revolution, since it is such an epochal realization and a monumental disappointment, exhibits the impulses and the deep upwellings much more markedly than does all the rest of the history preceding it. Consequently there is a kind of proportionate rightness in the much greater evenness of *L'Histoire de France*, if it is compared to *L'Histoire de la révolution française*. This summary condensation of forces, which Michelet has managed to capture in his handling of the ongoing presentation in time, makes the latter work what it is usually considered to be, his most salient achievement.

The detail here draws heavily, but variously, on a rhetorical handling that can be called metaphorical, with White.[18] But first of all the "metaphors" appear in different structural forms. Is the young man offering to be bled a metaphor for the future France wanting to resurrect the body if not the spirit of Mirabeau? Probably, since Michelet chose to dwell on this particular detail among the large repertory of incidents surrounding Mirabeau's deathbed. The bedside scene is also ironic, in that the young man cannot keep the spirit of Mirabeau alive any more than he can that leader's body. In any case this metaphor has a different structure from that of the dignitaries marching in procession, and from the procession itself. The *punctum* of Sieyès' arm-linkage with Charles Lameth is not metaphoric in this sense; it is an incident in the ongoing procession, and no more can be read into it than the (considerable amount of) possible interpretation derivable from any social gesture. It is correlated with, and made a transient moment of, the large and lengthy procession.

Michelet explicitly draws metaphorical inference from the torches late at night after the funeral, and his interpretive remarks about the proleptic significance of this sight assimilates it to temporal structure more fully, while giving it the different turn of metalinguistic effusion. It is one thing to say, "My love's like a red, red rose," and another to say, "Yes, her cheeks were very red, and a person looking at her would draw the pleasurable impression that she looks just like a red, red rose." Not only is the framing of the metaphor different; the correspondence between night torches and an ominous future development compares a large, complex visual moment to a large, later temporal unfolding; the young man offering the blood transfusion stands, synecdochally we may say, for the "people" as well as for a moment aimed to the future, while Mirabeau stands without synecdoche for "leader" as well as for a backward look at the past. The arm-linking of the two dignitaries, if it be construed an emblem of concord, works still differently (and if synecdochic, the synecdoche is different). And the inscription on the church cornice, if it be taken for an emblem of the fusion of church and state, has a structure different from all of these. Words set at a key point of an architectural construct are drawn from two partially discrete domains, "national great men" and "the faith," into a connection that forebodes a further connection. The domains are already only partially discrete since any political hero carries overtones of a religious hero, and Michelet draws on such similarities at points of the *L'Histoire de France*.

If the "people" in this work is metaphoric – and this seems to be White's chief claim – then it is metaphoric in still another sense, quite a different one. Taken as a term in a political ideology, the "people" is indeed one of the metaphors we live by.[19] Once Michelet has substantiated the term through his long narrative, and in his usage, the term ceases to be metaphoric in any ordinary sense. It simply converges with the deep sense of his narrative, just as "France" does, or "Deutschland" for Ranke, "the individual" for Burckhardt. The tropes with which he surrounds the word "people" are meant to single it out for attention as a factor and incidentally as an object of praise and wonder, but not to give it any of the various figural dimensions discussed above. All those are subjected deeply to time and have their predominant meaning as heightening salient moments of a temporal progression. And all of those figures, too, anchored in what may confidently be called facts, function at the point of the narrative as amplifying tropes; but in the sequence of the narrative, those various metaphors or quasi metaphors function as markers, framers, and vivifiers, but only as partially amplifying definers, of significant detail. It is their sequenced employment, and not their various metaphoric structures, that converge into the deep sense of the ongoing temporal narrative. Put differently, the convergence is too momentary and slight for all of them; and for "people" it is too permanent and total, to serve as especially characterizing the "argument" of the work.[20] Michelet's dexterity in handling these various types of metaphor, his skill at highlighting and varying the presentation of detail through their means, shows in bold relief if one compares him to Chateaubriand and Hugo on this subject. This is partly because of his superior skill on this ground. And it is partly because he is writing in a profoundly different mode, which he manipulates in a powerful oblivion to the "scholarly" convention of even-tempered presentation. His diachronic mastery is to be measured not just negatively against that common tone of scholarly neutrality. It is also to be measured positively; the force of succession is the main significative function of the metaphors. The difference among their linguistic structures – which, of course, could be further described and analyzed in Aristotelian or post-Aristotelian fashion – is secondary to that contributory delineation. It is this dexterity, indeed, more than the opinions they happen to share, that makes Michelet sound like Dostoevsky to one writer.[21]

The shift in and out of metaphor is also often accompanied by a shift of tone, which itself can be taken as a momentary emphasis in a complex series rather than as an extrapolated attitude. So in his chapter "The False Peace" (2:1) there is a touch of irony, but also of genuine pity, when he speaks of "*Le pauvre duc d'Orléans*" (1:165), who is about to cool his heels a whole day outside the castle to assure the king of his loyalty and thus unwittingly to provide himself with an alibi because it happens to be the original Bastille Day, but without deflecting the contempt and disgust of Mirabeau (166). Mirabeau measures surely this ineffectual clown; "*pauvre*" sets the note that leads to that significant response, while at the same time allowing the transient recognition of the duke's humanity. He, too, will be swallowed up in an execution before long. The text in any case moves on to other tonal shifts: "Versailles nageait dans la joie" (167), "Etrange et bizarre spectacle" (169).

At one end of his narrative register, Michelet is much more detailed than Burckhardt, while always actively varying and manipulating his presentation of detail. At the other end he allows himself longish effusions – which themselves can take the form of a list of details, as when he proudly runs through the achievements of the Assembly (1:402–403).

Always the self-transformation of the events in time lies in view, a broader but looser development than other historians may permit themselves. In the background lies the grand sweep recounted at an evener pace in *L'Histoire de France*, a sweep that Michelet intermittently allows himself references to, or even summarizes, as in the rapid long backward glance that centers on Joan of Arc (2:14). The progression that engages him amounts to a sort of subdued Hegelian dialectic, as he makes clear in the introduction:

Qui a vue une négation? Qu'est-ce qu'une négation vivante, une négation qui agit, qui enfante comme celle-ci? Un monde est né d'elle
hier... Non, pour produire, il faut être.

Who has seen a negation? What is a living negation, a negation that
acts, that gives birth like this one? A world was born of it yesterday
... No, to produce it is necessary to exist.

(1:25)

The principle of action over thought is Marxist here, too, though the staccato rhythms, the ellipses, and the quick changes of pace keep this summary
from the lockstep of any doctrinaire position and render it as just one more
wave in the onrushing stream of events. Very shortly he shall, almost
consistently, attribute the Church's failure at regenerating society to something like a suspension of dialectic: "Parti de l'arbitraire, ce système doit
rester dans l'arbitraire, il n'en peut sortir d'un pas." "Starting from the
arbitrary, this system had to stay in the arbitrary; it couldn't take a single
step out of it" (1:29). And in another perspective, there is the simple spirit,
"la loi est partout devancée par l'élan spontané de la vie et de l'action," "the
law is everywhere preceded by the spontaneous impulse of life and action"
(1:396). Everything depends on the unfolding development, which a state
can impede as well as a church, "Qui tua la République? Son gouvernement.
La forme extermina le fond" (2:794, apropos of the trial of Danton). Here
the rhythms are blunt and even; they are almost funerary. But the current
remains, of variable style and turbulent event. Fused, they call forth the
gathering presentation of mysteries proceeding in time according to aspectual laws, but no set law other than the events whose surge into the future
can be retrospectively captured by an adaptable management of the developing past.

PART II

STRATEGIES OF INCLUSION

WRITTEN HISTORY ASPIRES to the complete account, but it is constrained in the limitations of human knowledge, and also by the principles of its own domain, to define its own particular context, to content itself with partiality. All writing of history is synecdochic; it must approach its subject by the presentation of actual, particular events. In this it differs from both philosophy and poetry, which can mount comprehensive utterances.

Scriptural history aspires to unfolding the will of God – a kind of totality, since it is everywhere present. In the Old Testament, the doctrine of inspiration holds that the historian has been able to compile a text that does unfold the will of God. This presence of otality (God) as a constant but mysterious factor in the text as it proceeds is represented by the recurrence of the name for God, the tetragrammaton. In the New Testament the same aim is carried off by the specific set of events under presentation and discussion, a set of events in which God's coming to earth is given capital, millennial importance, one that constitutes a converging totality at the point of Apocalypse.

Philosophers can discuss the totality of what history means in various ways, producing the philosophy of history. These philosophers may, and characteristically do, write actual history that is governed by a totalizing, usually a dialectical, conception that orders the actual events they bring forward, and by implication several possible ones as well.

But the historian may eschew all these procedures. He characteristically does so, and envisages the coherence underlying his intrication of events by a careful angling of the partiality he has chosen; by a flexible management of synecdoches of which the sophistication becomes apparent if we compare such modern work with the capable accounts of even so masterly a brief historian as Sallust.

My final four chapters address these four approaches serially.

8

THE CONTRACTIONS AND EXPANSIONS
OF BIBLICAL HISTORY

T HE CRITERIA ARE INCIDENTAL by which we would deny not only a historiographic purpose but also a historiographic result to the biblical narrative about the successive events in the collective life of the Hebrews from the Exodus, or even earlier, to the destruction of the First Temple. While the Old Testament writer – whom we could minimally call a compiler – has a different relationship to his documents from that of Thucydides or Tacitus (who differ in this from each other), he does rely on documents that he finds trustworthy enough to be brought together even when there are overlaps or discrepancies in them. And he relies on what he cannot be faulted for regarding as evidence, the relationship of God to the Hebrews. This is so central to his conception of the unfolding of events that he would have been remiss in leaving it out – as remiss as a Braudelian would be for totally ignoring demographic data. Of course, his criteria of evidence differ from those that have been in force for some time, and probably not even a devout Jewish or Christian historian would either write under such rules of evidence or accept them here other than on faith. But if they are accepted as a prior assumption, the narrative then demonstrates the sense of key mutations in progressing events that one would deny to most medieval narratives or quasi narratives, even *The City of God*, which simply subsume all narrated events directly under the will of God, without any effect of truly sequent interpretation. Again, the devout modern historian might agree with this conclusion and still not endorse the *historiographic* practice of such writers. Any other features of the narratives in the books of Samuel and Kings can be assigned without much difficulty to the historiographic purpose, and refusing to give the designation "history" to this narrative of "instruction" (*torah*) raises more difficulties than it solves.[1]

One must still hold steadily in view when reading Samuel and Kings, or other parts of the Torah, that the writer puts at the center of his narrative an active agent, God, whose presence cannot be established by the canons of evidence that the modern historian uses. The translatability of the term "YHWH" into "manifest success after time," or "moral uprightness," or "unformulable instinct" or "unconscious command" will not do, because all of these and more are subsumable under the one all-embracing designation. This powerful undocumentable term coexists with the text's vision of mutation and process; and it also interacts with it, a large, all-encompassing factor. The emergence of the Torah as an interpretation of these interactions constitutes a large transformational idea – almost what Foucault calls an "*episteme*." And the narrative, again, shows how this idea develops.

Moreover, one cannot implicitly or explicitly invoke the "suspension of disbelief" one brings to a fictive work, because the rhetorical thrust of this text declares it not to be fiction, and what we know of the social developments it recounts from other sources tends to substantiate that declaration. To make about historiographic texts a distinction that is common to Frege and Austin, historiographic works in general assert the referentiality of their sentences and their sequence while at the same time stating that referentiality. The assertion must be dealt with in terms of the validity of the references, singly and globally. Finally, however many qualifications may be introduced between signifier and signified, the historiographic character of the historiographic text is not foregrounded if its asserted and stated acts of reference are not also foregrounded. And the transformational idea, the force of YHWH, defines and produces such possibilities of foregrounding.

As Auerbach trenchantly demonstrates, the narratives in the Torah are contracted, or "in the background." Yet the progression of time in these narratives is not evenly uniform, and there is a marked unevenness to their acts of foregrounding, which follow no simply formulable principle yet are too assured to be random. If twenty years are skipped in a phrase (1 Sam. 7:2), or if the accounts of the rules of the sons of Ahab are foreshortened by comparison with the account of David's rule, that unevenness of presentational distribution should be taken to indicate a lack of interesting development: those twenty years, those particular men, exhibited little that called for presentation by the writer.[2]

The contraction or foreshortening of presentation in this historical narrative is carried through by a seemingly flat linearity. And yet this linearity is modified in several ways. First, it is punctuated by the term for God, YHWH, a condensed and all-inclusive term as charged with meaning, and as "meaningless," as is Heidegger's definition of *Sein*. This term may be a verbal root, with reference to process or coming into being or energy – and including all the glosses listed above. In this sense, without reference to credence, it is a randomly recurring tonic assertion in a discourse where the other terms stay unjudgmentally close to designation, and hence to linear sequence. It is a constant reminder of what the linear sequence is supposed to be about, and of the principle that overridingly measures, and brings into being, the success or failure of a given ruler's enterprises. YHWH is thus incipiently dialectical as it maintains the tension of what the sequences must interact with, and it is at the same time implicitly summary of what they cannot escape being measured by.

Further modifying this linearity is the constant and unmistakable presence of a subtypological analogy. Typology is loosely but intermittently present here, as it might be in any narrative, historiographic or fictional. When David is singled out as the youngest and yet the heir, this repeats the typology of "the last shall be the first," a typology that is found as a fairy tale motif, and in other biblical cases, such as that of Samuel, who is chosen over the sons of Eli, or Jacob, or Joseph, or even Solomon when he is chosen over an elder son of David. This typology merges into the Christian typology that identifies Christ, the descendant of David, as "the stone that the builder rejected has become the cornerstone." And it still bears on small David's conquest over the giant Goliath, inverting the less myth-charged typology, or assumption, of valuing the tall, powerful man, a typology to which Samson corresponds, as in a more normal way does the towering Saul when he is chosen to rule (1 Sam. 9:2).

David's action against Goliath evidences other traits that transcend ty-pology – confidence, strategically angled humility, and generally an inspired sense of how the factors, first in a single military operation but later in general, can be reshuffled so as to bring about success under highly unfavorable conditions. Slings are used by these armies; David has found a particularly advantageous way to employ a sling. His choice of weapon indicates more than marksmanship, dexterity, or even just a physical flexibility. It is subtypological features of this sort that govern the analogy of David's career to those of other rulers. And here the "fictional" approach to his character through reference to character types merges with a study of his historical role as a king.

What gives force to the presentation of David is not just the typology that helps to focus him. The narrative sustains, in addition, a constantly qualified analogy between David and the others whose whole careers are presented. David is implicitly compared to the more circumscribed and deliberative Samuel (showing these traits in having to ask more than once about the voice of God at the beginning), to the alternately overassertive and underassertive Saul, and to the supremely confident but ominously self-indulgent Solomon, as well as to various officials who either reach or fail to reach David's balance and vision. David himself, indeed, served Saul and managed for years the varying pressure of that ruler's unpredictability. The first king did not work out but the second, David, became expansively the normative one. It is David's balance and vision as much as his anointing that give him the rule, though the anointing is an original act that supervenes because it is ordered by God. David's various actions spell out a justification for the anointing; they flesh it out and make it actual. The framework of analogy also pulls the "fictional" elements into further congruence with a long-range historical view.

The range and variety of David's actions must be intended here as the pattern for rule. All others are measured against it, especially the rule of Solomon. It is the Davidic genealogy that is singled out as crucial in the final verses of Ruth. And the descent of David has come through earlier complexities as the conclusion of the complex Judah–Tamar interactions (Gen. 38. 1–26; discussed in Robert Alter, 5–12). The typologies of folk motif are so incidental to this presentation that they must be counted the faintest of echoes.[3] And such literary patterns as "tragedy" do not really fit the case of Saul, all of whose behaviors can be referred to a relative incapacity for rule. This is a historical theme, rather than a "fictional" view of human frustration before a capricious and unfathomable God.

Four kinds of sequence braid the predominant linearities of this historical text together. First there is the large overall progression from final institution in the Holy Land (Judges) to final Exile (2 Kings). Second, there are the punctuating measures against developed presence or developed absence of the Divine Favor. Third, there are the territorial adjustments that accompany the large progressions, and also the institutional ones: the relationship between charismatic and institutionalized leadership in priests, prophets, and kings, as these will sometimes partially fuse and charge within the person of a single ruler; the emphases on territories within the Holy Land and the kinds and directions of pressures, usually military, from problematic or hostile neighbors. If the neighbors are not problematic, the text is silent about them; we hear nothing of Egypt in the books of Samuel, but only encounter Egypt when Solomon makes a dynastic marriage to an Egyptian princess at the beginning of his rule (1 Kings 3:1). Fourth, constantly playing against all these historical themes, is the career of an individual king in its "fictional" contours and style.

The first three sequences are dominated by the fourth sequence. The contours and style of an individual king are implicitly defined by the extent of his congruences and divergences from both the behaviors and the situations of other kings, especially his immediate predecessor and successor. The text, of course, does not use any version of this terminology; the presentation is carried through pure sequence. And so the question as to whether behaviors or situations must be assigned priority in some causal chain is often abrogated in favor of the first and second sequences: the particular point of a situation in the run of centuries, or its relation to the Divine Favor. Since the Divine Favor is presented as responsive to behaviors but may be accounted as the source of the situations, the question remains undecidable.

The compiler presents these factors not as a random sequence, however, and not as one that is simply patterned. What God responds to is not the single omission or commission of an act: It is as wrong for David to kill Uriah as it is for Saul to refrain from slaughtering Agag (1 Sam. 15:33); but these behaviors are not assessed just for the one moment. At the moment it is said that both are punished (1 Sam. 15:10; 2 Sam. 12:14). Rather, the divine response that bears on power involves not just a single act, and not a pattern like that of "tragedy." It involves the whole career, and the measure of the whole career is not the immediate response (as Saul loses the kingship) or even the ultimate one (as complications initiated by David's polygamy defer founding the Temple and bring about struggles over succession, the Divided Kingdom, and finally perhaps even the Exile). The measure of the whole career takes place through analogy to other careers, aligning the careers thereby in a mutually qualifying historical sequence. The measure we have for David, though he is himself the pattern of measure, is Samuel, Saul, Solomon, Ahab and others.

The analogies come first at momentary points in a career, incident by incident. David provides one overall analogy: David succeeds to a degree that no other king does, with the possible exception of his son Solomon. These two successes are in turn measured as mutually interdefining career-wholes, while standing for and embodying particular stages in the history of Israel: Solomon can deal with a wider area of influence and rule over a more prosperous and complicated government because David's balance and vision have succeeded in bringing the United Kingdom to that point. David has created the conditions under which Solomon can build the Temple. The many elements that compose the analogies may be highlighted in the following table (a lengthy one, but I shall be using it in what follows if not subjecting it to full structural analysis):

David	*Saul*	*Solomon*	*Other*
1. 1 Sam 16 anointed	succeeds		Moses
2. 1 6:14 plays lyre for Saul	obeys	takes over	Joshua
3. 17:12–49 kills Goliath	wins battles		Samson
4. 18:1–6 popular with Jonathan and others	strain with David		Joseph
5. 18:10 and passim evades Saul			Joseph

David	Saul	Solomon	Other
6. 18:17–30 loses Merab, gets Michal with foreskins		Egyptian marriage	
7. 19:1–20 Michal helps escape			Moses
8. 20:1–42 approaches Saul through Jonathan			
9. 21:1–9 gets bread and sword from Ahimelech			
10. 10–15 feigns madness to Achish of Gath	mad	wise	
11. 22:1–19 to Adullam, then Mizpeh. Doeg devastates Nob	Saul gives the order		Judges
12. 23:1–5 saves Keilah from Philistines			
13. 23:6–29 escapes Saul to Ziph, then Maon			
14. 24:1–22 spares Saul, reconciles, promises to protect his house	adopts David		Pharaoh adopts Joseph
15. 25:1–38 Abigail overrides Nabal to entertain David			
16. 25:39–44 marries her and Ahinoam, loses Michal			
17. 26 again spares Saul			
18. 27 to Achish as mercenary			
19. 28–29 serves but			

David	Saul	Solomon	Other
not trusted against Hebrews			
20. 30:1–20 rescues wives from Amelakites			
2 SAMUEL			
21. 1 mourns Saul and Jonathan			
22. 2:1–7 goes to Hebron			
23. 2:8–3:1 long war with Ishbosheth and Abner		tricks Shimei, Joab	
24. 3:2 has sons			
25. 3:22–4:12 enemies killed and mourned		expands cavalry (10:26)	
26. 5 is king, gets Jerusalem			
27. 6 gets ark and dances, Michal rebukes him			
28. 7 plans temple and gets promise		has dream, builds temple (1 Kings 3:5; 6–7)	
29. 8 conquers Edom, Moab, Syrians		diplomacy in Tyre (5) and Sheba (10); loses Edom, Syria (1 Kings 14–23)	
30. 8:15 appoints officials		appoints bureaucracy (1 Kings 1:4)	
31. 9 kind to Mephibosheth	harsh	harsh	

David	*Saul*	*Solomon*	*Other*
32. 10 conquers Syrians and Ammon	conquests	conquests	
33. 11 kills Uriah to get Bathsheba		strange women (11:1–13)	
34. 12 Nathan warns, child dies, Solomon born	Samuel warns		
35. 13:1–30 Absalom waits, kills Amnon			
36. 13:31–14:28 he flees, David mourns, guesses Joab role, restores Absalom			
37. 15 Absalom conspires, David flees		trouble with Jereboam	
38. 16:1–13 endures the curse of Shimei			
39. 16:14–28 Absalom gets David's concubines	Adonijah killed for requesting Abishag (1 Kings 2:13–25)		
40. 17–18:8 Absalom pursues David to Mahanaim	flees – pursues David	stable in place	
41. 18:8–33 Absalom dies, David mourns			
42. 19 David returns			
43. 20 guards concubines, conquers Sheba			

David	Saul	Solomon	Other
44. 21:1–18 turns seven of Saul's sons over to Gibeonites, spares Mephibosheth, buries bones of Saul and Jonathan			
45. 21:18–22 kills giants of Gath			
46. 22 song rejoicing over triumphs			
47. 23:1–7 sings oracle over future			
48. 23:8–39 triumphs and soldiers listed			
49. 24 census, plague, death.			

I KINGS

David	Saul	Solomon	Other
50. 1:1–10 Abishag fails to vivify David			
51. 1:11–50 agrees to accession of Solomon			
52. 2:1–10 he gives last commands, dies	suicide	dies honorably	

A rigorous thematic analysis could produce far more analogies than I have indicated here. Taken in its contour, the whole career of David (1–52) overlaps more than a third with the career of Saul (1–21). David is forced to operate under the duress of exclusion from the centers of power, and in stages (5; 9–13; 17–20), as Saul is never forced to do. In Saul's variation, he must deal internally with the loss of divinely constituted authority, all the while continuing nominally to rule. Absalom (37–41) and more briefly Adonijah (50–51) are excluded from the centers of a power to which they have some claim of succession, but they are types of the failed ruler. In this they are partly analogous to Saul, and even arguably to the son of David who does succeed to the throne, to Solomon, in so far as Solomon's stolidity and remoteness, the passivity that Fokkelman notes in the very grammar of the sentences that present him, suggests that he will not actively hold together the kingdom that his father had pulled together.[4]

Solomon has many more wives than David, but the text presents them first in a dynastic marriage at the beginning of his career and then in a summary of their multitude at the end (1 Kings 11:1–13), whereas sexual relations punctuate David's career at several key points (6–7; 15–16; 20; 27; 33–35; 43; 50–52). They are virtually absent from Saul's career in the presentation, and therefore in the view presented by the text of what is significant in the contour of that career. Saul is forced, however, to handle problems arising from the sexual activities of dependents (6); and one might include all the Absalom episodes under this heading, since the affection of David and Jonathan is explicitly compared to the love of women (21; 2 Sam. 1:26). Its character as "passing the love of women," however, is not set in a context by itself as a vivid personal fact, but rather comprised in a song, the one piece of quoted poetry in the entire series, which celebrates Saul along with Jonathan and all of Israel, a song designated explicitly as a quotation "from the Book of Jashar" (2 Sam. 1:18). David's contour does partially follow the pattern of Saul's in managing the sexual actions of dependents (20; 39; 43). So does Solomon's, still more simply and abruptly, when he puts Adonijah to death for requesting Abishag. Reactions to David, in fact, dominate the contour of Saul's career, and the charisma of the harper-warrior has a political as well as an amical impact on Saul's whole family. Michal, it may be said, reacts officially: We may conjecture that something in her discerns the imposing future king in David, and her lack of sympathy for the harper side surfaces in her revulsion at his triumphal dancing before the ark. She responds, in short, to the warrior side; and her brother Jonathan, the comrade-in-arms, responds to the harper as well, or his love might not be "passing the love of women."

Saul's children here have split and independently shaped their versions of his own reactions to David, in ways that shake his kingdom instead of solidifying it. Toward David he lacks the balance that he lacks in everything, being now too personally sympathetic in his political relations and now too imprudently hostile.

So, too, Saul in his military career: After his first successes (1 Sam. 11) he shows some prudence in managing his affairs, but he soon tips into imbalance when he precipitously performs sacrifices against Samuel's (and God's) express command (1 Sam. 13:5–13). Finally he fails to sacrifice Agag's herds as commanded, holding them instead for distribution as booty, and then fatally hanging fire before the political necessity, understood as a sort of absolute in this stern world, of killing the leader of an enemy army. Samuel, the priest-leader who advises him, gives a theatrical demonstration of Saul's failure here by hewing Agag to pieces just when he is withdrawing support, and so legitimation, from Saul (1 Sam. 15:33). The other kings that the text presents, who do succeed at sorting out the factors, throw the imbalance of Saul into relief. In his career's contour of repeatedly demonstrated imbalance, the handling of Agag and his flocks is only the culminating example. It makes little difference that Saul is willing to confess his sin; God will not be with him; or in more modern language, he has proved himself unfit to govern.[5]

One might, again, graph or plot these contours in all their congruence and variation, but both the congruence and the variation would constitute a chief segmentation – rather than any thematic summary like "succession narrative" – of the historiographic presentation here.

The contours proceed by what they subsume, the complexly intricated gestures of powerful individuals. After the great gain of perceiving the small-grained characterological (the "fictional") attributes here, we are obliged to assess their theoretical relation to the main rhetorical determinant of these narratives, the "historical." Fiction and history, to begin with, remain in a sort of fusion throughout the Torah, as I have elsewhere fairly summarily asserted in discussing the sacrifice of Isaac:

> Here, as nowhere in the mere art of fiction, are perfectly fused the romance of legend – all the symbolic meanings which Auerbach touches on in analyzing this passage (Gen. 22:1–13) – and the most delicate fictional perceptions. There is, for example, Abraham's finely realized set of relations with his servant and his son, existing mutely under the designations of the style – the polite dismissal of the servants before the sacrifice, the exaction of filial obedience in making Isaac carry the wood, the restrained answer to the breathless matter-of-factness of Isaac's questions, held back silently till the very ascent itself. And all the relations, heavenly and earthly, take on irony, pathos, and spiritual depth from the echoing progression of the three *Hinenni*'s ("Here am I") spoken by Abraham, first to God, then to Isaac, then to his guardian angel. Fiction as well as symbolism, and much else, lies in the tacit distinction of lambs: the white young animal in Isaac's mind; the human lamb in Abraham's; and what actually appears, the old curly-horned beast (ram, Hebrew *ayil*, "curled horned") . . .

This is history in which God's purpose is presented as so manifest that every act is symbolic. And one dimension to that symbolism, I would urge, is the fictive, the process of a secret life underlying the appearances of the narrative. The text leaves to our perceptions what it mutely presents – "in the background" as Auerbach says – the terrible intensity of this experience for Isaac. Doubtless his terror here helps to charge the yearning timidity with which he approaches the veiled Rebecca at twilight somewhat later. Doubtless it renders more pathetic and profound his later domination by Rebecca, in which an almost fictive situation combines to make Isaac, too, sacrifice his first-born, in his death-bed blessing, to allow the ascendancy of Jacob. And Jacob will show in his crafty side the third-generation version of Abraham's wisdom; he will go through, too, what, in fictional terms, is the metamorphosis of Abraham's encounter with God, wrestling with the angel, his head pillowed on stone, envisioning the ladder in heaven with "the angels of God ascending and descending on it."[6]

Abraham is presented as the father of his people, and Isaac as a necessary successor for those who will be under the eye and possibly the guidance of "the God of Abraham, Isaac, and Jacob." But these are nearly legendary figures. David emerges later on as more "historical" in our sense, and the "fictional" attributes are correspondingly given a more marked foreground-ing. This would be odd indeed, and digressive, if the character-observations, the "fiction," did not signify moments in the public, historical action. Part of the development shown in the long sequence from Exodus to 2 Kings is this gradually distinct emergence both of "history" and of "fiction." One cannot quite say of Abraham, or somewhat differently of David, however, that history and fiction are fused in their presentation, as they are in Homer's presentation of Agamemnon and Achilles. Homer is already "Aristotelian"; he offers a beginning, middle, and end. And so the *Iliad* may be assimilated to the canons of satisfactory imaginative ("fictional") shaping. Putting it differently, there are many public constraints but no public interpretation underlying the wrath of Achilles. In the Torah the span is too wide for an adduction of Aristotelian structuring. The beginning is the Creation itself, the middle is the vast but phased millennial development of the Hebrew people. And, taking the Old Testament by itself, no end is in view except perhaps the restoration of the Temple.

If the Old Testament is joined to the New, the Bible presents an Apoc-alypse, a sort of history of the future, which further and more emphatically fuses a number of presentational-rhetorical types.[7] The subtypology, how-ever, and the analogies, do continue a fairly consistent development in the text. Sets of relations between fathers and sons continue to obtain, and these undergo further changes in the sequences Eli–sons, Samuel–sons, Saul–Jonathan–grandsons, David–sons, Solomon–sons, and finally the ominous simplification between prevailingly evil and randomly good kings, father and son, from the division of the kingdom till the fall of the Temple. Relations between men and their wives also obtain in both a "fictional" or familial sense and, overridingly, in the "historical" sense that makes these relations crucial and symptomatic for the long-range national developments. We have not only Abraham–Sarah, Isaac–Rebecca, and Jacob–Leah–Rachel. After Samson–Philistine wives and Boaz–Ruth there is a sort of break by which we may infer that the failure to mention the wives of Eli and Saul implies not that their marriages lack "fictional" interest but that they are inconsequential for national development. David, suddenly, undertakes an intricately sequenced, various, and dynamic set of multiple marital ties; and even Abishag, whose sexual presence serves as a last simply therapeutic aid to the aged king, functions after his death in the political interactions (no. 39 in the tabulation). Solomon's ties are various and multiple but neither intricately sequenced nor dynamic.

The personal interactions here are fine-grained, complex, and so intricately involved with what happens before and after that terms like "foreshadowing," "irony," and "ambiguity" simplify them before the fact. At one moment the action is in "character" and seen so; in an overall motion, which God endorses, it will be "destiny." The technique for deploying these fine-grained actions of participants in prose is what we call "fiction," and that term serves as a kind of declared entitlement for Alter to carry out his many keenly perceived and finely discriminated inferences for the characters as they interact. Still, the term "fiction" is perhaps misleading if it be taken to imply "reflective of the private life," as all modern fiction is. These interactions, the contours and styles of these personages, are all at the service of the public life, unremittingly so. Hence, even though they are not "make-believe" – a sense of "fiction" hard to keep away from this text if its methodological probity be questioned – they cannot be assimilated to private, even if exemplary, texts like the supposed hybrid of the "factual novel," which deals with the private life. In some sense Balzac is "public"; he saw himself as a "sociologue." But he is also make-believe. And his ultimate reference is private.[8] If indeed "Philosophy is to poetry as history is to fiction,"[9] we have to be assumed to be dealing with whole procedures, and though mixes are possible (Lucretius) for the former, they are arguably not really so for the latter, however unstable the evidence for historiography may be in a given case.

To see how this assimilation of observed small-grained action to the historiographic purpose works, we might take a fairly protracted look at the events around the succession from David to Solomon:

1. Now king David was old *and* stricken in years; and they covered him with clothes, but he gat no heat. 2. Wherefore his servants said unto him, Let there be sought for my lord the king a young virgin: and let her stand before the king, and let her cherish him, and let her lie in thy bosom, that my lord the king may get heat. 3. So they sought for a fair damsel throughout all the coasts of Israel, and found Abishag a Shunammite, and brought her to the king. 4. and the damsel *was* very fair, and cherished the king, and ministered to him: but the king knew her not. 5. Then Adonijah the son of Haggith exalted

himself, saying, I will be king: and he prepared him chariots and horsemen, and fifty men to run before him. 6. And his father had not displeased him at any time in saying, Why hast thou done so? and he conferred with Joab the son of Zeruiah, and with Abiathar the priest: and they following Adonijah helped *him*. 8. But Zadok the priest, and Benaiah the son of Jehoiada and Nathan the prophet, and Shimei, and Rei, and the mighty men which *belonged* to David were not with Adonijah. 9. And Adonijah slew sheep and oxen and fat cattle by the stone of Zoheleth, which *is* by En-rogel, and called all his brethren the king's sons, and all the men of Judah the king's servants: 10. But Nathan the prophet, and Benaiah, and the mighty men, and Solomon his brother, he called not. 11. Wherefore Nathan spake unto Bath-sheba the mother of Solomon, saying, Hast thou not heard that Adon-ijah the son of Haggith doth reign, and David our lord knoweth *it* not? 12. Now therefore come, let me, I pray thee, give thee counsel, that thou mayest save thine own life, and the life of thy son Solomon. 13. Go and get thee in unto king David, and say unto him, Didst not thou, my lord, O king, swear unto thine handmaid, saying, Assuredly Solomon thy son shall reign after me, and he shall sit upon my throne. why then doth Adonijah reign? 14. Behold, while thou yet talkest there with the king, I also will come in after thee, and confirm thy words.

(1 Kings 1–14, King James version)

There is a capital importance to the transition under inspection here, from the most exemplary and inclusive king, David, to the son who will go on to build the Temple and give the United Kingdom at once its most stable and its final reign. In keeping with that capital importance – and not just for "characterization" – an unusual amount of detail is foregrounded here, and an unusual amount of dialogue. The scene planned with entirely appropriate care between Bathsheba and Nathan is given in three dialogue forms: the preliminary rehearsal just quoted, the speech of Bathsheba (15–21) and the speech of Nathan (22–27). Left in the background is the question of whether David really did promise Bathsheba that Solomon would succeed him. And the modern interpreter cannot do other than leave it in the background; there is no warrant for presuming that Nathan has made it up, and it would not accord with the style of his political behavior (to call it "character" would unduly personalize it) for him to do so. Whether he has made it up or not, however, comes to the same thing – which justifies the compiler's leaving it in the background.

David has always shown himself to be flexible enough to make the kind of farsighted decision that shows him to be an exemplary king, and there is no evidence here that his physical feebleness is accompanied by intellectual befuddlement, even though his withdrawal because of physical, and sexual, impotence has brought him to the point where he is not immediately abreast of news, the connection between his condition and his uninformedness being underscored by the repetition of the word "know" (4, 11). Looking at his decisions here in the context of earlier congeries of events (35 and 36 in the tabulation), David had showed himself willing to let his eldest be killed for sexual revenge, by the son who was next in line, and to restore Absalom after the death of Amnon, through the agency of Joab. It looked as though Absalom resembled him enough; the pattern of 37–40 sufficiently resembles the pattern of 8–20, and even Absalom's assumption of David's concubines (39) follows the model of David's taking over Saul's wives. He had acceded, channeling his sorrow and his "ire" into mourning again, when Joab had eliminated Absalom by killing him against David's express command (2 Sam. 18:12–13).

Now the elaborate, overlapping approach of Bathsheba and Nathan has been laid before him.[10] David had shown himself astute and adaptable at questions of succession twice before, passing over the inertial inclination toward primogeniture when the occasion demanded, and demanded in such a way that the death of the eldest son followed. That is indeed what happens here to Adonijah after the death of David and what Bathsheba correctly implies would happen to Solomon if Adonijah remained the ruler. Her statement that they would be "counted offenders" (*hatham*) (1 Kings 21) might gather up a past reference to the status of her adultery and its consequences that Nathan himself was so eloquent about (nos. 33 and 34 in the tabulation), but its main reference is to a public condition of marked outlawry that would soon bring their deaths, as Nathan warns (verse 12). And Adonijah does die, though after David's death, for the lesser offence of requesting as a partner (with implications for power and status) the very Abishag who has just been the king's "minister" even while failing to arouse him.[11]

But even though Adonijah is, in fact, now the eldest son and has the further advantage of never having been asked, "Why hast thou done so?" he has already shown himself as less capable at managing these strong prospects than proper governance would require. He has overreached through the end-run of already assuming the kingship, as the perfective verb "rule as king" keeps asserting. It is not a question of David's "ire," which David has shown himself able to manage with remarkable impartiality on earlier occasions. He forgave much more to Absalom. Further, when David does make his judgment, he deems it the best policy to install Solomon forthwith, and with full publicity, at a location closer to Jerusalem but within earshot of Adonijah's coronation ceremony. We may deduce the wisdom of David's choice among his options from their effects, both immediate (they are successful) and far-reaching (Solomon is successful in his reign). Once David has chosen first to have the succession take place immediately rather than after his death (parallelling Samuel's anointing of David while Saul is still alive, no. 1 in the table), and once he has chosen that Bathsheba's son will be king rather than the eldest son (the promise here being no more than a factor foregrounded by the king for policy reasons rather than an absolute condition; he is capable of reneging on a promise), then he at once sets out a sequence of events that parallel the policy deliberations of Bathsheba and Nathan in their crafted efficacity:

> 32. And king David said, Call me Zadok the priest, and Nathan the prophet, and Benaiah the son of Jehoiada. And they came before the king. 33. The king also said unto them, Take with you the servants of your lord, and cause Solomon my son to ride upon mine own mule, and bring him down to Gihon: 34. And let Zadok the priest and Nathan the prophet anoint him there king over Israel: and blow ye with the trumpet, and say, God save king Solomon. 35. Then ye shall come up after him, that he may come and sit upon my throne; for he shall be king in my stead; and I have appointed him to be ruler over Israel and over Judah.

Thus does David show the undiminished potency of his ruler's capacity.

Adonijah has made the mistake of connecting regal potency with sexual.[12] The sentence in the quoted passage that records David's failure to consummate union with Abishag is followed at once by what Adonijah assumes, almost as in the animal kingdom, would be its natural consequence, the loss of rule. Adonijah draws the consequence by emphasizing the personal pronoun, as grammar does not require, by putting the verb into the future imperfective (*ani emlok*), "It is I who will rule." Then he sets about installing himself in all the accoutrements of royalty, calling to himself David's most long-standing and powerful adviser, Joab, whose immediate acquiescence testifies to the plausibility of Adonijah's assumption.

If one inverts the proposition, it certainly holds: Power implies sexuality in that world as to some extent in ours. David has only to send out the word, and to all the "coasts" or borders (*gevur*); all nubile women are presumed to be available to the king for a service that involves something less even than simple concubinage. This situation is so taken for granted that to assume a possible jealousy on the part of Bathsheba would go too far. Bathsheba herself had been summoned to the king's bed and ultimately to marriage with him in a complex of events that leaves little room for personal predilection or courtly delay, even though punishable sin is involved. Uriah dies in battle (no. 33 in the table) as Nabal had died from shock over Abigail's behavior with David while he was still on the run but powerful enough to command services that Nabal withholds but Abigail proffers, leading David astutely to count her a fitly enterprising mate for himself (no. 15). Michal's "love" or "desire" (*ahav*, 1 Sam. 18:20) for David derives from the power that this princess may exercise over a newcomer to her father's court, and her immediate function (no. 7) is to serve as a key aid in David's escape. In his prolonged absence neither she nor her father has any compunction at matching her to another while David is still alive (no. 16), just as David has none at taking advantage of his polygamous prerogatives and marrying both Abigail and Ahinoam. The polygamous prerogative, indeed, takes various forms under various predilections. It is another aspect of the sexual-power situation that ultimately brings about the fall of the United Kingdom through Solomon's increasedly broad, though less dynamically modified, sexual activity. Personal predilection, family destiny, and situational definition of what it means here to be a ruler, interplay, and modify their interplay, in the sexual realm as elsewhere. In the succession scene here, sexuality is present only in Abishag's minimalized attention (though its political force is underscored) and as an aspect of enforceable memory; Bathsheba retains a power over David that Michal lost when she rebuked him for dancing before the ark (no. 27).

This text always shows the personal in a public dimension, and the personal always appears in circumstances of negotiation. To summon Bathsheba derives from David's royal prerogative, and once she has become pregnant, Joab and Nathan are involved. Amnon's refusal to negotiate for the hand of Tamar instead of to rape her reflects his situation (he is not king) as well as his character (he is arrogant in preemptively presuming on the royal prerogative he might exercise in the future). Even afterward he might have managed if he had not "hated" her (no. 35) but had instead carried through the negotiations she had originally pleaded for at the very moment when he showed sexual desire (incest not being a problem because marriage with half sisters was permitted, as Tamar's assumption shows). Often, as Fokkelman analyzes throughout, these personal-diplomatic situations occur in triadic patterns, and the small size of the group, the minimal size for political activity, is perfectly consonant with the small size of this kingdom. To show groups of three in dialogue, as in the passages quoted above, indicates not the fictionalization of these episodes but the effective angling of relations when the number of participants is moderately small.

There is a historiographic gain in the text's tendency toward schematizing. The moment appears as a model that is reduced to its power essentials, and the schematization lends itself to the constant reticulation of analogies that the repetitions noted by Alter also flesh out. The time process carries along the momentary schema, powerfully modifying it while endowing it with its utility as an ever-changing template for public behavior – ever-changing because the will of God can swerve at any time, as it may be assumed to have swerved away from Joab here. There is no reason on the face of it why Joab should have lost his balance to assess the plausible forces, with a small but capital mistake, throwing his lot in with the wrong side.

As Fokkelman also abundantly shows, the schematization enlists the smallest details of language. It tends to be reflected in a patterning of the syntax and in verbal repetitions on the smallest scale – tendencies fortified by the relatively small total vocabulary of biblical Hebrew. But at the same time the sentences move forward in their inexorable, and highly original, vision of the way time works itself out.

There is a feature of this text that Auerbach calls "background," Alter, "reticence," and Fokkelman, "abstruseness" (354), the powerfully managed foreshortenings and silences of the compiler. These effectually direct us to consider the actual data presented, which are sometimes quite detailed, as severally and together representing strongly charged peaks of public action. Seen thus in what it excludes, the text's act of selection throws attention markedly on what is said; seen for its inclusions, it implicitly declares the importance of a given detail.[13] Positively and negatively the very silences thus reinforce the historiographic set of these narratives.

The silences in this withholding of comment, actual or implied, on fore-shortenings and changes of tempo, permit a sort of double presentation. In the ongoing narrative an evenness of pacing governs the actual sequence of sentences. But the changes of role, tempo, and topic-emphasis stand out against this very evenness, throwing into relief the interactive dynamics among God, people, and leader. Each of these – God, people, and leader – is shown to act as a vector in response to the other two. The situation at a moment of time involves all three, and even the stability of a Solomon, in the context of constant analogy, has the effect of binding the forces, of holding God at the benevolent distance of being worshiped by the new Temple and the people in their busy, stable places within this quasi-bureaucratic regime.

A whole developmental picture can be built up, as Max Weber has done, of the social, and over time the historical, process that has here been de-scribed.[14] Weber constructs his act of synchronic historiography very much in the style, and under the presentational assumption, of Burckhardt and de Tocqueville (and we should not allow the modern classification "soci-ology" to obscure this); and he does so relying preponderantly on the Bible itself. In the light of the compiler's presentation, the kings are chosen and operate with the different emphases that Weber derives from the shepherd milieu for David and the peasant milieu for Saul, a derivation that gives an army of freebooters to the more nomadically oriented leader and a bureau-cratic army to the more stably established one. The replication between God and the people of the covenant that can be derived to obtain among them, the leagued society (*Eidgenossenschaft*), persists in Weber's presenta-tion, while undergoing changes. Indeed, Weber's treatise can exist both as historiography and as a hermeneutics of the society in the Bible because the Bible itself already incorporates a comparable sense of the progressions it narrates. To these progressions we may also adapt the "pure" types of Weberian authority, a "legal" authority based on edict, a "traditional" authority based on belief in past organization, and a "charismatic" authority based on emotional appeal.[15] Within what Weber describes as this covenantal society, of course, these types are "ideal-types" that do not appear in pure form. Here the very subjection of the leaders to the particular mix of God's favor will show the change. Until the later kings of Judah, there is a component of legalism in the choice of king that overrides primogeniture, but a component of traditionalism that makes primogeniture a factor, and at the same time there is a component of charisma that holds even for Saul, but especially for David, and somewhat less, or differently, for the more institutionalized and traditional Solomon. The social classes are all there, too, retrievable not by painful statistical analysis and the sifting of data, but in plain statements of the text itself. Among leaders, if kings, priests, and prophets may in a pure typology never actually adhere to the Weberian "ideal-types," their very changes of mix among the types stand out as defining the dynamic progression to which they are shown as subjected. Samuel, though not a king, has something like the constituted authority of one, while being a priest. Even Saul is also a prophet, while David, for all his charisma, seems not to be called one here. Charisma gradually leaves rulers, and also priests, removing wholly to prophets by the time of Elijah and Elisha. These prophets often show traces of the underclass, but since they are selected more or less out of the blue, without reference to prior affiliation or even virtue, they may also come from well-established strata, and even from the priesthood, as do both Jeremiah and Ezekiel.

Within the canon of the entire Old Testament the dynamics of power gradually seep out of the account, to provide the flat record of chronicle. And as this happens, a newer category takes over, overlapping in time with historiography. The section of prophecy has begun, and the prophets cease to be mere ecstatics like the Saul who is called a prophet but whose utterances are not even reported, or advisers like Nathan, or miracle-workers like Elijah and Elisha. Instead the dynamics of force have gone wholly inward. It has wholly abandoned the instituted authority of kings and priests, unless one of their number is recruited by God to become the single voice of the whole people – a subtypological variation of the roles of Abraham and Moses. This investment in the single voice is itself a historical phase, a large one, and the shift into the mode of prophecy, as the canon was organized, has itself a historiographic implication.

The contradictory dynamics of time may be taken to be schematized in the Hebrew verb system, as coordinated in this text, where perfective and imperfective aspectualize action and may change places under the set rule of the "vav consecutive." The remote past contains both threat and promise: the convenant and installation in the Holy Land on the one hand, and on the other hand the characterization of YHWH as jealous and exacting, while at the same time long-suffering. In this light the future is perpetually imperiled, and the present is caught up in a dynamics that involves both the righteousness (*tsedek*) of the ruler and his wisdom (*chokmah*) – if we may apply to the text itself these terms that recur in the Prophets. But the vocabulary is generally a recursive one, small enough to make any string of verses the sort of repetition-with-variation that sorts well with a historiographic presentation of events bearing the dual character of uniqueness and generality. In this vocabulary linearity of presentation and an implied assertion of both truth and factuality go hand in hand. The time here has been unfolded so as to show the perpetually pregnant time of the historiographer as well as the God-centered time of this people in its particular ethnological setting.

9

THE NEW TESTAMENT IN ITS
HISTORIOGRAPHIC DIMENSION

EVERY SECTION OF THE NEW TESTAMENT sets out
its presentation so that it is all sited in history and dependent on a
historical sequence. The establishment of the authority for a new
church and its doctrines is communicated through, and made dependent
upon, events in historical sequence that have been singled out and organized.
Thus the sense and senses of the New Testament are derived from a temporal
sequence of public import; they satisfy a definition of history.

In this the New Testament differs from the *Ecclesiastical History* of Eusebius or Augustine's *City of God*. In these, and other such histories, the
religious sense is not derived from the events. Rather, the religious sense
is a given, and the temporal sequences are so many illustrations or test cases
within that given. In such works as *The City of God*, the doctrine leaves no
room for a sense to accrue from the narrative, whereas in the New Testament a capital sense accrues, first from the exemplary narrated acts of
Christ's life from Nativity to Empty Tomb (Mark, taken as ending at 16:8)
or else from John the Baptist to Jesus' final appearances and Ascension.
Then, based on this set of epochal events, a sense continues to accrue in
the narrative of telling incidents from the life of the early church (Acts).

It would be a mistake, then, to confuse the historiographic acts of those
who wrote, and then of those who gradually compiled, the parts (the books)
of the New Testament with those later historians who take the Christian
revelation as a given and try to trace its presence, or a relation to its presence,
in every event. The New Testament writers did not begin with applying
these prior assumptions to history. Rather, they wished to ascertain the
presence of revelatory material within its historical context. And if the
Christian revelation was of capital importance, that importance was public
– in their view, universal. Consequently it was historical, even though
centered on one man and the doctrines he promulgated. It differs from
"aretology" – the tale of a supernatural wonder-worker – by its stated,
constant bearing on historical developments. This biographical centering,

the presence of miracles and other untestable events, and the heavy doctrinal emphasis, all tend to obscure the preponderant historical focus of the New Testament, which is at the same time so obvious as to be taken quietly for granted.[1] A chief component of the circumstances of that life in its context was the doctrines they implied or stated with relation to a complex, existing body of doctrine, the Old Testament in the interpretation of the time, as well as with relation to the history of Israel. All this the New Testament did, as millennia of commentary have shown, with considerable complexity.

Moreover, as the canon of the New Testament developed, several documents were excluded. These materials were tested, it would seem, for doctrinal soundness, but also for historical purchase on the crucial events. The final result, the New Testament as we have it, provides four very different, converging angles, in the four Gospels, on those events.

The three kinds of narrative in the New Testament are each of them differently oriented to temporal sequence: the Gospels, the book of Acts, and Revelation. The fourth kind of discourse to be found there, the Epistles, is also grounded into temporal sequence by its inclusion in the New Testament. In that context the Epistles become an extension to Acts, documents in the early history of the Church. Indeed, a letter is quoted in Acts (23:26–30). So many of the Epistles are defined by their immediate circumstances of sender and recipient that, once again, those that are not so defined must still be seen as sited in a comparable context.

The overlapping and mutually supplementary Gospels give the biographical details of Jesus' life, those that bear on what his life and his statements reveal. Hence, for example, there is no need for any evidence between the events around the Nativity and the Dispute in the Temple. The letters of Paul expound doctrine in the form of historically sited, dialogic communication – which, again, implicitly connects them to what is recounted in Acts, where a fair prominence is given to Paul's role. The Apocalypse, the fourth section, is not historiographic in a strict sense, though it is more specific as to sequence and singularity of event than are comparable prophecies in the Old Testament, which it heavily interweaves, as Austin Farrer has shown.[2] It communicates its eschatological expansions as a quasi-historical sequence, a sort of history of the future.

Of the Gospels, Luke, the longest of the Synoptics, is also the most detailed. But it is John, placed last by the compilers, the fourth of the four Gospels, who ends by stating the infinity of events from which he has selected, "And there are also many other things which Jesus did, the which, if they should be written every one (*kath'hen*, "one by one"), I suppose that even the world itself could not contain the books that should be written" (21:25). This places the historian's standard selective principle in a terminal, rather than an initial, position. It makes the act of its own selection a final reflection on the series it has presented, reorienting the series both toward actual happenings and to the sense that there is a meaning giving one thrust to all the details brought together, as tested implicitly by the less commanding ones that have been omitted in infinitely greater number.

In narrative history, however it may be summarized, a meaning always lurks under the story, a meaning that resists summary and abstract transpositions. An analogue for such a situation in these narratives of the Kerugma or "proclamation" is Jesus' double adduction of concealed meaning, and of open meaning, to the parables in the Kerugma itself. This aspectualization of the hidden against the open reflects, and itself helps to define, the aspectualization generally implied by the four different kinds of text in the New Testament, and the four complexly overlapping narratives in one of the kinds, the Gospels. The aspectualization, still more dynamic than that in the partial repetitions of Old Testament historical narrative, presses with special force on the question of how the parables are to be taken:

> And he taught them many things by parables, and said unto them in his doctrine (*didache*, "teaching").[3]
> . . . and when he was alone (*kata monas*), they that were about him with the twelve asked of him the parable (*parabolas*, "parables"). And he said unto them, Unto you it is given to know the mystery of the kingdom of God: but unto them that are without, all *these* things are done in parables: "That (*hina*) seeing they may see and not perceive, And hearing they may hear, and not understand; lest at any time they should be converted and *their* sins should be forgiven them." . . . But without a parable spake he not unto them: and when they were alone (*kat' idian*, "in private"), he expounded (*epeluen*, "explained," "untied") all things to his disciples.
>
> (Mark 4:2; 10–12; 34)

A crucial part of the historical narrative in the Gospels consists of Jesus' pronouncements, long and short. If, as the form-theorists maintain, the writer-compiler, Mark in this instance, drew on prior collections called something like "The Sayings of Jesus" as well as on prior narrative, then his conflation of them into the narrated sequence of a life would itself constitute a new form. And the parable itself is also a saying in a form that is hard to parallel in allegorical tales before the New Testament – so that doubly, here, the Gospel would be offering new wine in new bottles (Mark 2:22; Matt. 9:17). Even the echoes of the tone and message of the prophets are encapsulated by Jesus in more disjunct, more specifically oriented utterances, in more exact circumstances, and with the transcendent message declared as not just for a given century or generation, within the utterance, but for all time.[4]

Jesus immediately offers an interpretation of his parables, often, as though not only to enlist the rabbinical form *"midrash"* but also to aspectualize the puzzling situational caveat of the passage quoted above, itself permuted by the endorsing quotation from Isaiah (6:9–10). What exactly is Isaiah meant to endorse? Speculation on Mark's phrasing of this particular passage becomes exceedingly intricate, as Frank Kermode has lucidly summarized it.[5] The moment of this quotation aspectualizes it by referring it to another moment, that of Isaiah, which is itself comprised into the permanence of the canonical New Testament text. (This, interestingly, as Taylor points out,[6] follows the Targum version rather than the Septuagint or the Masoretic text of Isaiah – as though to bring Isaiah further into congruence with the voice of Mark's Greek.) "In order that" (*hina*) can be taken as "because"; and Matthew's version gives another word here, *"hoti,"* which tends more toward "because." And there are still finer shadings that Kermode notes.

The parable of the sower, it has been remarked, is a parable about parables. Its very form posits a certain closedness and circularity.[7] But unlike Kafka's parable about parables, it concentrates on the social effects of the "seed." A seed by definition is something whose function is not perceptible in itself but only in what happens to it, on a double time-line, one line of its generic potential for realization if it grows, and another line that traces "historically" the fate of an individual seed, or of groups of individuals, as in the parable. In an ideal circumstance the possible and the actual time-lines converge, as in the parable's fourth case, "And some fell on good ground, and did yield fruit that sprang up and increased, and brought forth, some thirty, and some sixty, and some a hundred" (8). "And these are they which are sown on good ground; such as hear the word, and receive *it*, and bring forth fruit, some thirtyfold, some sixty, and some a hundred" (20). The explanation links the seed with "the word" (*logos*, eight times in 4:14–20). "The word," too, is in no way modified but simply defined in terms of its effects on groups of auditors who are variously affected by the counteragency of Satan (referred to in 4:15).

Behold, there went out a sower to sow: And it came to pass, as he sowed, some fell by the wayside, and the fowls of the air came and devoured it up. And some fell on stony ground, where it had not much earth; and immediately it sprang up, because it had no depth of earth: But when the sun was up, it was scorched; and because it had no root, it withered away. And some fell among thorns, and the thorns grew up, and choked it, and it yielded no fruit. And other fell on good ground, and did yield fruit that sprang up and increased, and brought forth, some thirty, and some sixty, and some a hundred.

(4:3–8)

The explanation is interrupted by the caveat, and it is immediately preceded by the quotation from Isaiah, as though to emphasize the special access to meaning that is accorded this small group of auditors.

The somewhat different phrasings of these statements about constraints on the audience of Jesus' teaching as indicated by the form of the parables, serve to aspectualize not just the parables but the Gospels themselves as they focus toward revelatory meaning. Further aspectualized, too, is the presence of this particular explanation in the overall sequence selected by each of the Synoptics – a situation that bears not just on this explanation but on all the sequenced data of the presentation in each.

In Mark, as just excerpted, this explanation comes right after Jesus has chosen the disciples and acted to manage both the crowds around him and his family. It comes not quite a third of the way through the Gospel, and two parables are given at this point. In Matthew (13:1–52) it comes long after the Sermon on the Mount (5:1–7:27), and other statements follow on the choosing of the disciples before the parables are taken up. Matthew gives five parables here (13:18–34), amplifying them by three more parable-like similitudes (13:44–47). All this comes almost halfway through Matthew's narrative. Luke, at the parallel point, gives only one parable, that of the sower (8:3–18), after episodes involving women (7:36–8.3), about a third of the way through his narrative.

The passage in Mark indicates a relation between the utterances and those who are ready to hear them – the very subject of the preceding parable, which itself differently divides the auditors into four classes, rather than into those with whom Jesus is alone and the multitudes of those who are here said to be kept away by parable. There is a further, finer distinction made between those in a smaller group with him and the disciples (*kata monas*) and the still smaller group of the disciples by themselves to whom he gives explanations "privately" (*kath' idian*).

What an event-moment this is! "That seeing they may see and not perceive, And hearing they may hear, and not understand; lest at any time they should be converted and *their* sins should be forgiven them." First of all, this moment is puzzlingly hard. Taken just by themselves, its seemingly repellent conclusions cannot be generalized without undercutting the Christian message. Yet this moment is diplomatically and historically situated; it is a moment of confidentiality. In that light the label "closed" cannot be put on the parables in an absolute way – any more than the statement "the poor you have with you always" (Mark 14:7; Matt. 26:11; John 12:8) can be taken, systematically rather than historically, to modify the favorable destinies of the poor and those like them that are predicted in the Sermon on the Mount. If these disciples are to go forth and preach the gospel to the four corners of the earth – to disseminate the parables along with other sayings – to do so in a form deliberately framed to keep their meaning from auditors would be counterproductive. Jesus's own missions constitute such a "teaching," to use the very term with which this section has begun. And in what I have quoted above, the distinction between "parable" and "teaching," as part to whole, of verse 2, could be taken to contradict verse 34, "Without a parable spake he not unto them."

In a sense we make the best sense of this last statement, taken by itself, if we read it as itself a sort of parable, especially since the Gospels themselves plainly provide other public teachings than parables. Indeed, the contradiction between the situational openness of Jesus' teaching and the aspectual closedness of parable is even more pronounced in the "candlestick" parable (or metaphor). And this parable is given in the very verses that come between the first statement of closedness that I quote and the second: "Is a candle brought forth to be put under a bushel, or under a bed? And not be set on a candlestick? For there is nothing hid, which shall not be manifested; neither was any thing kept secret, but that it should come abroad. If any man have ears to hear, let him hear" (Mark 4:21–24). The candlestick exemplum and the statements about closedness cannot be reconciled, and they cannot be attributed to some flagrant and immediate incoherence. "If any man have ears to hear, let him hear," however, does rephrase the closedness of the parables in the somewhat different terms of a conditional accessibility. These insoluble difficulties are further modified if they are, as they should be, referred to the expansiveness of implication in this historical narrative, something that the very mode of history is gauged to express. (Is Nicias a good or a bad man in Thucydides? He is preeminently virtuous, but events prove him disastrously ineffective at both politics and military command, the two activities most important to Thucydides.)

In Matthew's version the closedness explanation is amplified and validated by a quotation from Psalms (78:2): "Without a parable spake he not unto them: That it might be fulfilled which was spoken by the prophet, saying, 'I will open my mouth in parables; I will utter things which have been kept secret from the foundation of the world' " (*kekrummena apo kataboles* – three words for the last twelve of the English; Matt. 13:34–35). This links Jesus' action of speaking not just with a prudential decision in a threatened situation, and not just with a judgment on the idle auditors in the large crowds, though these are historical aspects of his statement in context. The quotation from Psalms governs Jesus' statement by matching it to its Old Testament type, making it in turn the fulfillment of a prediction – and an act of statement – by that prophet-king who was then understood to be the author of Psalms, his forebear David.

This verse of the Psalm itself is set into "antithetical parallelism," since the first half is open and the second half mentions secrecy; but it is also in identical parallelism, since the basic statement here repeated is "open/utter." So the quotation does not just match the antithesis between the closedness of parable and the openness of letting a light shine forth to the world. Like the Gospels themselves, the quotation emphasizes openness so that its forward-looking declaration may be said to supplement, as well as to contradict, the "closedness" side of the statement it is immediately glossing, "without a parable spake he not unto them." Furthermore, as is highlighted in René Girard's use of this quotation for the title of a book largely about the Bible,[8] the quotation from Psalms concludes in a way that looks beyond the connection between David and Jesus, and looks also beyond the specific literary form of parable, to declare that the message, and the actions, here recounted are more revelatory than anything since Creation: they are "things which have been kept secret from the foundation of the world."

As in other history, then, there is an interdefinition among the events, including these important speech-events, which cannot be reduced to a set of propositions. An individual utterance (*rhema*) must be comprised within the overall interactive sense of the utterances (*logos*), but no materials for a systematic presentation are offered. It opens out in all directions. Indeed, *logos*, which here may always be taken to comprise its full range of Greek senses, is often used grammatically in an almost pronominal fashion that puts deep complexities on a par with the most casual usage. The aspects of simplicity and complexity for *logos* provide linguistic parallel to the historian's view of how Jesus' words and acts are to be taken. *Logos* not infrequently comes in sentences with the verb *legein*, "to speak," just, as it were, to indicate minimally what has been spoken – which, in the mouth of Jesus, is here given capital importance. *Logos* also, in John especially, becomes another name for Jesus himself in his presence, as well as for the utterances that unfold it. Here the Greek term *logos* is stretched beyond its own repertoire of intricate senses to take on a new sense; it stands for, and includes, a living human being who is the embodiment of the Word. "The Word was made flesh" (John 1:11).

All of Jesus' sayings are further aspectualized if they are set against what they lead to – and have causal links with – the Passion. As the text of Mark approaches that event, a further aspectualization takes place in his statements, since he begins to speak openly about the Passion itself, a new topic, and a new modality of extreme openness, as well as of explicit historical relevance, for his statements: "And he spake that saying openly" ("*kai parrhesia ton logon elalei*"; also "in freedom of speech he poured forth the logos," Mark 8:32). The Passion, through the deep legendary cast to its moments of historical siting,[9] becomes a giant, more intense, wordless parable, illuminated and foreshadowed by the "if it die" in the parable of the seed (John 12:23–26). It is also implied in the parable of the mustard seed (Matt. 13:31–32; Mark 4:30–32; Luke 13:18–19), and at points of several others, if not in all. At the earlier point of discussing the parables there is a moment of intimacy, "alone," when Jesus in effect consoles the few around him with their special access to his message. And then, almost immediately, there is the moment of emphasizing proclamation, which the candlestick metaphor endorses. The final statement in this small sequence may be said to embrace both openness and closedness: "And with many such parables spake he the word unto them, as they were able to hear *it*. But without a parable spake he not unto them: and when they were alone, he expounded all things to his disciples" (4:33–34). This, indeed, sees his larger audience in terms of the two parables given here about the sowers, while it reemphasizes the special access which the disciples' commitment gave them.

2

The whole text of Mark, and then of all the Gospels, taken in its represented sequence amplifies and dimensionalizes the historiographic thrust of its narrative.

Such aspectualization pervades the narratives individually and as they supplement one another. The view of "the kingdom of God," the various Christologies as they may derive from selection, emphasis, and phrasing,[10] come through in a constant ongoing dynamism of refocusing interadjustments. These transcend the dynamic of analogies in the accounts of Old Testament kings, who themselves are set as a template of multiple typological overlays upon these representations of Jesus. The Passion narrative itself comprises types and subtypes of matching Christ to set story figures and to Old Testament forms as it comes to culmination in each of the four Gospels.[11] The Passion engages all four in a converging parallelism (as a glance at any "Harmony of the Gospels" graphically shows). It functions as a full ongoing revelation, an intense act in which words have shrunk to the laconic "Last Words of Jesus." It is a full-dress induction of large-scale history into a picture which is drawn to modify that history crucially. It, too, is aspectualized: It is at once the fulfillment and the suppression of Jesus' teaching, transcended, the way the text presents it, by a Resurrection.

Seen in its historiographic dimension, then, the Passion narrative, too, comprises a grand aspectualization. Yet only by singling out that most important time as the only time for these narratives – only by overlooking various aspectualizations in their historiographic inclusiveness, from the genealogies in Matthew and Luke through Jesus' preaching, action, and miracle-working up to the Passion through each of the Gospels – could one assent to Martin Kähler's characterization that they are "passion stories with extended introductions"[12] They are, to be sure, weighted toward that end, but there is no basis for downplaying the sequences preceding it. In each of the Gospels the unique and the typical are brought into convergence, and the presence of miracles, which are unique for Christ but also typical of him, illustrate that convergence, in addition to providing both a positive stimulant and a negative irritant to the public context in which he is always acting and speaking. Even his sacrifice has both a negative and a positive aspect, since, as it is traditionally taken, it points up the apocalyptic negation toward which society may tend. As the writings of René Girard have shown, however, the actions, the doctrines, and the circumstances of Christ's Passion not only resume prior sacrifice patterns, which are so deep as to define any society. As the Gospels present it, his sacrifice also has the positive effect of redefining itself away from that pattern, uniquely, in a way that they are occupied in narrating. There, too, a typicality and a uniqueness are manifested, and one could extend Girard's comments by allowing both positive and negative functions to both the typicality and the uniqueness.[13]

So loaded with significance is all the binary coding that can be set into the Passion narrative.[14] But those codings have the limitation, if they are made exclusive, that they tend to misdefine that constant culiminating process by spatializing it into oppositions, when it is mainly given a historical and temporal sequence so as to demonstrate its transcendences. The capital force of the one sequence, comprising words, acts, and reactions, overarches all the binary codings that may be derived from the text. The process also overarches all the "prior" societal-mythical codings of Solar Myth, Hero, Suffering Servant, Overthrown King, and so on, both those of universal anthropological recurrence and those more specifically coded into the social norms of Hebrew society.[15] Christ's final suffering itself, the Passion narrative, only enters the text as a new prediction, as a sudden reversal, and as an enacted demonstration – as a historical outcome rather than as a closed, logical development of what precedes it.

In the historical thrust of the Gospels, the types and subtypes of figure are not superseded; but neither are they primary. At the same time the action is seen by the writers as too intense, too capital, and too millennial, for them to have access to the small touches of "personal" observation, to the "fictional" elements that do appear in the historical parts of the Old Testament, even though the momentary detail, particularly in the Passion narratives, is often much fuller than that in the Old Testament. Given the different slants of each evangelist, the least full, Mark, may have details that are not offered by the others. And, given the historiographic cast to the narrative, all details need not be accounted for, and an identity, that of Mark himself or another person, need not be assigned to someone who appears only once; the evangelist may use anonymity, or not foreground a naming, just as any other historian may do. The "boy in the linen cloth" of Mark 14:51–52 is given only the identity of his function. Puzzling over that identity further, in the face of no evidence, neither makes the boy mysterious nor particularly illustrates a hermeneutic relativism. He is not *the* young man but "a certain young man" or "some young man" (*neaniskos tis*), his anonymity stressed by the text. Moreover, the function of the young man, as it comes in context, once again cannot activate just the highlighting of reality by contrasted superfluous detail that Roland Barthes has called "the effect of the real." Indeed, in any history, while the "uncoded" detail casts an air of verification upon the coded remainder, the other details are not then inert.

Now this particular detail of the young man, taken in sequence as it comes between the arrest of Jesus and his arraignment before the high priest, does seem initially superfluous as it suddenly fills out a corner of the picture: "And there followed him a certain young man, having a linen cloth cast about *his* naked *body*; and the young men laid hold on him: And he left the linen cloth and fled from them naked." Taken, however, not in sequence, but in the connection of its vocabulary with other moments of the text, this moment, too, exhibits typological congruences and recurrences of image, as Austin Farrer points out: "... the linen winding sheet, the boy in linen, and the boy in a white robe. There is surely some symbolic motif here." And, weaving a plausible set of symbolic interpretations based on image and phrasing, he concludes: "Those who fled from Gethsemane lost their honour; Joseph vainly sought to spread human honour upon the crucified; the angel in the tomb revealed the unspotted honour of heaven. The three texts about the boy in the garden, Joseph's shrouding of Jesus, and the boy in the tomb, are held together by verbal echoes."[16] The sequenced "effect of the real" and the coordinated, coded symbols keep the intensity of the narrative high while combining to further its progression in the simple declarative sentences of its even presentation.

John, who is less full than Luke, at the same time enunciates not only the principle of severe selection at the end of his Gospel, as quoted above; at the beginning he asserts the positive principle of omnirelevance. This setting of principles before the facts he licenses by attributing it to any facts whatever, seen in the light of the Word: "Without him was not anything made that was made" (John 1:4). The term John uses is one that would accord as well or even better with the historical process than with any other kind of verbal organization: *egeneto*, "came about" or "came into being." "Apart from him there came into being no one thing that came into being."

The style of the Gospels also has the "flat" unitary surface of historical narrative, which it maintains even when it is delivering its tremendous kernels of doctrine or intense moments of crucial action. And this is so even in the conflations of other discourse that the "form critics" have traced into them. Indeed, this underlying compositional intricacy makes the easy, nearly colloquial flow of the narrative the more remarkable – even if one does not go so far as Klaus Berger, who distinguishes close to a hundred kinds of discourse that are harnessed or conflated in the New Testament.[17] This historical discourse is always public, and it may be said to conform to the tendency in history writing to measure relative successes and failures.

It does so by offering an ultimate failure that, seen in its true historical perspective, is a paramount success, significantly rooted in the types and predictions of the people among whom it occurs. "The stone which the builders rejected, The same is become the head of the corner" (Luke 20:17, quoting Psalm 118:22).

A by-product of the condemnation of Jesus by the unwilling Pilate – in an interlude worthy of a later diplomatic historian – is the new friendship that Pilate strikes up with the willing Herod (Luke 10:20). The history of Israel, the Sanhedrin, the local tetrarchy, the deep types of Near Eastern collective behavior, and the Roman Empire, are all measured by this "king" and in the light of his proximate future kingdom. The whole sequence of duplicitous action between Herod and the Magi, leading to the Massacre of the Innocents, is based on the fact that Jesus is a new king. At this point of the text, from Matthew 2:1 to 3:3., there are six occurrences of forms of "king" (*basileus*), "kingdom" (*basileia*), and "rule" (*basileuo*).

At one point in Luke (3:1) there is given the whole array of the names of those exercising constituted power – Tiberius, Herod, Philip, Pilate, Lysanias, Annas, and Caiaphas. And all the various constituted powers come into play to complicate the action, most predominantly as the forces gather to have Christ crucified. The disciples dispute about the relative power each will have after the death of Jesus (Luke 22:25–26). Even the humble social types of the Sermon on the Mount, "the poor, "those that mourn," and so on, are defined not only as private types, but often by the public consolation they are declared to accrue. The Beatitudes tend toward political deductions. They extend the principle behind Christ's suffering into the societal domain, insofar as they predict an evolution of public satisfaction, out of seemingly contradictory traits, for whole groups of people defined by those traits. But the relation between the political and the psychological, or private and public, or outer and inner, is defined by Jesus' answer to the Pharisees' question about when this "kingdom of God" shall come; to which he replies – indirectly, it may be noted, since no time is given – "The kingdom of God is within you" (Luke 20–21). The dynamic of this dialogue has certain parallels to the permutation of common terms with deep misunderstanding in the speeches of Thucydides as they, too, question an immediate future in terms of sovereignty.

Power, indeed, *dunamis*, is a term often used in the Gospels, and not infrequently with a political cast or dimension, though as always it has a range of senses, suggesting the power of God in history and elsewhere – demonic power, healing power, the very fact of Christ (Luke 1:17; 1:35), Christ's prophetic power, the specific deeds of Christ (Matt. 11:2–5; 13:58), the power of the disciples (Luke 24:28–29), the power of the community in relation to the power of God in history (Matt. 22:29).[18] Another term for power is *exousia* (also "authority"). Jesus is said to have given the disciples both *"dunamis"* and *"exousia"* (Luke 9.1). The centurion who claims to be unworthy because he is under authority (*exousia*) and has others under him is singled out as having a greater faith than any in Israel (Matt. 8:5–11). This *dunamis* or *exousia* ties in with a God-energized history, as in the Old Testament accounts of kings and prophets, but even more so when it intensively pours through, and momentarily overturns, one man who demonstrates that he is a super-prophet and is gradually realized as a super-king. This realization had not become incorporated in a large public life at the time of the writing, of course, and that situation makes the New Testament all the more an interpretation of factors in history. It has only its case to plead, and at that time not much other than narrowly regional results.

As befitting the energies of God at work in the events – itself *the* Old Testament historical format – the structure of each whole Gospel narrative, while closed with respect to the crucifixion, is open with respect both to the randomness of Christ's ministries and to the kinds of action it recounts. Miracles frame the dicta about parables; they are communications on still another plane and offer another kind of causal mystery. The healing miracles, indeed, while hardly the normal grist of historical narrative, have a triple historical force in the Gospels: They constitute an event with all the actions and reactions that surround them; they are meant to serve as a systematic, cumulative proof of Jesus' power; and they have an allegorical dimension when the blind are made to see, the lame to walk, and the possessed to be liberated.

Jesus at every point is in a tense, and political, relation to the official Judaic tradition that he is claiming to interpret correctly as well as to fulfill and transform. And matching the dynamic of his relation with those powers is the multiplicity of ways that he and his Gospel-historians call the Old Testament into play. This use of the Old Testament by the New, especially in the Gospels, is far more dynamic than the authoritative quotations from the Bible in ecclesiastical historians, Saint Augustine and others – or for that matter even the occasional passing references in the Old Testament to earlier points of the text. First of all there may be noted the very general use, always present to some degree in every adduction of the Old Testament by the Gospels, as when Luke gives John the Baptist a prediction that nests another prediction: "And all flesh shall see the Salvation of God" (Luke 3:6, quoting Isa. 40:5). This comprises every aspect of Christ's existence, and the entirety of humankind at what in Isaiah is some unspecified future time that Luke has John the Baptist bring suddenly closer. Distinct from this kind of quotation, since it is oriented toward rule and put in the mouth of an angel, is the assimilation of Jesus at the Annunciation both to the throne of David and to rule over all the Israelites: "The Lord God shall give unto him the throne of his father David: And he shall reign over the house of Jacob for ever; and of his kingdom there shall be no end" (Luke 1:32–33).

When Jesus himself adduces the story of Jonah and singles it out as the sign under which he works (Matt. 12:39–41; Luke 11:21–30), the typological mystery is by no means simple, and certainly no clearer than the parable. Jonah, the space of Nineveh (and implicitly that of the opposite end of the Mediterranean which he seeks out), and the time of his generation are all named. "The queen of the south" and her approach to Solomon, in an earlier generation, are further paralleled to that of Jonah – and to the time of the "greater" that Jesus here declares himself to be.

A legal use of the Old Testament comes into the picture, often, as in Luke 24:27;44, where the law of Moses is cited. Since it is cited as being fulfilled, the usage here conflates with the commonest type, the historical moment of the Gospel story that "fulfills" an Old Testament prophecy – though in this instance the "law" merges with "the prophets." The Old Testament gets an actual defensive, nearly magical use, when Jesus quotes it as a weapon against the devil (Matt. 4:2) – in an adaptation of a sort of Talmudic dispute, since the devil himself offers quotations in counterargument. Sometimes the references are very simple, as in the adduction of the Old Testament "God of Abraham, Isaac, and Jacob" at Luke 20:38. The "Suffering Servant" (Luke 17:20) is a general type included in the Old Testament and brought forward to bring the Passion once again into the perspective of the Prophets. The blood of Abel (Luke 11:51) is a historical precedent, while the story of Lot (Luke 17:29–31) is a historical warning, a cautionary tale built into the ongoing narrative. References to "the law and the prophets" – twice, for example, in the Sermon on the Mount – apply the combined constituents of the entire Old Testament not mainly to a moment of action but to the promulgation of a range of new doctrines. The reference makes the historical connection and emphasizes that Jesus claims to have come "not to destroy but to fulfill" both the law and the prophets. Each of these moments of citation is typologically charged in various dynamic ways, while at the same time it is subsumed into the ongoing narrative. The difference between the Old Testament context and its narrative adaptation in the Gospels is particularly marked for those quotations from Psalms that are echoed without explicit designation by the evangelist. The Psalm context of collective prayer becomes sharply individualized, typified, and subsumed across time, when excerpted at the significant moment and uttered by Jesus.

Time designations become more frequent as the narrative approaches the Passion, but the events are often left, as in the Old Testament, without a specific time reference. Time can be discontinuously linked with sign (*semeion*), as in Mark 13:4, "What *shall be* the sign when all these things shall be fulfilled" ("*mellei suntelesthai*," "are at the point of being brought to full conclusion"). Instead, the general notion of time (*hora*) and the timely (*kairos*) is touched on frequently, sometimes in the context of the special "sign" that is to be read into a moment, and sometimes not. Even Judas was watchful for the right time (*eukairos*, Mark 14:11) to betray Jesus. The evangelists indicate in different ways that Jesus is deeply aware of the timing that governs his activity. This fact, as they see it, gets underscored in Acts, in one of his last injunctions to the disciples, answering the question of when he will "restore again the kingdom of Israel" by declaring that their own actions – unlike his – must be in ignorance of such future circumstances, "It is not for you to know the times (*chronous*) or the seasons (*kairous*, "ripe moments"), which the Father has put in his own power" (Acts 1:6–7). "*Hora*," "hour" or "time," occurs frequently in the New Testament, and it is a term of special pregnancy, as Karl Georg Kuhn has pointed out.[19] *Hora* ranges from the time of day to the apocalyptic time of the nearness of the kingdom. Like all the terms for time, it occasionally embeds a metaphor of seasonal agricultural ripening. *Kairos*, the more marked term, occurs thirty-three times in the Gospels and forty-nine elsewhere in the New Testament. The least marked term of these, *chronos*, occurs least frequently (sixteen times in the Gospels).

The main historical vision of the New Testament bears upon Jesus' role in public life as the course of his life both reveals and begins that role. At the same time, concurrently and coherently, the evangelists build into their narratives the sort of wisdom about political-societal interactions that other historians show. There is an encapsulated near-Machiavellianism in the injunction to "make friends with the Mammon of unrighteousness" (Luke 16:9–14); and the notion that "one cannot serve both God and Mammon" (Matthew 6:24) has a political as well as a personal dimension. The psychology of Peter's denials of the Passion and Jesus' prediction of them is based on a wisdom about behavior in public under stress. It offers an unexpected congruence between social cynicism and the laws of the spiritual life. "Unto everyone which hath shall be given; and from him that hath not, even that he hath shall be taken away from him" (Luke 19:26); this, too, is less shocking as a social observation than it is as a religious principle. The religious context acts so that the social observation can be stretched for deep meaning. Coming just before the Passion in the parable of the steward, this piece of wisdom seems to be applied by Jesus to his own situation in still another shocking political statement, "But those mine enemies, which would not that I should reign over them, bring hither, and slay them before me" (27). The parable transposed economic management to the spiritual life; this conclusion expresses a political disposition of "enemies" in spiritual terms, but in congruence with the way kings typically deal with the material presence of enemies. And in his handling of the controversies with the official representatives of the Temple, Jesus exhibits not only theological acumen but diplomatic management when he answers the question about the source of his authority not with the sort of definition in which his teaching abounds, but rather with a related question, set to get the reaction that it does, of thwarting the priests and elders, "The baptism of John, was it from heaven or of men?" Political considerations – "the people will stone us" – inhibit them from the second answer, and their own theological orientation prevents them from giving the first. They say evasively that they do not know, whereupon they provide the license in diplomatic equality for Jesus to say the same thing, to protect himself just as they do, having been brought to provide the precedent through his dialogue (Luke 20:1–6). He applies the same diplomatic turn for his answer about Roman authority, "Render under Caesar the things that are Caesar's" (Matt. 22:21; Mark 12:17; Luke 20:25).

After the events recounted by the Gospels, when Jesus is absent even as the revenant of Emmaus, doctrines and actions are no longer united; they become largely split. Acts takes over for actions and Epistles for doctrines. Acts is built up of incremental happenings, each complete in itself while at the same time serving as an index of how far the small church has got to that point. Acts shows what the church could carry out and how it developed – beginning with the transmission of authority from Jesus and the miracle of Pentecost, which by Acts 20:16 is already a constituted feast. The particular features of the historical narrative are governed in their partial isolation and abruptness by the paradox of their continuity and discontinuity from Israel, as Bultmann notes.[20] Of this the Pentecost furnishes a Utopian, prospective image that is elaborately filled out in Revelation.

All these texts are, of course, not confined to historiography, but they find in that mode of discourse a grounding of their comprehensive form.

THE IMPLICATIONS OF SCOPE:
TOTALIZING EXPLANATIONS IN HISTORY

I

"THE PHILOSOPHY OF HISTORY" as a term characterizing the enterprises of Hegel, Heidegger, Dilthey, Weber, Nietzsche, and others, is accurate enough, though it has the unfortunate corollary of obscuring the historiographic set of some of these writers. Seen in terms of the objects of their discourse, the question might be posed not about whether, or how much, they foreground the theoretical component of discussion of history, but whether they include, or even tend toward a presentation of detailed patterns in social sequences through time. That is, whether they are writing history or not. Weber and Hegel do, each in his own way, Heidegger does not, and Dilthey does not, or at least he does not in any way that addresses public behavior. Nietzsche stops doing so on a large scale after the completion of *The Birth of Tragedy,* which offers, in post-Hegelian fashion, to read the development of Greece from Homer to Plato as an intellectual development governed not by one "spirit" (*Geist*), but by two, "intoxication" (*Rausch,* Dionysus) and "dream" (*Traum,* Apollo) in four stages of establishment, disjunction, fusion, and a final dissolution in "Socratism." *Geist* stands in Nietzsche's title, and he fleshes out what he means with enough detail to qualify the work as a history, though both philosophical and nonphilosophical writers of history may vary as to the amount of detail they deem necessary for presentation.

Those philosophically oriented historians who are also philosophers of history, tend to foreground in their work those assumptions and governing notions that appear in any historiography whatever, because the relation they establish between general and particular for facts or events, and between individual and society for actional complexes, tends toward a totalizing one. From the point of view of history writing, from the point of view of such objects of discourse, though it may be said that these writers are philosophical because they are totalizing, one could also say, so far as their abstract positions are concerned, that on the contrary they are totalizing because they are philosophical. Their inquiry into the patterns of the past induces them not only to find, but to assert, coherence as a general principle rather than as a final connection that has been intimated through skillfully connected divergences, the usual method. Without opting, or having to opt, for a priority of motive here, the tendency toward a total and moderately homeostatic, as well as a dialectical, view of social process in Weber, for example, more directly characterizes his historiographic works than does the particular rationale he elaborated to expound his views.

For history we should consider the effect of the totalizing on the presentation of historical sequence before we ask how the theories predict and accord with a writer's historiographic practice. In any case, the presentation of sequences in a diachronic frame continually modifies as well as exemplifies a theoretical method. Enchainment into the partial order of temporal sequence will further complicate the relation of general to particular in any historical work that is philosophical enough for the categories to exert constant pressure toward dialectical interdefinition in the events. Here, too, the paradoxes that bear on history writing are felt with especial force, since the extreme of order is constantly being constructed by the abstract terms as well as by the totalizing connections. But that extreme cannot be reached without the historiographic sequence disappearing into a formulable thesis about the angle and segment of social action. The questions the historian asks may be formulated in summary, but the answers never can, without the work's reaching the extreme of order that would remove it from the historiographic to the purely social-theoretical. At the same time in a philosophical historian the approach toward disorder or randomness undergoes a pressure also, though differently registered in the language of the philosophized historical discourse, because the totalizing perspective is obliged, as it were, to posit a prior randomness, and also to undercut the temporal order initially, in order for the categorization to take place. In all these procedures the circularity of any history writing, as it moves tensely between the poles of system and sequence, becomes especially apparent. And the reader is drawn toward the pole of system by treating the offered discourse as philosophy. In treating it as historiography, the reader is drawn toward questions about the legitimacy of the governing abstractions, and about their particular function in what seems at once unhistorical – even in one way or another arbitrarily question-begging – in its version of abstract substitutions for an implied historical demonstration.

Moreover, as Paul Ricoeur's discussion of mimesis may lead us to see, the mimesis in historiography is an Aristotelian one, the mimesis of an action that in turn implies intrication of events (they are then put into the order of quasi-causal relation as well as of subsumption of particular under general).[1] But the diction of the language in which history writing, like any other discourse, takes place, is inescapably "Platonic" as well, and especially in the philosopher of history who also writes philosophical history. His discourse may also include an imitation of (a reference to the idea of) a spatial object or a separate lexical abstraction. When Foucault speaks of "hospital" in a historiographic work, he is referring to a physical building in a specific location in Paris; and even his term "reason" may refer to a particular era's assumption of explanatory consistency. In such cases the historian is employing the "static" mimesis of Plato. And at the same time he is also employing the "dynamic" mimesis of Aristotle by referring to the particular concretization of purposes and assumptions at a moment of time that became the hospital, to the particular posture within a social dialectic at a moment of time that was and may still metatheoretically be characterized as "reason."

In this, surprisingly, the historiographic work is more complicated with respect to the mimetic function than is its cousin the fictional narrative, though both are alike in their relation to referents. Here history and fiction have only one difference: The referent in history is presumed to be actual where no such presumption (one way or the other) governs the referent in fiction. What this freedom from the presumption of actuality for the fictional work does is to simplify its mimesis toward the Platonic and static pattern. "I say 'flower,' " Mallarmé says, and a kind of abstraction, he argues, is immediately broached, the flower that is "absent from all bouquets."[2] But a bouquet at the funeral of a president, mentioned by the historian, is present both as a specific referent and in the time-dynamized implications of that bouquet's sequenced relation to sender, receiver, and particular context. If the writer of a novel says "house" or "Ellen" or "baptism," he is choosing the place and the name and the rite predominantly on the "Platonic" model. The house has only the attributes he chooses to give it (whether an actual one or not). The same is true for the person covered by the name and the gathering covered by the rite. But the historian inescapably adds an "Aristotelian" complication, an unavoidable real sequence as well as an unavoidable actual reference, to his use of such words.

As for persons, the agents in both history (even if distantly collectivized on *la longue durée*) and fiction may be typified, and in a sense cannot avoid being typifiable. But though the "actants" of Greimas, and other such typifying formulations, may overskeletalize the "syntax" of relations in a fictional plot, and though more may be happening and deeper senses meant in a novel than can be reached by such constructs – still the fiction from start to finish lends itself to such categorization because it is invented by the writer (even if he chooses faithfully to copy his own past with minimal inventive variation, as Gênet and Céline among many others would seem to do). In history writing, on the other hand, the very salience of the type in response to actual pressures of relation, makes it resist full formulation under the type's predictable behaviors. Elijah is a prophet, Solomon is a king, but these are still ideal-types in Weber's sense that do not predict the difference between Elijah and Elisha, or between both of these and Jeremiah, or between Solomon and David. Nor does either authority type predict the particular mix in the given instance of traditional, legal, and charismatic (in terms of still other Weberian ideal-types). Still less will the types predict an action when a given person, Saul, is designated as both prophet and king – except that a certain instability may obtain, as it markedly does in Saul's case. The business of the historian is not simply to use the types. If he does so, he verges toward chronicle on the one hand or tract on the other. He must continually test and define them through the temporal process. We know what a king is in such a context only after we have finished 2 Kings. But in fiction the "actants," so far as they go, are predictable, and there is no strain on their limits or on their approximations. They are, in a sense, always the same, undetermined as types by the given context where they appear.

The intrication of the historical work into both "static" and "dynamic" mimesis keeps a strain of implied justification upon each of the details it would include, and also markedly upon the seemingly even flow of its linear presentation. For that reason the implications of recourse to verbs of past time, well spelled out by Arthur Danto and Paul Ricoeur, will carry only so far. That feature of the historical work, like all its other features, gets a toughness of convincing applicability, the sense that it has carried out a mastery over seemingly contradictory or random sequences, from the double pull of the event-segment, the detail, or even the individual word, toward full (and thesis-bound) explanatory order on the one hand, and toward self-consistent but unique sequence on the other. Something like such a criterion of adequacy toward dialectical possibility is implied by Heidegger's insistence on the "authentic" *(eigentlich)* in any historiography deserving the name.[3]

Pressure toward a synchronic adequacy distanced from narrative sequence may even be provided by the various resources for quantification, and also by the available quantified data, to which the modern historian has access.[4] And at the same time the tension between narrative sequence and abstract thesis may be relaxed, or evaded, by the presentation of long-term series, substantiated with quantified data.

Braudel, indeed, insists on the presence of that tension as "levels" and "philosophy," and so he is theoretical even for his long-range quantifiable data.[5] Even for Braudel, without the tensions between sequence and thesis, or the diachronic and the synchronic, or the general and the particular, or concordance and discordance in the terms of Paul Ricoeur, it is hard to see how the categories that Braudel does honor, the individual and the social, can "make themselves be felt" or at least "reconciled."[6]

Evidence which would be at least subjectible to quantification, while notably kept in the focus of a dialectic that sustains and capitalizes on these various tensions, is variously presented by Max Weber and Michel Foucault. And their very abstentions from letting statistics do a large part of their job, coupled with the synchronizing social nature of their focus on evidence, throws into relief the freedom toward large-scale, and even toward totalizing, connections it is the main thrust of their presentations to make.

In this they are both implicitly and explicitly following the practice of writers so totalizing in their approach to historical sequence that the historiographic nature of their enterprise is sometimes displaced under the rubric "Philosophy of History" – a term Braudel is willing to apply to anyone not writing with his particular long-term set toward explanation. But Vico, Hegel, and the Nietzsche of *The Birth of Tragedy* address no less attention to sequence, and to the relation that particulars may have to sequence, than do Thucydides, Tacitus, and Gibbon. The high degree of foregrounded theorizing in such works, combined with a relatively light texture of presented detail, would tend to obscure the main historicizing focus of such writing, even for those who would stress the necessary substructure of assumption in any historiography – or who would even want to carry such assumptions through to their superstructure as well.

To speak of presuppositions, to relativize the necessary subjectivity of the historian with Carr and others,[7] has the corollary of obscuring the ways a total conception may be connected to the details of sequence, and also of obscuring the validity of those ways. In the deconstruction of Hegel carried out by Derrida's *Glas*, a – fairly traditional – relativism is pushed to an extreme; the idealizing Hegel is deconstructed by being reprinted without his sequence of argument, and also without his sequence of event (when some dimension of history is virtually always in question).[8] Here Hegel is further deconstructed by being juxtaposed chiefly against the skeptical hedonism of a Gênet who shares a comparable rhetoric while standing poles apart in his doctrine.[9]

As Paul Veyne says, "The frontier that separates history from science is not the one between the contingent and the necessary but the one between the whole and the necessary."[10] The totality cannot be abrogated because a "misplaced concreteness" necessarily shadows historiography. The writing takes place, and intends to refer to, especially significant sequences from that totality. The writer of fiction, on the other hand, even when he draws close to autobiography, as Gênet does, confects his own ongoing coherence. He starts by making it up, and a primary condition of his presentation allows his presented data the sorts of analytic classification that Roland Barthes presents when he speaks of "functions" and "indices," subclassifying the terms in a fiction as coordinating or subordinating into categories that define the relationship of the detail to the conceived coherence.[11]

This irreducible presence of a total complex of event to which the writer of history refers, makes his detail resistant to such coherence, all the more that in the ongoing collective life to which history must also refer, the temporality is irreducibly open-ended, whereas the writer of fiction, if he wishes to sidestep closure, must still build an open end into his work as a variant upon the expectation of closure.

2

Hegel sets himself the overall task of explaining how a connection obtains between the widely distant but integrated activities of the individual consciousness on the one hand and the time-bound totality of a culture or "state" on the other. The connection only begins by historicizing the epistemology of Kant.[12] At every point along the wide span of this continuum a dialectical process is in operation, always conceived as open-ended to the risk of being forestalled into incompletion or into some state less than "the absolute," "freedom," or full "self-consciousness." Even incomplete states, the master and the slave, the "*schöne Seele*," the "unhappy consciousness," are themselves seen both as a totality and as the result of a dialectical locking of onward motion in time. They have a specific historical location and dimension. But the achieved totality of Egypt, Greece, Christian civilization, or Hegel's modern state never settles into the status of a synchronic object; it remains profoundly historicized across the continuum it embodies from constituent units of consciousness, its individuals; to its realized and tested system of coordination, the society.

Hegel, according to his own classification, is not an "original" historian who discusses a delimited segment of national history (as he sees even Herodotus and Thucydides), nor is he a "reflective" one of the "universal" sort (Livy) or the "pragmatic" (Montesquieu).[13] His approach, rather, is the "philosophical," "the thoughtful contemplation of history," and in the passage where he concludes these distinctions he denies that the abstractness of philosophy is necessarily contradictory to the concreteness of the "data of reality."[14] The breadth, and the constant dialectical energy in the self-transcendences of the individual in Hegel's "becoming" (*Werden*), keep a historical process both actual and rational. All the dialectic of this process is implied in his much quoted statement "What is rational is real, and what is real is rational," "Was vernünftig ist, das ist wirklich; und was wirklich ist, das ist vernünftig."[15] And as he further says, "*The spirit performs in essences;* it makes itself according to that which it is in itself, to its action, to its work; thus it becomes an object to itself, thus it has itself as an existence in prospect," "*Der Geist handelt wesentlich,* er macht sich zu dem, was er an sich ist, zu seiner Tat, zu seinem Werk; *so wird er sich Gegenstand,* so hat er sich als ein Dasein vor sich."[16]

The relation between general and particular in such totalizing history, places a constant emphasis on the general, and it tends markedly toward the synchronic. But it remains as plausible as does more strictly narrative history, even though its texture of particulars is thinner and it is not based on the conventional documents. Any writing of history must doubly misplace a concreteness of that which it cannot know and also of what it chooses not to write about. Hegel's characterization of the spirit (*Geist*) of Egyptian civilization as "symbolic" of course cannot be "falsified" by presenting a counter-case as a control, but neither can Stephen Runciman's delineation of general forces bearing on political and military decisions in 1282 (the papacy, the Kingdom of Sicily, the Kingdom of Aragon, the Kingdom of France) or at a specific moment, say August 30, 1282.[17] Neither serves as a more reliable guide for the future: In spite of both the grammar and the aspiration of historians, that is even more true for historiographic progressions than it is for economic ones. And Hegel, in fact, is potentially even more predictive of the past than Runciman could be in the light of possible new evidence. An artifact dug up in Egypt since Hegel's time would be at least as likely to conform to Hegel's definitions as new documents would be to conform to Runciman's sequence of events, though, of course, this consistency of Hegel's derives from his greater prior generality.

That generality, however, roots itself from the beginning in the definition of the necessary historicity of the individual "subject." "The other side of his [the subject's] becoming, *history*, is that becoming which *knows* and *mediates* itself – the spirit that externalizes itself in time; but this externalization is indeed the externalization of itself."[18] In the *Aesthetics* and in the *Philosophy of History,* as intermittently elsewhere, Hegel provides an instantiation as well as a rationale of the historical relation between general and particular. As Hegel says with reference to the different relation between laws and feelings for the art in his time from the relation obtaining for the art of Greece and the High Middle Ages, "The imaginative-formative reflection of our life today, in relation both to will and to judgment, makes us necessarily hold fast to general viewpoints and to govern the particular in accordance with them."[19] Feeling at any time, though, is that which is incorporated into art. For Hegel this principle makes art uniquely appropriate for the characterization of civilization in its historical development. "The purpose [of art] is established therein: to awaken and enliven feelings, inclinations and passions *of all sorts, to fill* the heart and to let man, whether developed or still undeveloped, feel to the utmost what the human sensorium can bear, experience, and produce at its innermost and deepest."[20]

In his presentation of such totalities, however, Hegel is at pains to keep distinguishing the general (*Allgemeine*), the special (*Besondere*) and the particular (*Einzelne,* 115), and he holds a constant dialectical process in place for the realization and transmutation of the particular manifestations of the spirit into this or that form of art (208–211 and passim). In this vein he makes a large distinction between the symbolisms, conscious (*bewusste*) and

unconscious (*unbewusste*) (313–410). This brings him to particular characterizations that at every point have general bearing on the culture under
discussion, as may be illustrated by his handling of "metamorphosis," which
for him, in turn, as always, not only fuses the more general forms that it
comprises but also serves as a manifestation of the *Geist* that employs it:

> *Metamorphoses* are to be sure of a symbolic-mythological sort, but at
> the same time they expressly set the natural off against the spiritual,
> when to something natural that is under discussion – a cliff, animals,
> a flower, a spring – they give the significance of being a *realization*
> and a *punishment* for spiritual existences: Philomela, for example, the
> Pierides, Narcissus, Arethusa, that through a false step, a passion, a
> crime, fall into endless guilt or endless pain, whereby they have be-
> come something that is deprived of the spiritual life and is turned into
> a mere natural entity.
>
> On the one hand here the natural is not only treated externally and
> prosaically as a mere mountain, spring, tree, etc., but it is given a con-
> tent that belongs to a spiritual procedure or behavior. The cliff is not
> only a stone but also Niobe weeping for her children. On the other hand
> this human act, a certain guilt, and the transformation into a mere ap-
> pearance of nature is to be taken as a degradation of the spiritual.
>
> For this reason we must distinguish these transformations of human
> individuals and gods into things in nature very clearly from the au-
> thentic *unconscious symbolism*. In Egypt the godly is partly seen with
> immediacy in the closed inwardness, rich in secrets, of animal life;
> and partly the authentic symbol is a form of nature, which with a
> wider, related significance, although it may not constitute a really
> adequate entity, nevertheless is *shut up in immediacy . . .*
>
> In Ovid's "Metamorphoses," aside from the wholly modern treat-
> ment of the mythic, the most heterogeneous matter is mixed in.[21]

While, of course, discourse now current about Ovid or Egypt does not cast
itself in Hegelian terminology, there are many ways in which the discussion
of the role of animals in Egyptian religion or the particular mix of credence
and self-consciousness in Ovid has not advanced beyond Hegel's discussion,[22] and still less does such further discussion either contradict or
supersede Hegel. His force, the ring of truth to his generality as it is brought
to bear on such specific, large cultures in time, does not depend on its
freedom from disverifiability but rather on the acts of selection and attention
that precede the particular distinctions coordinated here for embodiment in
his act of totalized historical writing.

3

Max Weber is less unitary in his combination of general and particular than Hegel, while attentive in Marx's way to the dialectical interplay of syn-chronic factors. Weber increases the component of history in his writing by fine-tuning the dialectical interplay, and also, strikingly, by applying it more rigorously than does Marx.[23]

Weber's work, in fact, as has effectually been noted by Paul Veyne and others,[24] is prevailingly historiographic. His career runs from his large early treatise on recent economically motivated population shifts, through his expansive comparison of Roman with medieval bureaucratic and economic life, to the essentially historical studies that occupied the last twenty years of his life, the large-scale, detailed treatment of the de-velopment of individual religious traditions within their social contexts. Only the institutional classifications of the sort that (ironically) he himself studied would obscure the main historiographic thrust of his enterprise by allying it on the one hand to the new profession of sociology that he was instrumental in helping to found, and excluding it on the other hand from the scholarly, departmentalized history of Meinecke and Mommsen – who welcomed the young Max Weber as a Roman historian. When aligned with "Protestant Ethics and the Spirit of Capitalism," the equally large studies of the relation between religion and society in China, India, and ancient Israel – taken together the largest body of his work – consti-tute works of synchronic history quite comparable in focus and more ex-tensive in range than those of his predecessor Burckhardt. And in the proportions of Burckhardt's total production, too, the strictly historical works are scarcely more predominant over the book on Rubens, the re-flections on history, and the *Cicerone*, than are Weber's historical produc-tions over his theoretical treatises.

In Weber's works, the process of "socialization" (*Vergesellschaftung)* is subjected to historical developments as well as to the culture-specific con-straints that Hegel had emphasized. And the "ideal-types" are constantly modified by temporal mutations, especially since in principle they appear rarely if ever in a pure state. In *Das Antike Judentum,* for example, Weber constantly emphasizes the temporal stages while playing them dialectically against the Hebrew culture's own specific conception of its historicity (6–10). The relation of general to particular in this work, while a shade less given to narration, is comparable to that in *The Civilization of the Renaissance in Italy*. As Weber generally argues, values are weighed and at the same time measured against the abstract template of a neutralized attention to them; "the inclusion of value judgments in a purely objective analysis," he says,[25] "has produced a vitiation (*Schädigung)*" of the prior histories, which are uncomparative from culture to culture and undialectical in handling the given culture. At this initial point Weber explicitly introduces a perspectivization by comparing the Hebrew theodicy to that of the Jains, the Egyptians, and the Persians, as he later compares it to Hindu and Buddhist conceptions, while intermittently measuring the bearing of religious on economic attitudes in the post-Exilic world against those in the post-Reformation West.

One factor plays against another, creating a totality of conditions in whose dynamic interaction there implicitly resides the possibility of diachronic change, and so of history. "The natural, given contrasts in conditions of financial management have always expressed themselves in the oppositions between economic structure and social," "Die naturgegebenen Kontraste der Wirtschaftsbedingungen haben von jeher in Gegensätzen der ökonomischen und sozialen Struktur sich ausgedrückt"(13).

A more restricted version of Hegel's connection of individual psychological dynamics to social factors provides Weber with a focus to fine-tune their interactions. As he says, using the Hegelian term "immediate" in a more colloquial sense, "The most immediately understandable manner of the sense-directed structure of a procedure is indeed that procedure which has a strictly rational orientation toward means, those that are (subjectively) held as in a single signification adequate to attain (subjectively) clearly grasped purposes."[26] In Weber's view there is a large-scale reciprocity between the Hebrew people's conception of themselves and their conception of their relation to God, both conforming to, and developing along the lines of, a conception of the covenant.[27] This reciprocity derives from, and is in turn shown through Weber's presentation to be modified by, interactions with neighboring peoples in whose context the Hebrews are a "pariah people."

A special version of the ideal-type "peasant" provides coordinates for Saul's career, as the ideal-type "shepherd" does for David's (*Das Antike Judentum,* 53 and passim). And the settled versus the nomadic models are abstract patterns that interact to give the Hebrew communities and their tribal customs their particular character. Weber's abstract types of rule do not appear in a simple succession, as Plato, Vico, and even Tacitus present theirs. Rather, the "traditional" the "legal" and the "charismatic" are subjected to interactive processes that determine how they will dominate a society, or even combine in one for particular manifestations.[28] In warning against the dangers of an unreflective mixture of theory and history, Weber by implication sets the goal of a constantly monitored diachronic presentation that is at once theoretical and historical, eschewing for a constant dialectic the simple labeling of ideas in the past ("Die 'Objektivität' der Erkenntnis, 240). Indeed, in speaking of the interplay between demographic and ideological factors for the Mormons at Salt Lake, he implicitly sets an ideal that would modify even the practice of Braudel, "For we have here already to deal with the inseparable *intermodification* of ends, means, and corollary realization."[29]

4

Marx's acts of explanatory history writing offer a totalization, of course, and they do so in such a way as to step up the relation of general to particular by allowing no purchase for the play of other factors.[30] In Hegel's work the *"Geist"* of a given civilization subsumes particular manifestations with respect to itself. Other dimensions like political interactions or social structures, while they may not share in the full, deep self-realizations, may be conceived of as acting out their own sequences with only tangential reference to the defining spirit. Indeed, Hegel's notion of the hero in history, the Caesar, implies that the spirit can be aspectualized to unify in areas other than art, religion, and philosophy. In Marx, on the other hand, both the program for the future and the political (rather than historiographic) organization of the present totalize into economic struggle the relation in the past between general and particular. The Marxist catchphrase "it is no accident" well expresses the hermetically sealed character of this totalization; any manifestation in society finds the single dimension of its meaning in its function within a class warfare, in the process of which, on a time-plan almost as long as Hegel's, society interacts toward the quasi-Hegelian realization of the proletarian state. All the Hegelian functions are ambiguously treated as either deep-seated organizations or mere incremental additions, themselves economically determined: as "superstructure" (*Ueberbau*).

Later Marxians attenuate what is at once a theoretical emphasis on the economic in Marx – which gains its force from that totalizing emphasis – and from the practical writings, historiographic and other, which are aimed in that direction. Later Marxians attenuate this emphasis, by downplaying the passage in the 1859 preface to *A Contribution to the Critique of Political Economy,* where Marx makes the distinction between base and superstructure. To do so, however, effectually turns these Marxians away from Marx – a natural development in thought, which in no way undercuts the subtlety or totality (but it does undercut the exclusivity) with which Marx may be applied. Indeed, there is a crucial equivocation in this assimilation-by-implication of the exclusive totality in Marx's own thought to such developments, since the force of his own argument, Althusser and others have shown, takes its stand against Feuerbach (and Hegel) and any others who would want to qualify factors other than economic as decisive social determinants. They may justifiably be called "Marxian" if not fully "Marxist," since they have parted company with, and cannot therefore draw strength from, the exclusiveness implied in Marx's own totalizing analyses. Marx himself was a "vulgar Marxian" in their terminology, but his totalizing has

184

enough power to be turned to subtle uses, which could then be described as Weberian in the near neutrality of their analysis. In the attempt to provide a sort of Hegelian expansion for Marx, for example, John McMurtry expends considerable effort on a distinction between "ideology" and "forms of social consciousness" (*gesellschaftliche Bewusstein*) that he admits a century of commentators have mostly overlooked.[31] The distinction made by Jameson, following Althusser, between mechanical and expressionist – modified by structural – causality, does save the day, but by departing from Marx for kinds of analyses which effectually assert that any kind of coherent expression of an "unconscious" in the social context, connected to social determinants, must be described as Marxist – as it must in terms of its origins, since Marx was the first to do so – though, again, he was the first to do so with the totalized exclusion to economic factors as they define class warfare. But the term "Marxist" may or may not be applied systematically to such a position.[32]

Taken analytically, rather than programatically or politically, Marx carries out his totalizing discussions of the immediate past with a force that allows for the pattern-discrimination of interactions (often sinister ones) within modern society. In this he resembles Weber, and it is of course he who took the giant step of intensifying and further particularizing Hegel's "What is real is rational, and what is rational is real." He did so by focusing on the social interactions within a given society. The advantages of his motivated sharpness as well as the disadvantages of his rigorous exclusiveness appear with special salience in his rare, separate historiographic works, *The Eighteenth Brumaire of Louis Bonaparte,* and *Class Struggles in France 1848–1850.* In the former, he at once provides a trenchant analysis of how the aspect of class self-interest works deleteriously in a society and overdefines as a sequence from tragedy to farce what is anyway the constant possibility for ironic contrast between one set of events and another in a large sequence. His declaration comes at the very beginning here in a characteristic exaggeration that warps into the rhetoric of exhortation as well as sharpens his view for historiographic particulars:

> Hegel remarks somewhere that all facts and personages of great importance in world history occur, as it were, twice. He forgot to add: the first time as tragedy, the second as farce. Caussidière for Danton, Louis Blanc for Robespierre, the *Montagne* of 1848 to 1851 for the *Montagne* of 1793 to 1795, the Nephew for the Uncle. And the same caricature occurs in the circumstances attending the second edition of the eighteenth Brumaire![33]

The exclamation point, though it may even recall the stylistic crepitations of Michelet, is here applied at once to a series that has not yet been presented, whereas Michelet's exclamation points tend to be local and topical. As an unearned grace note, it is an exhortation rather than a historiographic inference. The statement also may be said to compress three series into two, since the "Eighteenth Brumaire" of 1851 is itself a product of the series from 1848 to 1851, in the analysis of which Marx had also published a treatise.

Further exaggerations ride the crest of Marx's intense dialectical discourse here: "what seems overthrown is no longer the monarchy but the liberal concessions that were wrung from it by centuries of struggle" (18); "On the side of the Paris proletariat stood none but itself" (23). In the process, however, Marx sustains a constant, particularized attention to the interactions of finance capital and the powerful coalitions connected with it, and the bourgeoisie, the petty bourgeoisie, the proletariat, and the lumpenproletariat, as well as to the occasional maskings of the economically oriented groups in political alignments. This attention, and the constant totalizing view that organizes it, allows him to speak of the petty bourgeoisie as a "transition class" splitting the army from the proletariat (54) and of their particular interaction as a "reverse" of the Revolution of 1848 (42).

The tendency toward exaggeration is more pronounced in these works, and in his later study of the Commune, than in his lengthy reportages during the same period to the *New York Herald Tribune*. But the dialectical analysis is much deeper in the historical works, since it is empowered by the totalizing perspective he is free to enlist, and the more remarkably so for having been written almost at once, pieces of historiography so close to the events that they qualify as reportage. When Marx understands himself to be under the aegis of scholarly rhetoric, in *Das Kapital*, the exaggeration markedly diminishes, but the historical analysis is also less intricated, though there, particularly in the discussion of the working day in England (3:8), the detail is comparably full and comparably prolonged. In *Das Kapital*, indeed, Marx draws most of his illustrations from England; he mentions France hardly at all, as though for that segment of history the work of analysis had been exhaustively performed in the two earlier studies.

That Marx considers such characterizations to be rhetorical additions, shows in his explicit abjuration of more than immediate content to "tragicomedy" in his introduction to *Class Struggles in France 1848–1850*: "Not in its immediate tragicomic gains did the revolutionary advance break a path for itself but on the contrary, in the fashioning of a closed, mighty counterrevolution, in the fashioning of an opponent through whose embattlement the crash party ripened into a truly revolutionary party."[34]

The rhetoric of Marx's historiography, then, is a surface rhetoric aimed at persuasion, rather than an endemic feature with the sort of profound implications that Hayden White draws when he astutely locates an "organic metaphor" in one paragraph of the "Communist Manifesto" (where of course the rhetoric is stepped up still further) and a transition into "mechanistic metonymy" in the next.[35] However, given the congruence between one aspect of Marx's analysis and another that is solidified by his totalizing approach in the generalized categories of class struggle as they bear on particular economic-political events at a moment of time, one may relate his affirmations, if not his rhetoric, fully to the system. So White impressively connects one kind of relationship to another: "These two kinds of relationships, *between the forms of value* on the one hand and *between the forms and the constant content of value* on the other, are precisely analogous to the relationships he took to exist between the phenomenal forms of historical (social) being on the one hand and its constant (human) content on the other" (288). And White matches the basic forms of value (elementary, total, generalized, and monetary) to the basic forms of society (primitive communist, slave, feudal, and capitalist) (294). All of this makes Marx markedly coherent, if no more metaphoric than any other totalizing social thinker may be said to be. This coherence holds in the face of the swarming heterogeneities that he himself presents, with all their representational variation.[36]

The middle distance between the whole society and the individual, and his economic focus, provides Marx with the extrapolable explanatory power that allows him to establish valid connections inside a given society, and on occasion to catch up a limited sequence into a totalizing presentation. And since general and particular are concretized – for being historicized, it should be said, rather than just because they are valid or because they lend themselves to revolutionary purposes – those terms themselves may be endlessly manipulated by Marxians.[37]

5

Vico, through his philosophical training, was aware of the possibility of generalizing, and through his profession as a teacher of Roman law he was committed to the necessity of providing particulars. His phases of history lean heavily on the diachronic and lightly on their cyclic recursion. They are fleshed out in the particulars of a fairly elaborate date chart provided for the Hebrews, the Chaldeans, the Scyths (blank on the chart), the Egyptians, the Greeks, and the Romans.[38] It is important theoretically not that Vico's dates would mostly have been off, but rather that he would have felt the necessity of providing the armature of their particularity.

The phases themselves are pre-Hegelian social matrices, and his definition of "nature" as the social origination of behaviors at a particular time brings it close to what Hegel called "*Geist,*" just as for Hegel "*Geist*" and "*Natur*" are not only separate but in final interrelation. "The nature of things," Vico says, "is nothing else than their origination at certain times and in certain aspects, which are always the way they are; and this way, not otherwise, are things born."[39] Vico constantly holds his notion of origination at a central point of reference for his phases, keeping both of them in view for a synchronic presentation of social units and a diachronic means of succession. "Poetic" in his vocabulary, by bearing the double sense of "deep-literary" (like Hegel's "*Kunst*") and "making" or "fashioning," becomes at once the cause and the effect of the totalized unification within a given phase, and by implication the key to the next phase, the moment the Foucault-like key of "poetic" formulation has changed.[40] Even the quasi-Platonic three phases of government – godlike monarchy, heroic aristocracy, and human democracy – come into being as a result of these prior definitions, which are definitions of thought that issue in particular systems to organize vocabulary. Where Hegel put art, Vico had already put language. In this perspective what he calls "philology" serves at once as a tool for historiographic particularization and a totalizing prior guarantee of general relevance and congruence. "Thus," he says "we must attribute the beginning of poetic wisdom to the metaphysical roughness [of things], from which, as from a trunk, there ramify on one branch, logic, morals, economics, and politics, all poetic; and on another branch, activating everything poetic, physics, which is the mother of cosmography, and thence astronomy, which validates its two children chronology and geography."[41]

Under the aegis of such coordinations, Vico goes on to declare a coherence in the theories of "civil theology," "authority," "history of ideas" ("*storia d'umane idee*"), "critical philosophy," "an ideal eternal history in accord with which the history of all nations proceeds in time," "a system of natural law for the *gentes* or 'peoples' "[42] and "the principles of universal history" (322–329).

This enunciation of "a mental language common to all nations," "*una lingua mentale comune a tutte le nazioni*" (255), provides not only the principle on which large phases in the development of civilization can be differentiated – phases that adjustments, further divisions, and amplifications will not refute. It also allows, as Vico claims, for the subsumption of the particulars of Greek or Roman law under the heading of a single guiding assumption. He provides not only the possibility of philosophical history but, in a form that was bound to be somewhat rough, its actualization as well.

6

Nietzsche, in his characteristically powerful shorthand, provided only the sketch of a historical series, most expansively in *The Birth of Tragedy*. In *The Use and Disadvantage of History* ("Vom Nutzen und Nachteil der Historie") – a title deliberately avoiding the balance that translators have given it – he proceeds in alternately negative and positive fashion: the critical historian of biblical times, David Strauss, is a "philistine"; the philosopher Schopenhauer, like Nietzsche himself, succeeds as a philosophical "teacher" because he is out of sorts with his time ("unzeitgemäss," the subtitle of this treatise). Wagner, cumulatively, through myth and through music, envisions the future because he understands the German past, Nietzsche asserts, at its fullest depth:[43]

> Und die Freien, Furchtlosen, in unschuldiger Selbstigkeit aus sich Wachsenden und Blühenden, die Siegfried unter euch?
>
> Wer so fragt, und vergebens fragt, der wird sich nach der Zukunft umsehen müssen; und sollte sein Blick in irgendwelcher Ferne gerade noch jenes "Volk" entdecken, welches seine eigne Geschichte aus den Zeichen der Wagnerschen Kunst herauslesen darf, so versteht er zuletzt auch *was Wagner diesem Volke sein wird:* – etwas, das er uns allen nicht sein kann, nämlich nicht der Seher einer Zukunft, wie er uns vielleicht erscheinen möchte, sondern der Deuter und Verklärer einer Vergangenheit.

> And the free, the fearless, the innocent selfhood growing and blossoming out of itself, the Siegfried among you?
>
> He who asks thus, and asks vainly, will have to consider the future; and should his gaze into some distance straightway discover that "Folk" which may read its own history out of the signs of Wagner's art, thus will he finally understand also *what Wagner will be for this Folk:* – something that he cannot be for all of us, that is, not the seer of a future that might perhaps appear to us but the indicator and explainer of a past.

This colleague of Burckhardt's would have been aware that he was totally and deliberately transmuting the past – the final word of this book – and the history that is deliberately personalized in this passage, to the point where general and particular are fused into myth and music, as past and future converge in the perceptive present of an individual who will gird himself to create the future by understanding the past. All the Hegelian dialectic of bringing the individual psyche into harmony with long-range social actions has here become so foreshortened that it leaves historiography behind in the very act of performing what it declares to be a consummate act of historiography.

7

Michel Foucault, in a sense, turns the Hegelian dialectic back onto the totalizing process when he distinguishes within a large social phase not a single leading idea or spirit, but rather a system that serves as a dialectical matrix. This system he calls an *"episteme."* An episteme is a sort of code of codes, doubling back on itself at once to produce and to analyze the particulars that come under its purview. This doubling process justifies the nomenclature of Foucault for the general, which he calls the "transcendantal" (seeing Kant, as it were, in the perspective of Hegel and Husserl) and the particular, which he calls the "empirical."[44] But, as in Marx or Hegel, the empirical implies no empiricism; rather it implies the historian's grist of detail that retains its authenticity while wholly caught up in the systematization that does not so much nullify it as fulfill it and give it meaning – in true post-Hegelian fashion. "So in every culture between the use of what one could call the organizing codes and reflections on order, there is the naked experience of order and of its modes of being."[45] Here in the definition the dialectic operating upon the dialectic does not touch base at any point on the details that, Foucault implies, will already have been subsumed, subject to the classification that will look as random as Borges' example of classification schemes from China, with which he begins his entire discussion (7).

Yet at the same time Foucault speaks of his having offered an explanation that is "very incomplete" (AS, 25), and he finds it theoretically as well as practically unnecessary to offer an account of the "continuous and insensible transition" from one phase to another, *"la transition continue et insensible"* (AS 182). His centering on discourse allows him to totalize while remaining partial and open-ended, because the relation of a categorizing discourse to its field of discussion is both total (insofar as it claims, by whatever episteme, to account for all the phenomena in the area) and partial (insofar as it has made a double choice both of the area of discussion and of the particular connections and kinds of connection that will be made within it).[46]

Foucault follows here the fairly standard division of Western history into medieval, Renaissance, nineteenth-century, and modern, but he totalizes it in ways that are original both with respect to the kind of data considered and the kinds of combination he extricates as crucially defining. For late medieval "signatures" and "representations" he lists from a "rich" repertoire of analogical figures ten examples (MC, 32) of which he singles out four as especially revelatory of the medieval combinatory system: *convenentia, aemulatio,* analogy, and "sympathy" (MC, 40). Every resemblance has such a signature (MC, 41), a fact that implies both a totalization and a particular mode for it. In the change to the classical age (roughly the seventeenth century) a new system comes into being, albeit partially and gradually, a "mathesis" in which "the sign ceases to be a figure of the world," "le signe cesse d'être une figure du monde" (MC, 72), and it is measured no longer by resemblance but by three principles of relation: the origin of its link to its object, the type of its link, and the certainty of the link. To qualify these three linkages as not parallel to one another, and possibly as not exhausting the repertoire of types, would not affect the validity of Foucault's analysis, or its explanatory power with respect to the "discourse" that is his central topic – and that admits of only partial parallels and characterizations.

This classifying mathesis he applies to three large areas of explanatory discourse that he finds particularly revealing for human societies: general grammar, natural history, and the analysis of riches. These classical subjects become possible, he argues, only when the episteme governing their sign-systems allows their universalizing and classifying, their "Cartesian" functions.

In the next age, the nineteenth century, they will be subjected to both Kantian modalization (we may infer) and Hegelian historicization. Their names become historical linguistics, organic biology, and economics. In the last, the conservative Ricardo and the revolutionary Marx, for all their opposition, present a common epistemic link between anthropology and history and more generally a focus on the category of labor (MC, 273). In the fourth age, the modern, artistic expression in the form of literature finally comes into its own (though he had used occasional examples earlier – Velázquez at length, Cervantes, Sade). In our time the empirico-transcendental has become more explicit, which permits such analyses as Foucault's own (MC, 394–395 and passim). As language itself becomes an object (MC, 307–314), the theologizing of Nietzsche, the axiomatization of Russell, and the unconscious-analyses of Freud, characteristically come into play, liberated, as always – but also totalized in type of relation – by the modern "redoubling of the empirical in the transcendantal," "*le redoublement de l'empirique dans le transcendantal*" (346)," the final term being given the orthography of Husserl and Heidegger, who are therefore by implication brought into the picture of still greater variation, still greater convergence, and still more active dialectic.

Foucault raises the question of "defining a totality," "*définir une totalité*" (AS, 10), implying some sort of possibility for doing so by a series of methodological questions hinging upon it. And then, paradoxically, he abjures that possibility implicitly by multiplying and relativizing the "fields" ("*champs*") of "enunciation" ("*énonciation*," AS, 77–79) and explicitly by declaring that he *is* partial in *Les Mots et les choses* for leaving out fields, and cases such as Euler, Lavoisier, and Vico; and he would have to be partial once he has decided not to aim for a *Weltanschauung* (AS, 207). Discourse itself, moreover, envisages as well as encompasses discontinuities, and it is doubly conditioned by the "principles" of reversal (*renversement*), discontinuity, specificity, and exteriority (OD, 53–62); and by the "constraints" of exclusion involved in taboos on the context of speech, a sharing in collective madness (*folie*) and a will to truth (OD, 12–21). This last constraint, which Foucault says he will emphasize, is a Nietzschean one, and it may be seen as the attempt to give a Nietzschean forward thrust to his own discourse, a forward thrust that becomes more apparent in his later works.

In his historiographic works, however, Foucault's actual demonstrations at once embody and escape his methodological paradoxes. There is a sequence of many systems in *L'Histoire de la folie* – from the Ship of Fools to the "great lockup," "*le grand renfermement*" (which is at once early classical and continuous to our time), to the taxonomic classification of madness, to the great delirium, to the beast-metaphor of the mad, through to the nineteenth-century model of the possibly curable illness. These systems run through the same time-frame as the phases of *Les Mots et les choses*, but the periods do not correspond; there are more of them from the sixteenth through the nineteenth centuries for madness than for the chosen intellectual disciplines, and the transition from the nineteenth to the twentieth century is not as marked – curiously, given the Freudian revolution that he himself uses as a chief example in *Les Mots et les choses*. Of course, there is a difference between the objects in view; but there is a resemblance of systemic totality between an episteme that organizes all its data and its signal fields of inquiry into a single mode and a social system that always sets "madness" and "reason" into interdependent alternation while changing the definition of each.[47] So *Surveiller et punir*, which is somewhat thinner in texture than the previous works (including *La Naissance de la clinique*), is correspondingly, or perhaps compensatorily, somewhat more rigorous in its totalization of the relation between power and knowledge (SP 32–39). In so far as it analyzes the theories of penologists like Beccaria, it is congruent with the epistemes of *Les Mots et les choses*, though fewer periods are involved – perhaps no more than two (a time before when the force was inscribed agonizingly on the body of the arrested, and afterward when he was under total surveillance and assessment) or else three (breaking the second period down into the merely punitive and the later purportedly rehabilitative "models" of incarceration). Insofar as it deals with deviants, this study is congruent with *L'histoire de la folie*, and insofar as it deals with the detained, with *La Naissance de la clinique*. Indeed, with the comparative references to schools, armies, and monasteries in "*Surveiller et punir* (155–190; 240), and taken together with the asylums and clinics of the earlier works, Foucault presents a picture of the drive toward totalitarianizing as well as totalizing in such enclosing institutions, a picture quite in harmony with the studies of Erving Goffman, though in the light of Goffman's fine-grained and multi-dimensioned gestural analysis, the prevailing mode of generalizing abstraction in Foucault comes into particular relief.

Again, *Histoire de la sexualité, I*, offers really just two periods, a Victorian repression when sex was unmentionable and punished outside the family,

and the present repressive tolerance when "freedom" is really just a eu-
phemism for the prying of a culture that wants to oversee everyone's sexual
life. The resultant discussion eventuates in a displacement of sex into language. This total scrutiny of displacement-by-knowledge amounts to a
"volonté de savoir" that is presumably more pernicious than the potentially
revelatory kind of the investigating theoretician–historian described under
this rubric in *L'ordre du discours*. Again, the study of sexuality exhibits
congruences with *Les mots et les choses*, insofar as knowledge and categorization are in question; with *L'Histoire de la folie* insofar as behaviors judged
within an episteme as beyond the pale may be subject to definition as insane;
and with *Surveiller et punir*, insofar as this most private of behaviors is here,
for that very reason, insidiously subjected (according to Foucault) to assimilation under power by analysis and control.[48] Here the body is a target in
all phases of history, not just in a particular phase. And the "classical"
period of the seventeenth century, rather than the Middle Ages, serves as
a prelude, rather than as a phase in itself, somewhat loosely defined not by
an elaborate episteme but rather as a libertarian area in a possibly cyclic
alternation between prudery and license.

Indeed, Piaget argues that Foucault provides no principle for getting from
the stage of dominance by a given episteme to the next.[49] Piaget argues also
that in individual cases the episteme is too loose to define accurately the
emplotment in a given work. Yet the very variability of their emplotment
would argue for their appositeness as a heuristic device at very least.

There are various shifts, as partially indicated here, in Foucault's approach
to theorizing, as his own qualifications about it imply. The theorizing, in
fact, not only fails to present a congruence from work to work – which
aspectualizes and richens his historiographic enterprise, seen as a whole.
Like Marx's, or for that matter Nietzsche's, it is aimed increasingly at the
reform of society. But, with an ambiguity foreign to Marx or even
Nietzsche, it also adopts the "objectivity" of other totalizers, Vico or Hegel.
And the late work in particular, from *Surveiller et punir* on, leaves hanging
the question of whether the totalitarianizing drive it demonstrates and by
implication excoriates is just a special case, though sweeping across history,
or a general illustration of the sort of episteme he has outlined in the earlier
work. Is the code of codes at work here, or has some homeostatic system
got out of hand? Solving this question would precede any assessment of
the exact totalizing implications of Foucault's presentation, which at
the same time suspends this question in its drive toward Marx-like
pamphleteering.

In a single work the theory may be leveled into at least three approaches.
In *L'Histoire de la folie*, for example, the governing level is the overall
presentation of the phases from the Ship of Fools to the modern therapeutic
models. Even within these levels there is aspectualizing, because enclosure

persists through several phases, as does the taxonomic classification of the insane; the terms "mania" and "melancholia" have been refined and related to each other but not dropped since their inception. And from the very beginning the Ship of Fools, as Foucault presents it, faces two ways: as a marginalization and mobility of the insane, on the model of the leper; and as a kind of incarceration. The whole ship moves, but the insane are enclosed on the ship. Lepers themselves, indeed, show both modes; as wandering pariahs at the edge of towns and as the inmates of leprosariums – which get transformed into insane asylums in one of Foucault's most telling bodies of data, at the time of "le grand renfermement." There is a further aspectualization if it is noticed that, seen this way, the stage of the "Ship of Fools" seems to be omitted.

Within the overall presentation of phases, and their summaries, there is another level of theorizing, the ad hoc marshaling of factors within a given phase. *In Les Mots et les Choses* and elsewhere, this marshaling can take numbered or even tabular form, as in the five forms of "liberation" that are matched point for point with five forms of "protection" (HF, 479); or the quadratured double table of the traits of classical, and then of nineteenth-century, intellectual enterprises (MC, 325). This table, consistent but more or less ad hoc, adds interpretive characterizations of linguistics, biology, and economics that do not appear in the other discourse of *Les Mots et les choses*.

A third level of theorizing is what might be called literary interpretation of the data. This kind of reading of data as though it were a metaphor is endemic to Foucault; it is one element in the long reading of Velázquez's *Las Meninas* at the beginning of *Les Mots et les choses*. Such interpretation is rare for the historiographer (until the advent of the current "new intellectual history," which has been influenced by Foucault). It enriches both the empirical and the transcendental in Foucault's work; it is an added dimension, rather than a necessary corollary of his method, and there is nothing like it in Hegel, Marx, Weber, Vico, or even Nietzsche.[50] A particularly full example of such "third level" theorizing comes up in the course of his discussion of the "Ship of Fools" (HF, 22):

> This navigation of the madman is at once rigorous sharing and absolute Passage. In one sense it only develops, all along a geography that is half real and half imaginary, the *liminal* situation of the madman on the horizon of the concern of medieval man – a symbolic situation, and one that is realized at once by the privilege given the madman of being *enclosed* at the *gates* of the city: his exclusion must enclose him, and if he must have no other *prison* than the *threshold* itself, he is held at the place of passage. He is put on the inside of the outside, and vice versa. A posture highly symbolic, which will remain his to our own

day, if we are willing to admit that what was once the visible fortress of order has now become the castle of our consciousness.

Water and navigation do have this role. Enclosed in the ship from which one cannot escape, the madman is entrusted to the river with a thousand arms, to the sea of a thousand ways, to that great uncertainty which is outside of everything. He is a prisoner in the middle of the freest and most open of routes: solidly chained to the infinite crossroads. He is the Passenger par excellence, that is, the prisoner of passage . . . One thing at least is certain: water and madness are linked for a long time in the dream of European man.[51]

The passage, which I have somewhat shortened and also excerpted from, illustrates a different modality from the other kinds of theory. Instead of offering an overall transcendental scheme, like the first level, and instead of reorganizing the particular data into other general categories like the second, it moves all the data into a quasi-Bachelardian universe of metaphorical–psychological correlation that may deeply bypass the phases, as the reference to the consciousness of our time and the quasi-Spenglerian sweep of "the dream of European man" may be taken to indicate.

At the same time it reverberates rhetorically into the long, and convincingly impressive, passages of particular instantiation – a fourth and tonic mode of discourse in this historiography – when Foucault lists the events of March 24, 1726, around the Deschauffours case in a large (but, given the flexibility of this rhetoric, not abrupt) transition that produces a discussion of the relation between medicine and reality from Greece to the seventeenth century (HF, 101). A little earlier he had made a similar transition from a discussion of the new "classical" conception of the sacred to an account of how the hospital administration organized itself to assign various classes of venereal disease cases to particular Paris hospitals (97–98). These shifts are rare in the historian, who usually marshals his particulars fairly evenly along a constantly interpreting narrative line, with occasional mild asides of theory, like Gibbon; or else, in a more philosophical vein, subsuming the particulars into a discussion at a fairly even plane of generality, like Hegel. Implied in the variety, and also in the unity of Foucault's approach, is a constant, but silent, sublation of the particulars into a theoretical domain that on only one level, the first above, aligns them rigidly into even dialectical phases. The sublation is silent but always present, like the time that shows its own even and constant presence by the rifts and discontinuities of which Foucault speaks in his two general books, and also by the very mismatches, and aspectualizations of his levels of theorizing, about which he does not need to speak, since, rather than evidencing contradiction, they have the positive function of carrying the temporal in his totalizing presentation, and, indeed, of historicizing it.

8

In the work of Spengler the totalization is far more comprehensive, and at the same time more detailed, than in any other philosophical historian, even though the actual philosophical justification is more random and casual than that of any other. Indeed, Spengler's sense of a feeling for destiny *(Schicksal)* is justified through the actualization of his own coding of codes, his own generalizations about complex particulars. His notion is a rough equivalent for the "genuineness" *(Eigentlichkeit)* of Heidegger, even though Spengler does not deal with the question of its circularity, and even though he asserts that his approach is a poetic one – in a sense much looser, and for that very reason more acceptable finally, than Vico's. Spengler's actual philosophical categories are a mixture of the *Sein* and *Werden* (being and becoming) that he claims to get from Goethe rather than Hegel, of an *Erfahren* and *Erkennen* that make no reference to Dilthey, and other terms that, again, essentially gain in validity for the looseness and randomness of their fit to his actual approach. The philosophical terms themselves are not gathered into a system, but the actual approach to cultures offered in his work is highly systematic, both diachronically and synchronically.

> The means whereby to identify dead forms is Mathematical Law. The means whereby to understand living forms is Analogy. By these means we are enabled to distinguish polarity and periodicity in the world.[52]

The statement trenchantly directs a traditional division, much like Dilthey's between *Natur* and *Geist*, toward the most comprehensive generalities. The principle of analogy, indeed, in Spengler's hands, does allow for the articulation of both periodicities and points on a periodicity, and the principle of analogy discriminates the points by which number systems can be compared with one another in each culture (though it is not applied, which is the task of the particular mathematics). Analogy on his largest scale provides a means whereby Egyptian conceptions of space can be distinguished from the "Magian," the "Apollonian" and the "Faustian." And so, in closer detail, Napoleon can be located in a developmental series as corresponding to Alexander; the classical avoidance of blue can be compared with the Western affinity for that color; Buddhism can be paralleled with socialism and Stoicism. The transcendental that will organize each of these phenomena and others into a generalized coherence can be seen as an authentic historical totality comprising "peoples, tongues, and epochs, battles and ideas, states and gods, arts and craft-works, laws, economic types and world ideas, great men and great events" (American ed., 1:3–4).[53]

Spengler calls this a comparative morphology, and while the somewhat extravagant scientist term overplays his conviction that laws are being adduced which, if akin to those for "dead forms," would cross the line from analogy to "mathematics"; still the sense of the term is justified and moderately accurate as a descriptive characterization of his totalizing activity.

The scholarly emphasis on "primary" rather than secondary sources, the empirical distrust for large-scale speculation, and a revulsion from the ambience of Nazism have often combined to prevent an assessment of the historiographic weight and character of Spengler's *Decline of the West*.[54] It was Spengler's misfortune to write just before public recognition of Einstein's theories, or even Freud's; the masterpieces of Proust, Joyce, Eliot, and Kafka; and the relegation of Germany to second rank among nations. Thus his prophecies on science (Newton and Gauss had made the last decisive contributions), imaginative literature, and political history have counted against him. And even his suggestive characterization of the uniquely Magian Christian Tsarism of Russian and his emphasis on Dostoevsky's expression of this as opposed to the political Tolstoy's is weakened for his not having revised his work to interpret the Russian Revolution more than negatively and briefly.[55] If Spengler is accorded enough impartiality to weigh justly his theoretical and prophetic errors, as we do Gibbon's, we may consider him on his own merits as a writer of history.

Spengler gave a new dimension to the genre of philosophic history, including in the sweep of his diachronic presentation much more detail than do Vico and Hegel. Nor is his work in any sense a prolegomenon to a work of specific research, like Buckle's. By massively fleshing out and varying the sources of data as he adapted Hegel's notion of a guiding and unifying spirit to an entire culture, he became the first to establish the spiritual unity within a given culture of its language, literature, art, architecture, religion, government, finance, law, mathematics, physical sciences, exploration, customs, strategy, social structure, and its own theories on all these institutionalized activities. He differs from earlier philosophical historians in furnishing copious and ordered detail for every theoretical point, so that his remarks on the events treated by Gibbon, for example, could be collected into a small volume that would bear favorable comparison for accuracy, minuteness, and breadth (though of course not for the same sort of structural unity) with the *Decline and Fall* itself.

Spengler's technique of multiple reference is never merely random, and it is sustained by a totalizing framework that allows him effactually to undercut the analogies stated casually by Ranke and others. He marshals potentially innumerable facts under a single ordered view in a sort of prismatic and periodized synchronicity, so that any paragraph in the book can easily be referred to any other but at the same time fits integrally into the book as a whole. This is what Eduard Meyer calls its "astonishingly comprehensive, strongly synchronizing cognition," "*erstaunlich umfangreiches, ihm staendig praesentes Wissen.*"

Only professional historians of the first rank – Thucydides, Tacitus, and Gibbon – can match Spengler's stylistic coordination at its best:

> It is, and always has been, a matter of knowledge that the expression-forms of world-history are limited in number, and that eras, epochs, situations, persons are ever repeating themselves true to type. Napoleon has hardly ever been discussed without a side glance at Caesar and Alexander – analogies of which, as we shall see, the first is morphologically quite inacceptable and the second is correct – while Napoleon himself conceived of his situation as akin to Charlemagne's. The French Revolutionary Convention spoke of Carthage when it meant England and the Jacobins styled themselves Romans. Other such comparisons, of all degrees of soundness and unsoundness, are those of Florence with Athens, Buddha with Christ, primitive Christianity with modern Socialism, the Roman financial magnate of Caesar's time with the Yankee. Petrarch, the first passionate archaeologist (and is not archaeology itself an expression of the sense that history is repetition?) related himself mentally to Cicero, and but lately Cecil Rhodes, the organizer of British South Africa, who had in his library specially prepared translations of the classical lives of the Caesars, felt himself akin to the Emperor Hadrian. It was the fate of Charles XII of Sweden that from his youth he carried Quintus Curtius's Life of Alexander in his pocket and wanted to copy this conqueror.[56]

I have deliberately chosen a passage where Spengler's range is not displayed with full brilliance to illustrate his stylistic control. After the first sentence of general statement, we descend imperceptibly to detail: commonplace analogies between cities, religious figures, periods in the history of ideas, financiers; the fondness of historical figures themselves for archetypes (which for Spengler are identical with prototypes, and this is the nub of his analogical technique). Spengler implies or easily states his judgment of these comparisons at the same time that he displays them. Through this and the following paragraphs runs the slight thread of his argument: Analogy has always been the basic tool and justification of historical writing; hitherto it has been used haphazardly; I am the first to apply it transcendentally to the whole of history.

As with Gibbon, the statement of fact is never placed by itself for sheer effect. It is always used, however lightly (and Spengler can be as light as Gibbon in this matter), as a term in a flow of argument, which is the undercurrent of the facts that are thereby joined together like the molecules of water in a running stream. The generality remains, through its application of periodicities to coded particulars, transformational but subtranscendental. Spengler controls the relation of his detail to the overriding spirit that it is subsumed to illustrate. There is always a schematic relation, however tenuous, to a unified view of the war, the year's process, the dynasty, or the idea.

Spengler's density of texture and unity of structure recall the critical history of philosophy that comprises the first book of Aristotle's *Metaphysics*. His particular acuteness shows up strongly if he is compared with the loosely totalizing Toynbee, whose seven-plus linear volumes recall the interminable extension of Herbert Spencer's *Synthetic Philosophy*, a work of which the latter volumes are not devoid of insight but certainly of justifiable structure. The abridgement that spread the popularity of Toynbee is not greatly inferior to the full-length *Study*. There is less detail, but the texture remains almost unchanged, whereas a condensation on the same scale of *Decline of the West* or of *Decline and Fall of the Roman Empire* would be unthinkable.

Spengler's marshaling of detail does not verge on mere factual extension like Toynbee's. It embraces an understanding and intimate acquaintance with the most complex institutions of several cultures: philosophical terminology and systems, jurisprudence, military strategy, architectural principles, monastic pedagogy, the evolution of a literary tradition and the individual artist's conception of it, burial customs and superstitions, interrelations in a pantheon, minor biographical facts, the topography and geography of cities, dress and ceremonial, the premises and methodology of mathematics and the most advanced physical sciences. This is so much the case, in fact, that Spengler's own lists, which I have quoted elsewhere in this chapter, are not nearly inclusive enough. It is, to begin with, Spengler's awareness of and ability to utilize the arcana of a hundred complex subjects in several cultures that gives his a range and depth of discussion equaled only by Aristotle in Western intellectual history.

As practice from Vico through Weber has shown, the philosophical historian to achieve integration and depth must deal primarily with these difficult configurations that compose the dynamic internal organization of a culture, and only incidentally with the external and extensive data of successive dynasties, migrations, wars, compacts, influences, and so on, that form the stuff of "yard-goods" history and for the most part furnish Toynbee with his material. Toynbee's texture is loose and thin, as his structure is merely extensive. Even in the field where his scholarship is paramount, the history of Greek thought, Toynbee furnishes the sort of illustration and comparison that remains tritely general without effectively linking the particulars into analogous historical sequences:

> Leaping next from Saint-Simon to Empedocles (a member of a
> society which is distinct and separate from, though "apparented" to

ours), we again find our rhythm pointed out – this time in the ebb and flow of the Physical Universe – by this Hellenic man of science. Empedocles attributes the changes in the face of the Universe, of which we are empirically aware, to the alternative ebb and flow of two forces which are complementary to one another and at the same time antithetical: an integrating force which he calls 'Love' and a disintegrating force which he calls "Hate."[57]

Then following a full page quotation of English prose translation, he continues:

The two alternating forces or phases in the rhythm of the Universe which Empedocles calls Love and Hate have also been detected – quite independently of the movement of Hellenic thought – by observers in the Sinic World, who have named them Yin and Yang. The nucleus of the Sinic character which stands for Yin seems to represent dark coiling clouds overshadowing the Sun, while the nucleus of the character which stands for Yang seems to represent the unclouded Sundisk emitting its rays.

And he extends this point for three more pages, concluding with a third parallel, which turns out to be none other than Spengler's favorite quotation from Goethe, the *Alles vergängliche ist nur ein Gleichnis* chorus at the end of Faust II. Here as elsewhere Toynbee's anxiety to achieve a scientistic methodology that will preserve his respectability among scholars makes him overapologetic about ideas that lack both the particular and the general applicability of Spengler's.

Compare the above passage with Spengler's use of Empedocles for cultural analogy:

The elements of Empedocles designate states of bodiliness, but the elements of Lavoisier, whose combustion-theory followed upon the isolation of oxygen in 1771, designate an energy-system accessible to human will, "rigid," and "fluid" becoming mere terms to describe tension-relations between molecules.[58]

Spengler was a trained mathematical theorist who wrote a doctoral thesis on Heraclitus. Here his professional knowledge of advanced chemistry and his first-hand intimacy with pre-Socratic philosophy have combined to produce one of his innumerable insights. It is only in this century that scholars have realized the extent to which Empedocles must be considered a physical scientist, and defining his science is still a live issue. Toynbee knows this and tells us so in a footnote to the first mention of Empedocles, but instead of integrating his comparisons to his historical view, he uses them to buttress the scientific nature of his own work. He prefers a disguised plea to an insight: "If Empedocles speaks of these eternal principles, Love and Hate, which Chinese philosophers and Goethe have independently discovered too, and is at the same time a thoroughgoing scientist, I may also utilize them and remain objective without laying myself open to accusations of impressionism."

What Kant says of a philosophical system can be applied in general to the work of the philosophical historian: "The whole is thus an organism *(articulatio)* and not an aggregate *(acervatio)*; it may grow from within *(per intussusceptionem)* but it cannot increase by external additions *(per appositionem)*."[59] For in technique, structure, and the dynamically configurated matter he discusses, Spengler's work is *articulatio*. Toynbee's tends toward *acervatio*.

Spengler's basic principle, culture as an organism, is not really false any more than it is finally true. It has a respected history in political theory in the "body politic" metaphor of Plato, Hobbes, and others, before the Darwinianism that provided a climate for him.[60] The metaphor has a certain instrumental value, and it is sometimes illuminating to speak of the birth, childhood, or old age of a culture. If one does not press this biological metaphor for a complete homology between the processes of an organism and those of a culture, its correspondence to the facts is hard to deny. Even Toynbee, who damns Spengler almost solely on his use of this metaphor, takes it over frivolously in criticizing Gibbon's conception of the age of the Antonines as a golden age when it was really an "Indian summer."[61]

Spengler's antitheses are heavy-handed but not false. Like the metaphor of the organism, they become in his hands the glass through which we see more clearly certain phases of the historical process. Destiny–Causality allows him to introduce a whole area of emotional life, folk history, and myth. The man of action–man of thought antithesis (merely a version of the medieval *vita activa–vita contemplativa*), though sketchier than the types of Weber, seems more in accord with political actuality than Toynbee's mimetic influence of the great genius, a still looser version of Weber's charismatic leader.

Of his three chief terms for civilizations since Egypt and early China, the term "Magian" – much contested but also suggestive in its power to collocate some aspects of Byzantine perception with the Arabic – would appear to be his own invention. The term "Apollonian" is, of course, borrowed essentially from Nietzsche, and it might be described as a fusion of Nietzsche and Winckelmann. It serves well to generalize and interrelate Greek mythology, Greek mathematics, Greek perceptions of time and space, and the Greek sense of the body. It may be said, in the light of Spengler's insistence on generalizing, that he allows us to see how even the Dionysian may be perceived as "Apollonian" in his sense (as opposed to dark forces in primitive cultures, or in our own – where the unconscious does not emerge into the celebratory light of day). As for "Faustian," this term carries its explanatory power well beyond this myth that Goethe's instinct for generalizable myths kept on his table throughout most of his working life. The Goethean striving, self-imperiling, encyclopedizing, and experience-tasting, as these attributes cohere in the figure of Goethe's Faust, lacks the suggestive power, as well as the historical dimension, of Spengler's "Faustian," which, of course, originated largely with Goethe. The science of Faust lacks even the contemporary vitalism and organicism of Goethe's own writings on plants, the perception of light, and the classification of animals, while Spengler is able to characterize, and reveal through the term, features of modern mathematics, chemistry, physics, and even biology, not only up to his time but (at least in the eyes of a nonscientist) even beyond. Modern atomic physics would seem to continue the Faustian pressure for further and further analyses, as it indeterminately recedes from the consciousness of the subjectively angled observer, and as it keeps dividing and reorganizing smaller, more transient, and more completely defined bodies into forces. Spengler wrote late enough that he could well have brought Einstein into his major work, but the Faustian characterization would seem to cover Einstein's relativity as it provides a scheme for the mathematical analysis of supremely powerful kernels of energy.

On the side of depth-psychological myth, too, Spengler, so to speak, Wagnerizes Goethe. The Northern myths, as he discusses the very rhythms in which the Eddas are cast (Am. ed., 1:186), can be perceived, through his collocation, to "radiate immensities of space and distance." These rhythms are indeed quite foreign to the "soft rustle" of the Homeric hexameter. The "Nordic" or "Faustian" feeling is also quite foreign to the Greek myths that the eclectic Goethe introduced or paralleled in *Faust II*. Euphorion and the Homunculus, indeed, are so unFaustian in Spengler's sense as to be instances of sentimentalized Hellenism rather than grounded and revelatory figures that could enable perception.[62]

There is a looseness in Spengler's sense of the principles under which he was writing, as he moves to either pole of "mathematics" or "analogy" in self-justification of the at once scientific-natural and artistic-spiritual character of his enterprise. So on the one hand he justifiably criticizes the historical analogies of writers like Ranke, who, though a "master of artful analogy," draws historical analogy "with a Plutarchian, popular-romantic touch."[63] When he says that they do not do so, "with the force of a mathematician," he implies that he himself does, and such a claim is easily refuted. Yet Spengler's claim of scientific rigor and artistic penetration, especially if compared with such later, fruitful double claims as those of Roland Barthes,[64] may be seen as in fact a justifiable description, if not a philosophical justification, of his method. The principle of analogy, matching one culture to another in the most specific details, deals not with events linearly, but with the codes that govern them. Spengler's coordination of these code-correspondences into fourteen "contemporary" spiritual epochs and eight cultural epochs overlays, and consigns to secondary or simplified status, his seasonal-Darwinian periodicity for cultures and civilizations from birth to death.[65] This simpler seasonal pattern is taken for granted, in fact, by nearly everyone who writes about whole cultures, and it is only Spengler's scientistic exaggeration of it that may be discarded. The simpler pattern, indeed, has the unfortunate by-product of obscuring his more complex, more intimately necessary, pattern of fourteen spiritual and eight cultural epochs. These allow him at once to internalize the organization of a given code at a given point in a culture and to generalize it from culture to culture, as though the whole demonstration of Foucault could be extrapolated to Classical antiquity, Egypt, China, and Arabia; or as though the "symbolic" Egypt of Hegel could be further dialecticized by being broken down into a number of phases and coordinated, both externally and internally.

9

A certain pressure bears upon the presentation of sequences in any historiography. This pressure cannot be dissociated from the sense, inescapable for reader and writer, that whatever light is shed upon the sequences will still not escape the paradoxes of misplaced concreteness and somewhat arbitrary causality. Time, even the Augustinian *distensio,* as it includes memory of the past and hope for the future, runs evenly in its course, and no writing can escape from the condition of time. Nor can it represent time's evenness without dissolving into the senselessness of total redundancy. Even partial redundancy, indeed, is fatal to the genuineness of a historical work. The instinct to avoid redundancy while producing order comes through in the writing as a sense that a futurity, as well as the misplaced concreteness of the past, hovers over the sequences as they are presented. At the same time the past does have an implacability in its order that is the more imposing because it cannot be fully represented. Something of such a sense inheres in Spengler's insistence on destiny (*Schicksal*) as opposed to causality, and in his quotation, at the very end of his large work, of a maxim from the Stoic Seneca, "*Ducunt Fata volentem, nolentem trahunt,*" "The Fates lead a willing man, drag an unwilling one."

In any totalizing historian all those conditions, and others, are more fully foregrounded by being rendered explicitly in the organizational principle of his work. That is, the general scheme both reveals the particulars and puts pressure on them. And further, this whole process, which has a synchronic air but may be deeply diachronic, as in Spengler or Vico, itself exhibits a congruence with the very conditions that any writing of history must both obey and evoke. Following Spengler, it may be said that it takes a Faustian (or in Hegelian terms a "Romantic") consciousness to perceive such processes, and to perform upon them the ratiocinations of a dialectical self-consciousness. At such ratiocinations, Weber, Hegel, and Foucault happen to be adept and Spengler happens to be clumsy, and yet he surpasses even those writers in the force of his generality and the sharpness of his particularity. The conditions, both general and particular, have already become operative in the Greek prose of the fifth century B.C. and immediately thereafter. A totalizing impulse is perceptible in Herodotus, and a modalizing one in Thucydides. Plato, also offers a "Spenglerian" large-scale cultural morphology in the primitivism of the cave and in the *Timaeus*; and he offers a Weberian (or Weber a Platonic) set of phases and ideal-types for governmental systems. From Vico through Foucault, and doubtless eventually beyond him, the modern totalizing historian has found various means for bringing the advantages of these approaches into a coherence that raises historiography to an admirable self-consciousness.

The intrication that Paul Ricoeur justifiably stresses in narrative history takes a different form in the totalizing historian; his pressure works primarily not to lay out sequence but to demonstrate the coherent relationship between sequenced facts or events (or congeries of them into codes or even intrigues) and the transforming principle he adduces. As with the synchronic historian, the understanding of a sequence in time becomes a by-product – though nonetheless an effective one – of the relation between particular and general.[66]

Here one may apply further than he himself does Ricoeur's italicized insistence that "my thesis concerning the ultimately narrative character of history is in no way confused with the defense of narrative history."[67] So Ricoeur finds an intrication even in Braudel by disengaging three levels that are conjoined in his work (1:290–303). The first level is an "immobile" one, the purely geographical one to which Braudel devotes the first three chapters of *The Mediterranean*. The second level is already implied (and therefore intricated) in this demonstration, the level of "geo-history" and "geopolitics" working between the poles of Turkey and Spain, centering on economic factors and relationships. The third level is the more usual history of events in the reign of Philip II with which Braudel concludes his work, indicating by various qualifications quoted by Ricoeur that he sees this third level as connected to, and a completion of, the other two. *Totale* and *globale* are also terms that Braudel invokes, justifiably for the massiveness of the work, if not for the logical substructure of his conception.[68]

Braudel is not a totalizer, but the partial convergence of his levels gives him an intrication that resembles the attempt to totalize, though by means of incremental matching or montage rather than by transcendental generalization. This would especially be the case since he does not merely aspectualize his presentation into a given set of loose prior categories (say, "political, economic, and social"), but rather offers the "new" approach of *la longue durée*, and then matches it, incrementally, with a complement. In *Civilisation matérielle, économie et capitalisme, XV–XVIII siècle*, Braudel has added, or at least indicated, a fourth whole level, the emphasized economic – itself interacting, of course, with the others. It turns out in the third volume of this work that the interaction of space and time produces not just a slow *longue durée*, but the surprising emergence of dominant cities, for short periods or longer.[69] In the successive dominances of individual cities in his "*économies-mondes*" (an expression that could be translated as "economy-world" in the singular, but also as "world economy"), the rules he adduces effectually pit slowness against arbitrary succession, partial dominations, and hierarchizations – the last serving as moderately new conceptual determinants in his large scheme. There is a struggle that verges on the political, and involves it, when one city "wins" or "loses" – say Paris over Lyon (278–287). And at the same time, the economic, partially shaped by the political, also will dominate it, as when Philip II moves his capital to Lisbon for three years (22).

That Braudel has done a heroic job of prior professional research in records or archives, as the totalizing historian (with the exception of Foucault) virtually never does, only slightly increases the plausibility of his method and the conviction carried by his results. A discourse cannot be judged by the labor that preceded it, even though academies do well to further orderliness by encouraging careful labor. But any discourse, historical or other, must be judged by the aptness of the statements and assertions it includes and coordinates, and not by the labor of prior substantiation, even though one can posit and even find cases of thin, inapt and repetitive history writing, the deficiencies of which may be traced to a reliance on a small, ill-selected group of secondary sources – as well as cases of history writing where all these deficiencies exist in spite of much careful substantiation in primary sources. The historian – Gibbon or Michelet or Parkman or Braudel – is drawn to such substantiation and is anchored, reassured, and honored by it. Yet the totalizer, coming from the direction of the general rather than the particular, may attain results of comparably equal conviction, not just by way of philosophical proposition but also toward the end of historical demonstration.

THE STRENGTH OF PARTIAL PURCHASES: KINDS OF SYNECDOCHE IN MODERN HISTORY WRITING

S YNECDOCHE APPLIES AS A TECHNIQUE not just to some historians but inescapably to all.[1] The predominance of the referent in the initial conception of a historiographic statement makes any detail a selection, a partial and therefore synecdochic datum, from a number of others that have been omitted. As Arthur Danto says (though not here enlisting this term), "There are wider and narrower contexts, but history as a whole is plainly the widest possible such context, and to ask the meaning of the *whole* of history is to deprive oneself of the contextual frame within which such requests are intelligible."[2] And the whole sequenced presentation of a historical work is also synecdochic, both with respect to what has been omitted and with respect to the overall sense that the narrative or other sequence implies but cannot directly state without dissolving into another form. All three of these synecdoches – the one of the detail and the two of the whole – are referential in character rather than (just) rhetorical. They differ in their initial (and therefore also in their final) structure from the predominantly rhetorical synecdoche in a poetic statement. Put differently, the poetic synecdoche sets up a kind of relation between signifier and signified that effectually closes around itself in order to highlight certain features within the statement. All three of the historical synecdoches refer outward, and consequently their relation between signifier and signified remains characteristically "flat" rather than rhetorically manipulated. Even under manipulation the historical synecdoches do not highlight features within the statement, except by the kind of abstraction that again may serve as a trigger toward extrapolation outward, to the referent. One can describe certain large aims of modern historical writing in terms of their various synecdochic implications, rather than in terms of the generic subclassifications usually applied to them.

So synecdoche is the outward sign of the discrepancy between the chaotic, undifferentiated matrix of all that ever happened and the authenticity that may accompany a gist that has been extricated from some of the connections obtaining within it. "Destiny" (or "Aptness," "*Das Geschick*") becomes history when it becomes destined," Heidegger says, when he has specified that this "destiny" "is neither the object of narrated history nor the completion of human activity." "Speech" begins by "bringing man on the route of uncovering. From this point forward the essence of history is defined."[3]

As with many areas of discourse in the modern world, the existence of a large, active body of practicing historians attached to departments of history and organized into a profession both sharpens and obscures the character of what they write. Braudel, for example, differs from Le Roy Ladurie and Philippe Ariès (and also from earlier members of the Annales school like Marc Bloch and Lucien Febvre) as much as any of these does from Michelet and Burckhardt, or Namier and E. H. Carr. The tracing of ideological sutures in the social relations of a late Catharist village, Montaillou, would not strike an observer who was unaware of institutional affiliations as deriving from the set of principles governing a vast demographic–economic survey of the Mediterranean – nor would works centering on *mentalités*, such as the ascertainment of underlying attitudes toward childhood as these get built into social institutions and various kinds of discourse. Still less would Braudel, Le Roy Ladurie, and Ariès seem, without our knowledge of the connection, to be utilizing the principles that underlie the careful ascertainment of doctrinal overlappings and uncertainties in contemporary documents bearing on "the problem of unbelief in the sixteenth century: the religion of Rabelais" (Febvre) or a diachronic survey of alignments and factors in feudal society (Bloch).

Of course, once we looked at historians in the manner of the institution-oriented professional historian so as to pay attention once more to these affiliations, we would reclassify all these as Annales historians. And so in a more general way we need neither to follow nor to qualify the profession's own, and characteristically frequent, division of its activities – into political history, economic history, social history, prosopography, history of science, intellectual history, local history, urban history, quantitative history, archeology, military history, psychological history, oral history, and the sociology of intellectual history.[4]

If we use these categories, Namier can be seen as a sort of prosopographer, in the light of his count of the makeup of Parliament at the time of George III; he looks at the nexuses of relations among small groups of policy makers in a way much like Ronald Syme's in *The Roman Revolution*. The prosopographic element remains a constituent in Namier's writing, as in his headcount of the peasants in the various European parliaments on the threshold of 1848.[5] Yet this book, as its title implies, comprises much intellectual history – though without offering the extended summaries of ideas that the genre usually implies. It is also a political history. Moreover, its constant attention to large groups within each society, and within the European community, particularly with relation to the determinants of different approaches to the revolution from one country to another, makes it a social history. Its fund of economic data and statistics makes it verge on (or at least show an awareness of) economic history and quantitative history. And the flow of its narrative, in accord with Namier's own insistence on the narrative component in history, makes it a somewhat synchronized narrative – in the fashion of Burckhardt or Foucault.[6] Still, none of these modes will really serve, even in combination, to characterize the blend of general and particular that Namier presents in this work. Revealingly, there is a constant, ironic interplay between documentation and qualification that links the footnotes to the text in something more than a merely subordinate or amplifying position.[7]

All history writing must be synecdochic. One could define the historian's awareness of the synecdochic nature of his work as an irony insofar as the juxtaposition of one selected detail to another frequently and characteristically entails some ironic reflection of the discrepancy between them. But the historian's irony also signals his sense that he has put particulars together in such a way that the synecdoche will have been transcended. The adjectives in the first sentence of the second footnote to this passage[8] step up the irony, and all the more as this footnote is the last one to the last paragraph of a chapter:

> About the same time the Turkish Ambassador in Vienna proposed to Czartoryski a transfer of the entire Polish emigration to Turkey, there to reorganize the army and administration. But when the Turks secured Russia's help against Egypt, they dropped the Poles, who now turned to Mehmet Ali. General Dembínski proceeded to Cairo. [*Footnote to a Polish text documenting nineteenth-century Polish emigration to Turkey.*] So went on the weary round of bizarre negotiations in exotic quarters, from which "only extreme misfortune could draw some illusory hopes." [*Footnote: "These schemes and their authors – high-minded, unbalanced, interested, or just trying to get rid of the Polish émigrés – vividly remind one of recent schemes for settling Jews in any Arctic or tropical Timbuktu so that they should not be a nuisance in Western countries, nor press for a return to their own National Home."*]

Namier has been presenting the Revolution of 1848 through a nexus of distorted particulars. But he presents it – much as Marx does – for a failed revolution, an irony built into its very conception so deep as to constitute a tautology; a failed revolution is not a revolution at all. And within the revolution there is a discrepancy of particulars, from France to Germany to Austria to Hungary to Poland. The work constitutes a series of fragmented synecdoches that turn out to be all we can have of the whole. The human ideals of self-determination and equality, which Namier seems to share, are aroused, deflected, disappointed, and yet somehow discernible in all these processes, both in the main action and in such characteristic and partially symmetrical byplays as the collusion between Austria and Turkey to dispose of the Poles, a contradiction to the ideals of 1848 that was a failure even greater than the revolution itself, though with the sinister corollary remarked on in the footnote about "recent schemes" – of which what Namier quotes, presumably out of the source documented in the prior footnote, is a fair summary. Hitler's project of transferring the Jews to Madagascar, if not to the Arctic, may have aborted, but into the death camps that Namier does not mention here. And the very last reference touches on the establishment of the State of Israel, which was still being delayed, after the Holocaust, through British agency rather than through that of the Turks, and of the Austrians who had once again been their recent enemies. The recent events of the footnote are in fact causal derivatives of the forces in 1848, as Namier only implies. This "humanitarian" footnote is more sinuously ironic than the flatly presented one that expands on the phrase "ferocious conflict" (136) to give the grisly details of the atrocities "of an ultra-modern type" inflicted on each other by the Magyars and the Serbs.

Throughout this set of events, indeed, as throughout Herodotus' and Tacitus' histories, there is a contrast and precarious balance largely unstated between carefully calculated attempts to establish humanitarian government and equally calculated attempts to subvert it through the ineradicable Machiavellian, or perhaps anti-Machiavellian, group interests and ferocities. The irony carries all this, and forces the synecdoches to carry it, as even the totalizing Herodotus manages to do through the constant analogies on which I have commented elsewhere.[9] There I matched a sweeping passage in Namier to the implied thesis of Herodotus:

> On the European Continent incomplete conquests fell into two patterns. The main stream of migrations, which had overrun Europe from East to West, was reversed about the eighth century: from West to East the French pressed against the Flemings and Germans, the Germans against the Lithuanians and Slavs, the Lithuanians and Poles against the Russians, and the Russians against the Finnish tribes, and ultimately also against the Mongols; each nation was yielding ground in the West, and gaining much more at the expense of its Eastern neighbours: in the East were wide spaces and a reduced capacity for resisting pressure. Similarly the Swedes spread across the Baltic, and the Italians across the Adriatic. The Flemish-Walloon problem in Belgium and the Franco-German problem in Alsace, the numerous problems of Germany's ragged Eastern border, Poland's problems both on her Western and on her Eastern flank, and the conflict between the Yugoslavs and the Italians, all originate in that great West to East shift

on the linguistic map of Europe. The other pattern of conquests whose consequences were formative of nineteenth-century European history, goes back to the continued Asiatic incursions, of the Avars, Magyars, and Turks into Southeastern Europe. The Germans met them at the gate of the Danube, between the Bohemian quadrilateral and the Alps: this is the origin of Austria whose core was the Ostmark round Vienna, with its flanking mountain bastions and its access to the Adriatic. Germans and Magyars in their head-on collision split off the Northern from the Southern Slavs and established their dominion over that middle zone; and next the subjection of the Southern Slavs and the Rumans was completed by the Turkish conquest of the Balkans.[10]

As Namier's title implies, his subject in view is the nineteenth century. This vast temporal overview is brought to bear on that time as an analogical overlay that provides a geopolitical template. The template itself is a distant result from a cause so deep and of such long range (over more than a millennium) as to be unconscious. This cause has demographic dimensions; we are well on our way to Braudel – or in another sense we are beyond him. The cause also has diplomatic dimensions that have been subsumed into the high level of generality here; we have not left the nineteenth-century diplomatic history still practiced in a syncopated and intensified form by Namier and many of his contemporaries. And at the same time the Namier who recommends Freud and speaks of the unconscious, must intend to assert here, and faintly to ironize, the unconscious element, the collective psychology, that itself can be described as an unperceived discrepancy, leading to a convergence, between the demographic and the diplomatic.

The level of generality here is high; but it is not totalizing. It makes claims not about any deep coherences in society but only about the large factors that govern shifts in political and linguistic populations. The sharpness of the disparity between these high generalities and the myriad particulars here being summarized can be taken as an implied assertion that the synecdoche, in the hands of a master, will have a nearly algebraic force.

Within the connections of the events narrated or discussed the sharpness of such general force is considerable in Namier's writing. It is less sharp, often, in that of A. J. P. Taylor, who gains a different force by a double or triple synecdoche, with ironic relations obtaining at every level. First, as the title of that book implies, his largest generality involves the development of the modern world "from Napoleon to Lenin," and this development shadows nearly all his writing. Then, more specifically, there is nearly always a bearing on the lead into or away from World War I. Finally the particular geographical area is shown as responding to tensions created by those first two levels.

Though the Crimean War seemed indecisive, great decisions followed from it. Without it neither Germany nor Italy could have been
united; without it Europe would never have known "the liberal era,"
that halcyon age which ended in 1914 and which, for centuries to
come, men will regard as "normal times," just as the barbarians looked
back to the peace and security of Augustan Rome.[11]

Taylor's range holds fixedly at bay the larger areas to which his double
synecdoches refer. That very fixity toward what is merely implied affords
him a certain freedom. Such a freedom keeps synecdochic, and ironic,
pressure on the outwardly restricted narrative of *Germany's First Bid for
Colonies 1884–1885:*[12]

> Had Bismarck at this time stated precisely to the British government
> that he desired colonies and specified the areas he wanted, he would
> have received his colonies and his grievance would have been at an
> end. But this was the last thing Bismarck wanted: no colonial griev-
> ance, no *rapprochement* with France.
>
> (34)

The hidden purposes thus coiling into multiple payoffs produce constant
ironies within the events that proceed to one side of the other policy issues
and general governmental concerns. Everything was done, it would seem,
to resolve this particular conflict. The son of the Iron Chancellor, Herbert
Bismarck, was given special privileges when First Secretary of his embassy
in England, but his blunderings, and his very ambitions, frustrated the extra
attention of the British. For the Germans, too, careful manipulations back-
fire in Taylor's presentation, "The result of this policy was the reverse of
what the Germans expected – England became not more, but less, friendly
to the powers of The Triple Alliance" (8). And again, through the endless
manipulation of unexpected factors, each party will rise to their challenge
and rise in vain – even the astute Bismarck: "He was very anxious to see
an agreement between France and England, which would leave England
much freer to oppose Russia and so relieve the pressure on Austria. The
time was therefore opportune for a settlement of the Zanzibar question,
which would show France she had nothing to hope for from Germany"
(94). These super-Thucydidean permutations among the relations of six
powers show them as having not even a momentary mastery over the
questions, the big questions and the large movements, that are shadowing
these events, and from which they draw their meaning. And the angles are
endless. The implications of another essay, "Prelude to Fashoda," carry
that sense, for the very precision with which Taylor delineates angles.[13] Of
the supposed differences between two French foreign ministers a common,

but futile, consistency of astute policy obtains, "Both men, as foreign ministers, knew that the entente would not be accepted by French public opinion unless the colonial germs were tolerable; hence they sometimes seemed to the British to be driving a hard bargain. Their ultimate objective, a general settlement, did not alter" (140).

The contours of time are again implied by the double synecdoche: Nineteenth- and Twentieth-century Europe and World War I stand as the enclosing wholes to which these parts gain the force of their reference. Namier, writing about the same periods, brings a more exhaustive irony to bear on the particular events, while his synecdochic implication is somewhat looser: now the whole of Europe from antiquity to the present, now the fate of an individual country over a characteristic span of fifty years or so.

In The Hapsburg Monarchy, Taylor addresses events that the sharp, concentrated essays of Namier often address.[14] A somewhat larger time frame, 1809–1918, loosens the diplomatic account somewhat (which, however, still manages an effect of coiled tightness). And the synecdochic suggestions are correspondingly looser, since they are almost spatial rather than temporal. The time covered is the whole time Taylor usually has in mind. World War I, again, stands as the great revelation, though it is only approached at the Austrian angle:

> The "Austrian mission" turned out to be nothing more than compelling Slavs to fight for German hegemony in Europe. Until the outbreak of war, it had been possible to dream of "federalism," of Magyar supremacy overthrown, and of a union of free peoples. Now these imaginary possibilities vanished, except in the minds of a few obstinate clericals or incorrigible theorists. An independent Habsburg Monarchy had ceased to exist. German victory might preserve its skeleton; the reality would be a German domination of Austria and a Magyar domination of Hungary, the radical programme of 1848. In 1848 the dynasty could still work with the subject peoples and even find true "Austrians"; now it was a thin disguise for Greater Germany and Great Hungary. The Slavs and Rumanians, who had clung for so long to Habsburg protection, had to become, willy-nilly, the enemies of the Habsburg Empire.
>
> (236)

The language of the next to the last sentence in this passage hints at an application to Hitler's goals for Grossdeutschland, and their permuted futility. The irony at once analyzes what has gone before, summarizes a moment, and reveals the dead hand of illusions that Taylor says, in introducing his revised edition, could not have preserved themselves by any strategy. "The conflict between a super-national dynastic state and the national principle had to be fought to the finish; and so, too, had the conflict between the master and subject nations" (7).

The synecdochic self-consciousness of Henry Adams' *History of the United States During the Administrations of Thomas Jefferson and James Madison* may be measured by the noticeable play of the writer's attention not only within individual chapters, but as this gets reflected, almost Burckhardt–like, in the leap from general chapters in the mode of Tocqueville's *Democracy in America,* chapters soon brought to bear upon a highly specific and extensively amplified diachronic series. This attention differentiates Adams' work from a more straightforward detailed narration of some sequenced segment of national import, where national import has guided the writer, such as Schiller's *Thirty Years' War,* Sallust's *Jugurtha,* or, for that matter, *The Peloponnesian War* itself.

Adams, unlike Michelet, is tracing neither a general history nor a great heroic moment. He does not write about the Revolution, and he also does not write about the Civil War, through which he had lived, and from which, by the time of writing the *History,* he had enough distance for assessment. He has chosen to record a crucial shift, the painful impressment upon the United States that it would have to make major provision for defense whether it wished or no; that embargoes could not be substituted for fighting. This is from one viewpoint a tame corollary, and a sort of negative aftermath, of the Revolution, but nothing so grand as the progression from, say, Robespierre to Napoleon. *L'Empereur* does figure in the *History,* but its massive, slow progress stays in its own sphere of preoccupation. There Napoleon figures throughout as a distant concentration of power, to be handled diplomatically in conjunction with Talleyrand over the Louisiana Purchase in the aftermath of the chaos after Toussaint L'Ouverture has been crushed; or to be approached a dozen years later by the American poet-diplomat Joel Barlow, who dies in Poland pursuing *l'Empereur* to and from Russia, having figured more than a thousand pages earlier as one of the Connecticut Wits. The irony of this event is not so much displayed; it is almost suppressed in favor of the events in America, to which it is itself both a magnified index and a synecdochic contrast. The narration can be as full as Gibbon or Ranke over a period of only seventeen years, and at the same time, in its conception, as synecdochically demonstrative as the foreshortened Taylor. Adams' events, as he handles them, wear the double face of the ordinary and the crucial. His patient Mirabeau, Albert Gallatin, is endlessly tested for his clarity and probity, which are allowed a display in the action, qualities less effectively displayed in the detail–dredged, fairly unsynecdochic biography of that statesman that Adams had earlier written – and which could serve as another foil to bring out the interplay in the *History.*

The double presence of aspiration proper to a revolution and the more normal stresses of government is given not just a temporal definition but an incipient temporal framework in Adams' first chapter:

> A government capable of sketching a magnificent plan, and willing to give only a half-hearted pledge for its fulfillment; a people eager to advertise a vast undertaking beyond their present powers, which when completed would become an object of jealousy and fear – this was the impression made upon the traveller who visited Washington in 1800, and mused among the unraised columns of the Capitol upon the destiny of the United States.[15]

This traveler is almost in Gibbon's situation at the Capitol of Rome as he decides to write the *Decline and Fall*, but it is a Gibbon in reverse, standing among the unfinished units of classicizing construction. The visible flat columns are displaced from their as yet unrealized architectural embodiment into an inherent contradiction between a "magnificent plan" and its "sketch." And Adams continues the voyage of the imagined traveler, who takes note not only of what he sees but of what he does not see. "As he travelled farther south his doubts were strengthened, for across the Potomac he could detect no sign of a new spirit." In the previous paragraph Adams had already depicted the desolation of Washington, "across a swamp, a mile and a half away, the shapeless, unfinished Capitol was seen, two wings without a body, ambitious enough in design to make more grotesque the nature of its surroundings." Still, "The conception proved that the United States understood the vastness of their task, and were willing to stake something on their faith in it." And yet further, "the contrast between the immensity of the task and the paucity of means seemed to challenge suspicion that the nation itself was a magnificent scheme like the federal city," and the whole of Adams' sense of sharp incongruity is built into the suspension between positive and negative senses in the one word "scheme."

On the one hand Jefferson's attempt to stay out of wars is a failure, while on the other hand the nation during all this time is getting vastly under way, assimilating characteristics that had not surfaced in the immediately preceding Federalist administrations, in Adams' view. The constant paradox allows the large inclusiveness to subserve both these theses, and so to call (or seem to call) for the constant supplementation of Adams' lavish detail, which is worked hard enough on both sides of the paradox to retain a synedochic salience. Thus does Adams avoid the impression of mere accumulation, of *acervatio*, that afflicts even such writes as Ranke. As George Hochfield says of the whole, "The all-embracing theme of the *History*, therefore, uniting its four minor or two major divisions in a single structure, is the failure of American democratic idealism, one aspect of which is the rise of American nationality""[16] This ambivalent United States is itself a synecdochic example in the larger world on which it impinges sporadically and typically, the world of England and France, of the Bey of Algiers and Toussaint L'Ouverture, of Spain and its many possessions, of Napoleon and Talleyrand.

E. H. Carr in *The Romantic Exiles* presents a narrative with still a different double synecdoche — between personal lives and romantic archetypes, and between personal lives and the early stages of the Russian Revolution. In the first volume of his large-scale *History of Soviet Russia, The Bolshevik Revolution,* these synecdoches seem to disappear. But the very relative absence of synecdoches, and the evenness of the political and economic sequencing, indicates a Roman-like massiveness to the giant state Carr treats at such length:

> The apparent unanimity of almost all the prominent members of the Russian party — for Lenin's followers were rank-and-filers with scarcely a known name among them — won almost universal support for the Mensheviks. Kautsky not only refused to publish in the German social-democratic journal *Neue Zeit* an article from Lenin defending the Bolshevik standpoint, but sent to the Menshevik *Iskra* for publication a copy of a letter roundly condemning Lenin's attitude. The most substantial attack on Lenin was an article in *Neue Zeit* in July 1904 by Rosa Luxemburg, who denounced his policy of "ultra-centralism" as bureaucratic and not democratic. Diagnosing a specifically Russian character in Lenin's project, she spoke bitterly of "the 'ego' crushed and pulverized by Russian absolutism" reappearing in the form of "the 'ego' of the Russian revolutionary" which "stands on its head and proclaims itself anew the mighty consummator of history"; and she offered a new argument when she attacked the absolute powers of Lenin's party leadership as likely "to intensify most dangerously the conservatism, which naturally belongs to every such body." Finally, Bebel, the veteran German party leader, made an offer of arbitration, which was hastily accepted by the Mensheviks and no less summarily rejected by Lenin.[17]

The prophecy of Rosa Luxemburg cuts both ways. We can read it as "such Cassandras are never heard," or as "of such ironies caught in prophecies-come-true are the early histories of successful revolutions made." The evenness of Carr's presentation forbids our slanting in either of these directions. At other points, and in the overall development of his narrative, Carr takes the position that Lenin's success demonstrates his penetration into long-range processes, and that the success, once again, validates if it does not justify the ruthlessness of his perpetual exclusions. At this point, though, the presented factors themselves prevent, or at least forestall, an adjudication between the obstinacy of Lenin and his astuteness, or between the tendency toward endlessly scissiparous schism in revolutionary parties and the correspondingly ruthless intolerance toward dissent of revolutionary administrations. The giant state effectually sweeps all these sidelights up in the presentation of a Carr who also brings the sidelights to bear. In so encompassing a view there is no room for any synecdoches other than the unavoidable ones consequent upon the historiographic enterprise, and the massiveness of Carr's assemblage of detail sets an illusion of completeness at the service of substantiating the massiveness of the state that is his subject.

In his own discussion of the three levels in *The Mediterranean* (1238), Braudel claims "a total history" while disavowing the totalizing efforts of those like Toynbee and Spengler.[18] But accumulations however massive, and however leveled, can never attain to the generality of the totalizing historians whom Braudel characterizes as "oversimple." Braudel's effect is to make the history of events, the last part of his work, itself an appendage to the demographic and economic presentation, which actually gains not totality but a hardness of covering adequacy by a failure to imply a synecdoche. It is resolutely nonsynecdochic; the inevitable selection and incompletion of his detail is implicitly referred to the possibility of corrections that would be incidental, like the date for major shift out of this period which he changes from 1620 to 1650 or so (1240) – but without changing any of his factorial deductions. His final chapter "Events, Politics, and People," then, sapped of all causal force, comes to seem, in the light of the economics and demography, not a possible synecdoche either but simply an alternately organized appendage of comparably determined data. "Why was the victory of Elizabeth's ships over Philip II's clumsy armadas not followed by the English supremacy that would have seemed logical?" he asks. And he almost immediately answers in terms of market: "There is only one plausible explanation: Holland, by her proximity to the Catholic provinces of the Netherlands and by her persistence in forcing the coffers of Spain, had better access than England to the Peninsula and the American treasure upon which her commerce depended" (635). "The blame (for a shaky credit situation)," he earlier says, "for the shortage must lie with the general economic situation rather than on Gresham's shoulders" (481–482). And he continues, "An entente between Philip II and Elizabeth was possible as long as the Crown and merchants of England could, by raising loans on the Antwerp bourse, obtain their share of the American treasure."

Economic considerations allow him to range much more freely than military and political ones do, and he gives very little attention to the Armada that preoccupies other historians, perhaps on the grounds that its defeat took place far north of the Mediterranean, in whose waters he concentrates his attention to the Spanish fleet.

There are no grounds for denying, in fact, equal plausibility to the conservative, closeup portrayal of this particular set of events in Garrett Mattingly's *Armada:*

By late Autumn, 1588, the affairs of Catholic France had come to deadlock. As the Armada advanced towards its rendezvous Henry of Valois had yielded more and more to Henry of Guise, but never quite the essentials. In August, when the rumors of a Spanish victory were thickest, he made Guise his lieutenant general, but he would not go back to Paris with him, and as the likelihood of a Spanish victory faded, slowly, slyly, the king's resistance stiffened. Slowly he began a cautious, indirect campaign to recover what he had lost.[19]

Mattingly's synecdoches proceed from a possible convergence of personality, religious affiliation, long-range power manipulation, and a still more obscure élan in which the legend of the victory over the Armada, which "raised men's hearts in dark hours," "became as important as the actual event." Just as these elusive yields from narrative history cannot be proved to be less important than the most exhaustive statistical surveys presented with the highest skill, so for Braudel what we call "piracy" is a form of economic activity favored by the geopolitical conditions of the Mediterranean and therefore persisting in the region from antiquity on. For Mattingly (86) it is one more factor in the interrupting process of particular interactions. Either view is defensible. These two virtually polar methods (since even Braudel's "Events, Politics, and People" has a texture that more resembles the rest of his history than it does Mattingly's) differ as much, we may say, in the extent and manner of their reliance on synecdoche, as they do in the area and technique of their presentation.

In the *Montaillou* of Le Roy Ladurie,[20] there is one synecdoche whereby the life of a very small, late village is taken to stand, with allowable individual variation, for a medieval life that in some features continues in time almost up to the present.[21] Then there is another "imbricated" synecdoche whereby through the prism largely of a single family Le Roy Ladurie surveys this village from various vantages – the homestead, the dominance of an individual family; pastoral management and migrations; ethnographic constituency; "mentality"; sexuality and marriage; age-grading; death; social structures; ideas about magic, salvation, religion, and the church; and others. Each of these synecdochic surveys is taken to add up, and to be complementary. The cycle concludes in his final chapter, "La maison et l'au delà," "The house and the world beyond." These presentational synecdoches, taken together, mount an integrative picture that lends them force for an implied further synecdoche, the relation between the part of this village and the whole of medieval France. This large picture he comes at, in both likenesses and differences, the other way round from the Burckhardt-like approach of Marc Bloch in *La Société féodale*. And the convergence of the two synecdoches can remain synchronic while largely implying a diachrony that is larger than the diachrony of the thirty years to which Ladurie confines his presentation.[22] The irony of the narrative-cum-documentation of Le Roy Ladurie's *Carnival in Romans* is increased by its synecdochic character in space – this uprising is a microcosm and also a pressure point of the unrest in all of France during the Wars of Religion; and also it is synecdochic in time: The issues associated with the collapse of the *ancien régime* before the French Revolution can be clearly discerned, this historian emphasizes (much as Michelet had), in the elements of the earlier class struggle of the sixteenth century.[23]

Irony enters more directly into such more directly synecdochic works as Robert Darnton's *Great Cat Massacre* and his *Business of Enlightenment*, where the given case mounts an extrapolable power that connects it to the larger events of the French Revolution,[24] without the apparent causal reticulation of A. J. P. Taylor's *Germany's First Bid for Colonies*. The prerevolutionary *mentalité* is approached through the response to social conditions implied in the intrication they undergo in the construction of documents – seventeenth-century fairy tales, an apprentice's account of a vicious carnivalesque massacre of cats, a bourgeois's description of the city of Montpellier, a policeman's file of data and anecdotes about writers, Diderot's borrowed classificatory framework for the *Encyclopédie*, one reader's response to Rousseau. Here the synecdoche of the written document as against the "full" life is doubled against the synecdoche of the single life in the mass – even as it provides a classificatory vision of the mass. These documents overlap (the policeman's with the bourgeois with Diderot, the fairy tale with the apprentice's tale), but they are themselves not commensurate. Their incommensurability and their remoteness from statistics and from large events throw their synedochic function into relief and work as flickering lights on the "whole" enigma of the nascent Revolution, as does the social structuring retrievable from the single archive of the list of subscribers to the *Encyclopédie* from the Société Typographique de Neuchâtel.

All these various synecdoches are global, and they involve a relation between the statements taken together and the large referent, rather than a rhetorical involution of the relation between signifier and signified, or some attitude one could characterize as "synecdochic." The historian, like any writer, may use synecdoches locally at points of his writing, as a rhetorical figure. But he will also use the "positive" synecdoche not of some implied ideological stance but rather of an inescapable reference to his larger referent, the limit to which is all of human action in time, by extensibility or by extrapolability or by some version of both. In addition to these "positive" synecdoches, there is the "negative" synecdoche of what must be left out through misplaced concreteness, and also the one implied in the act of selection. The Anglo-Saxon Chronicle, however, when it lists cattle but not people, is not synecdochic in the positive sense of Namier or Taylor; no larger reference is implied.

These implications of larger reference function variously within such achieved modern works as I have been discussing. For both Namier and Taylor what they say is extensible backward to Napoleon and forward to World War II and beyond. It is also extrapolable generally, as Thucydides wished his history to be, though there is a sense in Namier of more powerful extrapolability than in Taylor, whose very minutiae exude a sense of near uniqueness, a resistance to an extrapolability that is at the same time suggested, largely in the very inadequacy of the most astute human beings to match the complexity of factors presented, at least before the fact. Le Roy Ladurie's sequences are somewhat extensible, but not extrapolable at all. The large homeostasis that Braudel presents for the Mediterranean region is not extensible outside that region and beyond the particular time-frame he presents. At the same time a model is presented, an implicitly synecdochic one, for other demographic-geopolitical-economic complexes that might exhibit homeostasis. So Carr, whose Soviet state is not really extensible backward or forward, and not extrapolable in small ways, would have to be seen as extrapolable in large ways, or the sequence of events would make no sense.

No sequence is totally sealed off in space and time. In history writing the reader himself is somewhat outside the space and time of the work and, without further hermeneutic constructions, it may be said that his presence invokes a synecdoche. In history writing, only through some synecdochic mechanism, however faintly suggested, can the past be recaptured. As Taylor says himself of *Germany's First Bid for Colonies*, and of his work generally – stressing, as it were, the irony in his synecdochic juxtapositions – "It is sound scholarly history and at the same time very funny, a specialty of mine."[25]

As Jack Hexter says, "History-as-problem proceeds under the sign of elegance."[26] One corollary of such elegance is the awareness that the historian builds into his text of the constant synecdochic pressure he must bring to bear on his problem. Here the principle of elegance-in-economy that Hexter stresses will make him pare down, while the principle of maximum relevance will make him build up. So each detail will have been, so to speak, doubly tested, in ways that show through the appositeness of his sequential presentation. This elegance will be felt in such constantly problematized modern works as Lawrence Stone's *Crisis of the Aristocracy, 1558–1641*, as Hexter presents it, or in Ariès's *L'Homme devant la mort*. In such works the narrative component has been minimized, and correspondingly, very little irony of event enters the presentation. An equivalent for irony, however, may be perceived in the play of intellection through the material, and in the vivifying contrast between the momentary act of solving the problem in part and the tension within the solved parts as they carry, in their necessary synecdoche, the index of their partiality.

In all these works the elegance obtains through the appropriate management of the synecdoche, in which the consciousness of a managed partiality carries the implication, whatever the particular structure of the work, that a surplus of meaning inheres in the connections that have been established. With such communications of surplus the best historians have continued to endow us.

NOTES

I. INTRODUCTION

1. R. G. Collingwood, The *Idea of History* (Oxford: Clarendon Press, 1956 [1946]), 115. The sentence is repeated at 215, on Collingwood's own account.

2. Louis O. Mink elaborates and criticizes these notions in *Mind, History, and Dialectic: The Philosophy of R. G. Collingwood* (Bloomington: Indiana University Press, 1969).

3. Morton White, *Foundations of Historical Knowledge* (New York: Harper, 1965). This bias also controls some of the attention of Arthur Danto in *Narration and Knowledge* (New York: Columbia University Press, 1985), where his chapter "Narrative Sentences" (143–182) addresses this question atomistically, sentence by sentence.

4. W. H. Dray, "Conflicting Interpretations in History: The Case of the English Civil War," in Gary Shapiro and Alan Sica, eds., *Hermeneutics* (Amherst: University of Massachusetts Press, 1984), 239–258. Dray's own book, *Laws and Explanation in History* (Oxford: Clarendon Press, 1957), formulates answers – tentative ones, I am arguing, as they would have to be – to the question of how historiography mounts causal explanations.

5. Ibid., 258–270.

6. See Rex Martin, *Historical Explanation* (Ithaca, N.Y.: Cornell University Press, 1977), 19–29.

7. Paul Ricoeur, *Temps et récit III* (Paris: Seuil, 1985), 110.

8. *Temps et récit, I* (1983), 102–103.

9. Lionel Gossman, *The Empire Unpossess'd: An Essay on Gibbon's* Decline and Fall (Cambridge University Press, 1981).

10. *Temps et récit I*, 165–174.

11. Hayden White underscores the arbitrariness of Braudel's dismissal of narrative history (White, *The Content of the Form* [Baltimore: Johns Hopkins University Press, 1987]). "The reasons they adduce for their dissatisfaction with narrative history are jejune." "It is difficult to know what to make of this strange congeries of opinions" (33). And, contra the exclusions against narrative of the Annales school, "narrative figurates the body of events that serves as its primary referent and transforms these events into intimations of patterns of meaning that any literal representation of them as facts could never produce" (45). And as Paul Veyne says (*Comment on écrit l'histoire* [Paris: Seuil, 1971],

151) of the variety of work produced by Braudel's associates, "What relationship can obtain among works at first sight so heterogeneous?" "Quelle parenté peut-il y avoir entre des travaux si hétérogènes à première vue?"

12. A number of questions bearing on this topic are discussed by Jack Hexter, *Doing History* (Bloomington: University of Indiana Press), 1971.

13. Carl G. Hempel, "The Function of General Laws in History," in Patrick Gardiner, ed., *Theories of History* (Glencoe: Free Press, 1959 [1942],) 344–355 (351).

14. Hayden White (*Metahistory* [Baltimore: Johns Hopkins University Press, 1973]) would want to apply them more generally as deep structures organizing a work. Paul Ricoeur (*Temps et récit*) brings many philosophical questions but fewer specific characterizations to bear for his "mise en intrigue."

15. Hayden White, *Tropics of Discourse* (Baltimore: Johns Hopkins University Press, 1978), 13–19. If they are taken as "ideal-types" in Weber's sense, the concurrence of two or more of White's tropes would not present a problem for theory.

16. All citations from *Tropics of Discourse*.

2. THE PROBLEMATIC EMERGENCE OF HISTORY WRITING AS A SEPARATE GENRE

1. Hayden White argues for a provisional countercase in which annals and chronicles would provide their own template of valid explanation, "If it were only a matter of realism in representation, one could make a pretty good case for both annals and chronicle forms as paradigms of ways that reality offers itself to perception ("Narrativity in the Representation of Reality," in *The Content of the Form*, 1–25). Still, qualifying this possibility does not have to entail relegating the global referent of a historical work "that is and can only be imaginary" (24). "Also imaginary" need not amount to "only imaginary."

2. For the implications of this term, see "Inquiry: Herodotus," in Albert Cook, *Myth and Language* (Bloomington: Indiana University Press, 1980), 145–189. In that book I discuss how the linearity of Herodotus works as a way of disengaging discourse from the myth-dominated circularity of Homer; I derive the procedures of Herodotus out of the implications of that disengagement. As Michel de Certeau says, in *L'Ecriture de l'histoire* (Paris: Gallimard, 1975), temporality "is less the result of research than its condition" (20). He further quotes Gérard Mairet, "Le Discours et l'historique," in *Essai sur la représentation historienne du temps* (Paris: Mame, 1974), as setting down the postulate that the historian "substitutes for the knowing of time the knowledge of that which is in time" (168).

3. Roland Barthes, "L'Effet de Réel," in *Le Bruissement de la langue: Essais critiques IV* (Paris: Seuil, 1984), 167–174. More specifically addressing himself to the writing of history ("Le Discours de l'histoire," 153–156), Barthes also invokes "l'effet de réel" here, and declares that "the 'real' is never more than an unformulated signified concealed behind the apparent omnipotence of the referent," "le réel n'est jamais qu'un signifié informulé, abrité derrière la toute-

puissance du référent" (165). Yet his handling of historical details one by one, and consigning the overall discourse to a "feigned performative discourse," "un discours performatif truqué" (165), does not serve really to define the area of historical discourse, or to characterize its objects – a task that the invocation of standard distinctions between signifier, signified, and referent can neither aid nor block. Barthes invokes metaphor and metonymy, the imaginary, Jakobson's shifters, and three classes (161–163), the last of which is the "functions" of Propp, serial types that in fact hypostatize events and actors too quickly to be of any use in the definition or discussion of historiography. The first two classes – an implication in the signified through metaphor and syllogistic or enthymematic discourse – may be found in the writings of historians but cannot really be taken to characterize them specifically; these traits can be found separately or together in other kinds of writing. Barthes is better in his specific discussions of Michelet, as cited in Chapter 7 of this volume. Here Barthes quotes Augustin Thierry, rather than any recent or more complex theoreticians, to characterize narrative history – and then at the same time scores Thierry for being naive. Too close an identification of historiography with fiction will obscure the cognitive functions of both, and just because there is a partial structural similarity between them.

In a rapprochement of history and fiction, Hans Robert Jauss offers three "illusions" of classic narrative history ("Der Gebrauch der Fiktion in Formen der Anschauung und Darstellung der Geschichte," in Reinhart Koselleck, Heinrich Lutz, and Jörn Rüsen, eds., *Theorie der Geschichte: Formen der Geschichtschreibung* [Munich: DTV, 1982], 415–451): (1) The illusion of the complete circuit, "Die Illusion der vollständigen Verlaufs"; (2) illusion of the initial beginning and definitive end, "Illusion des ersten Anfangs und definitiven Endes"; (3) illusion of an objective image of the past, "Illusion eines objektiven Bildes der Vergangenheit." Although Jauss gives all three of these a hermeneutic function, they are neither exactly commensurate nor mutually exclusive. More important, the term "illusion" is quite misleading, a capitulation to the definition of a relation between signifier and signified that nullifies the important referent and ultimately renders the whole discourse a sort of fantasy.

4. M. L. West, ed., Hesiod, *Works and Days* (Oxford: Clarendon Press, 1978), ll. 106–201.

5. Hesiod, *Works and Days*, 106.

6. For the differences of implication between this verb and another compound for the same root used by Herodotus (*apokoruphou*, 5.73), see Cook, *Myth and Language*, 159.

7. Roland Barthes, *La Chambre claire: Notes sur la photographie* (Paris: Gallimard, 1980); translated as *Camera Lucida* (New York: Hill & Wang, 1981), passim.

8. Even a brief summary will suggest both the similarities and the dissimilarities in which the age of gold is most like that of silver, the bronze age like the age of heroes, and the iron age a sort of cumulative opposite to all four taken together, though the ages are presented as progressively worse:

> gold – like gods, unperturbed, unaging, joyous, dying in sleep, free of work, peaceful, rich, acting as daimones for men.

silver – having an easy life course, proud to each other, impious, happy
   mortals.
bronze – warlike, proud, not grain-eating, strong, stout, having bronze
   homes and weapons, suddenly dying.
heroes – more just and noble, demigods, warlike, headed to the Isles of the
   Blest at death.
iron – toiling incessantly, care-laden, mixing the evil and the noble, inhos-
   pitable, unfilial, slandering, impious, quarrelsome, pride-honoring.

The correspondences among the ages are partially but not symmetrically
structured. The age of heroes, with respect to its time-definition, is least
assimilable to the others since it is defined as of an explicit time, that of the
Seven Against Thebes and the Trojan War. At the same time the age of the
heroes is the only one of the five whose attributes overlap into a number of
the others; and all of the traits of the heroes can be matched in the ages of
gold, or silver, or bronze. Again, the age of iron is most distinct for its
difference both from any set of ideals and from all the other four.

9. Percy Lubbock, *The Craft of Fiction* (London: Jonathan Cape, 1954 [1921]),
   passim.
10. In all these terms and categories, I am indebted to Naomi Schor's work *Reading
   in Detail* (New York: Methuen, 1987). She astutely accounts for desublimation
   and its opposite in fictional discourse – another difference between detail there
   and in the discourse of history: "What is then illuminated in *Le Curé de Tours*
   is the danger that is always hidden in synecdoche; the part may be out of
   proportion with the whole, and when that happens, one comes under the sway
   of the sublime. For if synecdoche presupposes a classical ideal of proportion-
   ality, indeed of harmony, the sublime always implies a radical disproportion
   between part and whole" (146). But the synecdoche in history, selected from
   real rather than invented data, begins "deflated" of the sublime; its misplaced
   concreteness leaves the "radical disproportion" inescapably in place. And yet
   it somehow manages to convey a sense of something lurking under a story,
   an effect that is conceptually, and also discursively, coherent.
      On the other hand, the complications of this question for fictional detail
   may be indicated by Stendhal's statement that "one spoils such tender sentiments by recounting them in detail," "on gâte des sentiments si tendre à les
   raconter en détail" (*Oeuvres intimes,* ed. Henri Martineau [Paris: Pléiade,
   1955], 395), a notion that assigns a desublimating, rather than a sublimat-
   ing, function to the inclusion of detail in a narrative. Here, too, since Stendhal is not urging that the sentiments not be recounted, he implies a sort of
   saturation point beyond which added details begin to spoil the lift of subli-
   mation in the story.
      In speaking of the particular in history, Michel de Certeau calls it "the limit
   of the thinkable" *(L'Ecriture de l'histoire,* 99 and passim). But this point, derived
   from the necessity to match any fact to some general classification in order to
   understand it at all, would not apply just to the historical detail. It is the
   condition of the word in language, the datum in perception, and so on.
11. The notion may be found throughout Weber's works. It is discussed at some

length in "Die 'Objektivität' sozialwissenschaftlicher Erkenntnis" (1904), in Max Weber, *Soziologie, Weltgeschichtliche Analysen, Politik,* ed. Johannes Winckelmann (Stuttgart: Kröner, 1956), 186–262.

12. Aristotle *Poetics* (1451b 2–3) trans. Gerald F. Else; Cook, *Myth and Language,* 299 n. 6. Aristotle asks a version of the modern question, what the reference, and hence the sense, of the whole utterance amounts to. As Lionel Gossman points out, there was also a long tradition in antiquity, notably exemplified by Quintilian and Cicero, of treating history in its rhetorical and literary dimension. Lionel Gossman, "Reproduction or Signification," in Robert H. Canary and Henry Kozicki, eds., *The Writing of History: Literary Form and Historical Understanding* (Madison: University of Wisconsin Press, 1978), 3–40. Further, as Thomas MacCary says (personal communication):

> Aristotle's "things that could happen" and Thucydides' "things that ought to have been said," are the same, revealing a way of thinking totally alien to us. To call it Greek idealism might be the best we can do, but consider what Aristotle says about the death of Sardanapalus (*Politics* 5.10): "Sardanapalus rendered himself contemptible by being seen carding wool with the women, and was murdered by one who saw him. At least that is the story told; and if it is not true of him, it is pretty sure to be true of someone else." It is not the individual that matters, but the pattern he follows – or should have followed.

And again:

> Thucydides is not himself without constants; he refers to *anthropeia physis* as such. To say this is just doing to Thucydides what Derrida did to Husserl – find the metaphysical flaw in the phenomenological argument. It also shows that Thucydides, with his philosophy of change, looks beyond Plato to Aristotle. His constant is characterized by change: human nature constantly finds the lowest level of its immediate circumstances; that is how it defines itself.

13. E. A. Speiser, "Ancient Mesopotamia," in *The Idea of History in the Ancient Near East,* ed. Robert G. Dentan (New Haven: Yale University Press, 1955), 35–76. But certainly the accounts by such kings as Esar-Haddon do not, in translation at least, carry any sense more than the intent to memorialize great deeds. They almost wholly resemble such later records as Augustus' *Res Gestae* on the *Monumentum Ancyranum,* which is contemporary with Livy but lacks wholly even that historian's rather miscellaneous sense of sequences in time.

14. This situation is described by E. G. Pulleybank, "The Historiographical Tradition," in *The Legacy of China,* ed. Raymond Dawson (Oxford: Clarendon Press, 1964): "The sheer quantity of Chinese historical writing needs to be stressed" (143–164). And by the eighteenth century a Chinese compendium listed fifteen categories of historiography (156). In the earliest of these works there is evidently an element of sub-Plutarchian measurement of encomium that assesses the figures discussed in the light of standard ideals. As Dore J. Levy reports in "The Trojan and the Hegemon; or, the Culture Hero as Slave of Duty," *Comparative Literature Studies,* 22 (1985): "The heroes of early Chinese historiography tend to be conceived in terms of abstractions of ritual completeness; that is, those aspects of social conduct which they exemplify in their careers" (136–146).

15. Gregory of Tours, *Historia Francorum,* in Bruno Krusch and William Levison,

eds., *Scriptores rerum Merovingicarum. Monumenta Germaniae historica*, 2nd ed. (Hannover: Hahn, 1951), 1:i, Book 5, ll. 1–6, p. 193. Gregory makes a general reference to Matthew on a time of troubles, and the passage he quotes is 10.21, "And the brother shall deliver up the brother to death, and the father the child: and the children shall rise up against their parents, and cause them to be put to death."

16. Einhard, *Vita Karoli Magni*, in *Monumenta Germaniae historica. Scriptores rerum Germanicarum* 25, ed. G. Waitz, 6th ed. (Hannover: Hahn, 1911), as reprinted and translated in *Einhard's "The Life of Charlemagne,"* ed. Evelyn Scherabon Firchow and Edwin H. Zeydel (Coral Gables, Fla.: University of Miami Press, 1982). In this instance it is their translation that I follow. Generally, however, all translations not otherwise attributed are my own.

17. Charles Foulon, "Wace," in R. S. Loomis, *Arthurian Literature* (Oxford: Clarendon Press, 1959), 94–103.

18. As Wace says, "En cele grant pais ke jo di / Ne sai si vus l'avez oi, / Furent les merveilles pruvees / Et les aventures truvees / Ki d'Artur sunt tant recuntees / Ke a fable sunt aturnees. / Ne tut mençunge, ne tut veir, Tut folie ne tut saveir." "In this great country what I say / I do not know if you have heard / The marvels were undergone / And the adventures were discovered / That of Arthur are so much told / And have been assigned to fable. / Not wholly lie, not wholly witness / Wholly folly or wholly knowledge" (9787–9794). Wace emphasizes veracity in his proem: "Ki vult oïr et vult saveir / De rei en rei e d'eir en eir, / Ki cil furent e dunt il vendrent . . . / Ki anceis e ki puis i fu, / Maistre Wace l'ad translaté / Ki en conte la verité." "Who wants to hear and wants to know / From reign to reign and time to time / Who they were and whence they came / . . . / What was before, what afterward / Master Wace has translated it / He who tells the truth of it" (1–8).

19. Arthur's identification as "Riothamus" is under current discussion in Geoffrey Ashe, *The Discovery of King Arthur* (London: Debrett's Peerage, 1984).

20. Caxton's "Preface," in Sir Thomas Malory, *Works*, ed. Eugène Vinaver (Oxford: Clarendon Press, 1971), xiii.

21. A partial scenario of this operatic play / stage epic is published in Robert Wilson, *The Civil WarS* (Frankfurt: Suhrkamp, 1984).

22. For a defense of Pound's historiographic focus from a slightly different point of view, see Michael F. Harper, "Truth and Calliope: Ezra Pound's Malatesta," *PMLA* 96, no. 1, (January 1981), 86–103. See also Marianne Korn, ed., *Ezra Pound and History* (Orono, Me.: The National Poetry Foundation, 1985).

23. Pound, *The Cantos* (New York: New Directions, 1972), passim.

24. For the facts here I am drawing on Carroll F. Terrell, *A Companion to the Cantos of Ezra Pound, Vol II* (Berkeley: University of California Press, 1984), ad loc.

25. Dominick La Capra, *History and Criticism* (Ithaca, N.Y.: Cornell University Press, 1985), well emphasizes that the linguistic revision of older rhetoric ("inventio," "dispositio," "elocutio"), the application of "generative tropes," and the orientation toward persuasion (which is another aspect of Aristotelian rhetoric) in the aesthetics of reception theory – all account for just a part of historical discourse rather than the whole. La Capra would amplify classical

rhetoric by a "dialogic" model based on Bakhtin. "Historiography is dialogical in that, through it, the historian enters into a 'conversational' exchange with the past and with other inquirers seeking an understanding of it. The problem is the nature of the conversation." This is fruitful orientation for understanding the paradox that obtains between verification and rhetoric, sustaining the rhetorical side by pointing out, as he does, the ways in which "performative" and other functions of language than the constative are integral to the historian's presentation. It remains, though, preliminary to the task of addressing the paradox. This "exchange" or "dialogic" model that he proposes, with its eight or more features, would still pose problems in accounting specifically for the object, or the overall referent, of historical discourse as distinguishable from other types of discourse – since his model would account equally well for other types also.

26. As Croce puts it somewhat too exclusively and negatively, "The concept of cause is and must remain extraneous to history because it was born on the terrain of the natural sciences and has its function in their domain," "il concetto di causa è e deve rimanere estraneo alla storia, perché nato sul terreno delle scienze naturali e avente il suo ufficio nel ambito loro" (*La Storia come pensiero e come azione* [Bari: Laterza, 1938], 16). Or as Michel de Certeau puts it, from a somewhat different angle, "On the one hand the real is the *result* of the analysis, and on the other hand it is its *postulate*," "D'une part, le réel est le *résultat* de l'analyse, et, d'autre part, il est son *postulat*," *L'Ecriture de l'histoire*, 47.

27. R. G. Collingwood, *The Idea of History*, 215. However, one might assimilate this remark to the practice of the Annales historians by extending thought to what they mean by "*mentalités*," though even then Braudel's practice would be hard to account for.

28. The list is given in W. W. How and J. Wells, *A Commentary on Herodotus* (Oxford: Clarendon Press, 1928), 1:51.

29. Charles Fornara, *Herodotus: An Interpretative Essay* (Oxford: Clarendon Press, 1971), 41–42, 44, 52–54, 66–73, 78–91. Kurt A. Raaflaub shows how these references and further analogues between past and present set the two into interpretive interactions along lines that give Herodotus' thought some of the force of similar thinking in tragedy and epic. ("Herodotus, Political Thought, and the Meaning of History," *Arethusa*, 20.1 and 2 (Spring and Fall 1987), 221–248).

30. Extended examples for Freud appear in Sigmund Freud, *Three Case Histories* (New York: Collier, 1963 [1909–18]).

31. Deborah Boedeker demonstrates Herodotus' intrication of his sources to set up multiple political and religious dimensions of another political figure's actions, in "The Two Faces of Demaratus," *Arethusa* 20.1 and 2 (Spring and Fall 1987), 185–201.

3 · PARTICULAR AND GENERAL IN THUCYDIDES

1. A. W. Gomme, A *Historical Commentary on Thucydides* (Oxford: Clarendon Press, 1959–70), I, 135, on 20.1 "It should be remembered that *tekmērion* is

not *evidence* but the *inference* drawn from the evidence." The rigor Thucydides marshaled when sifting evidence for a particular fact shows, for example, in his use of Homer's authority for the relation of the Greeks' early defenses to their later ones in the Trojan War, as Edwin Dolin lucidly and complexly demonstrates ("Thucydides on the Trojan War: A Critique of the Text of 1.11.1," *Harvard Studies in Classical Philology*, 86 [1982]), 119–149).

2. Eric Havelock, *Preface to Plato* (Cambridge, Mass.: Harvard University Press, 1963).

3. It is startling that F. M. Cornford (*Thucydides Mythistoricus* [London: Edward Arnold, 1907]) would have used this sentence as the epigraph for a work that then goes on effectually to misread its strictures. With the benefit of modern thematic analysis we may make the story of Pausanias (1.129–135) conform to a mythic pattern, as Cornford does but Thucydides does not. Still less would Thucydides effectually capitalize *apatē* as the goddess "Deception" in the first events surrounding Alcibiades (5.35–46).

For the overall "mythic" cast of the Peloponnesian War itself, Cornford offers a convenient reference point to deny. This contemporary of Freud, as we may say, saw in Thucydides' *History* a sort of return of the repressed, tragedy coming back in another form. Yet as everyone realizes, we cannot seek the sense of this work in a crude equation of Athens' downfall through *hybris* and *ate* with that in Greek tragedy. Indeed, the formula does not work too well for Greek tragedy either. Thucydides is not *mythistoricus*. For one thing, the word *ate* does not occur once in the whole of his work, and the six references to *hybris* are all limited to a very specific occasion. (I have tried to deduce the implications of the exclusively poetic use of *ate* in Albert Cook, *Enactment: Greek Tragedy* [Chicago: Swallow Press, 1971] 69–76. For further examination of the personal psychological implications of this complex word, see William F. Wyatt, Jr., "Homeric Ate," *American Journal of Philology* 103 [1982], 247–276). This is Thucydides' – and for that matter the historian's – normal use of such abstractions, even though there is a slight poetic cast to Thucydides' vocabulary. (Dionysius of Halicarnassus was the first to notice the poetic cast of Thucydides' vocabulary, which is also touched on by Gomme [*Historical Commentary*, I, 135, note on *agan* in 1.70.1]. See also John H. Finley, Jr., *Thucydides* [Cambridge, Mass.: Harvard University Press, 1942], 265). But whatever the dominant substratum we attribute to Thucydides' narrative, the relation he establishes between particular and general in his narrative radically divorces it from the procedures of myth-evocation.

It is the modern era, and not the Athens of the Peloponnesian War, that sees a tragic cast to history. This is the mode of Hegel, Marx, Nietzsche, and Heidegger, become explicit and somewhat narrowed in influential force though wide in scope for Alfred Weber, *Das Tragische und die Geschichte* (Munich: Piper, 1959 [1943]).

4. Though Herodotus is more explicit in this and other ways, the actual differences between the two historians with respect to the gods are relatively minor. As Ronald Syme points out ("Thucydides," in the *Proceedings of the British Academy* 48 [1962], 39–56), in Thucydides an appeal to the gods often fails. But that is

true in Herodotus as well, with the frequent elaborate mismatching of oracle to circumstance.

5. Gomme, *Historical Commentary*.
6. Quoted in ibid., 2:90.
7. See also 2.14.1, "in the time of Cecrops." As Gomme says (ibid., 2:48), "Another example to show that Thucydides did not doubt the truth in outline of the Greek 'myth,' though he might interpret the story in his own way."
8. Wolfgang Schadewalt, *Die Anfänge der Geschichtsschreibung bei den Griechen* (Frankfurt: Suhrkamp, 1982), 251–252.
9. Gomme, *Historical Commentary*, I, 153; 2:154–155.
10. Ibid., 1:209, on 1.5.7–7, with examples.
11. Albert Cook, *Myth and Language*, 158–162.
12. See Finley, *Thucydides*, 46–70.
13. This is Schadewalt's phrase, by way of qualifying Reinhardt's and Schwartz's comparisons of Thucydides to Machiavelli.
14. Gomme, *Historical Commentary*, 1:19.
15. A. W. Gomme, A. Andrewes, and K. J. Dover, *A Historical Commentary on Thucydides* (Oxford: Clarendon Press, 1970), 4:433–436, on 7.57–59.
16. Cornford, *Thucydides Mythistoricus*, 132.
17. Eduard Schwarz, *Das Geschichtswerk des Thukydides* (Hildesheim: Olms, 1960 [1929]), 27.
18. See Walter Müri, "Beitrag zum Verständnis des Thukydides" (1947), in Hans Herter, ed., *Thukydides* (Darmstadt: Wissenschaftliche Buchhandlung, 1968), 135–169. Syme, "Thucydides," remarks on Thucydides' predilection for the term. An expansive examination of this and related "psychological" words is given in Pierre Huart, *Le Vocabulaire de l'analyse psychologique dans l'oeuvre de Thucydide* (Paris: Klincksieck, 1968).
19. Otto Regenbogen, *Kleine Schriften* (Munich, 1961).
20. Lowell Edmunds, *Chance and Intelligence in Thucydides* (Cambridge, Mass.: Harvard University Press, 1975), 155.
21. Nathan Rotenstreich, *Between Past and Present* (New Haven, Conn.: Yale University Press, 1958), 296.
22. See Albert Cook, *The Classic Line* (Bloomington: Indiana University Press, 1966), 70–71.
23. Gomme, *Historical Commentary*, 2:13.
24. H. D. Westlake, *Individuals in Thucydides* (Cambridge University Press, 1968), 15.
25. Ibid., 231.
26. See Peter R. Pouncey, *The Necessities of War: A Study of Thucydides' Pessimism* (New York: Columbia University Press, 1980), and Gomme, *Historical Commentary*, 2:195.
27. Schadewalt, *Die Anfäng der Geschichtsschreibung*, 301, and Gomme, *Historical Commentary*, 25–29; also Karl Reinhardt, *Das Vermächtnis der Antike* (Göttingen, 1960).
28. Müri, "Beitrag zum Verständnis Thukyidides," 155ff.
29. Paul Ricoeur, *The Contribution of French Historiography to a Theory of History* (Oxford: Clarendon Press, 1980), 19.

30. N. G. L. Hammond, "The Particular and the Universal in the Speeches of Thucydides," in *The Speeches in Thucydides* (Chapel Hill: University of North Carolina Press, 1973), 49–59.
31. Finley, *Thucydides*, 253–269.
32. G. E. L. Lloyd, *Polarity and Analogy: Two Types of Argumentation in Early Greek Thought* (Cambridge University Press, 1966).
33. Günter Wille, "Zu Stil und Methode des Thukydides" (1963), in Hans Herter, ed., *Thukydides*, 691.
34. Schadewalt, *Die Anfänge der Geschichtsschreibung*, 391–394. Schadewalt diagrams the narrative according to three foci of exposition, "Wesensdeutung," "Machtmotiv," and "Pathologie Athens."

4. REFERENCE AND RHETORIC IN HISTORIOGRAPHY (GIBBON)

1. As Hexter says, "Communication through historiography requires historians to put into written words what they know experientially and diffusely about the past, to organize it into coherent and sequential statements in order to make it fully accessible first to themselves and then to others. Their communication with others, the history they end up writing, thus starts four removes from the episodes in the past that concern them. Between the two lie the historical record, the historians' experiential knowledge acquired through their exploration of that record, and their attempts to communicate to themselves what they know" (*Doing History*, 372). And again "The serious historiographic problem is not how to avoid the mix [of analysis and story-telling] in order to maintain the superiority of one mode over the other, but how to proportion it and how to manage it" (379).
2. Hayden White, *Metahistory* (Baltimore: Johns Hopkins University Press, 1973). "Modes of emplotment," like "Romantic," do not either predict or necessarily correlate with "modes of argument" like "formist," "modes of ideological implication" like "anarchist," or "tropes" like "metaphor." Each term in itself is either too complex or too vague to be more than roughly applicable to the work of a given historian, and the headings are too diverse for illuminating connections to obtain more than occasionally between terms under one heading or another. For more specific qualifications of White, see this volume's Chapter 7, on Burckhardt and Michelet.
3. Albert Cook, *The Meaning of Fiction* (Detroit: Wayne State University Press, 1960). In this discussion I have also considered, in rudimentary fashion for historiography, the implications of the common ground between historiography and fiction, "Philosophy is to poetry as history is to fiction." In my chapter "Balzac: History as Rhetoric," I have discussed Balzac's whole appropriation as a pretense, but also with some documentary force, of the posture of the historian. Balzac's kind of emplotment, I would argue, is more easily assimilable to White's kinds of plot than those in a historian. And fiction offers a different relationship between rhetoric and validation than historiography does. Further, White wants to identify metonymy with cause, *post hoc, ergo propter hoc*. But cause always shows through any historian, not just White's "metonymic" ones. And it never shows through fully, or the historian has

transformed his work into a brief arguing a case.

Balzac is comic, tragic, and satiric all at once, whereas Michelet and Burck-hardt, for example, are, properly speaking, none of these. In the nature of my own presentation here, it should be said, I shall be continually qualifying or even arguing against points that White makes. Still, it is from his resolute and comprehensive attempt to provide rhetorical dimensions or even deep structure for works of historiography that I take my departure. My relation to White is not that of Paul Ricoeur to Derrida in *La Métaphore vive*, where he wishes to provide the means for refuting fundamental ideas. Nor is it that of Derrida to Husserl, against whom he provides local refutation with general implications within his own quasi system. Rather, I wish to incorporate White's arguments while qualifying them and redefining or refining some of his specific analyses. For a perspicacious assessment of contradictions in White, see David Konstan, "The Function of Narrative in Hayden White's *Metahistory*," *Clio* 11, no. 1 (Fall 1981), 65–78.

4. See Albert Cook, *The Classic Line*.

5. For the resistance of music to irony, see Jackson Barry, *Dramatic Structure* (Berkeley: University of California Press, 1970), 156.

6. Hexter (*Doing History*) once again makes telling points, "This procedure [the attempt of Morton White and other analytic philosophers to account for the principles of historiography] has been less than satisfactory, since it requires them quite arbitrarily and without evidence to assign to many [features of historiography] an altogether aesthetic rather than a noetic function. . . .

   "The philosophers have proceeded as they have for the very good reason that to do otherwise would be to raise extremely perplexing questions about the nature of knowing, understanding, meaning and truth to which, as of now, neither they nor anyone else has any very plausible answers" (393). Ideas of cause, as well, remain both inescapably germane and unresolvably perplexing in the best historiography.

   In this light Hayden White's quasi-structuralist attempt to assign the meaning in historiography to a supposed deep structure of rhetorical types is the inverse of Morton White's attempt to assign that meaning to testable analytic sentences. Both writers separate verification from rhetoric in ways partially belied by the actual acts of understanding carried through in historiographic works.

7. Louis O. Mink, "Narrative Form as a Cognitive Instrument," in Robert H. Canary and Henry Kozicki, eds., *The Writing of History*, 129–150 (145).

8. As Burckhardt says in *The Civilization of the Renaissance in Italy* (New York: Harper, 1975), 102, "We might find something to say against every line of the *Istorie Fiorentine*, and yet the great and unique value of the whole would remain unaffected."

9. Any historiography must be at several hermeneutic removes from its data, as Hexter declares (see note 1). This situation is highlighted by the text's implied insistence on the reliability of its individual verbal references. The removes from data – or from "episodes" – may be variously tabulated. The first remove is the necessary limitation on evidence available from the total chaos, or tau-tological order through identity with itself, of all that ever happened. The second remove is the selection made from the available evidence (diplomatic

letters are chosen instead of popular broadsides, or the two are overlooked in favor of population statistics). The third remove (related to the first) is the slant in the documents or data at hand; population statistics have something lying behind them precisely as do diplomatic letters, though in statistics it is the relation to other patterns and in documents the relation to the concealed purposes of the writer of the document. At a fourth remove is the interpretative strategy used to organize after this selection. If a compilation is being made, a fifth remove is present, that of the compiler, as in the case of Samuel and Kings. Since we do not know how extensive and reliable his sources were, mentioned and unmentioned, or how large a segment they constitute of the total sources available to him, we are unable to assess his relation to removes one through four. A sixth possible remove, textual reliability, is actually trivial; we may assume that texts are roughly accurate. Every interpreter of a historiographic text is himself at least at a fifth remove, and possibly more.

The shifts among the various removes are so flexible that there is little need to adjudicate among them or to yield to their accessibility to relativization. Such hermeneutic discussions, for all their philosophical viability and even plausibility, have the effect of arresting discourse wholly upon themselves. But there is more, or at least there are other things, to say.

10. Nancy S. Struever, *The Language of History in the Renaissance: Rhetoric and Historical Consciousness in Florentine Humanism* (Princeton, N.J.: Princeton University Press, 1970), 198. While this principle is well put, we may question Struever's causal attribution to humanist discourse of getting Machiavelli and, later, Gibbon beyond rhetorical practice. Machiavelli in fact was well versed in the classical historians and did not need the humanists for the specific task of attaining a viable historiography; and the usual classical rhetoric itself, however its tangentiality be managed, can never produce the sorts of tensions between verification and time contours that the great historian manages.

11. Roland Barthes, *La Chambre claire*.

12. Roland Barthes, *S/Z* (Paris: Seuil, 1970).

13. Albert Cook, *Myth and Language*.

14. "Should I not have deduced the decline of the Empire from the Civil Wars, that ensued after the fall of Nero or even from the tyranny which succeeded the reign of Augustus? Alas! I should: but of what avail is this tardy knowledge? Where error is irretrievable, repentance is useless." *The English Essays of Edward Gibbon*, ed. P. B. Craddock (Oxford University Press, 1972), 338, as cited by G. W. Bowersock, "Gibbon on Civil War and Rebellion in the Decline of the Roman Empire," in Bowersock, John Clive, and Stephen Graubard, eds., *Edward Gibbon and the Decline and Fall of the Roman Empire* (Cambridge, Mass.: Harvard University Press, 1977), 27–36. I would assert that Gibbon's sense, here expressed, that his history was unrevisable, derives not only from his conception of what publication entails but also from an instinctive tact toward the proportions, and narrative meaning, of his history. After all, it is possible to revise, even radically.

15. Marshall McLuhan, "John Dos Passos: Technique vs. Sensibility," in A. Walton Litz, ed., *American Fiction* (Oxford University Press, 1963), 138–149. "Gibbon's late use of baroque perspectivism, the linear handling of history as a

dwindling avenue, concurred with the eighteenth-century discovery of the picturesque, or the principle of discontinuity as a means of enriching artistic effect."

16. Paul Ricoeur, *Contribution of French Historiography*, 19.

17. Paul Ricoeur, *Temps et récit*. Paul Veyne, *Comment on écrit l'histoire*, "Ou bien les faits sont considérés comme des individualités, ou bien comme des phéno-mènes derrière lesquels on cherche un invariant caché" (18). Veyne is led by this opposition to define an event as that which does not go without saying, "an event has sense only in series," "un événement n'a de sens que dans une série" (38). This begs several important questions, and permits him to range between universal and particular: "The traits retained as pertinent, with relation to which an individual fact is described, are universals," "Les traits, retenus comme pertinents, par rapport auxquels on décrit un fait individuel, sont des universaux" (62). "That is historic which is not universal, and which is not singular (*singulier*). For it not to be universal, there must be difference; for it not to be singular, it must be specific" (76). But as Ricoeur says of Veyne (*Contribution*, 45), "It is when history ceases to be eventful that the narrativist theory is truly put to the test." And as Hermann Lübbe says from a different angle ("Was aus Handlungen Geschichten macht," in Jürgen Mittelstrass and Manfred Riedel, eds., *Vernünftiges Denken* [Berlin: de Gruyter, 1978], 237–250), "one can argue endlessly without theoretical gain about the role of ac-cidence (*Zufall*) in history" (247). As he also says, emphasizing that history escapes the rationales of its participants, "Histories are procedures that do not adapt to the rational manipulations (*Handlungsraison*) of the participants. They are not rational with respect to manipulation" (238).

18. *Comment on écrit*, 139.

19. Reinhart Koselleck, "*Uber die Theoriebedürftigkeit der Geschichtswissenschaft*," in Werner Conze, ed., *Theorie der Geschichtswissenschaft und Praxis des Geschichts-unterrichts* (Stuttgart: Klett, 1972), 10–28, reprinted in *Wege der Forschung, Ge-schichtsschreibung*, 37–59, "It is significant that history 'as such' has no object at all – it is then itself, by which it cannot resolve the question of its object of research, but can only be doubled back (*sondern nur sprachlich verdoppelt lässt*), 'history of history.' In this way it is clear to what degree 'history itself' (*Ge-schichte schlechthin*) was in its very origin (*ursprünglich*) a metahistorical cate-gory" (40–41).

20. Much like (for example) Milton, Gibbon long cast about for a subject and a style. "The style of an author should be the image of his mind, but the choice and command of language is the fruit of exercise. Many experiments were made before I could hit the middle tone between a dull chronicle and a rhetorical declamation: three times did I compose the first chapter, and twice the second and third, before I was tolerably satisfied with their effect . . . the fifteenth and sixteenth chapters have been reduced by three successive revisals from a large volume to their present size; and they might still be compressed without any loss of facts or sentiments" (*Autobiography* [Oxford University Press, 1907], 177). "It has always been my practice to cast a long paragraph in a single mould, to try it by my ear, to deposit it in my memory, but to suspend the action of the pen till I had given the last polish to my work" (ibid., 185).

21. One sense that must usually be disallowed for Gibbon is the one first re-
corded in Smollett, 1771, "6, to beguile, while away." I fear that this is
the sense mainly understood by Hayden White ("neither should we dismiss
too easily Gibbon's own characterization of his Decline and Fall . . . as the
product of an effort to divert and amuse himself" [*Metahistory*, 55]).
White's plea at once misattributes the modern sense to Gibbon and falsifies
his enterprise by vastly oversimplifying its verbal procedures in the guise
of attending to their complications. Gibbon had to find his way to such
expression. Gibbon does use this word in all or many of its senses, including the modern sense. The older, more serious sense, however, is quite
distinct in the *Autobiography*. "No plan of study was recommended for my
use; no exercises were prescribed for his inspection; and, at the most precious season of youth, whole days and weeks were suffered to elapse
without labour or amusement" (*Autobiography*, 42).

     Such mismatches between White's categories and the actual statements of
the historians he cites are a risk of his matching procedure. Here they derive
from trying to make Gibbon's multiplex and partially intermittent irony do a
single job. Indeed, in this light, what Peter Gay says is apposite (*Style in History*
[New York: Basic, 1974], 51), "for Gibbon, then, gravity and levity coexisted
without strain." Gay, however, goes on to overemphasize levity when he says
that "while both together define his historical vision, it is with levity that
Gibbon was most at home." Some yearning for levity under the repressions
of strict (but gracefully managed) professionalism must lurk beneath this over-
valuation of the element of levity in Gibbon when the gravity is also clearly
to be perceived. What does "at home" mean here, when Gibbon obviously
eases in the gravamen of his immense rhetoric with a sternness that characterizes
him as much as does the sharp levity in which he obviously delights? What
would be needed to bring the structures of levity and gravity together would
be not a psychoanalysis (for which the evidence is probably too slight) but
rather a psychoanalytically oriented structuration of the interaction of tones in
Gibbon's style. That is not my task here, though I would hope that what I
have to say here would bear upon such questions, as upon others.

22. Martin Heidegger, *Sein und Zeit* (Tübingen: Niemeyer, 1963 [1927]), 372–403.
As Heidegger himself says at various points of his work, the presentation of
human existence in time has to proceed in circular fashion (152, 158, and
passim). The attribution of "authenticity," even for someone who assents to
Heidegger's "laying bare" of man's existence in time, would then itself be
circular, or summarizable in the same key terms. It would not operate to
explain in other terms how a historical work attains its authentic presentation
in time of what suggests causality but does not establish it as other than a
revelation-through-sequence in the narrative.

     At the same time Heidegger effectively characterizes the inextricability of
general and particular in the historian's writing:

> When historiography, itself arising from a genuine historicity, uncovers
> the existence that existed at that time [Heidegger refers to the past as
> "Gewesenheit" instead of the usual term "Vergangenheit"], then it has

already laid the general open in the singular. The question whether historiography has as its object only the ordering of "individual" occurrences or "laws" as well, is radically erroneous.

Wenn die Historie, selbst eigentlicher Geschichtlichkeit entwachsend, wiederholend das dagewesene Dasein in seiner Möglichkeit enthüllt, dann hat sie auch schon im Einmaligen das "Allgemeine" offenbar gemacht. Die Frage, ob die Historie nur die Reihung der einmaligen, "individuellen" Begebenheiten oder auch "Gesetze" zum Gegenstand habe, ist in der Wurzel schon verfehlt (395).

23. Harold L. Bond, *The Literary Art of Edward Gibbon* (Oxford: Clarendon Press, 1960), 144.

24. Paul Ricoeur, *Tempts et récit*, I, 85: "Le temps devient temps dans la mesure où il est articulé sur un mode narratif, et que le récit atteint sa signification plénière quand il devient une condition de l'existence temporelle."

25. John William Miller, *The Philosophy of History* (New York: Norton, 1981), 147.

26. Many such discussions can be found, for example, in Koselleck, Lutz, and Rüsen, eds., *Theorie der Geschichte*. Rüsen's own contribution, for example ("Die vier Typen des historischen Erzählens," 514–605), begins with a criticism of Hayden White's typology and continues with his own, of traditional, exemplary, critical, and genetic history. These respectively eternalize time, spatialize it, allow it to be assessed as thought, and time-orient it as thought (*als Sinn verzeitlicht*). The application of these four categories to actual histories would almost surely, as with White, find them overlapping, interlocking, and overdefining the delicate procedures under way in the given narrative, and would ultimately lead to misdefinition.

5. SCALE, PSYCHOLOGICAL STEREOTYPING, AND STYLE IN TACITUS' *ANNALS*

1. Initium mihi operis Servius Galba iterum Titus Vinius consules erunt. nam post conditam urbem octingentos et viginti prioris aevi annos multi auctores rettulerunt, dum res populi Romani memorabantur pari eloquentia ac libertate: postquam bellatum apud Actium atque omnem potentiam ad unum conferri pacis interfuit, magna illa ingenia cessere; simul veritas pluribus modis infracta, primum inscitia rei publicae ut alienae, mox libidine adsentandi aut rursus odio adversus dominantis: ita neutris cura posteritatis inter infensos vel obnoxios. sed ambitionem scriptoris facile averseris, obtrectatio et livor pronis auribus accipiuntur; quippe adulationi foedum crimen servitutis, malignitati falsa species libertatis inest. mihi Galba Otho Vitellius nec beneficio nec iniuria cogniti. dignitatem nostram a Vespasiano inchoatam, a Tito auctam, a Domitiano longius provectam non abnuerim: sed incorruptam fidem professis neque amore quisquam et sine odio dicendus est. quod si vita suppeditet, principatum divi Nervae et imperium Traiani, uberiorem securioremque materiam, senectuti seposui, rara temporum felicitate ubi sentire quae velis et quae sentias dicere licet.

2. Urbem Romam a principio reges habuere; libertatem et consulatum L. Brutus instituit. dictaturae ad tempus sumebantur; neque decemviralis potestas ultra biennium, neque tribunorum militum consulare ius diu valuit.

> non Cinnae, non Sullae longa dominatio; et Pompei Crassique potentia
> cito in Caesarem, Lepidi atque Antonii arma in Augustum cessere, qui
> cuncta discordiis civilibus fessa nomine principis sub imperium accepit.
> sed veteris populi Romani prospera vel adversa claris scriptoribus me-
> morata sunt; temporibusque Augusti dicendis non defuere decora ingenia,
> donec gliscente adulatione deterrerentur. Tiberii Gaique et Claudii ac Ner-
> onis res florentibus ipsis ob metum falsae, postquam occiderant recentibus
> odiis compositae sunt. inde consilium mihi pauca de Augusto et extrema
> tradere, mox Tiberii principatum et cetera, sine ira et studio, quorum causas
> procul habeo.

3. The contradiction between Tacitus' ideal of the capable authoritarian emperor
   and the latitude implied by *libertas* is resolved for him by the case of Nerva,
   who "was to mix characteristics previously dissociated, the principate and
   liberty," *Nerva Caesar res olim dissociabiles miscuerit, principatum ac libertatem*
   (Agricola 3). *Libertas* has a large range. In the third line of the introduction to
   the *Histories*, quoted above, it is paired with *eloquentia* both as an ideal attitude
   in the writer ("honesty") and as a quality in him which will allow him to
   assume this attitude.

   As Ronald Syme points out in *Tacitus* (Oxford: Clarendon Press, 1958),
   413, Tacitus mostly omits *auctoritas*, or uses it ironically (1.24; 11.25; 14.39),
   or pairs it or replaces it with its somewhat pejorative synonym *potentia* (413).

   On Tacitus' diction generally, E. Lösfeld ("On the Style of Tacitus," *Journal*
   of Roman Studies 38 [1948], 1–8) points out his specific emphases of diction, in
   the use of "*claritudo*" for "*claritas*," "*glisco*" for *cresco*," and the like. Lösfeld
   also indicates his tendency to avoid balanced clauses and to bury his psychology
   in passing maxims.

   Friedrich Klingner ("Sprache und Stil des Tacitus am Anfang des 13 An-
   nalenbuches," *Hermes* 83 [1955], 187–200) lists points at which Tacitus has
   deflected traditional usage for forceful effect.

4. Nam cunctas nationes et urbes populus aut primores aut singuli regunt:
   delecta ex iis et consociata rei publicae forma laudari facilius quam evenire,
   vel si evenit, haud diuturna esse potest. igitur ut olim plebe valida, vel
   cum patres pollerent, noscenda vulgi natura et quibus modis temperanter
   haberetur, senatusque et optimatium ingenia qui maxime perdidicerant,
   callidi temporum et sapientes credebantur, sic converso statu neque alia re
   Romana quam si unus imperitet, haec conquiri tradique in rem fuerit, quia
   pauci prudentia honesta ab deterioribus, utilia ab noxiis discernunt, plures
   aliorum eventis docentur.

5. Syme, *Tacitus*, 573.
6. Inez Scott Ryberg, "Tacitus's Art of Innuendo," *Transactions of the American*
   Philological Association 73 [1942], 383–404.
7. Ryberg (ibid.) gives the comparative detail for Livia (389–391) and for Seneca
   (399–404).
8. R. G. Collingwood, *The Idea of History*, 38–40. Collingwood consistently
   oversimplifies Tacitus, while measuring him by antipsychological principles
   that if consistently applied would invalidate most great historiographers. For
   example, "his characters are seen not from inside," he asserts, with understanding and sympathy, "but from outside as mere spectacles of virtue or vice"
   (39). The philosophical problems raised by such an assertion are considerable,
   even before one gets to the point of assessing its hermeneutic validity.

9. ... sic Tiberius finivit octavo et septuagesimo aetatis anno.

Pater ei Nero et utrimque origo gentis Claudiae, quamquam mater in Liviam et mox Iuliam familiam adoptionibus transierit. casus prima ab infantia ancipites; nam proscriptum patrem exul secutus, ubi domum Augusti privignus introiit, multis aemulis conflictatus est, dum Marcellus et Agrippa, mox Gaius Luciusque Caesares viguere; etiam frater eius Drusus prosperiore civium amore erat. sed maxime in lubrico egit accepta in matrimonium Iulia, impudicitiam uxoris tolerans aut declinans. dein Rhodo regressus vacuos principis penatis duodecim annis, mox rei Romanae arbitrium tribus ferme et viginti obtinuit. morum quoque tempora illi diversa: egregium vita famaque quoad privatus vel in imperiis sub Augusto fuit; occultum ac subdolum fingendis virtutibus donec Germanicus ac Drusus superfuere; idem inter bona malaque mixtus incolumi matre; intestabilis saevitia sed obtectis libidinibus dum Seianum dilexit timuitve: postremo in scelera simul ac dedecora prorupit postquam remoto pudore et metu suo tantum ingenio utebatur.

10. Syme, *Tacitus*, 42.

11. Tiberii Gaique et Claudii ac Neronis res florentibus ipsis ob metum falsae, postquam occiderant recentibus odiis compositae sunt. inde consilium mihi pauca de Augusto et extrema tradere, mox Tiberii principatum et cetera, sine ira et studio, quorum causas procul habeo.

12. The fact that Lévi-Strauss, for example, introduces these categories in his own discourse, allows Jacques Derrida (*L'Ecriture et la Différence* [Paris: Seuil, 1967], 409–428) the latitude for a metacommentary of endlessly qualifying combination upon them.

13. Syme, *Tacitus*, 253: "What survives... indicates a structure of three groups, each containing six books." Syme goes on to discuss the bases of this division, indicating (262) that the exordium of Book 13 marks a new section for Nero.

14. Ceterum Augustus subsidia dominationi Claudium Marcellum sororis filium admodum adulescentem pontificatu et curuli aedilitate, M. Agrippam, ignobilem loco, bonum militia et victoriae socium, geminatis consulatibus extulit, mox defuncto Marcello generum sumpsit; Tiberium Neronem et Claudium Drusum privignos imperatoriis nominibus auxit, integra etiam tum domo sua...

at hercule Germanicum Druso ortum octo apud Rhenum legionibus inposuit adscirique per adoptionem a Tiberio iussit, quamquam esset in domo Tiberii filius iuvenis, sed quo pluribus munimentis insisteret. bellum ea tempestate nullum nisi adversus Germanos supererat, abolendae magis infamiae ob amissum cum Quintilio Varo exercitum quam cupidine proferendi imperii aut dignum ob praemium. domi res tranquillae, eadem magistratuum vocabula; iuniores post Actiacam victoriam, etiam senes plerique inter bella civium nati: quotus quisque reliquus qui rem publicam vidisset?

Igitur verso civitatis statu nihil usquam prisci et integri moris: omnes exuta aequalitate iussa principis aspectare, nulla in praesens formidine, dum Augustus aetate validus seque et domum et pacem sustentavit. postquam provecta iam senectus aegro et corpore fatigabatur aderatque finis et spes novae, pauci bona libertatis in cassum disserere, plures bellum pavescere, alii cupere.

15. See the characterization of the *Res Gestae* in Ronald Syme, *The Roman Revolution* (Oxford: Clarendon Press, 1974 [1939], 522–524, with references. Of course, as Syme notes, this very lengthy inscription on the Monumentum Ancyranum

was meant for public consumption. So it cannot really compare with historiography, except to sharpen a sense of how individualized Tacitus has made his private interpretation of comparable public events.

16. Syme, *Tacitus*, 190. "Of Tacitus' bold independence in the selection of material and the construction of a narrative, the proof is overpowering."

17. In 12.40, Tacitus speaks explicitly of justifying a break in the annalistic sequence. He breaks it on other occasions also, to round out a story.

18. Tacitus has a tendency to note innovations, especially where they indicate a special twist of decline. There are frequent stresses on aspects of novelty as he depicts the downward spiral of the *maiestas* trials. When Seneca is brought in to write a speech for Nero (13.3), Tacitus remarks that this is the first instance of such a surrogate (with the irony that Nero especially prides himself on being a writer).

19. . . . stimulabat Claudium consuleret rei publicae, Britannici pueritiam robore circumdaret: sic apud divum Augustum, quamquam nepotibus subnixum, viguisse privignos; a Tiberio super propriam stirpem Germanicum adsumptum: se quoque accingeret iuvene partem curarum capessituro.

20. Syme, *Tacitus*, 26.

21. Viktor Pöschl says that Tacitus' judgments appear from a mass of insights, in Pöschl, ed., *Tacitus* (Darmstadt: Wissenschaftliche Buchhandlung [Wege der Forschung 97 (1969), "Der Historiker Tacitus," 161–176]). Pöschl, however, himself oversimplifies the intermittent foreshortening of Tacitus when he says, "Detail takes a back seat. 'The praetor cares not for small details' is a main principle," "Das Detail tritt zurück. *Minima non curat praetor* ist ein Hauptprinzip." The opposite is actually the case; as the last books show, Tacitus is careful enough of detail to deploy it unevenly through the work. This has the effect of heightening what Pöschl himself well characterizes as "recognizing the significance of the irrational moment."

22. In his discussion of the end of *Annals* 13, Charles Segal demonstrates how what some have found a puzzlingly irrelevant detail, the *prodigium* of the rebirth of a sacred fig tree, touches many thematic keys, even in its very discontinuities ("Tacitus and Poetic History: The End of Annals XIII," *Ramus* 2, no. 2 [1973], 107–126), "Initially the fig tree looks as if it were shoring up Nero's lies [but the] irony of this omen also touches upon the discrepancy between the apparent and the actual meaning of divine signs which XIV also develops. This discrepancy, in turn, is parallel to the discrepancy between Nero's rhetoric and his acts (113–114)." Segal goes on to locate this prodigium in a series, by no means anaphoric or merely repetitious, of other prodigies in Tacitus, which come thick and fast in Book 14.

23. Pleraque eorum quae rettuli quaeque referam parva forsitan et levia memoratu videri non nescius sum: sed nemo annalis nostros cum scriptura eorum contenderit qui veteres populi Romani res composuere. ingentia illi bella, expugnationes urbium, fusos captosque reges, aut si quando ad interna praeverterent, discordias consulum adversum tribunos, agrarias frumentariasque leges, plebis et optimatium certamina libero egressu memorabant: nobis in arto et inglorius labor; immota quippe aut modice lacessita pax, maestae urbis res et princeps proferendi imperi incuriosus erat. non tamen sine usu fuerit introspicere illa primo aspectu levia ex quis magnarum saepe rerum motus oriuntur.

24. Syme. *Tacitus*, 116.

25. Arnold Gerber and Adolf Greef, *Lexicon Taciteum* (Leipzig: Teubner, 1903), s.v.

26.   multitudo ingens haud proinde in crimine incendii quam odio humani generis convicti sunt. et pereuntibus addita ludibria, ut ferarum tergis contecti laniatu canum interirent, aut crucibus adfixi aut flammandi, atque ubi defecisset dies in usum nocturni luminis urerentur.

27. Syme, *Tacitus*, 111, 115, and passim, spells out the kinds of concerns that could be attributed in any case to a historian who wrote a small treatise on rhetoric, the *Dialogus*.

28. Tacitus often shows events slipping away from the nomenclature used to describe them. Paralleling Thucydides (3.82), he explicitly has Otho characterize the process, at Galba's hands, "What others call crimes he calls reforms, while with false names he speaks of severity for cruelty, economy for avarice, and calls discipline the tortures and affronts against you," "*nam quae alii scelera, hic remedia vocat, dum falsis nominibus severitatem pro saevitia, parsimoniam pro avaritia, supplicia et contumelias vestras disciplinam appellat*" (*Histories* 1.37).

29.   causae variae traduntur: alii taedio novae curae semel placita pro aeternis servavisse, quidam invidia, ne plures fruerentur; sunt qui existiment, ut callidum eius ingenium, ita anxium iudicium; neque enim eminentis virtutes sectabatur, et rursum vitia oderat: ex optimis periculum sibi, a pessimis dedecus publicum metuebat. qua haesitatione postremo eo provectus est ut mandaverit quibusdam provincias, quos egredi urbe non erat passurus.

                                                                 (1.80)

30. Gerber-Greef, s.v., lists well over a hundred uses of *species* in Tacitus, in a variety of senses – outward appearance, form, manifestation, show, pretext, ideal, and the like.

31. Syme, *Tacitus*, 192.

32. F. R. D. Goodyear, *Tacitus* (Oxford: Clarendon Press, 1970), 32. "Dramatic contrast is another important part of Tacitus' technique, for instance in the opposition of Tiberius and Germanicus." For the elaboration of networks of contrasting terms as they are brought to bear on "good" or "evil" characters, see Joseph Lucas, *Les Obsessions de Tacite* (Leiden: Brill, 1974).

33.   De comitiis consularibus, quae tum primum illo principe ac deinceps fuere, vix quicquam firmare ausim: adeo diversa non modo apud auctores, sed in ipsius orationibus reperiuntur. modo subtractis candidatorum nominibus originem cuiusque et vitam et stipendia descripsit ut qui forent intellegeretur; aliquando ea quoque significatione subtracta candidatos hortatus ne ambitu comitia turbarent, suam ad id curam pollicitus est. plerumque eos tantum apud se professos disseruit, quorum nomina consulibus edidisset; posse et alios profiteri, si gratiae aut meritis confiderent: speciosa verbis, re inania aut subdola, quantoque maiore libertatis imagine tegebantur, tanto eruptura ad infensius servitium.

34. Paul Veyne, *Comment on écrit l'histoire*, 81, 139.

6. TEMPORALIZING THE ABSTRACTION OF INDETERMINACY: MACHIAVELLI AND GUICCIARDINI

1. For Machiavelli, at least, this profound shift in attention and in the power of modulating assumptions was noticed as early as the sixteenth century by Jean

Bodin, "And Machiavelli was the first, I believe, to write a great deal about the Republic after the barbarian had just heaped it all together; and there is no doubt that he would have written more, truer and better, if he had joined into his practice the writings of the ancient philosophers and historians," "multa quoque Machiavellus, primus quidem, ut opinor, post annos mille circiter ac ducentos quam barbaries omnia cumularat, de Republica scripsit; nec dubium est, quin multo pluria verius ac melius scripturus fuerit, si veterum philosophorum et historicorum scripter [*sic*] cum usu coniunxisset" (Jean Bodin, *Methodus ad facilem historiarum cognitionem*, [Paris, 1566]; vi, 155 in the Amsterdam edition [1650]. I owe this citation to Franco Fido, who provides a full account of the understanding of Machiavelli in different eras (*Machiavelli* [Palumbo, n.d.]). The "conjunction" of philosophers and historians is quite interesting here, even though we may discount, as humanist piety, the negative constraint on Machiavelli.

2. Reinhart Koselleck adduces Guicciardini as well as Bodin for an openness to future developments that he finds entailed in a notion of historicity (*Futures Past: On the Semantics of Historical Time*, trans. Keith Tribe [Cambridge, Mass.: MIT Press, 1985], 13).

3. Paul Ricoeur, *Temps et récit*, passim.

4. J. G. A. Pocock, *The Machiavellian Moment* (Princeton, N.J.: Princeton University Press, 1975). As Pocock says of the predecessors to Machiavelli and Guicciardini, "the knowledge of particulars was time-bound, just as the phenomena of which it was knowledge ... were time-bound themselves" (5). Pocock stresses the dependence of their vocabulary on the dialectical presentation – in words like "providence," "fortune," "virtue" and the like. Indeed, the historical vision in Machiavelli and Guicciardini does qualify as a "historicism," effectually modifying the contention of Friedrich Meinecke that such a term could apply only after the developments he traces in eighteenth-century writers (*Die Entstehung des Historismus*, [Munich: Leibniz, 1946]), even though Meinecke's general discrimination holds about a difference in historical outlook from the late eighteenth century on. Still, to defend such a view, Meinecke must downplay the historicism of Machiavelli as a relativism he links to that of Montesquieu, effectually stressing the synchronicity of both writers (150, 164), stating the half-truth that Machiavelli's purpose was entirely the same as Montesquieu's, "He stressed the typical and the recurrent in these procedures, exactly the way Machiavelli had once done, so that he too could reach the point of winning maxims out of history for political activity," "Er betonte das Typische und Immerwiederkehrende an diesen Vorgängen, ganz wie es Machiavelli einst getan hatte, weil es ihm wie diesem darauf ankam, Maximen für das politische Handeln aus der Geschichte zu gewinnen" (164). All historians are interested in recurrences; but they also give an attention to diachronic process, as Machiavelli does, and later Gibbon; but Montesquieu does not.

5. Ricoeur, *Temps et récit* 1:111; 104. "La dialectique entre narrativité et temporalité"; "C'est cette capacité de l'histoire à être suivie qui constitue la solution

poétique du paradoxe de distension-intention. Que l'histoire se laisse suivre convertit le paradoxe en dialectique vivante." Ricoeur applies a Kantian process of judgment and a Husserlian description of "within-timeness" to the act of history writing as it brings about a *"synthèse de l'hétérogène,"* a phrase he italicizes (1:103). As for Ricoeur's own study, its three large volumes, meant to cover both historiography and fiction, offer moderately little illustration or comment on individual historians. Applying his notion to himself, it is as though the *distensio* of theory operated to block the reintegration of narratives into his deep consideration.

6. Pocock, *The Machiavellian Moment*, ix.

7. Both these points are made by Harvey C. Mansfield, Jr., *Machiavelli's New Modes and Orders: A Study of the* Discourses on Livy (Ithaca, N.Y.:Cornell University Press, 1979), 53–54. Both Machiavelli and Guicciardini came to full-blown history only at the end of long political and literary careers. The *History of Florence is* Machiavelli's last work, the *History of Italy*, Guicciardini's. The latter writer worked his *Ricordi* over and over into greater complexity and cross-assertion, a process that Mark Phillips shows him bringing in the *Storia d'Italia* to its full culmination. (Mark Phillips, *Francesco Guicciardini: The Historian's Craft* (Toronto: University of Toronto Press, 1977).

8. Francesco De Sanctis, *Storia della letteratura italiana* (Milan: Feltrinelli, 1956 [1877]), "I fatti sono il punto fermo intorno a cui gira" (517).

9. Apposite here, though not given my specific application, is Harvey Mansfield's observation (*Machiavelli's New Modes,* 8), "Overestimating the difficulty of understanding Machiavelli comes to the same thing as underestimating the difficulty as it becomes apparent that the creativity claimed by interpreters comes to nothing more than forced enthusiasm for Machiavelli the harbinger of modernity."

10. "Queste populazione furono quelle che destrussono lo imperio romano; alle quali ne fu data occasione dagli imperadori, i quali, avendo abbandonata Roma, sedia antica dello Imperio, e riduttisi ad abitare in Gonstantinopoli, avevano fatta la parte dello imperio occidentale più debole, per essere meno osservata da loro e più esposta alle rapine de' ministri e de' nemici di quelli" (1:1). I am here using, with modifications, the translation of M. Walter Dunne (New York: Harper: 1960 [1901]).

11. Fermato così lo stato, dopo sei anni, che fu nel 1381 ordinato, visse la città dentro insino al '93 assai quieta. Nel qual tempo Giovan Galeazzo Visconti, chiamato Conte di Virtù, prese messer Bernabò suo zio e per ciò diventò di tutta Lombardia principe. Costui credette potere divenire re di Italia con la forza, come gli era diventato duca di Milano con lo inganno; e mosse, nel '90, una guerra grandissima a'Fiorentini; e in modo variò quella nel maneggiarsi, che molte volte fu il Duca più presso al pericolo di perdere, che i Fiorentini, i quali, se non moriva, avevano perduto. Non di meno le difese furono animose e mirabili ad una republica, e il fine fu assai meno malvagio che non era stata la guerra spaventevole; perchè...il Duca... morì: la qual morte no gli lasciò gustare le sue passate vittorie, e a' Fiorentini non lasciò sentire le loro presenti perdite.

12. I am here quoting the translation of James B. Atkinson, *The Prince* (Indian-

apolis: Bobbs-Merrill, 1976): "chi non fa e' fondamenti prima, li potrebbe con una gran virtù farli poi, ancora che si faccino con disagio dello architettore e periculo dello edifizio" (7).

13.   "In modo che, se a fare perdere Milano a Francia bastò, la prima volta, uno duca Lodovico che romoreggiassi in su' confini, a farlo di poi perdere, la seconda, gli bisognò avere, contro, el mondo tutto, e che gli eserciti suoi fussino spenti o fugati di Italia; il che nacque dalle cagioni sopradette. Nondimanco, e la prima e la seconda volta, gli fu tolto."

                                                                              (3)

14. Peter E. Bondanella, *Francesco Guicciardini* (Boston: Twayne, 1976), 26, 96, notes Guicciardini's departure from his predecessors in this regard.

15. Montaigne, *Essais*, II, 10. Both these criticisms would strike the modern reader of history as off the mark, since Guicciardini is far less digressive, or illustrative, in incidental detail than most modern historians, and the indirectness of his lessons would tend to be taken as a quality of the work rather than as an indication of the amorality of the writer.

16.   . . . dal bene si scende al male, e dal male si sale al bene. Perché la virtù partorisce quiete, la quiete ozio, l'ozio disordine, il disordine rovina; e similmente dalla rovina nasce l'ordine, dall'ordine virtù, da questa, gloria e buona fortune.

17. "Nè si può chiamare in alcun modo una repubblica inordinata, dove siano tanti esempi di virtù, perchè i buoni esempi nascono dalla buona educazione, la buona educazione dalle buone leggi; e le buone leggi da quei tumulti che molti inconsideramente dannano."

18. One among many examples of this interaction among groups elsewhere than in Rome is this passage from the *Istorie Fiorentine* (2:9):

      Vinti i Grandi, riordinò il popolo lo stato; e perché gli era di tre sorte popolo, potente, mediocre e basso, si ordinò che i potenti avessero duoi Signori, tre i mediocri e tre i bassi; e il gonfaloniere fusse ora dell'una ora dell'altra sorte. Oltradi questo, tutti gli ordini della giustizia contro ai Grandi si riassunsono; e per fargli più deboli, molti di loro intra la popolare moltitudine mescolorono. Questa rovina de' nobili fu sì grande e in modo afflisse la parte loro, che mai poi a pigliare le armi contro al popolo si ardirono, anzi continuamente più umani e abietti diventorono. Il che fu cagione che Firenze, non solamente di armi, ma di ogni generosità si spogliasse.

      The nobility being thus overcome, the people reformed the government; and as they were of three kinds, those in power, the middle, and the lower class, it was ordered that those in power should appoint two signors; the middle, three; and the lower, three; and that the Gonfalonier should be chosen alternately from either party. Besides this, all the regulations for the restraint of the nobility were renewed; and in order to weaken them still more, many were reduced to the grade of the people. The ruin of the nobility was so vast, and depressed them so much, that they never afterward ventured to take arms against the people, but soon became humbled and abject in the extreme. This was the cause that Florence deprived herself not only of arms but of all generosity of character.

19. *Discorsi*, I, 43, "Innanzi che seguano i grandi accidenti in una città o in una provincia, vengono segni che li pronosticano o uomini che li predicono."

20. Federico Chabod, *Scritti su Machiavelli* (Turin: Einaudi, 1964), 372, "A procedure by dilemma that always puts forward the two extreme and antithetical

solutions, letting the middle fall . . . and proceeds stylistically by disjunction."
The notion of disjunction here is quite apposite, more so than the uniform
reason given for it. Looking for uniform reasons in Machiavelli has the effect,
here as often, of misdescribing his work for having underplayed the historicizing element in it.

21. Both points are made, without explicitly joining or contrasting them, by Peter
E. Bondanella, *Francesco Guicciardini*, 91–92.

7. THE CROSSCURRENTS OF TIME: BURCKHARDT AND MICHELET

1. There are gloomy statements about contemporary politics and human progress
generally to be found in Burckhardt's letters and elsewhere. Hayden White is
misled by these to characterize, and again often to misdescribe, Burckhardt's
historical writings (*Metahistory*, 234–262). There is no necessary homology,
and as it happens no direct homology in this case, between the random remarks
of Burckhardt the citizen of Basel and the measured compositions of Burckhardt the great historian, though it would be an interesting biographical study
to plot the relations between the two. Burckhardt did indeed make many
comments, mostly in letters, on a wide range of events. For a compendium
of these, see Jacob Burckhardt, *Betrachtungen über die Schweiz und Europa*, ed.,
Hans A. Wyss (Basel: Urs Graf, 1941).

  While Burckhardt uses irony, as most historians tend to do, he does so on
the whole less frequently, and far less saliently, than the "romantic" Michelet.
Nor is his approach ironic because it is synchronic. As for Burckhardt's supposed rejection of metaphor, of which White makes much, his strictures in
the *Cicerone* against allegory in Giotto – and Dante – have no particular bearing
on his historiography. It is the standard romantic deprecation of allegory to
be found in nineteenth-century literary criticism from Goethe on. One of
Burckhardt's best-known chapter headings, "The State as a Work of Art," is
highly metaphorical, and it is even assimilable to allegory. Curiously, in fact,
it echoes the historical bearing of political allegory that Walter Benjamin finds
in German "Trauerspiel."

  On the general question of congruence between a writer's personal views
and his historiography, as H. Stuart Hughes says (*Oswald Spengler* [New York:
Scribner, 1952], 32–33), "Most of [the heirs of *Historismus*] kept their historical
consciences and their political convictions in separate drawers . . . As a result,
the historian of the latter half of the century thought and wrote on two widely-
separated planes." For a general account of Burckhardt's thinking on such
subjects with relation to his activities in his later years, see Werner Kaegi, *Jacob
Burckhardt, Eine Biographie* (Basel: Schwabe, 1973), 5:447–642; and (1977), 6:11–
47.

2. Jacob Burckhardt, *Weltgeschichtliche Betrachtungen* (Basel: Benno Schwabe, 1956
[1905]), Werke 4. (I cite this volume or another of this edition of Burckhardt's
collected works by page number only in the text.)

  > durch den kosmopolitischen Verkehr des 19. Jahrhunderts überhaupt die
  > Gesichtspunkte unendlich vervielfacht . . .
  > Endlich kommen hiezu die starken Bewegungen in der neueren Philo-

sophie, bedeutend an sich und beständig verbunden mit allgemeinen welt-
geschichtlichen Anschauungen.
So haben die Studien des 19. Jahrhunderts eine Universalität gewinnen
können wie die früheren nie. . . .

> Wir handeln ja, wie gesagt, nicht sowohl vom Studium der Geschichte,
> als vom Studium des *Geschichtlichen.*

(11–12)

3. See Karl Löwith, *Jakob Burckhardt: der Mensch inmitten der Geschichte* (Lucerne: Vita Nova, 1936), 62–65. It is not in his turns of phrase but in his overall organization that Burckhardt creates an ironic – never a satiric – cast to his writing. He does, to be sure, find satire in the Renaissance to be an especially revelatory expression and evidence, devoting a whole chapter to it, "Modern Wit and Satire," the last chapter of Part Two, "The Development of the Individual." As he says in its last words, "historical criticism will always find in Aretino an important point of orientation (*Stellung*)."

4. It is the temperance and sanity of Rubens, amid the delineation of complex scenes, that Burckhardt admires (Jacob Burckhardt, *Recollections of Rubens* [London: Phaidon, 1949 (1898)] 15).

5.
> Der Geist ist die Kraft, jedes Zeitliche ideal aufzufassen . . . Was einst Jubel und Jammer war, muss nun Erkenntnis werden, wie eigentlich auch im Leben des Einzelnen. Damit erhält auch der Satz *Historia vitae magistra* einen höheren und zugleich bescheideneren Sinn. Wir wollen durch Erfahrung nicht sowohl klug (für ein andermal) als weise (für immer) werden.

(Weltgeschichtliche Betrachtungen, 6–7)

6.
> Da das Geistige wie das Materielle wandelbar ist und der Wechsel der Zeiten die Formen, welche das Gewand des äusseren wie des geistigen Lebens bilden, unaufhörlich mit sich rafft, ist das Thema der Geschichte überhaupt, dass sie die zwei in sich identischen Grundrichtungen zeige und davon ausgehe, wie erstlich alles Geistige, auf welchem Gebiete es auch wahrgenommen werde, eine geschichtliche Seite habe . . .
>
> Die Wirkung des Hauptphänomens ist das geschichtliche Leben, wie es tausendgestaltig, komplex, unter allen möglichen Verkappungen, frei und unfrei daherwogt, bald durch Masse, bald durch Individuen sprechend, bald optimistisch, bald pessimistisch gestimmt, Staaten, Religionen, Kulturen gründend und zerstörend, bald sich selbst ein dumpfes Rätsel, mehr von dunklen Gefühlen, die durch die Phantasie vermittelt sind, als von Reflexionen geführt, bald von lauter Reflexion begleitet.

(4–6)

This passage seems most closely to describe Michelet among Burckhardt's contemporaries.

7. Jacob Burckhardt, *The Age of Constantine the Great* (New York: Doubleday, Anchor Books, 1956, [1852]), 281. "Dies ist eine ganz überflüssige Mühe." Burckhardt here calls it superfluous as well as futile: irrelevant as well as unascertainable.

8. Burckhardt says "*konnte* anlangen." Though *konnte* has some of the lightness of a colloquial expression here, still it suggests a result that combines character and historical forces to produce a cyclic recursion at this point.

9. "Let us rather pause at the days of Leo X, under whom the enjoyment (*Genuss*) of antiquity combined with all other pleasures (*Genüssen*) to give to Roman life a unique stamp and consecration" ("*zu jenem wundersamen Eindruck verflocht,*

welcher dem Leben in Rom seine Weihe gab" – Burckhardt speaks of a "wondrous impression," 192). I cite page numbers after the translation published in New York by Harper (Colophon Books, 1958). I usually revise this translation, sometimes considerably.

10. *Werke*, 4:27.

> Die 'Verwirklichung des Sittlichen auf Erden' durch den Staat müsste tausendmal scheitern an der innern Unzulänglichkeit der Menschennatur überhaupt und auch der der Besten insbesondere. Das Sittliche hat ein wesentlich anderes Forum als den Staat; es ist schon enorm viel, dass dieser das konventionelle Recht aufrecht hält. Er wird am ehesten gesund bleiben, wenn er sich seiner Natur (vielleicht sogar seines wesentlichen Ursprungs) als Notinstitut bleibt.

11. To illustrate this point I should like to quote him at some length, on the festivities of triumph and carnival:

> In the first place it was the practice, both at the carnival and on other occasions, to represent the triumphs of specific ancient Roman commanders. Thus at Florence was shown that of Paulus Aemilius (under Lorenzo the Magnificent) and that of Camillus (on the visit of Leo X), both conducted by the painter Francesco Granacci. In Rome the first complete exhibition of this kind was the triumph of Augustus after the victory over Cleopatra, under Paul II, where, besides the comic and mythological masks (which, as a matter of fact, were not wanting in the ancient triumphs), all the other requisites were to be found – kings in chains, silk tablets with decrees of the Senate and people, a Senate clothed in the ancient costume, praetors, aediles, and quaestors, four chariots filled with singing masks, and doubtless, cars laden with trophies. Other processions rather aimed at setting forth, in a general way, the universal empire of ancient Rome; and in answer to the very real danger which threatened Europe from the side of the Turks, a cavalcade of camels bearing masks representing Turkish prisoners appeared before the people. Later, at the carnival of 1500 Cesare Borgia, with a bold allusion to himself, celebrated the triumph of Julius Caesar, in a procession that was eleven magnificent chariots strong, doubtless to the vexation of the pilgrims who had come for the Jubilee. Two *trionfi*, famous for their taste and beauty, were given by rival companies in Florence to celebrate the election of Leo X to the Papacy. One of them represented the Three Ages of Man, the other the Ages of the World, ingeniously set forth in five scenes of Roman history and in two allegories of the Golden Age of Saturn and of its final return. The imagination displayed in the adornment of the chariots when the great Florentine artists undertook the work made the scene so impressive that people found a permanent, periodic repetition of such spectacles desirable. Hitherto the subject cities had been satisfied merely to present their symbolical gifts (costly stuffs and wax candles) on the day when they annually did homage. The guild of merchants now built ten chariots (to which others were afterward to be added), not so much to carry as to symbolize the tribute, and Andrea del Sarto, who painted some of them, no doubt did his work to perfection. Such cars, whether used to hold tribute or trophies, now formed a part of every celebration, even when there was not much money to be laid out. The Sienese announced, in 1477, the alliance between Ferrante and Sixtus IV, with which they themselves were associated, by driving a chariot round the city, with "one clad as the goddess of peace standing on a hauberk and other arms."
>
> (3:287–288).

This large passage of one longish paragraph comes to a diapason in the detail that could well be taken emblematically for the whole mood of the moment, and of the time, a detail that happens to be a quotation from Vasari. In the process most of the orders have been adduced – as implicitly celebrating themselves – under which the Renaissance achievements were realized: popes, artists, merchants, rulers. The very first illustration – and the word *erste* comes up twice – couples the ruler, Lorenzo the Magnificent, and the pope, Leo the Tenth. They are set in parentheses that at once coordinate them with each other and subordinate them to the point of the sentence, which culminates in a reference to the leadership of an artist. At the moment he is not in parenthesis because it is his scene. The passage follows a general characterization, which in turn succeeds some comparable illustrations. It roams easily backward and forward in the narrow compass of the time it has set itself, while generally coupling the ancient and the Renaissance along the lines of the earlier section on that topic. An imagined recapitulation of personal and large historical time cycles is brought to bear not in any interpretative gesture but rather as a citation of what has been celebrated, the four ages of man, the ages of the world. The first introduction of the word *Masken* couples it with adjectives that are emphasized by being separated by a copula, *heitern* and *mythologischen*. It is further heightened by occasioning a parenthesis that gives no specific detail but rather an assurance that the model of antiquity has been faithfully adhered to. The threat of the Turks, so important to the diachronic historians including Braudel, here is apotropaically given a symbolic denigration. We hear little about the Turks in Burckhardt. In this particular sequence an effect almost of montage is achieved by the constant listing in detail of the ancient types that are adopted for these Renaissance *trionfi*. "*Vier Wagen voll singender Masken und ohne Zweifel auch Trophäenwagen*" appends an inference about completion to the indications of sounds as well as sights.

12. Jules Michelet *L'Histoire de la révolution française,* ed. Gérard Walter (Paris: Gallimard, 1952 [1869]) I, 291. This edition is cited unless otherwise specified.

Stephen Bann, *The Clothing of Clio* (Cambridge University Press, 1984), sees Michelet as combining the "*syntagm* (the linear order of terms 'in presence')" and the "*system* (the associative order of potential terms 'in absence')" (36) favored by his predecessors. "Michelet's history [is] not simply . . . the successor of those of Barante and Thierry, but . . . a third stage in the cycle: . . . an attempt at a synthesis between syntagm (*récit*) and system" (48). Bann links all these procedures to nineteenth-century photography, art, and literature.

Hayden White offers many apt features to characterize Michelet, though as always his categories are not finely tuned enough, and at the same time are too commonplace, to catch the contours of Michelet's handling of diachrony. And White also overemphasizes the tendentious element in Michelet, again by applying his discrete utterances too univocally to the work:

> Herder characterized the objects occupying the historical field in the mode of Metaphor, and then proceeded to a Synecdochic integration of the field by the explanatory strategies of Organicism and the emplotting strategies

246

of Comedy. Michelet began in the same way, but the patterns of integration which he discerned in that field were represented from a perspective given to him by his Ironic awareness of their evanescent and transitory nature. The "Romance" of the French people's struggle against tyranny and division and their attainment of a perfect unity during the first year of the Revolution is progressively distanced by the growing awareness in Michelet of the resurgence and (at least temporary) victory of the blocking forces.

(161)

This is very astute. At the same time, though, White goes so far in his global characterization of "Romantic" tendentiousness to Michelet that he denies him the very attributes I shall try to show he possesses: "As in all dualistic systems of thought, there was no way in his historiographic theory for conceiving of the historical process as a dialectical or even incremental progress toward the desired goal." White well discerns the dualism pervading Michelet, but it by no means prevents this contemporary of Marx from being implicitly dialectical. And Michelet's whole work, here and in the *Histoire de France*, is nothing if not incremental. A corrective to White's insistence on Michelet's tendentiousness is Barthes's implied assertion of his neutrality (Roland Barthes, *"Littérature et discontinu,"* in *Essais critiques* [Paris: Seuil, 1964], 180):

> Proceeding in his time . . . to an "Essay of Representation" of France, Michelet organized our country like a chemical body, the negative at the center, the active parts at the edge, equilibrated across this central void, precisely *neutral* (for Michelet on his part did not fear the neutral) from which royalty had emerged.

> Procédant en son temps . . . à un "essai de représentation" de la France, Michelet organisait notre pays comme un corps chimique, le négatif au centre, les parties actives au bord, s'équilibrant à travers ce vide central, *neutre* précisément (car Michelet, lui, ne craignait pas le neutre), dont était sortie la royauté.

(Barthes is actually referring to Michelet's spatial survey of France, indicating incidentally that even there, as his statements show, the historian keeps diachrony constantly in mind.)

13. I, 490–491. "Thousands of priests wrote Robespierre in strong gratitude," "Des milliers de prêtres écrivirent à Robespierre leur vive reconnaissance." Beyond the irony of the tenderness for the rights of priests in the severely anticlerical Robespierre – a man known for his ruthlessness to the rights of anybody – there is the implicitly ecclesiastical behavior of these Jacobins whose chief he became, on which Michelet remarks later on, "The Jacobins seem to consider themselves the direct heirs of the priests. They imitate their provocative intolerance, through which the Clergy has aroused an abundance of heresies," "Les Jacobins semblent se porter pour héritiers directs des prêtres. Ils en imitent l'irritante intolérance, par laquelle le Clergé a suscité tant d'hérésies" (537).

14. As Roland Barthes says in his quasi-Bachelardian study (*Michelet* [Paris: Seuil, 1975], 49), "Here is a history that grows, swept in a torrent by the sap of justice. But sometimes the plant stops growing, or indeed, on the contrary,

grows too fast, monstrously," "Voilà donc l'Histoire qui pousse, traversée 'en torrent' par la sève du Juste. Mais quelquefois la plante s'arrête de pousser, ou bien, au contraire, pousse trop vite, monstrueusement."

15. 16:321. This passage is cited by Linda Orr, *Jules Michelet: Nature, History, and Language* (Ithaca:, N.Y.: Cornell University Press, 1976), 29. It is cited in a context where it is given the dimension of an analogy between forces in the natural world (*L'Oiseau, L'Insecte*) and human forces, an analogy embodied in Michelet's late writings as a naturalist.

16. As Michelet later says, speaking of "The principle of expedients, interest, which called itself *public safety* and ruined France," "le principe d'expédients, intérêt, qui s'appela le *salut public,* et qui a perdu la France, "Ruined because this tyranny [the Terror] had the end result of putting its enemy in Paris and its chief on St. Helena, "Perdu en ce que cette tyrannie eut pour dernier résultat de mettre son ennemi à Paris et son chef à Sainte Hélène."

17. Victor Hugo, *Littérature et philosophie mêlées, Oeuvres complètes* (Paris: Hetzel, n.d.), 21, 273–313.

18. Hayden White, *Metahistory*, 150 and passim. White is fairly vague in the attribution, though. And again it could be said that Michelet's use of detail is, as always in achieved historiography, synecdochic: He has chosen his details from the large abundance of what was known about the funeral of Mirabeau – and very differently from Victor Hugo, as I have indicated. It is metonymic, too, for being presented in careful sequence. And irony of event is implied in the concord among the named dignitaries, a concord soon to be doubly blasted in their individual declines or deaths, and in the increasingly marked and somber divisions among the revolutionaries.

19. Such metaphors, not the most interesting or the most complex cases, are discussed in George Lakoff and Mark Johnson, *Metaphors We Live By* (Chicago: University of Chicago Press, 1980). Other general analyses of such metaphors are offered in Mark Turner, *Death Is the Mother of Beauty* (Chicago: University of Chicago Press, 1987) and Samuel Levin's forthcoming book on metaphor from Yale University Press.

20. The aphorism about man as a solidified gas is a sixth type of metaphor, an attribution of psychological properties on the basis of physical laws and facts whose recent discovery itself attests metaphorically to the intellectual dimension of the creative force in the Revolution. Michelet's "argument," in so far as he may be said to offer one, is not only "formist" in White's terms (and therefore, he argues, especially akin to a "Romantic" "mode of emplotment" as well as to a "Metaphoric" master-trope). It is also "Mechanistic," "Organicist," and "Contextualist" as well. Any historiography, again, in the elusiveness of the knowledge coded into but not fully extrapolable from its narrative presentation, tends to use all four of these "modes of argument," and sometimes simultaneously. White half allows for this possibility, but he cannot wholly allow for it without rendering his categories fairly useless as instruments of discrimination.

21. Alain Besançon, "Michelet and Dostoevskyism in History," *Clio* 6, no. 2 (Winter, 1977), 131–148.

8. THE CONTRACTIONS AND EXPANSIONS OF BIBLICAL HISTORY

1. *Torah,* from *yarah,* "to instruct," designates not just the Pentateuch but all the books of the Old Testament from Genesis to Nehemiah (in ancient Hebrew usage the term distinguishes these portions from "Prophets" and "Writings"), classified together by tradition and presenting a continuous temporal sequence of events. Hence all the books of the "Torah" may be argued to have a historical, and even a historiographic, bearing.

2. The compiler in the handling of his documents is willing to dovetail and parallel partially conflicting accounts without comment. Given the intelligence manifestly at work both in the portions and in the whole, it is inconceivable that the compiler would have been unaware that just a few verses before he had given another, different account of the matter, say the meeting of Saul and David (1S 16.19–23; 17.55–58). As Robert Alter says (*The Art of Biblical Narrative,* citing R. Gros Louis, "The Difficulty of Ruling Well: King David of Israel," *Semeia* 8 [1977], 15–33), "Saul, in his different roles as troubled individual and jealous monarch, responds in different ways to these two aspects of David. 'Saul the man can love his comforter and recall the refreshment brought to him by his music; Saul the king cannot bear to hear the Israelite women singing, "Saul has slain his thousands, and David his ten thousands." ' "

   As for the particular foregrounding or highlighting that makes the foreshortening uneven, it should be noted that this historian avoids the more usual, and indeed virtually the universal, practice for such narrators, a deadly evenness of progression.

3. J. G. Frazer gives proportionally little space to Samuel and Kings in his *Folklore in the Old Testament* (London: Macmillan, 1918), 503–557. There he discusses only the simple phrase "bundle of life," applied by Abigail to David (1 Sam. 25:29), with parallels: the tradition of oracles paralleling the Witch of Endor; and the sin of the census (2 Sam. 24), with abundant parallels. Frazer does earlier mention (4), as a motif, the displacement of an elder son in favor of a younger, though this process manifests so many variations through the Torah, a basic typological form upon which individual instances play interrelated, analogical variations, as they do against the supposed rule of primogeniture itself.

4. On passivity, see J. P. Fokkelman, *Narrative Art and Poetry in the Books of Samuel,* (Assen: Van Gorcum, 1981), 1:369.

5. Meir Sternberg, *The Poetics of Biblical Narrative* (Bloomington: Indiana University Press, 1980), 482–492, demonstrates at some length how the small details of the narrative here present a "pattern of coordination" around the thesis of God's justification in the rejection of Saul. "Isn't there a glaring disproportion between achievement and reward, sin and penalty? These are the normative questions that the reader is sure to pose. And these are indeed the very questions that the narrator prepares to meet and resolve, by way of subtle persuasive art rather than blunt ideological fiat" (484).

6. Albert Cook, *The Meaning of Fiction,* 306–307.

7. Northrop Frye in general tends to slight the historiographic set that governs

the longest by far of the three traditional sections of the Old Testament (and much of the New). In *The Great Code: the Bible and Literature* (New York: Harcourt Brace, Harvest, 1983), he adduces a typology of seven "phases," no one of which can account for the set of history: Creation, Revolution, Law, Wisdom, Prophecy, Gospel, Apocalypse. Frye's three functions of language – the metaphoric, the metonymic, and the descriptive – though they are useful generally for classifying forms of expression, happen not to be very applicable in dealing with other than poetic texts in the Bible. They do not help much with Samuel and Kings, which combine, problematically, a supermetaphoric overriding term, YHWH, with language as flatly designative or "descriptive" (or indeed "metonymic") as historiography may get. We must deal with the fact that the Biblical text as we have it, in startling contrast to the Greek and other cultures that we know, begins not with poetry but with prose. (This makes Frye's talk about Greek developments needlessly complicating.) It verges on tautology to call prose "metonymic," since many kinds of prose, as he acknowledges, do enlist metaphor. And anyway all prose must be me-tonymic in one sense because words are inescapably contiguous for being in sequenced order. Frye further offers three classes of metonymy – the meta-phoric, the analogical that "puts the verbal expression . . . for something that by definition transcends adequate verbal expression," and that in which "the word is 'put for' the object it describes." These, indeed, are so all-inclusive, while at the same time being both vague and uncoordinated, that it is hard to see how they can be used for the convincingly systematic study of any linguistic utterances, biblical or other. Frye says that the second category is "roughly the sense in which I use" metonymy. But "a mode of analogical thinking and writing in which the verbal expression is 'put for' something that by definition transcends adequate verbal expression" may be taken to cover any human utterance whatever. And it can also be made to cover the ineffability of what human language cannot express at all; "metonymy" here may be seen to do duty for the old "inexpressibility trope" of medieval poetics.

In his particular discussion, as in his overall scheme, Frye gives very short shrift to historiographic texts. Furthermore, he both distorts and overinterprets them in a simple archetypal direction. Thus he must go to a gloss to see Absalom hanging by "his golden hair," since the text says "his head" ("*rosho*," 2 Sam. 18:14); we may assume the text to be careful enough to have fore-grounded the hair if that had been the intent. "Absalom's curious helplessness in what seems a relatively easy situation to get out of suggests a ritual element in the story of his death," Frye continues (180). But in Absalom's situation, indeed, there is next to nothing of the "scapegoat" and "martyr," and he is neither the prophet (like even the failed Saul) nor the king normal in such cases. There are in fact military reasons why Absalom should stay in the tree when surrounded by an enemy; and one may also infer a fatigue that would make flight difficult after a long battle. In any case, the text is dense with historiographic complication and interreference, here as elsewhere. If there are – and there may be – typological echoes (though one has to cross to Frazer's Balder to get the analogue of golden hair/crucifixion), the question is not their presence, faint at best in this instance, but their relation to the text's predominant significations. If Saul is chosen just for being "goodly" and "tall" (1 Sam. 9:2) and David chosen for this "heart" (1 Sam. 16:7) while also being "ruddy" and "goodly," then in this sequence the beauty of Absalom's hair that the text earlier dwells on (2 Sam. 14:26) may be taken as an ominously synecdochic excerption both from the handsomeness of the whole man and the relation of the whole man to a discretion that would handle his relation to power. When David loves him so, Absalom's obvious best strategy would be to wait till he could succeed to the kingship, since if he were alive, it would seem that Bathsheba could not dislodge him in favor of Solomon (she has enough difficulty when Absalom's death has removed him from the competition). Just as Absalom resembles his father in being able to prolong rebellion but differs in his incapacity to adapt to changing situations and properly scrutinize subordinates or allies, so he resembles his father in being handsome but differs in the way he uses his looks.

Frye also oversimplifies and misinterprets the sparing of Agag (1 Sam. 15:29) "out of human decency" (181) by a Saul who has been notably fierce in battle (1 Sam. 14:47–48) and shows scorched-earth savagery to those he construes as enemies, razing the priestly city of Nob (1 Sam. 22:19). Frye fails to mention that the human sacrifices at the rebuilding of Jericho (1 Kings 16:34) are explicitly designated earlier as a curse (Josh. 6:26). The passage says not, as Frye alleges, that "any rebuilding of the city would have to sacrifice his eldest son to lay the foundation" (185), but rather that a rebuilding would be "in" the sons (the sacrifice being so abominable that only the word "in" hints at it). And this is a fair share of Frye's discussion involving Samuel and Kings. I go on at this length about Frye's discussion to indicate the kinds of slippages that keen-sighted writers may permit themselves when dealing with the Bible, slippages they would never permit themselves in discussing Blake or Shakespeare.

8. See Albert Cook, *The Meaning of Fiction*, chap. 5, "Balzac: History as Rhetoric."

9. Ibid., p. 69.

10. As Alter says, stressing the repetitions-with-variations of the second and third speeches (not in the verses quoted above), "The differences between Nathan's version and Bathsheba's version are wonderfully in character for both. Bathsheba's presentation reveals the distressed mother and suppliant wife emphasizing the injustice done to her son, the imminent danger threatening mother and son, the absolute dependence of the nation on the powerful word of the king. Nathan, by what he adds, sharpens the more general political aspects of the threat from Adonijah, beginning emphatically with 'me your servant' (Bathsheba prudently left Nathan out of her account) and closing the series with a symmetrical counterpart, 'Solomon your servant.' Most crucially, Nathan adds a little vignette of Adonijah's company eating and drinking and shouting 'Long live King Adonijah,' a scene certainly calculated to rouse the ire of the still reigning king" (98–99). Alter's ensuing discussion is equally apposite.

11. Fokkelman (347) quotes M. J. Mulder on the political importance attached to the particular term here use, *sokenet*.

12. This is an overprimitive assumption on Adonijah's part, as the evidence in Gray's gloss would implicitly urge (John Gray, *I and II Kings: A Commentary* [Philadelphia: Westminster, 1963], 76), "Field anthropology among primitives indicates that the authority and even the life of the king depends on his virility, and there may be more than a coincidence in David's appointment of a co-regent after he failed to pass the test of virility."

13. Fokkelman in using the term says on the one hand, "I value this abstruseness as a literary asset and find it unnecessary to seek a 'solution.' " But then on the other hand he does just that when he puzzles over why David's promise to Bathsheba is not mentioned earlier in the text. Why not presume the compiler left the question out as not bearing on the complexities of what he does present? Fokkelman reviews the literature on this question in the light of "*Thronfolgegeschichte.*" As he well says, "The idea that the oath is pure invention on the part of the faction (i.e., Nathan) is hard to reconcile with the portrait and allure of Nathan presented in II Samuel." And he points out that Nathan continues to "sound respectful."

14. Max Weber, *Das Antike Judentum (Gesammelte Aufsätze zur Religionsoziologie,* vol. 3) [Stuttgart: Zechnall, 1922]).

15. "Die drei reinen Typen der legitimen Herrschaft," in *Soziologie, Analysen, Politik* (Stuttgart: Kröner, 1956 [1904]), 151–156.

9. THE NEW TESTAMENT IN ITS HISTORIOGRAPHIC DIMENSION

1. As Hans W. Frei says (*The Eclipse of Biblical Narrative* [New Haven: Yale University Press, 1974], 10) "A realistic or history- like (though not necessarily historical) element is a feature, as obvious as it is important, of many of the biblical narratives that went into the making of Christian belief. . . . But since the precritical or interpretive procedure for isolating it had irretrievably broken down . . . this specifically realistic characteristic, though acknowledged by all hands to be there, finally came to be ignored, or – even more fascinating – its presence or distinctiveness came to be denied for lack of a 'method' to isolate it."

In the analysis of Louis Marin, *The Semiotics of the Passion Narrative, Topics and Figures* (Pittsburgh: Pickwick Press, 1980), the very place names in the passion narratives of each of the synoptics are not only "layered" with signification but ordered into levels of structured opposition and transformation, naming, mapping, and coordinating the space through which Jesus moves. "A 'travail' of contraries develops. A fixed production of meaning, and an 'act of meaning' . . . are disconnected by . . . this symbolic thing, which is at the same time full and double, in itself and different from itself . . . 'the other of the discourse' that they cause and which unceasingly annuls them . . . Such is the function of the reference in the discourse of the narrative . . . no longer narrative, but meta-narrative, of the narrative of an exchange and a communication" (4–5). Conflating Lévi-Strauss, Derrida, and Peirce, Marin is able complexly to map transformations in the pattern of signification, demonstrating further, in spite of local overtypifications, how much implication has been built into this narrative. And the historiographic thrust of the utterance is still another, overriding signification to the patterns he elaborates.

2. Austin Farrer, *The Rebirth of Images* (Boston: Beacon, 1966 [1949]).

3. "Teaching," the reading of the Revised Standard Version, is better than "doctrine" for *didache*. (See G. Kittel and Gerhard Friedrich, *Theologisches Wörterbuch zum Neuen Testament* [Stuttgart: Kohlhammer, 1927–1973], s.v.) *Didache* is simply the noun of *didaskein*, the verb "to teach" that is used earlier in the sentence. *Didaskalia* is the term closest to the English "doctrine." I have, however, left the King James rendering in all cases. Readers unfamiliar with it should note that its italics indicate not emphasis but the opposite – that the English is adding something not be be found in the Greek.

4. On the newness of the parables, see Joachim Jeremias, *Rediscovering the Parables* (New York: Scribner's, 1966), 10: "Jesus' parables are something entirely new. In all the rabbinic literature not one single parable has come down to us from the period before Jesus; only two similes from Rabbi Hillel (c. 20 B.C.), who jokingly compared the body with a statue, and the soul with a quest. It is among the sayings of Rabban Jochanan ben Zakkai (d. c. A.D. 80) that we first meet with a parable . . . As its imagery resembles one of Jesus' parables, we may well ask whether Jesus' model (together with other factors, such as Greek animal fables) did not have an important influence on the rabbi's adopting parables as a narrative form." For a discussion of parable as a mode and genre, see Albert Cook, "Parable," in *Myth and Language*, 234–247.

5. Frank Kermode, *The Genesis of Secrecy: On the Interpretation of Narrative* (Cambridge, Mass.: Harvard University Press, 1979).

6. Vincent Taylor, *The Gospel According to St. Mark* (London: Macmillan, 1952), 256.

7. Austin Farrer, *A Study in St. Mark* (London: Dacre, 1951), 240–248. As Farrar says (240), "The parable of the sower is not a characteristic parable, nor is it a parable which could well stand first in the Gospel. For it is a parable about hearing such doctrine as depends for its effect on a responsive ear, and especially, perhaps, parabolic doctrine. The evangelist will not record a parable about hearing before he has given us any parables which set before us the sort of thing we ought to hear. In particular, the sower is not characteristic of the difficulty of parables; it is a simple parabolic exhortation to us to receptiveness and responsiveness, in order that the word, parabolic or otherwise, may have its fruit in us." Farrer's whole commentary abounds in farseeing resolutions, as "The parables could not be more illuminating than they are, but the rays they shed fall into the abyss of Godhead (244)." "The lamp need not be stowed under the bushel in order to shine, but the seed must be buried in order to bear (245)."

8. René Girard, *Des Choses cachées depuis la fondation du monde* (Paris: Grasset, 1978). Actually, Girard takes the quotation completely out of context to apply it to his own overall interpretation of Scripture – an interpretation, however, of which the sweep, if not the specific message, is effectually authorized by the sweeping outward look both of the Psalm and of the text of Matthew at this point.

9. The legendary underlay to these events – which some depth psychologies, in

fact, attribute to the events in any life – has been spelled out in great detail by those modern commentators who lead up to and qualify Rudolph Bultmann, *Die Geschichte der synoptischen Tradition* (Göttingen: Vandenhoek & Ruprecht, 1970 [1931]). As in depth psychology, however, the presence of legendary congruences can be taken to indicate not that the events did not (or did) happen, but rather their intensity in context.

10. I am here following Edwin Hoskins and Noel Davey Bailey, *The Riddle of the New Testament* (London: Faber, 1958), to name a specific source for what has been a general focus of much discussion about the Gospels (and the New Testament as a whole) over the past century.

11. Nearly every phrase and every momentary detail of the Passion narrative, for example, has been linked to types and subtypes of wording and action by the critics of the past century. Just for its relation to Old Testament types, as Martin Dibelius says ("Historisches Problem der Leidengeschichte," in Meinrad Limbeck ed., *Redaktion und Theologie des Passionsberichtes nach den Synoptikern* [Darmstadt: Wissenschaftliche Buchgesellschaft (Wege der Forschung 481), 1981], 66), "From Psalm 22 (Septuagint 21) derives the division of his garments (19), the mockery and headwagging of passers-by (8), and the last cry of Jesus (2); that Jesus finally cried out we read in Psalm 22.25 and Psalm 31 (Septuagint 30.23). This Psalm also contains Jesus' last cry in Luke's presentation, as well as many details in the progress of events up to the crucifixion (6; 12–14); in Psalm 69 (68) we read of the mockery of the thieves (10) and of the drink of vinegar (22)."

12. Quoted in Meinrad Limbeck, *Redaktion und Theologie des Passionsberichtes*, 17.

13. René Girard, *Le Bouc émissaire* (Paris: Grasset, 1982), 161, "l'idée faussement chrétienne qui fait de la passion un événement unique dans sa dimension maléfique alors qu'il est unique seulement dans sa dimension révélatrice," "the idea falsely called Christian that makes the passion an event unique in its malificent dimension when it is unique only in its revelatory dimension." But it is unique in both, as (paradoxically) typical in both.

14. See Roland Barthes, Jean Starobinski, and others, in François Bovon, ed., *Analyse structurale et exégèse biblique* (Neuchâtel: Delachaux & Niestlé, 1978), for an outstanding example of these illuminating but limited procedures.

15. As Rudolf Bultmann says (*Theology of the New Testament* [New York: Scribner's, 1951], 116–117), "In the present context it does not matter whether the allegorical sense of a text was regarded as its only meaning or as a deeper meaning existing side by side with the literal one. In this context the distinction can also be ignored between allegory (the art of finding prediction or deeper truths of any sort in the wording of Scripture) and typology (the interpretation of persons, events, or institutions of the past as foreshadowing prototypes)." Bultmann is here speaking specifically of the presence of the Old Testament in the New, but his principle can be taken still more generally.

16. Austin Farrer, *The Glass of Vision* (London: Dacre, 1948), 143–144. Farrer goes on to provide a further linking around the name of Joseph, and the typological echoes resulting from the fact that Joseph of Arimathea who begged to bury Jesus repeats the request of Joseph to Pharaoh over (Jacob) Israel; and the loss of a coat in flight is common both to this passage and to the Potiphar's wife

episode. Some of these connections may seem arbitrary, but the range of possibility is too rich for all to be arbitrary. And as Farrer says elsewhere (*A Study in St. Mark*, 141), "Christ dies now in himself; at a later day he will suffer in his apostles. For the present it is not theirs to die. The young man puts off his *sindon* and escapes alive. Christ is destined, at this season, to wear the *sindon* alone. The Arimathaean wraps him in it; it is his shroud."

17. Klaus Berger, *Formgeschichte des neuen Testaments* (Heidelberg: Quelle & Meyer, 1984). He offers as types "comparison," "example," three uses of "metaphor," five aspects of "parable" (*Gleichnis*), "allegory," "proverb," "speech," "argumentation," etc., etc. Berger, however, like Northrop Frye, severely slights the historiographic element by making it only one of this very large number of strands, when (I am arguing) it is in fact the predominant one. One must supplement Berger's atomizing precision with Bultmann's sort of unitary reminder (*Theology of the New Testament*, 86), "As more and more exact and stable formulas grow out of the kerygma and gradually crystallize into creeds, so there develops out of the kerygma *the literary form: Gospel*" (italics Bultmann's). Bultmann goes on, however, to list a moderately arbitrary series of seven sequential steps through which this (supposed) development took place.

18. I am summarizing the discussion of *dunamis* in the *Theologisches Wörterbuch zum neuen Testament*, s.v.

19. Karl Georg Kuhn, "Jesus in Gethsemane," in Meinrad Limbeck, ed., *Redaktion und Theologie des Passionsberichtes*, 95–96.

20. Rudolf Bultmann, *Theology of the New Testament*, 96–97: "It must be recognized, however, that the *relation of the Church to Israel's history* is a peculiarly paradoxical one because the course of events from Jacob-Israel down to the present is not a continuous history but one broken by the eschatological occurrence in Christ. That is, the eschatological Congregation is not simply the historical successor and heir of the empirical Israel of history but the heir of the ideal Israel. . . . It was indeed the elect People of God; but its election always hovered above and ahead of it, so to say, as goal and promise."

10. THE IMPLICATIONS OF SCOPE: TOTALIZING EXPLANATIONS IN HISTORY

1. Paul Ricoeur, *Temps et récit*, 1:85–136, and passim.

2. Stéphane Mallarmé, *Oeuvres complètes* (Paris: Pléiade, 1945), 368.

3. Since Heidegger's hermeneutic approach is meant to lay bare rather than to justify, the circularity in his definition of history, as in all his other areas of discourse, is a necessary corollary of his method. His requirement that history be "authentic," since it is couched in the terminology of his system, has the advantage of fuller, and even of more precise, articulation than, say, Carr's strictures in the process of a telling refutation of Karl Popper (E. H. Carr, *What Is History?* [New York: Random House, Vintage Books, 1961]. In Heidegger's words, "*Mit der Existenz des geschichtlichen In-der-Welt-seins ist* Zuhandenes und Vorhandenes je schon in die Geschichte der 'Welt' einbezogen," "*With the existence of historical Being-in-the-World is* that which is both instrumental and environmental already drawn into relationship with the history of

the 'world' " (Martin Heidegger, *Sein und Zeit*, 388). And further, "Die Ver-
lorenheit in das Man und an das Welt-Geschichtliche enthüllte sich früher als
Flucht vor dem Tode. Diese Flucht vor . . . offenbart das Sein *zum* Tode als
eine Grundbestimmtheit der Sorge. Die vorlaufende Entschlossenheit bringt
dieses Sein zum Tode in die eigentliche Existenz," "This abandonment into
the averaged man and with respect to the world-historical bared itself earlier
as a flight before death. This 'flight before' . . . bares the Being *toward* death as
a base-definition of Care. The preceding resolution brings this being-toward-
death into genuine existence" (390). In an "ungenuine historicity" all this
process is "hidden." (*verborgen*, 391). Heidegger uses Yorck (in his correspondence with Dilthey) as an intermediate figure to qualify the standard
definitions of historicity, which at their highest level Dilthey exemplifies (399–
404). Dilthey proceeds, it may be observed, with a more absolute distinction
than Hegel's between science and the social sciences, between *Naturwissen-
schaften* and *Geisteswissenschaften*. In *Der Aufbau der Geschichtlichen Welt in den
Geisteswissenschaften*, vol. 7 of *Gesammelte Werke* [Stuttgart: Teubner, 1958
(1883)], Dilthey characterizes the "operational coherence" (*Wirkungszusam-
menhang*) of the "*Geisteswissenschaften*" as dependent on categories that resemble
the Heideggerian constructions without their thrust into the deepest feelings
(even though "*Fühlung*" is one of Dilthey's categories). Terms like *Erleben* and
Verstehen (152–188) "experience" and "understanding," do not cohere fully
enough in Dilthey to carry the epistemological weight that will more than
loosely characterize what he is discussing, even though his focus and his reliance
on such terminologies may be followed by Gadamer and others to characterize
the hermeneutic act. Dilthey deals, it may be said, with the discourse but not
directly or really systematically with its subject. He is too dependent, Heidegger says, on "psychology" (398); and so, as Heidegger quotes Yorck,
Dilthey's enterprises "emphasize too little the generic distinction between the
ontish and the historical," "zu wenig die generische Differenz zwischen On-
tischem und Historischem betonen" (399).

Given the necessary circularity of Heidegger's definitions, the term "genuine" aptly characterizes an achieved historicity; and therefore Theodor Adorno's criticism of Heidegger's approach entirely misfires in *Negative Dialektik*
(1966) – and even more in *Jargon der Eigentlichkeit* (*Jargon of Authenticity*, 1965),
both in *Schriften* 6, (Frankfurt: Suhrkamp, 1973), in which Adorno does correctly score a host of vulgarized uses leading after Nietzsche up to and away
from the Nazi use of *eigentlich*. He leans on Heidegger's interactions with the
Nazi authorities (46–47) and provides a loose social context of moral implication rather than an argument that may hold against Heidegger. At the same
time is should be said that in Adorno's writings on music, and notably in
Versuch über Wagner, a genuine sort of totalizing history has been achieved that
has affinities with the work of both Nietzsche and Max Weber in its ability
consistently to generalize connections, or even homologies, down to small
details, between musical practice and a social dialectic.

4. Jacques Le Goff and Pierre Nora, eds., *Faire de l'Histoire: nouveaux problèmes*
(Paris: Gallimard, 1974,) especially François Furet, "Le Quantitatif en histoire,"
52–71.

5. Fernand Braudel, introduction to *La Méditerranée et le monde méditerranéen à l'époque de Philippe II* (Paris: Armand Colin, 1966 [1949]). English version, *The Mediterranean in the Age of Philip II* (New York: Harper, 1972), 1:21 (my translation): "I affirm, against Ranke and Karl Brandi, that narrative history is not a method or the objective method par excellence, but indeed also a philosophy of history," "J'affirme, contre Ranke ou Karl Brandi, que l'histoire-récit n'est pas une méthode ou la méthode objective par excellence, mais bien une philosophie de l'histoire, elle aussi."

6. Fernand Braudel, "Les Temps de l'Histoire," in *Ecrits sur l'histoire* (Paris: Flammarion, 1969), 35, "The difficulty is not to reconcile, on the level of principles, the necessity of individual and of social history; the difficulty is in being able to feel both at the same time, and, in the passion for one, not to disdain the other." "Et la difficulté n'est pas de concilier, sur le plan des principes, la nécessité de l'histoire individuelle et de l'histoire sociale; la difficulté est d'être capable de sentir l'une et l'autre à la fois, et, se passionant pour l'une, de ne pas dédaigner l'autre." Braudel comes perilously close to falling under this final stricture himself, though he could scarcely avoid doing so, one may presume, while at the same time maintaining the advantageous fixity of his own perspective.

7. E. H. Carr, *What Is History?*, especially 3–35.

8. Jacques Derrida, *Glas* (Paris: Editions Galilée, 1974). For an account of the strong and multiple positive element in this arresting work, see Geoffrey Hartman, *Saving the Text* (Baltimore: Johns Hopkins University Press, 1981).

9. So the connection of the ideal-type origination of law with the ideal-types of origination for history and literature, made in Derrida's recent lectures on Kafka's *Vor dem Gesetz*, have the purity of a ground-clearing that remains in effect negative because it (of course deliberately) holds back from enunciating the principles by which we might assess the procedures of the totalizing historian.

10. Paul Veyne, "L'Histoire conceptualisante," in Le Goff and Nora, *Faire de l'Histoire*, 63: "La frontière qui sépare l'histoire et la science n'est pas celle du contingent et du nécessaire, mais celle du tout et du nécessaire."

11. Roland Barthes, "Analyse structurale des récits," in *Poétique du récit* (Paris: Seuil, 1977), 7–57. Barthes continues to speak of "*unités*" here, as he does in S/Z. But his repertory of unities has shifted, and if we take his two repertories together, we must characterize each as an ad hoc taxonomic census of possible terms rather than as the realization of necessary ones. In "La lutte avec l'ange," (F. Bovon, ed., *Analyse structurale et exégèse biblique*, 27–40), Barthes adduces three types – still another partially different typology – of nomenclature: (1) that whose analysis is undecidable in its relation to the moment (like a standard epithet); (2) actantial terms (functions); and (3) sequential ones (actions). The fact that Barthes often changes his categories, and that they are therefore obviously ad hoc and arbitrary, however, does not make them less applicable as generalizations of sign-functions within a code. Such ad hoc classifications are the staple of any good critical discourse. In Barthes's case they apply best to works of popular entertainment, the James Bond stories of Barthes's constant and deliberate illustration, which depend on the surface features of sign-codes.

We want to know about these, but also about the deep drift of the story; what invests power in Tolstoy or Beckett is some difference from Ian Fleming. And the same is true for the difference between Villani and Machiavelli. It is such differences that we should ultimately be addressing.

12. As Alexandre Kojève says in *Introduction à la lecture de Hegel* (Paris: Gallimard, 1947), "The philosophy of Spirit culminates in the philosophy of history, which describes the real becoming of the Absolute," "La Philosophie de l'Esprit culmine dans la Philosophie de l'histoire, qui décrit le devenir réel de l'Absolu" (37), and also "Hegel is the first to identify Concept and Time," "Hegel est le premier à identifier le Concept et le Temps" (365); "So the terms *Zeit* and *Geschichte* are rigorously equivalent," "Les termes 'Zeit' et 'Geschichte' sont donc rigoureusement équivalents" (397). Kant's own typology in "Idea of a Universal History from a Cosmopolitan Point of View" (1784; translation by W. Hastie printed in Patrick Gardiner, ed., *Theories of History*, 22–33) is so simply schematic as to be unworthy of a great philosopher.

13. G. W. F. Hegel, *Philosophie der Geschichte* (Stuttgart: Reklam, 1961 [1837]), 39–47.

14. G. W. F. Hegel, "Dem Gegebenen und Seienden," in ibid., 48.

15. G. W. F. Hegel, *Grundlinien der Philosophie des Rechts* (Hamburg: Meiner, 1955 [1821]), 14.

16. *Philosophie der Geschichte*, 130–131.

17. Stephen Runciman, *The Sicilian Vespers* (Harmondsworth: Penguin, 1960 [1958]), 250.

18. "Die andere Seite aber seines Werdens, die *Geschichte*, ist das *wissende*, sich *vermittelnde* Werden – der an die Zeit entäusserte Geist; aber diese Entäusserung ist ebenso die Entäusserung ihrer selbst." G. W. F. Hegel, *Phänomenologie des Geistes* (Hamburg: Meiner, 1952 [1807]), 563.

19. G. W. F. Hegel, *Aesthetik* (Frankfurt: Europäische Verlagsanstalt, n.d. [1842]), 22. "Die Reflexionsbildung unseres heutigen Lebens macht es uns, sowohl in Beziehung auf den Willen als auch auf das Urteil, zum Bedürfnis, allgemeine Gesichtspunkte festzuhalten und danach das Besondere zu regeln."

20. Ihr Zweck wird daher darin gesetzt: die schlummernden Gefühle, Neigungen und Leidenschaften *aller Art* zu wecken und zu beleben, das Herz zu *erfüllen* und den Menschen, entwickelt oder noch unentwickelt, alles durchfühlen zu lassen, was das menschliche Gemüt in seinem Innersten und Geheimsten tragen, erfahren und hervorbringen kann.

(55)

21. Die *Metamorphosen* . . . sind zwar symbolisch-mythologischer Art, zugleich aber stellen sie dem Geistigen das Natürliche ausdrücklich gegenüber, indem sie einem natürlich Vorhandenen, einem Felsen, Tiere, einer Blume, Quelle die Bedeutung geben, ein *Herunterkommen* und eine *Strafe* geistiger Existenzen zu sein: der Philomele z.B., der Pieriden, des Narziss, der Arethusa, welche durch einen Fehltritt, eine Leidenschaft, ein Verbrechen in unendliche Schuld oder einen unendlichen Schmerz verfallen, dadurch der Freiheit des geistigen Lebens verlustig und zu einem nur natürlichen Dasein geworden sind.

Einerseits also wird hier das Natürliche nicht nur äusserlich und prosaisch als blosser Berg, Quell, Baum, usf. betrachtet, sondern es wird ihm ein Inhalt gegeben, der einer vom Geist ausgehenden Handlung oder Begebenheit angehört. Der Felsen ist nicht nur Stein, sondern Niobe, die um ihre Kinder weint. Andereseits ist diese menschliche Tat irgendeine Schuld und die Verwandlung zur blossen Naturescheinung als eine Degradation des Geistigen zu nehmen.

Wir müssen deshalb diese Verwandlungen menschlicher Individuen und Götter zu Naturdingen sehr wohl von der eigentlich *unbewussten Symbolik* unterscheiden. In Aegypten wird teils in der geheimnisreichen, verschlossenen Innerlichkeit des tierischen Lebens unmittelbar das Göttliche angeschaut, teils ist das eigentliche Symbol eine Naturgestalt, welche mit einer weiteren, verwandten Bedeutung, obschon sie nicht deren wirkliches adäquates Dasein ausmachen soll, dennoch *unmittelbar zusammengeschlossen* wird...

In Ovids "Metamorphosen" ist ausser der ganz modernen Behandlung des Mythischen das Heterogenste miteinander vermischt.

(*Aesthetik*, 381–382)

22. See Albert Cook, "Ovid: The Dialectics of Recovery from Atavism," in *Myth and Language*.

23. One could describe Weber's work either as a modification of Marx in the direction of "value-free" delineation, as a complication of it by adding psychological and social factors to the economic ones, or as a combination of Marx's dialectical approach and Hegel's, the material and the spiritual (*geistliche*) entering into an interaction that could also be characterized as a balance struck between Marx's approach and Dilthey's. Weber himself sometimes approaches a Marxist explanation, as in his assignment of class-oriented economic motivation to the Bedouins (*Das Antike Judentum*, 88). Correspondingly, he tends both to praise and to qualify Marx, as in "Die 'Objektivität' der sozialwissenschaftlicher Erkenntnis" (*Soziologie, Analysen, Politik*, 250):

There was intentionally avoided a demonstration with respect to what for us is the most important case of ideal-typical constructions: Marx. This was done so as not to complicate the presentation by bringing in interpretations of Marx, and not to anticipate the discussions in our journal, which will make a regular object of critical analysis out of the literature that increases about and in connection with this great thinker.

Absichtlich ist es vermieden worden, an dem für uns weitaus wichtigsten Fall idealtypischer Konstruktionen zu demonstrieren: an *Marx*. Es geschah, um die Darstellung nicht durch Hineinziehen von Marx-Interpretationen noch zu komplizieren und um den Erörterungen in unserer Zeitschrift, welche die Literatur, die über und im Anschluss an den Grossen Denker erwächst, zum regelmässigen Gegenstand kritischer Analyse machen wird, nicht vorzugreifen.

24. Paul Veyne "L'oeuvre historique de Weber," in *Comment on écrit l'histoire*, 197–200, with the arresting superlative, "The most exemplary historical work of our century is that of Max Weber."

25. "... das Hineintragen von Werturteilen in die rein objective Analyse" (*Das Antike Judentum*, 2). Weber associates the unreflected (*unreflektiert*) with the undefined (*unbestimmt*) in the writing of history ("Die 'Objektivität' der Erkenntnis," 238).

26. Die unmittelbar 'verständlichste Art' der sinnhaften Struktur eines Handelns ist ja das subjektiv streng rational orientierte Handeln nach Mitteln, welche (subjektiv) für eindeutig adäquat zur Erreichung von (subjektiv) eindeutig und klar erfassten Zwecken gehalten werden." ("Ueber einige Kategorien der verstehenden Soziologie," in *Soziologie, Analysen, Politik*, 102). *Zweck* is a word

that retains a Hegelian coloring, and, of course, also an Aristotelian and a Kantian one.

27. *Das Antike Judentum*, passim, and especially 81–87 and 125–140.

28. "Die drei reinen Typen der legitimen Herrschaft," in *Soziologie, Analysen, Politik*, 151–156.

29. "Denn schon hier handelt es sich um den unaustragbaren *Ausgleich* von Zweck, Mittel und Nebenerfolg." ("Der Sinn der 'Wertfreiheit' der Sozialwissenschaften," in *Soziologie, Analysen, Politik*, 283.)

30. As Arthur Danto well says, "Marxism is a philosophy of history, and indeed exhibits both theories: the descriptive and the explanatory [in Danto's sense]" (*Narration and Knowledge*, 2). Danto, however, like Marx (though with a different aim), casts as necessary rather than just as possible the projection of a historiographic view from the past into the future. Lévi-Strauss traces in Sartre, and differently in Marx, an opposition between analytical and dialectical reasoning ("Histoire et Dialectique," *La Pensée Sauvage* [Paris: Plon, 1962], 324–357).

31. John McMurtry, *The Structure of Marx's World View* (Princeton, N.J.: Princeton University Press, 1978), 123–156. McMurtry effectually admits that it requires considerable ratiocination to expand this phrase beyond its enmeshment in economic factors.

32. Raymond Williams, to effectuate his own interesting connections between literary production and writing, must first clear the ground by heavily attenuating the distinction between base and superstructure (*Culture and Society* [New York: Harper, 1958], 265–284; and *Marxism and Literature* [Oxford University Press, 1977], 75–82).

Effectually divorced from an actual political program, the Marxism in the universities of our time employs Marx in what may be called a Weberian way as an instrumental vocabulary for analyzing social interactions, especially in the cultural sphere. Such discussions can have a great deal of explanatory power, as they adopt the mode of Plekhanov's translation of cultural phenomena into social terms with the kind of complexity that Adorno's work exemplifies. (G. V. Plekhanov, *Pisma bez Adresa* [Letter without an Address] and *Iskusstvo i Obshchestvennaya Zhizn* [Art and Social Life], [Moscow: Khudozhestvennaya Literatura, 1956 (1899, 1911)]. The schematic simplicity of Plekhanov would strike the modern Marxian, I believe, as amateurish to the point of uselessness. His lack of sophistication may serve to indicate the poverty of such discussions in [diverging] Marxist circles after Marx – a lack that cannot be simply ascribed to the times, since Ruskin and Matthew Arnold, for example, do not function in that particularly elementary mode.)

These modern writers can enlist distinctions that become very fine-grained, as in Frederic Jameson's discriminations of the six ways Althusser and Lukàcs may be said to differ in their interpretation of Marx's own discrimination of factors (*The Political Unconscious* [Ithaca, N.Y.: Cornell University Press, 1981], 49–52): representation (*Darstellung*) and historiography; "character" and the social history of classes; praxis versus structure, and the possible "contamination" of the latter by individual action or by reification; synchronic treatment of the foregoing categories versus diachronic transitions; contradiction versus mediation in dialectic; and the "totality" of Althusser versus the "expressive totality" of Hegel, Lukàcs, and Sartre. All of this not only belongs to the superstructure but also refers to it, whereas Marx's own writings are largely preoccupied with the "base." More directly than the social scientist who is perforce an analytic follower of Marx when he discusses the interactions of social classes, such literary critics use what they fairly arbitrarily classify as Marxist explanation to provide a general and dialectical framework for the discussion of particular literary works. This is the case, too, for many of the treatises of Lukacs, Goldmann, Eagleton, and such specific studies as Edward Ahearn, "Using Marx to Read Flaubert: The Case of *Madame Bovary*," in Will L. McLendon, ed., *L'Hénaurme Siècle*, (Heidelberg: Carl Winter, 1984), 73–91; to be included, along with material on Balzac, Faulkner, Joyce, James, Baudelaire, Austen, Melville, and others in a book on the Marxist interpretation of literature to be published by the Yale University Press.

33. Karl Marx, *Der 18te Brumaire des Louis Bonaparte*, in *Werke* (Berlin: Dietz, 1960), 8:115. *The Eighteenth Brumaire of Louis Bonaparte* (New York: International Publishers, 1963), 15.

> Hegel bemerkt irgendwo, dass alle grossen weltgeschichtlichen Tatsachen und Personen sich sozusagen zweimal ereignen. Er hat vergessen hinzuzufügen: das eine Mal als Tragödie, das andere Mal als Farce. Caussidière für Danton, Louis Blanc für Robespierre, die Montagne von 1848–1851 für die Montagne von 1793–1795, der Neffe für den Onkel. Und dieselbe Karikatur in den Umständen, unter denen die zweite Auflage des achzenten Brumaire herausgegeben wird!

A note in the German volume indicates Engels' reference to the third part of Hegel's *Philosophie der Geschichte* as the source of this passage. There, however, Hegel uses the term "tragedy," and he might well have avoided the term "farce," since his comparison is of the Persian Empire to the Roman, and so the repetition would have the slightest of causal connections, whereas Marx's repetition stays within one society; and a multiplicity of causal connections can, of course, be asserted between the Revolution and the Second Empire.

34. "Nicht in seinen unmittelbaren tragikomischen Errungenschaften brach sich der revolutionäre Fortschritt Bann, sondern umgekehrt in der Erzeugung einer geschlossenen, mächtigen Kontrerevolution, in der Erzeugung eines Gegners, durch dessen Bekämpfung erst die Umsturzpartei zu einer wirklich revolutionären Partei heranreifte," *Die Klassenkämpfe in Frankreich 1848 bis 1850*, in Karl Marx, *Werke*, 7:11. Here too, though, exaggeration is frequent, as when Marx declares that in the light of 1848 "the various classes of French society must count their evolutionary epochs by weeks when before they counted them by half-centuries" (61). And he ironically claims that the royalists hold the kingship as the one rational goal the way Kant (not Hegel!) held the republic to be the one rational form of government (76). Marx also leans, within these events, on ironies of repetition (91). And he does at least once refer to "historical irony" ("*geschichtliche Ironie*," die Klassenkämpfe, 40).

35. Hayden White, *Metahistory*, 310–311.

36. I am here indebted to the penetrating if partial study of Jeffrey Mehlman,

Revolution and Repetition (Berkeley: University of California Press, 1977). By effectually holding Hegel in view, Mehlman is even able to compare Marx to Georges Bataille (27–30).

37. As, for example, Louis Althusser, *Pour Marx* (Paris: Maspero, 1965). As he says in this connection, "It is essential not to confuse the real distinction of the abstract (Generality I) and the concrete (Generality III), which concerns theoretical practice alone, with another distinction, an ideological one, which opposes abstraction (constituting the essence of thought, science, theory) to the concrete (constituting the essence of the real)." "Il est donc essentiel de ne pas confondre la distinction réelle de l'abstrait (Généralité I) et du concret (Généralité III) qui concerne la seule pratique théorique, avec une autre distinction, idéologique celle-lá, qui oppose l'abstraction (constituant l'essence de la pensée, science, théorie) au concret (constituant l'esence du réel)" (190).

38. Giambattista Vico, *La Scienza Nuova e Opere scelte*, ed. Nicola Abbagnano, (Turin: Unione Tipografico, 1966 [1722]), 208–209. This edition reproduces the original diachronic date chart, which is balanced synchronically by a complex allegorical table of the book's thesis in the frontispiece (176).

39. "Natura di cose altro non è che nascimento di esse in certi tempi e con certe guise, le quali sempre che sono tali, indi tali e non altre nascon le cose" (252).

40. John Baker, in a manuscript essay on Vico, amplifies considerably the explanatory value of Vico's "poesia," comparing its power to that of Kant's a priori, while distinguishing it in its essentials from Hegel, Herder, and others.

41. "Dobbiamo per tutto ciò dar incominciamento alla sapienza poetica da una rozza lor metafisica, dalla quale, come da un tronco, si diramino per un ramo la logica, la morale, l'iconomica e la politica, tutte poetiche; e per un altro ramo, tutte eziando poetiche, la fisica, la qual sia stata madre della loro cosmografia, e quindi dell' astronomia, che ne dia accertate le due sue figluole, che sono cronologia e geografia" (309–310).

42. In his professional capacity Vico addresses the international law of Grotius, whom he cites (186).

43. Friedrich Nietzsche, *Werke*, ed. Karl Schlechta (Munich: Hanser, 1966 [1877]), 1:434. For a larger discussion of Nietzsche's attitudes to time and temporal succession in the context of his entire philosophical work, see Albert Cook, "The Moment of Nietzsche," *Carleton Germanic Papers* 7 (1979), 1–25, expanded in chap. 12, "The Moment of Nietzsche," *Thresholds: Studies in the Romantic Experience* (Madison: University of Wisconsin Press, 1985), 220–243; 291–300.

44. Michel Foucault, *Les Mots et les choses* (Paris: Gallimard, 1966), English translation, *The Order of Things* (New York: Random House, 1970), hereafter cited as "MC." Other Foucault titles will also be abbreviated: *L'Histoire de la folie* (Paris: Gallimard, 1972 [1963], "HF"); *L'Archéologie du savoir*, (Paris: Gallimard, 1969, "AS"); *L'Ordre du discours* (Paris: Gallimard, 1973, "OD"); *Surveiller et punir* (Paris: Gallimard, 1975, "SP"); and *Histoire de la sexualité I: La volonté de savoir* (Paris: Gallimard, 1976, "HS"). These works appear in English translation as: *Madness and Civilization* (New York: Pantheon, 1965); *Archeology*

of Knowledge (New York: Pantheon, 1972); *Order of Discourse* (New York: Pantheon, 1966); *Discipline and Punish* (New York: Pantheon, 1977), and *History of Sexuality, Vol. I* (New York: Pantheon, 1978).

45. "Ainsi dans toute culture entre l'usage de ce qu'on pourrait appeler les codes ordinateurs et les réflexions sur l'ordre, il y a l'expérience nue de l'ordre et de ses modes d'être," 12–13. Paul Veyne ("Foucault révolutionne l'histoire" in *Comment on écrit l'histoire*, 201–242) characterizes Foucault as having achieved a sort of transcendental neutrality in the general focusing of details: "A rough stone only becomes the key of vault or buttress when it takes its place in a structure" (227). Nothing exists transhistorically and explaining a pretended object consists of showing on what historical *context* it depends" (228). He goes on to assert Foucault's effectual superiority to a Marx as a historian (240).

46. As Hayden White says of Foucault's discourse (*The Content of the Form*, 112) "What is at work here is some principle of subordination, the vertical equivalent, we might say, of the horizontal principle of exclusion operative in the external restraints."

47. Foucault rhetorically oversimplifies the relation between these two works, "L'histoire de la folie serait l'histoire de l'Autre...l'histoire de l'ordre des choses serait l'histoire du Même," "The history of madness would be the history of the Other...the history of the order of things the history of the Same" (MC, 15). Deleuze and Guattari go even further in asserting an intrinsically unstable relationship between codes and particulars, or words and things, speaking specifically of Foucault: "In short, one must never confront words and things that are supposed to correspond, nor signifiers and signified that are supposed to conform to one another, but rather distinct formalizations in a state of unstable equilibrium or reciprocal presupposition," "Bref, il ne faut jamais confronter des mots et des choses supposés correspondants, ni des signifiants et des signifiés supposés distinctes, en etât d'equilibre instable ou de presupposition reciproque." (Gilles Deleuze and Félix Guattari, *Mille Plateaux* [Paris: Minuit, 1980], 87.)

48. Foucault's second and third volumes on sexuality raise comparable questions and enlist comparable procedures, extending "Classical" back to Greece, with a sexual reading of the difference between classical and Christian. All this is more conventional than the first volume or than his earlier works and exhibits his adaptive shift of templates for totalization.

49. Jean Piaget, *Structuralism* (New York: Basic, 1970).

50. However, totalizing systems, for that very reason, can be made congruent with each other. So the synchronic and nonhistoricizing system of Talcott Parsons, as it derives from Weber, can be made congruent with Weber quite easily. Interestingly, Arthur Kroker has worked out correspondences, and the shifts to validate them, between Parsons (therefore Weber, we may say) and Foucault, in "Modern Power in Reverse Image: The Paradigm Shift of Michel Foucault and Talcott Parsons," in John Fakete, ed., *The Structural Allegory* (Theory of History and Literature, vol. 2 [Minneapolis: University of Minnesota Press, 1984]), 74–103.

51.   Cette navigation du fou, c'est à la fois le partage rigoureux et l'absolu
Passage. Elle ne fait, en un sens, que développer, tout au long d'une
géographie mi-réelle, mi-imaginaire, la situation *liminaire* du fou à l'horizon
du souci de l'homme médieval–situation symbolique et réalisée à la fois
par le privilège qui est donné au fou d'être *enfermé* aux *portes* de la ville:
son exclusion doit l'enclore; s'il ne peut et ne doit avoir d'autre *prison* que
le *seuil* lui-même, on le retient sur le lieu du passage. Il est mis à l'intérieur
de l'extérieur, et inversement. Posture hautement symbolique, qui restera
sans doute la sienne jusqu'à nos jours, si on veut bien admettre que ce qui
fut jadis forteresse visible de l'ordre est devenu maintenant château de notre
conscience.
    L'eau et la navigation ont bien ce rôle. Enfermé dans le navire, d'où on
n'échappe pas, le fou est confié à la riviére aux mille bras, à la mer aux
mille chemins, à cette grande incertitude extérieure à tout. Il est prisonnier
au milieu de la plus libre, de la plus ouverte des routes: solidement enchaîné
à l'infini carrefour. Il est le Passager par excellence, c'est-à-dire le prisonnier
du passage... Une chose au moins est certaine: l'eau et la folie sont liées
pour longtemps dans le rêve de l'homme européen.

52.   *Der Untergang des Abendlandes: Umrisse einer Morphologie der Weltgeschichte* (Munich: Beck, 1980 [1923]); *The Decline of the West* (New York: Knopf, 1946
[1932]), American ed. 1:4. "Das Mittel tote Formen zu erkennen, is das mathematische Gesetz. Das Mittel lebendige Formen zu verstehen, ist die Analogie.
Auf diese Weise unterscheiden sich Polarität und Periodizität der Welt" (German ed., 4) .

53.   "Völker, Sprachen und Epochen, Schlachten und Ideen, Staaten und Götter,
Künste und Kunstwerke, Wissenschaften, Rechte, Wirtschaftsformen und Weltanschauungen, grosse Menschen und grosse Ereignisse" (4). In another such
list he speaks of "culture as the . . . total of its visible, tangible and comprehensible expressions – acts and opinions, religion and state, arts and sciences,
peoples and cities, economic and social forms, speech, laws, customs, characters, facial lines and costumes" (Am. ed., 1:55). "Kultur . . . als die Summe
ihres versinnlichten, räumlich und fasslich gewordenen Ausdrucks: Taten und
Gesinnungen, Völker und Städte, wirtschaftliche und gesellschaftliche Formen,
Sprachen, Rechten, Sitten, Charktere, Gesichtszüge und Trachten" (Ger. ed.,
75). The study of kinesics by Birdwhistell, Schafflen, and others has strikingly
born out Spengler's inclusion of facial lines in this list.

54.   I am here adapting and expanding some paragraphs from my essay "The Merit
of Spengler," *The Centennial Review* 7, no. 3 (Summer 1963), 306–316.

55.   Am. ed., 1:309; 2:195–196 and passim. Ger. ed., 395, 792, and passim.

56.   Am. ed., 1:4.

        "Das Bewusstsein davon, dass die Zahl der weltgeschichtlichen Erscheinungsformen eine begrenzte ist, dass Zeitalter, Epochen, Lagen, Personen,
sich dem Typus nach wiederholen, war immer vorhanden. Man hat das
Auftreten Napoleons kaum je ohne einen Seitenblick auf Cäsar und Alexander behandelt, von denen der erste, wie man sehen wird, morphologisch
unzulässig, der zweite richtig war. Napoleon selbst fand die Verwandschaft
seiner Lage mit derjenigen Karls des Grossen heraus. Der Konvent sprach
von Karthago, wenn er England meinte, und die Jakobiner nannten sich
Römer. Man hat, mit sehr verschiedenem Recht, Florenz mit Athen, Buddha mit Christus, das Urchristentum mit dem modernen Sozialismus, die
römischen Finanzgrössen der Zeit Cäsars mit den Yankees verglichen.
Petrarca, der erste leidenschaftliche Archäologe – die Archäologie ist ja

selbst ein Ausdruck des Gefühls, dass Geschichte sich wiederholt – dachte
in bezug auf sich an Cicero, und erst vor kurzem noch Cecil Rhodes, der
Organisator des englischen Südafrika, der die antiken Cäsarbiographien
in eigens für ihn angefertigten Uebersetzungen in seiner Bibliothek besass,
an Kaiser Hadrian. Es war das Verhängnis Karls XII von Schweden, dass
er von Jugend auf das Leben Alexanders von Curtius Rufus in der Tasche
trug und diesen Eroberer kopieren wollte.

(Ger. ed., 4–5).

57. Arnold Toynbee, *A Study of History* (Oxford University Press, 1934), 1:200–204.

58. Am. ed., 384. "Die Elemente des Empedokles bezeichnen ein körperliches
Sichverhalten, die Elemente der Verbrennungstheorie Lavoisiers (1777), die
der Entdeckung des Sauerstoffs (1771) folgte, ein dem *menschlichen Willen zugängliches* Energiesystem. Fest und flüssig werden Bezeichnungen für spannungsverhältnisse zwischen Molekülen" (Ger. ed., 492).

59. Immanuel Kant, *Kritik der Reinen Vernunft* (1781), "Tranzendentale Methoden
Lehre," 3, "Die Architektonik der Reinen Vernunft," trans. J. M. D. Meiklejohn (New York: Wiley, 1943), 467.

60. H. Stuart Hughes, *Oswald Spengler* (New York: Scribner, 1952), 31–32.

61. Toynbee seems not to see that in this term Spengler was himself revising the
conventional "Golden Age" and "Silver Age" designations for Rome.

62. It goes without saying that like all totalizers Spengler would not admit such
unanalyzable exceptions to his categories as I have been suggesting here; so
nothing happening or finding expression in Faustian culture could be
unFaustian.

63. "Die Vergleiche Rankes, eines Meisters der Kunstvollen Analogie . . . Sie sind
bei ihm wie bei andern aus einem plutarchischen, d. h. volkstümlich romantischen Geschmack gezogen," "nicht mit der Strenge des Mathematikers" (4, 5.
Here, as occasionally elsewhere, I have slightly revised Atkinson's English
translation).

64. In *S/Z* and elsewhere Barthes claims a scientific validity for his ad hoc typologies, while at the same time taking the stage as a writer who is inspired,
to use old-fashioned terms; to be a privileged producer of "texts" comes to
the same thing. As for Spengler, the double claim is especially fruitful (if
indefensible as a grounding for the uses of language) because it permits at once
a high organization to an analysis and a "prior" flexibility toward the choice
of areas for application and for terms.

65. Moreover, Spengler is no grossly sociologizing Darwinian on the pattern of
Herbert Spencer. Darwin himself is acutely seen as a post-Kantian formulator
of the "will to life," coordinated with and distinguished from others: "It is
the same creative will-to-life that was Schopenhauer-wise denied in Tristan
and Darwin-wise asserted in Siegfried; that was brilliantly and theatrically
formulated by Nietzsche in Zarathustra; that led the Hegelian Marx to a
political-economic and the Malthusian Darwin to a zoological hypothesis
which together have, without its being noticed, transformed the world-feeling
of the Western European megalopolitan" (Am. ed., 1:45). "Es ist derselbe
schöpferische Lebenswille, der im Tristan schopenhauerische verneint, im Siegfried darwinistischbejaht wurde, den Nietzsche im Zarathustra glänzend und

theatralisch formulierte, der durch den Hegelianer Marx der Anlass einer na-
tionalökonomischen, durch den Malthusianer Darwin der einer zoologischen
Hypothese wurde, die beide gemeinsam und unvermerkt das Weltgefühl des
westeuropäischen Grossstädters verwandelt haben." (Ger. ed., 63). The quib-
ble that indeed the effect of Marx and Darwin had not been unnoticed on the
collective psyche even in Spengler's time should not obscure the powerful
correlation of their own with other idea-systems in this passage.

66. Paul Ricoeur, "Narrative Time," in *Critical Inquiry* (Autumn 1980), 169–190:
"The dialectical character of 'now that' appears only that it is unfolded nar-
ratively in the interplay between being able to act and being bound to the
world order. This interplay accentuates what distinguishes within-timeness
from abstract time and what makes the interpretation of within-timeness lean
toward the representation of abstract time" (177). In the totalizing historian,
as the narrative unfolding has been displaced, we may say that the "within-
timeness" of Ricoeur does not disappear but leans harder; within-timeness and
abstract time are forced toward interdefinition without the explicit "configuration" that Ricoeur summarizes from Louis O. Mink (*Journal of Philosophy*
69, no. 9 [1972], 735–737). Ricoeur, developing what he calls the Aristotelian
mise en intrigue of *Temps et récit*, goes on to praise Heideggerian repetition as
getting closer to historicity than does the implicit dechronologization of Greimas, Barthes, and Propp (184). Greimas' *actants*, indeed, verge on tautology,
because in the guise of analyzing nodes of action in fiction they simply sche-
matize the obvious constituents of any naming of action in any linguistic mode.
This kind of "grammar" adds nothing to our ability to discuss fiction, or any
discourse, with respect either to communicated meaning or particular rhetorical
structures. For an argument about the comparable emptiness of Propp's categories in this regard, see Albert Cook, *Myth and Language*, 20, 284.

67. Paul Ricoeur, *Temps et Récit*, 1:133, "Ma thèse concernant le caractère ul-
timement narratif de l'histoire ne se confond aucunement avec la défense de
l'histoire narrative."

68. As Hexter describes Braudel's three levels (Jack Hexter, "Fernand Braudel and
the *Monde Braudellien*," *On Historians* [Cambridge, Mass.: Harvard University
press, 1979], 61–148): "In the crunch Braudel himself recognizes that between
the Platonic poles of total stability and instantaneous change there are *durées*
of the most varied length.: 'ten, a hundred.' . . . The three *durées* are somewhat
arbitrarily attached to specific subject matters: *longue durée* to the geographic,
social and cultural; *moyenne* to the economic and sometimes to the social: *courte*,
in fact if not in theory to the political" (137).

69. Fernand Braudel, *Civilization matérielle, économie et capitalisme, XV–XVIII siècle*,
vol. 3: *Le Temps du monde* (Paris: Armand Colin, 1979).

II. THE STRENGTH OF PARTIAL PURCHASES: KINDS OF
SYNECDOCHE IN MODERN HISTORY WRITING

1. Hayden White (*Metahistory*, 28–36 and passim) would use synecdoche as a
term to distinguish just one (somewhat shifting) class of historians. White
moves too quickly from a literary definition of synecdoche to a historical.

Thus he more or less arbitrarily links this technique to a "comic" emplotment, an "organicist" argument, and a "conservative" mode of ideological implications. This categorization obliges him to engage in considerable epicyclic ratiocination to deal with his form of synecdoche in cases like those of Ranke (177–178) and Marx (285–286), since, to begin with, neither is "comic" in any more general sense than that they can be characterized as hopeful (but also hardheaded); and certainly Marx is not in any obvious sense conservative.

2. Arthur Danto, *Narration and Knowledge,* 13.
3. Martin Heidegger, "Die Frage nach der Technik," in *Vorträge und Aufsätze* (Neske: Pfüllingen, 1954), 32. "Wir nennen jenes versammelnde Schicken, das den Menschen erst auf einen Weg des Entbergens bringt, das *Geschick*. Von hier aus bestimmt sich das Wesen aller Geschichte. Sie ist weder nur der Gegenstand der Historie, noch nur der Vollzug menschlichen Tuns. Dieses wird geschichtlich erst als ein geschickliches." Further, "Historical representation takes History as an object, within which a happening takes place that in its changeableness at the same time passes away," "Das historische Vorstellen nimmt die Geschichte als einen Gegenstand, worin ein Geschehen abläuft, das in seiner Wandelbarkeit zugleich vergeht" (48). There are further distinctions drawn between "*Historie*" and "*Geschichte*" as the essay continues (63–64), and all these amplify the discussions already cited along these lines from *Sein und Zeit.*
4. I have taken this list, not as exhaustive but as loosely indicative, from the table of contents of Felix Gilbert and Stephen Graubard, eds., *Historical Studies Today* (New York: Norton, 1972). That marked changes may happen quickly is illustrated by the absence of gender studies from this list. A comparable categorization of the historiographic enterprises in the ancient world has been deduced from their terminologies and practices by modern scholars, as these are summarized by Charles William Fornara (*The Nature of History in Ancient Greece and Rome* [Berkeley: University of California Press, 1983]), 1: genealogy or mythography, ethnography, history, horography or local history, and chronography.
5. Lewis Namier, *1848: The Revolution of the Intellectuals* (New York: Doubleday, 1964 [1946]), 22.
6. See "History," in Lewis Namier, *Avenues of History* (London: Hamish Hamilton, 1952), 1–10.
7. I owe this point to an unpublished paper on Namier by Susan Fischman.
8. Lewis Namier, *1848,* 57.
9. Albert Cook, "Inquiry: Herodotus," in *Myth and Language.*
10. Lewis Namier, "Basic Factors in 19th-Century European History," in *Vanished Supremacies* (New York: Harper, 1963 [1958]), 167–168.
11. A. J. P. Taylor, "Crimea: the War That Would Not Boil," in *From Napoleon to Lenin* (New York: Harper, 1966 [1952], 60–70 (60).
12. A. J. P. Taylor, *Germany's First Bid for Colonies 1884–1885: A Move in Bismarck's European Policy* (New York: Norton, 1970).
13. A. J. P. Taylor, "Prelude to Fashoda, the Question of the Upper Nile, 1894–5," in *Essays in English History* (Harmondsworth: Penguin, 1976), 129–168.

14. A. J. P. Taylor, *The Hapsburg Monarchy, 1809–1918* (New York: Harper, 1965 [1948]).
15. Henry Adams, *History of the United States of America During the Administrations of Thomas Jefferson and James Madison* (New York: Library of America, 1984 [1884]), 24.
16. George Hochfield, *Henry Adams* (New York: Barnes & Noble, 1962), 63.
17. E. H. Carr, *A History of Soviet Russia* (Harmondsworth: Penguin, 1966 [1950]), 1:45–46.
18. Fernand Braudel, *The Mediterranean and the Mediterranean World in the Age of Philip II* (New York: Harper, 1973 [1949–1966]), 1238–1240. Other references here will be by page number to this edition.
19. Garrett Mattingly, *The Armada* (Boston: Houghton Mifflin, 1959), 376.
20. Emmanuel Le Roy Ladurie, *Montaillou, Village occitan de 1294 à 1324* (Paris: Gallimard, 1975).
21. Le Roy Ladurie points out how the difference of emphasis in education for the sexes – the girls learning to sing and dance, the boys to work and make practical decisions – has persisted from this time, while the mingling of sexes in the medieval tavern, on the evidence of Montaillou, had disappeared by the nineteenth century, when the bistro had become a male sanctuary (398–399).
22. The late Reinhardt Kuhn had begun a study of historiography in which he emphasized the elaborate shifts in language at the base of Le Roy Ladurie's evidence: In the inquisitional records, initial depositions are taken in medieval French, translated into Latin, and then rendered and categorized in Ladurie's modern French, with occasional Latin citations for key terms. This process of translation, too, could be described as a synecdochic matching, of expressions from one language to expressions in another (since translation can never be total, a part – even ninety-nine percent – must stand for a whole in the target language).
23. Emmanuel Le Roy Ladurie, *Carnival in Romans* (New York: Braziller, 1979) (*Le Carneval du Romans* [Paris: Gallimard, 1979]).
24. Robert Darnton, *The Great Cat Massacre* (New York: Basic, 1984); *The Business of Enlightenment* (Cambridge, Mass.: Harvard University Press [Belknap], 1979).
25. A. J. P. Taylor, *A Personal History* (New York: Atheneum, 1983), 123.
26. Jack Hexter, *On Historians*, 144.

INDEX

Index

Index

Index